AMC'S BEST DAY HIKES IN THE
WHITE MOUNTAINS

Four-Season Guide to 60 of the Best
Trails in the White Mountains

4th Edition // Robert N. Buchsbaum

T0036798

Appalachian Mountain Club Books // Boston, Massachusetts

AMC is a nonprofit organization, and sales of AMC Books fund our mission of protecting the Northeast outdoors. If you appreciate our efforts and would like to become a member or make a donation to AMC, visit outdoors.org, call 800-372-1758, or contact us at Appalachian Mountain Club, 10 City Square, Boston, MA 02129.

outdoors.org/books-maps

Distributed by National Book Network.

Front cover of Old Bridle Path by Paula Champagne/AMC
Back cover photograph of Lost Pond Trail by Paula Champagne/AMC
Title page photo of Low's Bald Spot © Dennis Welsh
Interior photographs by Robert N. Buchsbaum, unless otherwise noted. Reproduced by permission.
Maps by Ken Dumas © Appalachian Mountain Club
Cover design by Jon Lavalley
Interior design by Abigail Coyle
Illustrations by Nancy Childs

Library of Congress Cataloging-in-Publication Data

Names: Buchsbaum, Robert, author.
Title: AMC's best day hikes in the White Mountains : four season guide to 60 of the best trails in the White Mountains / Robert N. Buchsbaum.
Other titles: Best day hikes in the White Mountains
Description: 4th edition. | Boston, Massacusetts : Appalachian Mountain Club Books, 2022. | Includes index. | Summary: "A four-season guide to 60 of the best day hikes in the White Mountains of New Hampshire"--Provided by publisher.
Identifiers: LCCN 2021060924 (print) | LCCN 2021060925 (ebook) | ISBN 9781628421378 (trade paperback) | ISBN 9781628421385 (epub) | ISBN 9781628421392 (mobi)
Subjects: LCSH: Hiking--White Mountain National Forest (N.H. and Me.)--Guidebooks. | Trails--White Mountain National Forest (N.H. and Me.)--Guidebooks. | White Mountain National Forest (N.H. and Me.)--Guidebooks.
Classification: LCC GV199.42.W47 B83 2022 (print) | LCC GV199.42.W47 (ebook) | DDC 917.42/20444--dc23
LC record available at https://lccn.loc.gov/2021060924
LC ebook record available at https://lccn.loc.gov/2021060925

The paper used in this publication meets the minimum requirements of the American National Standard for Information Sciences-Permanence of Paper for Printed Library Materials, ANSI Z39.48-1984. ∞

Interior pages and cover are printed on responsibly harvested paper stock certified by The Forest Stewardship Council®, an independent auditor of responsible forestry practices.
Printed in the United States of America, using vegetable-based inks.

5 4 3 2 1   22 23 24 25 26

This book is dedicated to all the volunteers who maintain the trails, allowing us to enjoy the wonderful vistas, waterfalls, ponds, flowers, and creatures of the White Mountains.

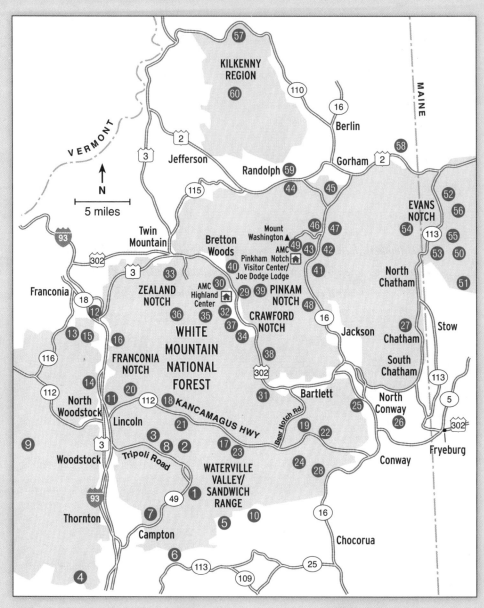

VERMONT

MAINE

KILKENNY REGION

57

60

110

16

Berlin

2

Jefferson

Randolph 59

Gorham 2 58

115

EVANS NOTCH

52

56

44

45

Twin Mountain

302

3

Bretton Woods

Mount Washington ▲

46

47

113

54

55

Franconia

18

12

ZEALAND NOTCH

33

AMC Highland Center

30

29

39

40

Pinkham Notch Visitor Center/ Joe Dodge Lodge

AMC Notch

49

43

42

41

PINKAM NOTCH

North Chatham

53

50

51

36

35

32

37

34

CRAWFORD NOTCH

48

16

27

Chatham

Stow

13

15

16

WHITE MOUNTAIN NATIONAL FOREST

Jackson

116

FRANCONIA NOTCH

38

South Chatham

113

14

302

Bartlett

North Conway

5

112

11

20

31

112

18

KANCAMAGUS HWY

Bear Notch Rd.

25

302

North Woodstock

Lincoln

21

19

22

26

Fryeburg

3

3

8

2

17

23

24

Conway

9

Woodstock

Tripoli Road

28

49

1

WATERVILLE VALLEY/ SANDWICH RANGE

93

7

5

10

16

Thornton

Campton

6

Chocorua

4

113

109

25

N

5 miles

93

302

3

2

3

Legend:

❄ Alpine zone (an ecological zone characterized by the lack of trees; ground cover and plants are typical of the Arctic Circle)

🧗 Exposed ledges (trail crosses an exposed ledge—a consideration in severe weather or in wet or icy conditions; hikes that end at a scenic ledge but do not cross an exposed ledge en route are not marked with this icon)

🏃 Steep or difficult terrain

🏊 Difficult brook crossing

🚶 Good for kids

🐕 Dog-friendly

♿ Accessible

♨ Waterfall

💧 Pond, stream, spring, or other water feature

❄ Snowshoeing

⛷ Cross-country skiing

🏠 Shelter or hut

🎆 Scenic views

△ Designated tentsite

🌲 Wilderness area (federally designated areas of restricted human activity, with specific rules and regulations)

🏊 Swimming

🎪 Picnic area

🚶 Visitor center

🚌 Public transit

$ Fee

CONTENTS

7 // EVANS NOTCH — 259

8 // NORTH COUNTRY — 293

NATURE AND HISTORY ESSAYS

AT-A-GLANCE TRIP PLANNER

Trip number	Trip name and location	Difficulty rating	Round-trip distance	Elevation gain	Estimated time
THE SOUTHWESTERN WHITE MOUNTAINS AND WATERVILLE VALLEY					
1	Cascade Path, Waterville Valley *Waterville Valley, NH*	Easy	3.4 mi	800 ft	2 hrs
2	Davis Boulders and Goodrich Rock *Waterville Valley, NH*	Moderate	4 mi	750 ft	2–3 hrs
3	East Pond and Little East Pond *Livermore, NH*	Moderate	4.8 mi	1,000 ft	4–5 hrs
4	Stinson Mountain Trail *Rumney, NH*	Moderate	3.6 mi	1,400 ft	3 hrs
5	Mount Israel *Sandwich, NH*	Moderate	4.2 mi	1,700 ft	3.5 hrs
6	Percival-Morgan Loop *Holderness/Campton, NH*	Moderate	5.4 mi	1,600 ft	4.5 hrs
7	Welch-Dickey Loop *Thornton, NH*	Moderate–Strenuous	4.4 mi	1,800 ft	3.5–5 hrs
8	Mount Osceola *Livermore, NH*	Strenuous	5.8 mi	2,050 ft	5–6 hrs
9	Mount Moosilauke *Woodstock/Benton, NH*	Strenuous	8.3 mi	2,650 ft	6 hrs
10	Whiteface–Passaconaway Loop *Waterville Valley, NH*	Strenuous	12.6 mi	2,950 ft	7–8.5 hrs
FRANCONIA NOTCH					
11	Flume Gorge *Lincoln, NH*	Easy	2 mi	500 ft	2 hrs
12	Bald Mountain and Artist's Bluff *Franconia, NH*	Moderate	1.6 mi	600 ft	2 hrs
13	Coppermine Trail to Bridal Veil Falls *Franconia, NH*	Moderate	5 mi	1,100 ft	3–4 hrs
14	Mount Pemigewasset Trail *Lincoln, NH*	Moderate	3.6 mi	1,300 ft	3 hrs
15	Lonesome Lake and Hut *Lincoln, NH*	Moderate	3.2 mi	1,000 ft	3–4 hrs
16	Cloudland Falls and Franconia Ridge via Falling Waters Trail, Greenleaf Trail, and Old Bridle Path *Lincoln, NH to Franconia, NH*	Moderate–Strenuous	8.9 mi (loop); 2.6 mi (round trip)	3,950 ft (loop)/900 ft (round trip)	7 hrs (loop); 2 hrs (round trip)

Trip highlights	Trip features
Pleasant, easy walk to beautiful series of small waterfalls	
Incredible rock formations including one of the largest glacial erratics in the White Mountains	
Mountain ponds with wildflowers, ferns, mushrooms	
Sweeping view from the summit. Interesting geology	
Great views of Sandwich Range and lakes	
Fun climb with extensive views of Squam Lake	
Excellent views, popular family hike	
Spectacular mountain vista at summit	
Follows rushing mountain stream to alpine summit with extensive views	
A rigorous hike up two 4,000 footers providing great distinct views	
Waterfalls, stunning gorge, covered bridges	
Ideal family outing with views and nearby picturesque swimming beach	
One of the most beautiful waterfalls in the White Mountains	
Good for kids, excellent views, wildflowers, and mushrooms	
Beautiful swimming lake, great views, overnight accommodation	
Longer option is one of the White Mountains' most spectacular alpine hikes. Shorter waterfall option	

OFF THE KANCAMAGUS HIGHWAY

17	Sabbaday Falls *Waterville Valley, NH*	Easy	0.6 mi	100 ft	0.5–1 hr
18	Forest Discovery Trail *Lincoln, NH*	Easy	1.4 mi	200 ft	1–2 hrs
19	Rocky Gorge and Lovequist Loop around Falls Pond *Albany, NH*	Easy	1 mi	150 ft	0.5–1 hr
20	Lincoln Woods Trail to Black Pond and/or Franconia Falls *Lincoln, NH*	Moderate	6.6, 6.8., or 8 mi	500 ft	3–5 hrs
21	Greeley Ponds *Lincoln/Livermore, NH*	Moderate	3.2 or 4.6 mi	450 ft	2–4 hrs
22	Boulder Loop Trail *Albany, NH*	Moderate	3.1 mi	950 ft	2–4 hrs
23	UNH Trail to Hedgehog Mountain *Albany, NH*	Moderate	4.7 mi	1,400 ft	3.5–5 hrs
24	Champney Falls and Mount Chocorua *Albany, NH*	Moderate to falls; strenuous to Mount Chocorua	3.5 mi to falls; 7.6 mi to summit	600 ft to falls; 2,250 ft to summit	2.5 hrs to falls; 6 hrs to summit

CONWAY–NORTH CONWAY

25	Diana's Baths *Conway, NH*	Easy	1.2 mi	minimal	0.5–1 hr
26	Black Cap *Conway, NH*	Moderate	2.2 mi	650 ft	1–2 hrs
27	Mountain Pond Loop Trail *Chatham, NH*	Moderate	2.7 mi	minimal	1.5–3 hrs
28	White Ledge Loop *Albany, NH*	Moderate	4.4 mi	1,450 ft	3–5 hrs

CRAWFORD NOTCH AND ZEALAND NOTCH

29	Saco Lake and Elephant Head *Carroll, NH*	Easy	1.2 mi	150 ft	1 hr
30	Ammonoosuc Lake via Around the Lake Trail *Carroll, NH*	Easy	1.2 mi or 1.8 mi	250 ft	1–2 hrs
31	Sawyer Pond *Livermore, NH*	Moderate	3 mi	350 ft	1.5–2 hrs
32	Mount Willard *Carroll, NH to Hart's Location, NH*	Moderate	3.2 mi	900 ft	3–4 hrs
33	Sugarloaf Trail *Bethlehem, NH*	Moderate	3.4 mi	700 ft– 1,100 ft	3–4 hrs

Gorge with interesting geology, ideal for families with very young children	
Interpretive trail with view of nearby forests and mountains; benches along trail	
Good for families; small gorge, pond, fishing, picnics	
Old logging railroad along river to pond and waterfall, wading	
Classic mountain ponds, rugged slopes, split-log bridges	
Rocky ledges, fine views, covered bridge nearby	
Great vistas, three overlooks, interesting wildflowers	
Great for families up to the waterfalls; spectacular mountain scenery from Mount Chocorua	
Popular family destination, wading, universally accessible	
Popular family hike, fine vista	
Pond with beaver houses, spruce-fir forest, boulder piles	
Excellent family outing; hemlock forest, esker, great views	
Easy hike to pond and vista, especially good for small children	
Quiet pond with moose, beavers, wood ducks, wildflowers	
Swimming, picnicking, camping, fishing, bird-watching	
One of the most beautiful views in the White Mountains	
Great views, glacial boulders, smoky quartz in abandoned quarry	

34	Arethusa Falls and Frankenstein Cliff *Hart's Location, NH*	Moderate	3 mi or 4.9 mi	950 ft or 1,650 ft	2 hrs or 4–5 hrs
35	Mount Avalon *Carroll, NH to Bethlehem, NH*	Moderate	3.7 mi	1,550 ft	3–4 hrs
36	Zealand Trail to Zealand Falls Hut and Zealand Pond *Bethlehem, NH*	Moderate	5.4 mi	650 ft	3–4 hrs
37	Ethan Pond and Ripley Falls *Hart's Location, NH to Bethlehem, NH*	Moderate	6 mi	1,850 ft	5 hrs
38	Mount Crawford *Hart's Location, NH to Hadley's Purchase, NH*	Strenuous	5 mi	2,100 ft	5 hrs
39	Mizpah Spring Hut and Mount Pierce *Carroll, NH to Hart's Location, NH*	Strenuous	6.6 mi	2,450 ft	5–6 hrs
40	Mount Eisenhower via Edmands Path *Crawford's Purchase, NH*	Strenuous	6.6 mi	2,750 ft	6 hrs

PINKHAM NOTCH AND GORHAM

41	Lost Pond *Pinkham's Grant, NH*	Easy	1 mi to pond, 1.8 mi entire trail	minimal	1–2 hrs
42	Square Ledge *Pinkham's Grant, NH*	Moderate	1.2 mi	400 ft	1–2 hrs
43	Lila's Ledge and Brad's Bluff *Pinkham's Grant, NH*	Moderate	2.8 mi	650 ft	2–3 hrs
44	Waterfall and Vista Loop in the Northern Presidential Range *Randolph, NH*	Easy–Strenuous	1.5 (easy loop); 4 mi (strenuous loop)	400 ft (easy loop); 1,450 ft (strenuous loop)	1–2 hrs (easy loop; 3–4 hrs (strenuous loop)
45	Pine Mountain from Pinkham B (Dolly Copp) Road *Gorham, NH*	Moderate	3.5 mi	850 ft	2–3.5 hrs
46	Low's Bald Spot via Old Jackson Road *Pinkham's Grant, NH to Sargent's Purchase, NH*	Moderate	4.4 mi	1,050 ft	3–4 hrs
47	Nineteen Mile Brook Trail to Carter Notch Hut *Bean's Purchase, NH*	Moderate	7.6 mi	2,000 ft	7 hrs
48	Glen Boulder *Pinkham's Grant, NH*	Strenuous	3.2 mi	1,750 ft	3–4 hrs

Tallest waterfall in New Hampshire, great views of Crawford Notch

Pass attractive cascades to excellent vista

Premier location for beavers, birds, and other wildlife, spectacular notch view

Remote mountain pond favored by the legendary Ethan Allen Crawford

Stunning vistas, mountain birds

Great birds, old-growth red spruce forest, wildflowers, alpine vista

Well-graded trail to alpine zone with spectacular vistas and rare alpine plants

Beaver wetland, wildflowers, views of Mount Washington

Great first experience for young children on a steep trail to vista

Two overlooks above Pinkham Notch and interesting geology

First part has great waterfalls and picnic spot; second part offers great views

Fascinating geology and excellent views for moderate effort

Great view, interesting mushrooms, wildflowers

Hike along a brook to stunning mountain scenery, two pristine lakes

Steep hike to prominent glacial erratic in alpine zone

49	Tuckerman Ravine and Mount Washington *Pinkham's Grant, NH to Sargent's Purchase, NH*	Strenuous	8.4 mi	4,250 ft	8 hrs

EVANS NOTCH

50	Shell Pond *Stow, ME to Stoneham, ME*	Easy	3.1 mi	200 ft	2–3 hrs
51	Lord Hill *Stoneham, ME*	Easy	2.8 mi	750 ft	2–4 hrs
52	The Roost *Batchelder's Grant, ME*	Moderate	2.1 mi	700 ft	1–1.5 hrs
53	Deer Hill *Chatham, NH to Stow, ME*	Moderate	4.3 mi or 5.1 mi	1,250 ft or 1,600 ft	3–4 hrs or 4–5 hrs
54	Basin Trail to Basin Rim *Bean's Purchase, NH*	Moderate	4.6 mi	800 ft	3.5–5 hrs
55	Blueberry Mountain via Stone House Trail *Stow, ME to Stoneham, ME*	Moderate	4 mi	1,150 ft	3–5 hrs
56	Caribou Mountain *Batchelder's Grant, ME*	Strenuous	6.9 mi	1,950 ft	6 hrs

NORTH COUNTRY

57	Devil's Hopyard *Stark, NH*	Easy	2.6 mi	200 ft	1–2 hrs
58	Mount Crag *Shelburne, NH*	Moderate	2.4 mi	700 ft	2 hrs
59	Lookout Ledge *Randolph, NH*	Moderate	2.6 mi	950 ft	2.5–3.5 hrs
60	Unknown Pond from Mill Brook Road *Stark, NH to Kilkenny, NH*	Moderate	4.4 mi	1,450 ft	3.5 hrs

Tallest mountain in New England, incomparable views, alpine community, very challenging

Loop around beautiful pond with potential wildlife sightings

Rock collecting, vista of pond

Terrific views of Wild River and Evans Brook valleys

Maple, beech, birch, hemlock, blueberries, great views

Impressive glacial cirque and cliffs

Blueberries, great views, a gorge, and deep pool

Beautiful cascades and views, alpine plants

Narrow, picturesque gorge, universally accessible along pond

Well-graded trail leading to great view of the Androscoggin Valley

Wonderful view of Northern Presidentials

Remote, boreal mountain pond

ACKNOWLEDGMENTS

I thank the Appalachian Mountain Club for giving me the opportunity to write this book. I have had the pleasure of working with gifted editors and other staff at AMC Books. Gordon Hardy guided me through the first edition of *Nature Hikes in the White Mountains*, and I am forever grateful for his faith, encouragement, advice, and good humor. Mark Russell oversaw the second edition. Sarah Jane Shangraw led the evolution of *Nature Hikes* into *Best Day Hikes in the White Mountains*, Dan Eisner and Kimberly Duncan-Mooney managed the second edition of that work, and Victoria Sandbrook Flynn and Shannon Smith worked on the third edition. This latest edition is under the supervision of Tim Mudie. Walter Graff and Nancy Ritger at Pinkham Notch provided helpful recommendations for the original work on trails appropriate for children and contributed some ideas on how to approach this topic. Much of what I have learned about the White Mountains comes from my past association with the wonderful group of AMC volunteer naturalists.

Many people have provided advice and support through my years of writing about day hikes and nature in the White Mountains. I don't have enough space to acknowledge all who contributed, but a few stand out. Steven D. Smith, coauthor of AMC's *White Mountain Guide* (31st edition), reviewed all the trail descriptions in addition to providing wise counsel on the general perspective of the book and suggesting several hikes. I am indebted to Lesley Rowse and Gary Inman for their advice on trails, particularly in Evans Notch; for sharing their knowledge of the White Mountains; and for letting my family invade their home on numerous occasions. Ed Quinlan and Leslie Nelkin also opened their house to us, accompanied us on many hikes, and offered feedback. Sarah Allen and her children, Sam and Jack Van Etten, joined us on multiple hikes. AMC New Hampshire Chapter members David Ross, Jane Gibbons, and Wanda Rice gave valuable feedback and suggestions on choices of hikes in the previous edition. Information on the influence of storms and climate change on forest history was provided by David Publicover and Sarah Nelson of AMC's Research Department. J. Dykstra Eusden reviewed the geology section in Appendix B, and Woodrow Thompson and Thom Davis kindly addressed various questions I had about regional geology. David Govatski provided historical details on Low's Bald Spot. Much of the information about the origins of place names in the White Mountains was taken from John T. B. Mudge's *The White Mountains: Names, Places, and Legends* (The Durand Press, 1995). Numerous AMC staff and volunteers contributed photos used in the book. Of course, the author takes all responsibility for any errors.

Very special thanks are due to my wife, Nancy Schalch, and our children, Alison and Gabriel. For the earlier editions, Nancy was my chief hiking companion, cheerfully doing more than her share of the childcare on our trips so I could concentrate on writing notes and taking photographs. She provided continual encouragement and logistical support, reading and making useful comments on the entire manuscript. Alison went on her first hike when she was 2 months old and, fortunately for us (and for this book project), instantly took a liking to being out on the trails and now in her mid-20s spends a good amount of time hiking in the White Mountains. She has played an essential role in this edition, checking out some of the trails that needed updates and providing commentary on two additions: Glen Boulder Trail and the Whiteface-Passaconaway Loop. Gabriel was not here when the first version of this book came out, but he has more than made up for it with his enthusiasm for the natural world and helping us explore old and new trails. He also provided comments on Glen Boulder Trail. It has been great to see the pendulum swing over the years, from Nancy and me encouraging the children to keep up on the trails to them now wondering what could possibly be taking their parents so long to get up the mountain.

Robert Buchsbaum
Beverly, Massachusetts, 2021

INTRODUCTION

The White Mountains compose a region of bare mountain summits; extensive views; deep, glacially scoured ravines; fascinating plants and animals; enchanted evergreen forests; and cold mountain streams tumbling over boulders in fantastic patterns. The region provides some of the very best hiking opportunities in the United States. It has the largest alpine (above treeline) area in the East, where on a clear day the panoramic views can seem endless. Many wonderful hikes take you to lower mountains where the vistas are almost as extensive and to more intimate trails along rivers and streams that lead to waterfalls and ponds. Whether you are looking for a full day of hiking or a short walk with young children, the White Mountains have something suitable.

For this book, I have selected a variety of trails with different levels of difficulty, so families with young children who are beginning hikers as well as people looking for a long day hike up a steep slope should be able to find something appropriate for their interests and skill levels. The trails all have some natural highlight, whether it is a scenic vista, an interesting geological feature, or a particularly rich abundance of birds or other wildlife. Most of the hikes are within the White Mountain National Forest, the largest national forest in the northeastern United States and part of the U.S. Forest Service. Other hikes are in New Hampshire state parks or on private conservation land. I have tried to select trails that are well maintained by trail crews of the national forest, AMC, and other hiking clubs.

HOW TO USE THIS BOOK

With 60 hikes to choose from, you may wonder how to decide where to go. The locator map at the front of this book will help you narrow down the trips by location, and the at-a-glance trip planner that follows the table of contents will provide more information to guide you toward a decision.

In the at-a-glance trip planner and at the beginning of each trip description, you will find a series of icons that indicate safety concerns, if the hike is a good outing for kids, dogs, snowshoeing, and cross-country skiing, if at least some part of the trail is universally accessible, and more. The precautions on brook crossings and steep or rough trails are very much influenced by weather. Note that winter activities may be appropriate for only part of the trail or may be impossible if the road to a trailhead is not plowed, so be sure to read the descriptions.

Information on the basics follows: location, difficulty rating, distance, elevation gain, estimated time, and available maps. The difficulty ratings are based on the author's perception and are estimates of what the average hiker will experience. You may find the hikes to be easier or more difficult than stated. The estimated time is also based on the author's perception. Consider your own pace when planning.

The elevation gain is the sum of all the uphill climbing that is required to complete the hike. It takes into account the various ups and downs of the terrain. Information is included about the location of the hike in AMC's *White Mountain National Forest Map & Guide* (4th edition), the maps of AMC's *White Mountain Guide* (31st edition), the relevant U.S. Geological Survey (USGS) topographic map, and the town(s) in which the hike is located.

The "Directions" section explains how to reach the trailhead by car. Some trips have a public transportation icon, which means the trailhead is near a stop on the AMC Hiker Shuttle. Global positioning system (GPS) coordinates for parking lots are also included. When you enter the coordinates into your GPS device, it will provide driving directions. Whether or not you own a GPS device, it is wise to consult an atlas before leaving your home. The "Directions" section also describes whether the road to the trailhead is maintained in winter, a key consideration if you are hiking from roughly November through early May.

In the "Trail Description" section, you will find instructions on following the trail or trails. The section describes where to turn at any trail junction, where to watch for occasional challenges (such as a stream crossing that could be difficult after a rainstorm), and where to be particularly careful to avoid losing the trail. You will also learn about the natural and human history along your hike, along with information about flora, fauna, and any landmarks and objects you may encounter.

The trail maps that accompany each trip will help guide you along your hike. An additional resource is AMC's *White Mountain National Forest Map & Guide*. This provides a thorough overview of the region and contains brief descriptions of almost all the hikes described here.

Following the trail description, there is a section called "Other Activities," which describes nearby swimming and fishing opportunities, places of natural or historical interest, other local hikes, and possible winter activities. Each trip ends with a "More Information" section that provides details about the locations of bathrooms and other amenities, the land ownership of the trail, and any fees required. Phone numbers and websites (if available) are included here.

The trail descriptions are grouped by geographic region within the White Mountains. The hikes within each region are ordered by level of difficulty, with those rated easy first, those rated moderate next, and those that are more challenging last. At the beginning of each regional section is a summary of local resources. If you are interested in nearby campgrounds, stores, restaurants, and so on, refer to this background information.

Also included in this book is an appendix full of advice on hiking in the White Mountains with children. Another appendix on natural history emphasizes flora, fauna, and geological features that are visible on many trails.

Before starting out, read the trail description to decide if the hike is right for you. Remember that the difficulty rating naturally involves some subjectivity. "Easy" means that the terrain is relatively level and the hike is less than 3 miles long or that the hike is somewhat steep but very short. "Moderate" means the terrain may be rocky or there is a steeper grade. The hike may be 2 to 5 miles long. "Strenuous" means the terrain can be difficult and is generally inappropriate for young children, the elevation gain is greater than 2,000 feet, and the hike may be 5 to 10 miles long. The estimated times are for hiking and factor in some additional minutes for stops to admire the scenery or have lunch.

I hope you enjoy this book and that it is a useful companion on many great hikes in the White Mountains.

TRIP PLANNING AND SAFETY

The White Mountains region is the most popular hiking destination in New England, and serious accidents are uncommon. However, keep a couple of things in mind to ensure a safe, positive experience. The trails in the White Mountains, although generally well marked, are not manicured. A trail will sometimes cross directly over streams without any bridges; have exposed tree roots and rocks; lead to windy, exposed locations; or require scrambling up and over boulders. Another safety consideration is the weather, notoriously fickle in the White Mountains, particularly at higher elevations. You may be several hours from "civilization," out of range of cell phone reception and other amenities, when a thunderstorm or even a summer snowstorm hits, so it is wise to be prepared. You will be more likely to have an enjoyable, safe hike if you take proper precautions. Before heading out, consider the following:

- Select a hike that everyone in your group is comfortable taking. Match the hike to the abilities of the least capable person in the group. If anyone is uncomfortable with the weather or is tired, turn around and complete the hike another day.

- Check the weather. In the White Mountains, the weather can change rapidly. Bright, sunny days can turn into cold, soaking rains, so hikers need to be prepared with rain gear and extra clothes. At low elevations, bad weather can be merely uncomfortable, but above treeline, the consequences can be deadly. Lives have been lost due to hypothermia and lightning strikes, almost always involving people who ignored weather warnings, did not carry a map and compass, and did not have the proper gear. You must be willing to turn back if the weather begins to sour. If you are planning a ridge or summit hike, especially in summer, start early so you will be off the exposed area before the afternoon hours when thunderstorms most often strike. Before heading out, particularly if planning a hike above treeline, you should get a weather forecast at AMC facilities at Pinkham and Crawford notches or at White Mountain National Forest ranger stations. In winter, it is particularly critical to check on weather and snow conditions.

- Plan to be back at the trailhead before dark. Before beginning your hike, determine a turnaround time. Don't diverge from it, even if you have not reached your intended destination.

- Check current trail conditions at AMC's website, outdoors.org.

- Bring a pack with the following items:

- Water: Two quarts per person is usually adequate, depending on the weather and the length of the trip. Consider bringing a water filter as backup for longer trips.
- Food: Even if you are planning just a 1-hour hike, bring high-energy snacks, such as nuts, dried fruit, or granola bars. Pack a lunch for longer trips.
- Map and compass: Be sure you know how to use them. A handheld GPS device may be helpful but is not always reliable, particularly under a thick canopy of spruce and fir trees.
- Headlamp or flashlight, with spare batteries
- Extra clothing: rain gear, wool sweater or fleece, hat, and mittens
- Sunscreen
- First-aid kit, including adhesive bandages, gauze, nonprescription painkiller, and moleskin
- Pocketknife or multitool
- Waterproof matches and a lighter
- Trash bag
- Toilet paper
- Whistle
- Insect repellent
- Sunglasses
- Cell phone: Be aware that cell phone service is unreliable in the backcountry. If you are receiving a signal, use the phone only for emergencies to avoid disturbing the backcountry experience for other hikers.
- Binoculars (optional)
- Camera (optional)

- Wear appropriate footwear and clothing for the season. Wool or synthetic hiking socks will keep your feet dry and help prevent blisters. Comfortable, waterproof hiking boots that are broken in before your hike will provide ankle support and good traction. Avoid wearing cotton clothing, which absorbs sweat and rain and contributes to an unpleasant experience. Polypropylene, fleece, silk, and wool all wick moisture away from your body and keep you warm in wet or cold conditions. It is always wise to bring a windbreaker and extra clothes when hiking to summit ledges, even at low elevations in summer. The weather on ledges can be cool and windy compared with that in the forest. You'll enjoy lunch breaks at the summits much more if you have additional layers to wear.

- To limit bug bites, wear pants and a long-sleeved shirt or use insect repellents. Blackfly season in the White Mountains runs through much of May and June, and mosquitoes can be a problem in low, swampy areas from late spring through much of summer. After you complete your hike, check for deer ticks, which carry the dangerous Lyme disease.

- If you are ahead of the rest of your hiking group, wait at all trail junctions until the others catch up. This avoids confusion and keeps people from getting separated or lost.

- If you see downed wood that appears to be purposely covering a trail, it probably means the trail is closed due to overuse or hazardous conditions.

- If a trail is muddy, walk through the mud or on rocks, never on tree roots or plants. Waterproof boots will keep your feet dry and comfortable. Staying in the center of the trail will keep it from eroding into a wide hiking highway.

- Leave your itinerary and the time you expect to return with someone you trust. If you see a logbook at the trailhead, be sure to sign in when you arrive and sign out when you finish your hike.

- If your hike takes you out into the sun, wear a sun hat and sunscreen.

- Poison ivy is uncommon in the White Mountains, but it does grow along some lowland trails. To identify the plant, look for clusters of three leaves that are shiny in the sun but dull in the shade. If you do come into contact with poison ivy, wash the affected area with soap as soon as possible.

- Wear blaze-orange items in hunting season. In New Hampshire, deer hunting season typically runs from early November through early December.

- Rainstorms and spring snowmelt can make stream crossings difficult or even hazardous. Rocks that are fun to scramble up in dry weather can become slippery when wet or icy. I have noted these in the hike descriptions, so you can choose your hike wisely under these less-than-ideal conditions.

- Annoying insects are likely to be the only wildlife "threat" you will encounter. Bears are extremely rare and will almost always take pains to stay away from humans. To avoid surprising a mother with cubs, it is a good idea to make some noise while hiking.

- You may need more than 2 quarts of water per person for some of the longer hikes in this book, particularly if the weather is warm. Water in mountain lakes and streams is considered unsafe to drink, so fill your water bottle before beginning your hike. Read the hike description to determine if you will be passing a reliable and safe source of water along the trail (for example, an AMC hut).

- Getting lost is an unpleasant experience. At higher elevations of the White Mountains and in bad weather, it can be dangerous. The trails in this guide are generally well marked with signs and blazes (painted spots on tree trunks or rocks); however, intersections with logging roads or unmarked trails, and occasional faded blazes, might lead to some confusion. On open ledges and summits, trails are often marked by cairns, which are carefully placed piles of rocks. Read the trail description before you depart so that you are prepared for any quirks. If you think you are off the trail, the best thing to do is to backtrack until you find the last blaze. Keep track of the blazes as you hike, which is a job you might share with children so they feel responsible for the successful navigation of the trip. Remember to stay on the trail, not only to remain safe but also to protect plants and wildlife.

WHAT TO BRING ESPECIALLY FOR KIDS

First of all, bring all the items necessary for hikes without children. A child who is cold or hungry is not going to be a good hiking companion. Remember that children are more likely to get chilled if you end up carrying them, so bring extra clothing, especially for backpack-sized babies.

One important safety item for children is a whistle. Train children beforehand to stay within sight, but make sure all children have a whistle. If they are separated from the group, they should stay put and blow the whistle at regular intervals. Remind them that the whistle is not for play but should be used only when they sense they are lost.

Food is another critical ingredient of a successful hike with kids. Lunch is a great motivator and reward. Occasional snacks,

It's never too early to get your kids outside.

such as granola bars, fruit, or cookies, can nip any crankiness before it goes too far.

Have kids carry a pack of their own when they are old enough. In addition to extra clothes and perhaps a small water bottle, make sure each child's pack has something essential for one of the group's activities (for example, a special snack, bags for blueberries, or a lunch treat). If children insist they won't need jackets, suggest that they can sit on them during breaks or lunch.

Consider bringing along a child carrier, especially for longer hikes. It is a lot easier than carrying a tired child on your shoulders—and safer too.

Other small items that are good to have: a hand lens or magnifying glass to aid in studying tiny things; binoculars if your destination has a view; a tea or soup strainer to make searching for aquatic life along ponds and streams more fun; and a bug box to enable children to examine insects closely. Finally, allow younger children to bring a favorite toy or stuffed animal in their own day packs.

See Appendix A (page 311) for more advice on hiking with children.

HIKESAFE

The U.S. Forest Service and the New Hampshire Fish and Game Department have developed hikeSafe, a program to encourage hiker responsibility in the White Mountain National Forest. The hikeSafe "Hiker Responsibility Code" states that you are responsible for yourself, so be prepared:

- With knowledge and gear. Become self-reliant by learning about the terrain, conditions, local weather, and your equipment before you start.
- To leave your plans. Tell someone where you are going, the trails you are hiking, when you'll return, and your emergency plans.
- To stay together. When you start as a group, you should hike as a group and end as a group. Pace your hike to the slowest person.
- To turn back. Weather changes quickly in the mountains. Fatigue and unexpected conditions can also affect your hike. Know your limitations and when to postpone your hike. The mountains will be there another day.
- For emergencies, even if you are headed out for just an hour. An injury, severe weather, or a wrong turn could become life threatening. Don't assume you will be rescued; know how to rescue yourself.
- To share the hiker code with others.

The New Hampshire Fish and Game Department sells an annual voluntary hikeSafe card to raise money for the department's search-and-rescue fund. Cardholders will not be held responsible for search-and-rescue costs if rescued; they will still be charged if their actions are deemed reckless or intentional. The card is good from time of purchase through the end of the calendar year and costs $25 for individuals and $35 for families. Cards may be purchased online at wildlife.state.nh.us/safe.

PARKING AND ENTRANCE FEES

The White Mountain National Forest Recreational Fee Program has existed since 1997. Your vehicle must display a sticker for you to park at certain marked trailheads within the national forest. These are generally the trailheads that have bathrooms, picnic tables, and other amenities. In 2021, the cost of the sticker was $5 for a one-day pass, $30 for one year, and $40 per year for two cars in the same family. Day passes are available at self-service pay stations at some trailheads. Day and yearly passes are available at ranger stations, information centers, and numerous businesses throughout the region. Ninety-five percent of every fee directly supports the White Mountain National Forest.

Holders of Interagency, Golden Age, or Golden Access passes do not have to pay the fee, but the card must be displayed on the car's dashboard. You can obtain these passes at White Mountain National Forest ranger stations and information centers.

Certain sites operated by concessionaires within the national forest charge a day-use fee. These include Russell Pond (off Tripoli Road) and South Pond (North Country).

Changes to the fee program, including an increase in the amount of the fees and the elimination of some of the sites that require fees, have been proposed. You can obtain the latest information at fs.usda.gov/main/whitemountain/passes-permits/recreation.

Franconia Notch and Crawford Notch state parks do not generally charge an entrance fee for day use by hikers. If you park at the beach at Echo Lake in Franconia Notch State Park, there is a charge of $4 per adult and $2 per child. Franconia Notch State Park charges an entrance fee of $16 per adult and $14 per child for walking the trails of Flume Gorge (Trip 11).

AMC LODGES AND HUTS

Hikers staying overnight in the White Mountains can opt for backcountry stays at AMC's huts or frontcountry comfort at AMC's Joe Dodge Lodge in Pinkham Notch or Highland Center in Crawford Notch. Two shuttle routes operate daily from June through September and on weekends until mid-October, connecting the lodge-and-hut system to major trailheads across the White Mountain National Forest. For more information about AMC's lodges and huts, visit outdoors.org/destinations; a shuttle schedule is available at outdoors .org/shuttle. For shuttle reservations, call 603-466-2727.

DOGS ON THE TRAILS

Dogs can be great hiking companions. They are permitted on trails in the White Mountain National Forest, but they must be under verbal or physical control at all times. Hikers with dogs should recognize that while dogs will likely bring smiles to the faces of many other hikers, some people may find dogs intimidating, especially when dogs surprise them on a trail. When in campgrounds, dogs must be leashed. The rules for New Hampshire state parks vary by park. Franconia Notch and Crawford Notch state parks both allow dogs in designated areas, so check when you arrive at those parks. Be aware that dogs, like people, will have more stamina for hiking if they have been getting regular exercise before you attempt to scale a mountain with them.

LEAVE NO TRACE

The Appalachian Mountain Club (AMC) is a national educational partner of Leave No Trace, a nonprofit organization dedicated to promoting and inspiring responsible outdoor recreation through education, research, and partnerships. The Leave No Trace program seeks to develop wildland ethics—ways in which people think and act in the outdoors to minimize their impact on the areas they visit and to protect our natural resources for future enjoyment. Leave No Trace unites four federal land management agencies—U.S. Forest Service, National Park Service, Bureau of Land Management, and U.S. Fish & Wildlife Service—with manufacturers, outdoor retailers, user groups, educators, organizations such as AMC, and individuals.

The Leave No Trace ethic is guided by the following seven principles:

1. **Plan Ahead and Prepare.** Know the terrain and any regulations applicable to the area you're planning to visit, and be prepared for extreme weather or other emergencies. This will enhance your enjoyment and ensure that you've chosen an appropriate destination. Small groups have less impact on resources and on the experiences of other backcountry visitors.

2. **Travel and Camp on Durable Surfaces.** Travel and camp on established trails and campsites, rock, gravel, dry grasses, or snow. Good campsites are found, not made. Camp at least 200 feet from lakes and streams, and focus activities on areas where vegetation is absent. In pristine areas, disperse use to prevent the creation of campsites and trails.

3. **Dispose of Waste Properly.** Pack it in, pack it out. Inspect your camp for trash or food scraps. Deposit solid human waste in cat holes dug 6 to 8 inches deep, at least 200 feet from water, camps, and trails. Pack out toilet paper and hygiene products. To wash yourself or your dishes, carry water 200 feet from streams or lakes and use small amounts of biodegradable soap. Scatter strained dishwater.

4. **Leave What You Find.** Cultural or historical artifacts, as well as natural objects such as plants and rocks, should be left as found.

5. **Minimize Campfire Impacts.** Cook on a stove. Use established fire rings, fire pans, or mound fires. If you build a campfire, keep it small and use dead sticks found on the ground.

6. **Respect Wildlife.** Observe wildlife from a distance. Feeding animals alters their natural behavior. Protect wildlife from your food by storing rations and trash securely.

7. **Be Considerate of Other Visitors.** Be courteous, respect the quality of other visitors' backcountry experience, and let nature's sounds prevail.

AMC is a national provider of the Leave No Trace Master Educator course. AMC offers this five-day course, designed especially for outdoor professionals and land managers, as well as the shorter two-day Leave No Trace Trainer course, at locations throughout the Northeast.

For Leave No Trace information and materials, contact the Leave No Trace Center for Outdoor Ethics, P.O. Box 997, Boulder, CO 80306; 800-332-4100 or 302-442-8222; lnt.org. For a schedule of AMC Leave No Trace courses, see activities.outdoors.org.

1 // THE SOUTHWESTERN WHITE MOUNTAINS AND WATERVILLE VALLEY

The southwestern corner of the White Mountains provides a variety of hiking opportunities, from short walks along beautiful cascading streams to 4,800-foot Mount Moosilauke. The region includes the towns of Plymouth, Rumney, Campton, Thornton, Waterville Valley, and Sandwich. From I-93, it is a relatively short drive from the big metropolitan areas of the East Coast compared with driving to other parts of the White Mountains. The region loses its snow cover earlier in spring and cools down later in fall than more northerly sections of the White Mountain National Forest, making for a more extended hiking season.

Waterville Valley, tucked in among 4,000-foot peaks, is a centerpiece of this region. The location still feels secluded and quiet despite the presence of a major ski resort and conference center. If you are coming from the south, reach Waterville Valley from I-93 by traveling about 11 miles northeast on NH 49 (Campton, Exit 28). This well-paved, scenic road parallels Mad River. If approaching from the north, travel about 10 miles east through Thornton Gap on Tripoli Road (Exit 31 off I-93), an unpaved road for much of its length. Tripoli Road is not plowed in winter, so the trailheads along this route (Trips 3 and 8) cannot be reached by car during that time.

The valley's loop hike to Welch and Dickey mountains is one of the most popular family hikes in the White Mountains (see Trip 7). An extensive network of easy and moderate trails lead along streams and to scenic vistas.

The Squam Range in the southern part of this region provides views of several lakes, including Squam Lake and Lake Winnipesaukee. Percival-Morgan Loop (Trip 6) overlooks Squam Lake south of Waterville Valley.

Facing page: Hiking up the ledges near the summit of Mount Whiteface. *Photo by Alison Buchsbaum.*

SUPPLIES AND LOGISTICS

Plymouth is one of the larger towns in the White Mountain region, with restaurants, gas stations, malls, and Plymouth State University, a campus of the University System of New Hampshire. The resort community of Waterville Valley has downhill ski slopes, a convention center, and condominiums. The town caters to outdoor activities, so you'll have no trouble buying last-minute supplies before your hike or ice cream at the end. If you are coming from the north, you may find it convenient to get your supplies off Exit 32 (Lincoln/North Woodstock), where there are various stores along NH 112.

NEARBY CAMPING

Numerous national forest campgrounds are in the region. NH 49 in the Waterville Valley area provides access to three. These are Campton Campground (1.7 miles from I-93; 58 sites open in summer and a group camping area open year-round), Waterville Campground (10.0 miles from I-93; 27 sites open year-round), and Osceola Vista Campground (off Tripoli Road just beyond the village of Waterville Valley and the ski area; 11 sites open late May to early October). Russell Pond, a terrific spot for swimming and paddling, can be reached from Tripoli Road a few miles from I-93. It has 86 sites. The campgrounds in Franconia Notch and the western part of the Kancamagus Highway are 30 to 45 minutes from the trails in this region.

1 CASCADE PATH, WATERVILLE VALLEY

This pleasant, easy walk leads to a beautiful series of small waterfalls in Waterville Valley near the resort community. Several connecting trails provide a potentially longer hike.

Features 🏊🚶🐕 〰️ 🔍

Location Waterville Valley, NH

Rating Easy

Distance 3.4 miles round trip

Elevation Gain 800 feet

Estimated Time 2 hours

Maps *AMC White Mountain National Forest Map & Guide*, 4th ed., J7 and Waterville Valley Inset; AMC *White Mountain Guide*, 31st ed. Map 3 Crawford Notch–Sandwich Range, J6; USGS Topo: Waterville Valley, Mount Tripyramid

Contact White Mountain National Forest: fs.usda.gov/whitemountain, 603-536-6100; Waterville Valley Athletic & Improvement Association: wvaia.org

GPS Coordinates 43° 57.61′ N, 71° 30.52′ W

DIRECTIONS

Waterville Valley is at the end of NH 49, about 11 miles northeast of Exit 28 (Campton) off I-93, or about 10 miles east of I-93 through Thornton Gap on Tripoli Road (Exit 31). To find the trailhead, continue on NH 49 (Valley Road) past the town square and turn right onto Boulder Path Road, following the signs to Snow's Mountain and Waterville Valley Athletic & Improvement Association hiking trails. Park in the large lot just past the tennis courts about 0.1 mile north of West Branch Road. Follow the sign to Cascade Path. New development may affect the location of the trailhead, so pay close attention to the sign.

TRAIL DESCRIPTION

Cascade Path begins by climbing along the left (north) side of the winding Cascade Ridge Road. At 0.2 mile, the trail, now ascending an old ski slope, passes the junction with Boulder Path. It passes through a small patch of woods, crosses the road once more, and enters the woods on the left (north) side of the old slope after about 0.3 mile. Do not turn off too soon on the cross-country ski trail.

The yellow-blazed hiking trail intersects a cross-country ski trail a short way in and then ascends a low ridge and passes Elephant Rock Trail at 0.5 mile. Just beyond, look for

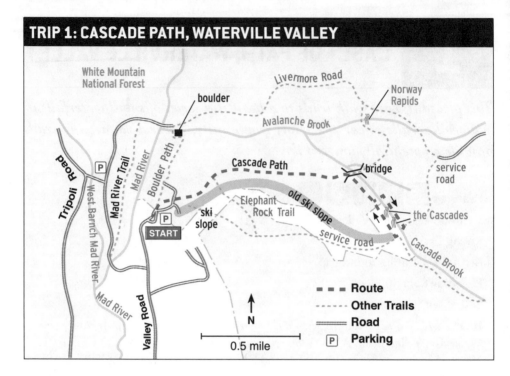

White Mountain National Forest

Livermore Road

Norway Rapids

boulder

Avalanche Brook

Tripoli Road

Mad River Trail

Mad River

Boulder Path

Cascade Path

bridge

service road

West Barnch Mad River

ski slope

Elephant Rock Trail

old ski slope

the Cascades

START

service road

Cascade Brook

Mad River

Valley Road

- - - Route
- - - - Other Trails
==== Road
P Parking

N

0.5 mile

hemlocks with their short, flat needles. One hemlock root hugging a rock near the trail may particularly catch your eye.

The trail descends gradually, crossing several small wooden bridges. It reaches Cascade Brook at 1.2 miles, where a cross-country ski trail comes in from the left. A patch of pretty wildflowers blooms in the middle of the trail just before the brook. Look for blue-bead lilies (*Clintonia*), bunchberries, lance-leaved twisted-stalks, and asters. You could turn around here, although the cascades are not much farther and are really worth seeing. Norway Rapids Trail, also with yellow blazes, heads left across the brook, but continue straight on Cascade Path.

Along the brook you will pass a marvelous example of a tree that grows on top of a rock. The woods here are dominated by northern hardwoods: beech, sugar maple, and yellow birch. Red and painted trillium, blue-bead lily, Canada mayflower, goldthread, and mountain wood sorrel put on particularly showy displays in spring. In late summer, most of the flowers are gone, but the rich woods provide a great habitat for mushrooms. Amanitas, most of which are deadly poisonous, are particularly abundant. One of the most common and attractive is fly agaric, which is your classic toadstool with a broad red cap (occasionally yellowish) covered with flecks of whitish scales. A pure white amanita is called destroying angel, which certainly brings home the message that picking any mushroom should be best left to the experts—and even they occasionally make mistakes. Boletes also grow here; they have tiny pores instead of gills on their undersides.

Just below the first cascade, the main part of the trail crosses the stream to its east side, which could be tricky at high water. With a trail on the west side as well, you have a choice.

Waterfall along Cascade Path. *Photo by Edward Quinlan.*

Both sides become rougher at this point. The east side of the brook offers swimming opportunities, although the water is always frigid. If you remain on the west side, you are higher above the brook with great perspectives on the cascades, which go on for a good distance, shooting through small gorges and tumbling into deep pools. Just when you think you've reached the last waterfall, you walk up a little farther and discover yet another.

Although pools below several of the cascades may look inviting, use care, common sense, and a conservation ethic. Some are difficult to reach because of the steep sides of the banks. Others show signs of erosion where too many people have scurried down the sides to get to them, inadvertently destroying the vegetation.

Much of the streambed around the cascades consists of flat slabs of granite. A flat slab just below the bridge at the top of the trail makes an excellent lunch rock. Note there and elsewhere how the granite fractured along smooth joints when it was eroded by streams.

When you reach an unpaved maintenance road at 1.7 miles, retrace your steps to return to the trailhead. If the crossing at the base of the first cascade is passable, you could loop back on the path on the other side of the brook.

DID YOU KNOW?

Cascade Path, built in the 1850s, was one of the first trails constructed in Waterville Valley, according to Steven D. Smith's *The Waterville Valley Guidebook* (Town of Waterville Valley, 2020). It was part of the first trail network in the Northeast, built by Nathaniel Greeley (see Laura and Guy Waterman's *Forest and Crag: A History of Hiking, Trail Blazing, and Adventure in the Northeast Mountains*, SUNY Press, 2019). Individual trails had long existed, but Greeley's work represented the first interconnected network.

Waterville Valley remained a quiet summer resort until 1966, when the ski area at Mount Tecumseh was developed.

OTHER ACTIVITIES

Many connecting trails could make for a longer loop hike. When you reach the maintenance road at the end of Cascade Path, you can turn left onto the maintenance road, follow it for 0.6 mile, and then turn left onto Livermore Road (another unpaved road—no motorized vehicles). After 1.5 more miles, turn left onto yellow-blazed Boulder Path. The namesake boulder, a huge glacial erratic in Slide Brook, is just a short distance from the turn. The path crosses the brook, which will require wading. (If the crossing looks too challenging, then complete the loop on Livermore Road instead.) After the crossing, the trail follows the brook for about 100 yards past various wildflowers, such as pink lady's slipper and Canada mayflower, and oak ferns. It then ascends away from the brook and reaches an old woodland road. Turn right and follow the road back to a cul de sac. Walk alongside the cul de sac back to Cascade Path to complete the loop (4.9 miles for the complete loop).

Norway Rapids Trail (yellow blazes) also links Cascade Path to Livermore Road. It turns left (northeast) at 1.2 miles along Cascade Path, crosses a bridge over Cascade Brook and runs for 0.5 mile to Livermore Road, passing impressive rapids on Slide Brook. Crossing Slide Brook requires wading, which should not be attempted in high water.

If you turn right onto the maintenance road at the top of Cascade Path, you reach the top of Snow's Mountain Ski Area in 0.8 mile and can enjoy some views. Descend on Elephant Rock Trail back to a left turn onto Cascade Path.

Livermore Road is appropriate for skiing and snowshoeing. In addition, Waterville Valley offers a host of other skiing and snowshoeing opportunities.

The resort village of Waterville Valley, famous for skiing in winter, has restaurants, a grocery store, golf, fishing, and other amenities.

MORE INFORMATION

Most of this hike is within the White Mountain National Forest. Parking is free.

AQUATIC INSECTS IN THE WHITE MOUNTAINS

A number of aquatic insects are common inhabitants of the White Mountains. Most are easy to find in streams, ditches, and temporary woodland pools, and some, such as mosquitoes and blackflies, actually come looking for you.

Mosquitoes begin life in small, temporary pools, such as those that form in depressions on a path after a heavy rain, or in holes in trees. The wormlike larvae (called wrigglers because of their corkscrew movements) survive best in these isolated pools because they are easy prey for fish, salamanders, and just about everything else that lives in more permanent bodies of water. Wrigglers typically hang down from the water surface, with their posterior end taking in air while they feed on detritus (dead leaf fragments and other organic matter) underwater. They abandon this posture and scatter toward the bottom when your shadow or any other "threat" appears over their little pool. A larva goes through several stages before forming a pupa (which also swims in the pool). The adult mosquito emerges after the pupal stage and leaves the pool to mate and search for nectar (males) or a blood meal (females).

The crane fly is a graceful fly with very long legs. You are likely to see one hovering above the water, occasionally landing on people and causing instant panic because it looks like the world's largest mosquito. But don't worry, crane flies are harmless. Their larvae feed on detritus in streams and are important in nutrient recycling.

Blackflies spend their larval stages attached to rocks along flowing waters, passively feeding on organic matter that passes by. Unfortunately for us and other mammals, they abandon that lifestyle as adults. Although males feed solely on nectar or plant sap, females require a blood meal for optimum egg development.

Predaceous diving beetles spend most of their lives in water. You might find them in any deep pool in a stream or even in ditches along the sides of trails. They are blackish and oval and swim strongly underwater, feeding on invertebrates and even larval fish. Don't try to pick up one with your hands because they can give a surprisingly nasty bite (their larvae are named "water tigers"). Adults can fly, which is how they reach some of those out-of-the-way pools in the woods.

Water striders walk on the water' surface, supported by surface tension—the same force that keeps cocoa powder on the surface of hot water until it is stirred. Tiny hairs on the bottoms of their legs repel water and prevent them from sinking. If for some reason their

legs do penetrate the surface, the insect "falls" underwater and must crawl up on some vegetation to dry off before it can walk on water again. If the light is just right, water striders appear to have foot pads under their legs. These are actually indentations of the water surface itself under the weight of the insect.

Humans are much too big and heavy to walk on the water, but for many tiny creatures, the water surface can be an impenetrable barrier. Water striders feed on small invertebrates that fall onto the surface film and get stuck. They lay eggs underwater, and the newly hatched young must swim to the surface and break through to survive.

Whirligig beetles spin around in dizzying patterns on the surface of the water, particularly when they are disturbed by your presence. They actually have two pairs of eyes, one that can look up at the sky to detect predators and another that looks into the water. They hold their antenna on the water surface and are very sensitive to vibrations that might indicate potential prey struggling there.

2 | DAVIS BOULDERS AND GOODRICH ROCK

This hike takes you to two of the most impressive rock formations in the White Mountains. Goodrich Rock is one of the largest glacial erratics in New Hampshire. Davis Boulders are equally impressive, with the trail winding through a hillside of glacial erratics, one of which is named the Lemon Squeezer and another the Old Old Wooden Ship (yes, it is really "Old Old"). The hike starts out on a short section of Livermore Road and then follows a longer section of Greeley Ponds Trail and finally Goodrich Rock Trail.

Features

Location Waterville Valley, NH

Rating Moderate

Distance 4.0 miles round trip

Elevation Gain 750 feet

Estimated Time 2–3 hours

Maps *AMC White Mountain National Forest Map & Guide,* 4th ed., J6 and Waterville Valley inset; AMC *White Mountain Guide,* 31st ed. Map 3 Crawford Notch, Sandwich Range, J6; USGS Topo: Waterville Valley

GPS Coordinates 43° 57.96′ N, 71° 30.83′ W

Contact White Mountain National Forest: fs.usda.gov/whitemountain, 603-536-6100; Waterville Valley Athletic & Improvement Association: wvaia.org

DIRECTIONS

Waterville Valley is at the end of NH 49, about 11 miles northeast of the Campton exit off I-93 (Exit 28) or about 10 miles east of I-93 through Thornton Gap on Tripoli Road (Exit 31). Parking for this hike is available at the large Livermore parking area, also known as Depot Camp. To find the trailhead coming from NH 49, turn left on Tripoli Road before you reach the town center. In 1.3 miles, take the right fork to stay on Tripoli Road where the left branch goes to the downhill ski area. After 0.6 mile, turn right onto West Branch Road, cross the river on a bridge, and then turn left almost immediately into the parking area. If you take Tripoli Road from I-93, the parking area is about 0.6 mile on the left after you pass the entrance to Osceola Vista Campground.

TRIP 2: DAVIS BOULDERS AND GOODRICH ROCK

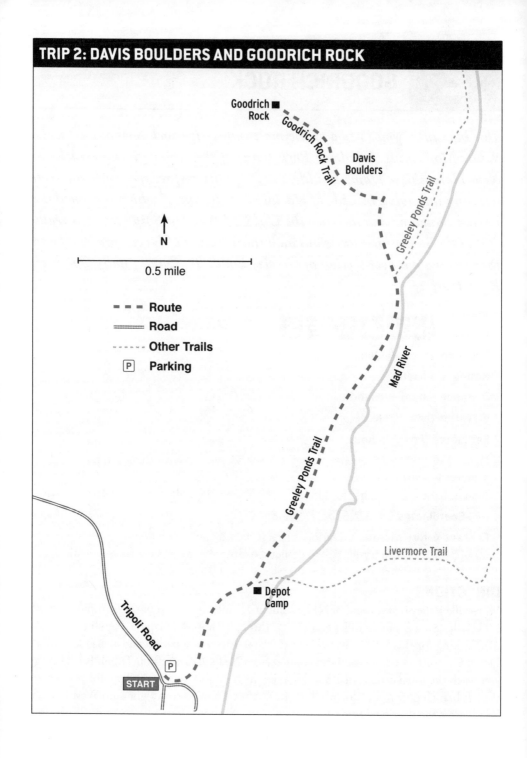

Goodrich
Rock ■

Goodrich Rock Trail

Davis
Boulders

Greeley Ponds Trail

↑
N

|———————————————|
0.5 mile

- - - Route
═══ Road
----- Other Trails
P Parking

Mad River

Greeley Ponds Trail

Tripoli Road

Livermore Trail

■ Depot
Camp

P

START

TRAIL DESCRIPTION

From the Livermore parking area, go past the kiosk and head left on Livermore Trail, a wide old logging road, also called Livermore Road. After about 0.2 mile, cross a ski trail and then an open space that was the actual site of Depot Camp, a logging camp in the early 1900s. The open field has fireweed, a tall (up to 4-foot) herb that has flowers with four beautiful magenta petals. This plant thrives in recently cleared areas, such as those created by fire, lumbering, or windstorms. Goldenrods and raspberry brambles also abound in this open field. The trail then crosses a bridge over a branch of Mad River and reaches the junction of Greeley Ponds Trail at 0.3 mile.

Turn left onto yellow-blazed Greeley Ponds Trail a short distance after crossing a tributary to Mad River. This gentle, wide trail is also a former logging road. You first pass through a patch of boreal forest with red spruce and balsam fir, not typical at this relatively low elevation. The trail then returns to the northern hardwood forest and veers slightly right where an old stone wall crosses the roadbed. Flowering wintergreen, wood ferns, and shining club moss provide the understory with greenery well into winter.

At 1.2 miles (0.9 mile along Greeley Ponds Trail), the route approaches the main branch of Mad River to your right, and you see the signs for Davis Boulders and Goodrich Rock to your left. Turn left onto Goodrich Rock Trail (yellow blazes). Immediately you start ascending up the relatively steep side of the glacially scoured valley. Climb about 250 feet, with the final ascent on stone steps. The trail becomes more level and at 1.7 miles enters the realm of Davis Boulders. This fantastic landscape features huge boulders carried to this site by the last glacier and strewn throughout the forest. Kids and adults will love climbing through the narrow cleft in the rocks called the Lemon Squeezer and having their pictures taken. Be careful in a few places, particularly if the rocks are wet.

Many of the boulders are covered with rock tripe, a lichen that resembles a piece of shoe leather. This lichen is said to be edible, but only as an emergency food. Also growing on the rocks is an evergreen fern aptly named rock fern. See if you can find circular clusters of spore cases (called sori) underneath its fronds. Equally impressive are the trees, primarily yellow birches, growing on top of the boulders. Their roots seem to embrace the rocks as they anchor themselves on the ground.

The remainder of the hike is within the boreal forest with red spruce and balsam fir. At 2.0 miles you reach Goodrich Rock, which one of my hiking companions described as "the mother of all erratics" (see "Why Glaciers?" page 167). Follow the trail around to the back of the boulder to a 20-foot wooden ladder. Climb the ladder to the top of the rock for an excellent view to the south over Waterville Valley to Sandwich Mountain and Mount Tecumseh, but be careful in wet weather, particularly on the descent. This is a great place for lunch or a snack.

Retrace your steps and descend via Goodrich Rock Trail to Greeley Ponds Trail. Take a few minutes to enjoy the access to Mad River at this junction. Then return via Greeley Ponds and Livermore trails to the parking area.

Climb the ladder at Goodrich Rock for a great view of Waterville Valley.

DID YOU KNOW?

According to Steven D. Smith's *The Waterville Valley Guidebook* (Town of Waterville Valley, 2020), the Goodrich family were summer residents of Waterville Valley starting in the late 1800s. They were active AMC members and responsible for many of the trails built in the valley. Arthur Goodrich, the first of the Goodriches to discover the charms of the area in 1875, published the first guidebook to Waterville Valley trails in 1892. He and his brother Charles first reported the rock that bears the family name. Arthur's son Nathaniel became a famous climber and is credited in a 1931 issue of the AMC's journal *Appalachia* with proposing a goal of climbing ("peak bagging") all 4,000-footers in the White Mountains.

OTHER ACTIVITIES

Multiple interesting short walks off Livermore Trail are within easy access of this hike. If you have not had your fill of glacial erratics, check out the Boulder, which is 0.2 mile farther east along Livermore Trail from its intersection with Greeley Ponds Trail. This boulder is just off the main route on Boulder Path and sits in the middle of Slide Brook. Walk an additional 0.1 mile along Livermore Trail to Big Pine Trail. Take the 0.2-mile spur (yellow blazes) to see four huge white pines that miraculously escaped the lumber cutters. They are within the Mad River floodplain, so there is one short, somewhat steep pitch.

Livermore and Greeley Ponds trails are appropriate for skiing and snowshoeing. In addition, Waterville Valley offers a host of other skiing and snowshoeing opportunities.

The resort village of Waterville Valley, famous for skiing in winter, has restaurants, a grocery store, golf, fishing, and other amenities.

MORE INFORMATION

White Mountain National Forest lists Livermore Trail (Livermore Road) as an accessible trail. See fs.usda.gov/Internet/FSE_DOCUMENTS/stelprdb5377702.pdf.

Bathrooms are available at the trailhead.

The Livermore parking area has a day-use fee of $5. Although it is a large lot, it can become filled on weekends, including during the cross-country skiing season.

3 EAST POND AND LITTLE EAST POND

Nestled behind Mount Osceola and Scar Ridge at 2,600 feet, East Pond and Little East Pond are two aquatic gems. They are connected by a loop trail that passes through rich woodlands carpeted with wildflowers, ferns, and mushrooms and crosses over several streams.

Features

Location Livermore, NH

Rating Moderate

Distance 4.8 miles loop

Elevation Gain 1,000 feet

Estimated Time 4–5 hours

Maps *AMC White Mountain National Forest Map & Guide*, 4th ed., I6 and Waterville Valley inset; AMC *White Mountain Guide*, 31st ed. Map 4 Moosilauke–Kinsman, J5; USGS Topo: Waterville Valley and Mount Osceola

GPS Coordinates 43° 59.63′ N, 71° 35.00′ W

Contact White Mountain National Forest: fs.usda.gov/whitemountain, 603-536-6100

DIRECTIONS

The trailhead for East Pond Trail is off Tripoli Road, about 5.2 miles from its junction with I-93 at Exit 31. If you are coming from Waterville Valley, the trailhead is about 6 miles west of the junction of Tripoli Road and NH 49. Make sure to stay to the right when the road to the ski area splits off to the left. Turn north off Tripoli Road onto a gravel side road and continue for about 100 yards to the parking lot (4.8 miles from the road to the ski area if you are coming from Waterville Valley). Tripoli Road is not plowed in winter.

TRAIL DESCRIPTION

This loop hike uses East Pond Trail, East Pond Loop Trail, and Little East Pond Trail. The entire loop may be long for younger children, so you can shorten the hike by walking only to East Pond, a moderate uphill of 800 feet over 1.3 miles.

East Pond Trail starts out on an old, wide logging road. After a few minutes, the logging road swings off to the right, and East Pond Trail continues straight, remaining on a wide path. Look for the yellow blazes.

After 0.3 mile, you reach the junction with Little East Pond Trail, near where the tripoli mill once stood (more on that later). This is a good spot to see wildflowers and ferns, notably wild sarsaparilla, red trillium, golden alexanders, blue-bead lily, and long beech fern.

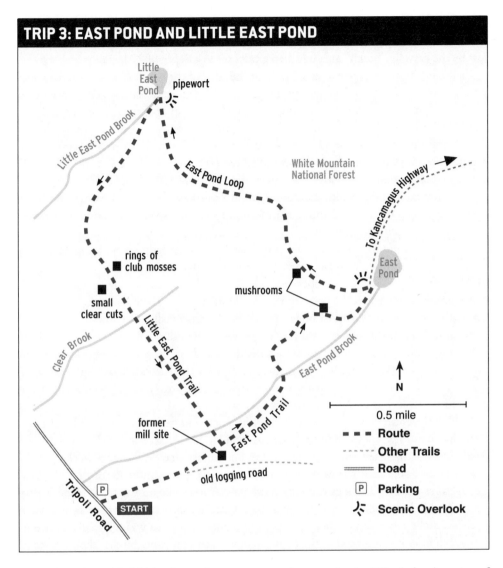

Striped maple and hobblebush are the common understory shrubs. Watch for the ruins of the mill (foundation, stones, pieces of metal) about 200 feet in the woods to the right.

Continue straight on East Pond Trail along the old logging road on a gradual ascent. The trail remains wide and, for the most part, offers easy walking. Cross East Pond Brook at 0.7 mile on a solid bridge. Pass a sign stating that you have entered the East Pond Forest Protection Area at about 1 mile. The forest has become spruce-fir at this point. At 1.3 miles, just below East Pond, you reach a three-way junction. East Pond Loop Trail diverges sharply left toward Little East Pond. East Pond Trail continues at a slight left and follows the west shore of the pond. Take a short spur to the right to reach the shore of East Pond at an open area. This is the best spot to view the pond, swim, and picnic.

East Pond is about 6.5 acres and at an elevation of 2,600 feet. A saddle in Scar Ridge forms the backdrop of the pond as you look out from the southern end. The water is shallow by the gravelly "beach" area but then grades off to a depth of 27 feet.

There's much for everyone to enjoy right at the edge of the pond. If you swim, you'll be joining the abundant resident red-spotted newts. These aquatic salamanders have green bodies with red spots, and they use their flattened tails to propel themselves through the water. In an unusual twist for an amphibian, immature newts—just recently graduated from being aquatic larvae—typically leave the water and live on land for several years in a juvenile life stage, during which they're called red efts. You may have seen these brightly colored critters (orange-red bodies with green spots—the reverse of the adult color pattern) on the forest floor of the White Mountains, often a considerable distance from water. They eventually return to the water and transform into newts that spend their adult lives swimming in places such as East Pond.

Newts have a number of companions in East Pond. Frog tadpoles are quite abundant from late spring through midsummer. Leeches also inhabit the pond. A beaver lodge is visible near a big rock on the opposite shore. Dragonflies patrol for unwary insects, and water striders skim across the pools in the small outlet creek. The most common shrub is leatherleaf, a typical resident of boggy pond shores. Shadbush and withe-rod, a type of viburnum also called northern wild raisin, can also be found.

For additional perspectives, follow East Pond Trail along the west side of the pond for about 200 yards. (It eventually swings away and meets the Kancamagus Highway in 3.7 miles.) Explore some short spur paths to informal camping areas near the pond shore. Keep a watchful eye skyward for ravens, hawks, and other birds.

To hike the entire loop, return to the trail junction and head west on East Pond Loop Trail. It is about 1.5 miles (one hour) from East Pond to Little East Pond via East Pond Loop Trail. This trail has a few small ups and downs but almost no overall change in elevation.

East Pond Loop Trail passes through a forest of red spruce and balsam fir with occasional paper birches. The logs of many more paper birches lie on the forest floor. Thirty years ago, birch dominated this section of the forest, but spruce and fir have clearly taken over—actually returning to their former prominence. This area was originally spruce-fir forest, but after it was logged in the early twentieth century, paper birches took over until they were toppled by windstorms.

The first part of this trail has almost no understory vegetation, probably due to the intense shading by the spruce and fir trees. Sunny gaps created by wind throws provide partial views of Mount Osceola, Scar Ridge, and the Sandwich Range. Hay-scented fern, a large, lacy fern that smells like freshly cut grass when it dries out in fall, often colonizes forest gaps. Hay-scented fern grows as a dense colony because new individuals are produced from old ones by underground runners. So the patch you see is really one individual plant, because the ferns are all connected underneath.

East Pond Loop Trail is a particularly good place to find witch's butter if you are hiking midsummer through autumn. This bright-yellow or yellow-orange fungus grows on dead logs. It is also called jelly fungus because it looks like a blob of jelly on a log and is somewhat sticky. Like most fungi, witch's butter gets its nutrition by breaking down dead organic matter, such as a log upon which it grows.

View of Scar Ridge from East Pond.

Listen for birds that are characteristic of spruce-fir forest in this stretch of the trail. Argu-ably the most beautiful song is the ascending flutelike call of the Swainson's thrush. You may also hear the staccato two-note *che-bunk* of the yellow-bellied flycatcher, or its more musical slurred, whistle-like call. Magnolia warblers are also common here.

About 0.5 mile from Little East Pond, cross a streambed that is likely to be dry in middle to late summer. As you enter an area with abundant hobblebush, blue-bead lily, and painted trillium, you are getting close to Little East Pond. When the trail reaches the junction of Little East Pond Trail (2.8 miles), a short spur path to the right leads you to the south end of the pond.

Little East Pond (3.5 acres) is shallow and dotted with waterlilies and pipeworts. Pipe-worts look like long pins, with small white balls atop thin stalks. The "pinheads" are flower clusters. The shoreline is boggy, with abundant sphagnum, leatherleaf, mountain holly, Labrador tea, and marsh Saint-John's-wort. Right by the trail sign, look for a patch of snowberries and bunchberries growing under small balsam fir and red spruce. The roots of a large, upturned tree form an interesting background for a family photograph.

From Little East Pond, return to Little East Pond Trail to continue the loop. It is 1.7 miles to the junction with East Pond Trail. The route first descends somewhat steeply through spruce and fir (400-foot decline over 0.4 mile), initially along the outlet to Little East Pond. It then makes a sharp left turn, levels out, and follows the grade of an old log-ging railroad through a rich northern hardwood forest. Along with hobblebush and striped maples, notice the young sugar maples coming up. Unlike many species of trees, which will die if they are kept in the shade too long, sugar maple saplings are able to survive under the forest canopy, biding their time and waiting for their moment in the sun when one of the giants around them falls. Then, finally bathed in full sunlight, the little trees grow fast toward the forest canopy. You can also find an occasional white ash along with the maple, yellow birch, and beech.

Striking "fairy rings" of shining club moss appear along Little East Pond Trail. These roundish patches of low, dark green plants resemble bottle brushes with their small, dense, needlelike leaves on upright stems. Like hay-scented fern, this club moss grows by one individual spore germinating and then sending out runners that create new upright plants.

The trail crosses Clear Brook (rock-hop) at about 3.8 miles. It crosses other smaller brooks and travels on split logs through muddy areas. Rock-hop across East Pond Brook (4.4 miles) just before reaching the junction with East Pond Trail. Turn right to return to the parking area (0.3 mile from the junction) on Tripoli Road. The total loop is 4.8 miles.

DID YOU KNOW?

Tripoli (or tripolite), the source of the name of the road, is a rock, also called diatomaceous earth, that can be made into a fine powder with a variety of uses. These include a polish in toothpaste, an abrasive in cleaners, an element in water filters, and an aid in controlling insects and other pests. Tripoli is composed of the silica derived from the skeletons of diatoms, which are microscopic marine algae. The rock was mined from the bottom of East Pond in the early part of the twentieth century and hauled down to the tripoli mill near the trail junction for processing.

OTHER ACTIVITIES

You can swim with the newts in East Pond. Bring water shoes because the pond bottom has gravelly and muddy spots (and unfortunately you also need to watch for broken glass). If you see leeches, keep moving—they are reportedly less likely to latch on to a moving target.

MORE INFORMATION

Parking at the trailhead is free. Restaurants and hiking supplies are available in Waterville Valley.

4   STINSON MOUNTAIN TRAIL

Stinson Mountain is a long ridge that dominates the landscape just north of Plymouth, New Hampshire, and west of I-93. The summit offers a sweeping view south over the Lakes Region and toward Mount Cardigan.

Features

Location Rumney, NH

Rating Moderate

Distance 3.6 miles round trip

Elevation Gain 1,400 feet

Estimated Time 3 hours

Maps *AMC White Mountain National Forest Map & Guide*, 4th ed., K3; AMC *White Mountain Guide*, 31st ed. Map 4 Moosilauke–Kinsman, K3; USGS Topo: Rumney

GPS Coordinates 43° 50.94′ N, 71° 48.10′ W

Contact White Mountain National Forest: fs.usda.gov/whitemountain, 603-536-6100

DIRECTIONS

Stinson Mountain is in the extreme southwestern part of the White Mountain National Forest, not far from Plymouth, New Hampshire. From Exit 26 (milepost 82) off I-93, follow NH 25 west. In 4.0 miles go around a traffic circle, staying on NH 25. In another 1.0 mile, pass Polar Caves. At 8.5 miles from I-93, turn right onto Main Street toward Rumney Center, which you reach in 0.7 mile. Continue straight through the main intersection onto Stinson Lake Road and go 4.5 miles. Just before you reach Stinson Lake itself, turn right onto Cross Street and take it for 0.8 mile (it becomes a dirt road) until it reaches a T junction with Doetown Road. Turn right toward the parking area, 0.3 mile down the road. Space is available for about four vehicles, and there is some room farther down along the side of the road for more cars to park.

TRAIL DESCRIPTION

Stinson Mountain Trail is a great half-day hike, suitable for younger children but still enough of a climb to engage experienced hikers. The ascent is pleasant and relatively easy, with no particularly steep sections.

From the parking area, the trail enters the woods and climbs gradually uphill through northern hardwoods. Many large sugar maples line this part of the route, but also look for white ash, a tree whose bark has an attractive lattice pattern. Another distinctive feature of white ash is its compound leaves (consisting of multiple leaflets all originating from one

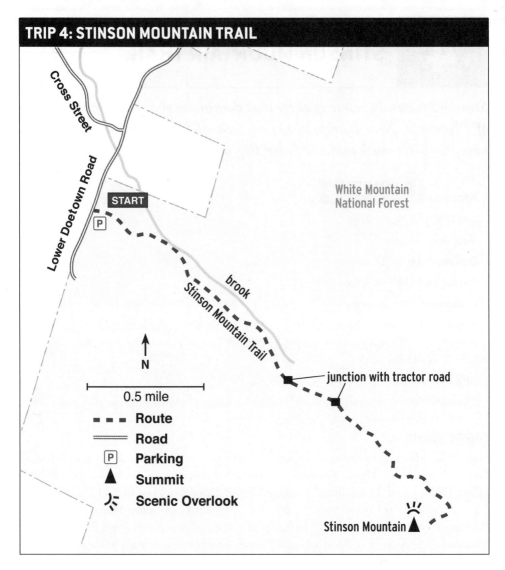

Cross Street

Lower Doetown Road

START

P

White Mountain
National Forest

brook

Stinson Mountain Trail

N

junction with tractor road

0.5 mile

- - - **Route**
=== **Road**
P **Parking**
▲ **Summit**
࿅ **Scenic Overlook**

Stinson Mountain ▲

bud) that are attached to the branches in pairs opposite each other. Birds singing in spring and summer include hermit thrushes, red-eyed vireos, black-throated blue warblers, and black-throated green warblers. Look for American toads and garter snakes scooting across the trail as you ascend. Yellow blazes are only occasional, but the route is easy to follow as long as you don't get sidetracked on one of the logging roads that it intersects.

After about 0.9 mile, turn left onto an old tractor road (now used by snowmobiles; watch out during winter) and follow it for 0.2 mile. In late summer and early fall, the white flowers of whorled aster put on a lovely display here.

At 1.1 miles at a trail sign, Stinson Mountain Trail branches off to the right from the snowmobile road just before a wooden bridge and climbs more steeply. Hobblebush will be evident along this section of the trail. Note the gradual change from northern hardwoods to spruce-fir forest. You'll find colonies of hay-scented fern in every small clearing where sunlight reaches the forest floor. Birds on this higher section could be Swainson's thrushes, magnolia and yellow-rumped warblers, white-throated sparrows, and dark-eyed juncos. A short distance from the summit, the trail intersects the upper part of the same snowmobile road. Continue straight to the open summit. A right turn will also get you there via a short loop.

At the open summit, the old concrete footings from a fire tower provide a handy perch from which to enjoy the views to the south and east. Squam Lake to the southeast is the largest body of water visible. To the southwest, the summit of Mount Cardigan (3,150 feet) is prominent. Wind turbines on Tenny and Fletcher mountains are to the west. You can get a look at Stinson Lake and Mount Moosilauke by a short spur path to the north. This spur can be a little difficult to distinguish from some dead-end trails in the northwest direction, but keep trying. Restricted views of Franconia Ridge and the 4,000-footers along the Kancamagus Highway are to the east and northeast.

Aside from the views, the layering and folds in the rocks at the summit are bound to catch your eye. The bedrocks of Stinson Mountain are metamorphic rocks that were deposited as layers of sand and mud under a prehistoric ocean about 400 million years ago. These sediments first became layers of sandstone and shale. They were later folded and re-formed as metamorphic schists and gneisses when these rocks were under intense heat and pressure and actually became flexible as they were compressed between two moving continents.

The short trees at the summit include balsam fir, red spruce, and heart-leaved birch. Lowbush blueberries and raspberries are there, but neither is abundant enough to satisfy

The view north from Stinson Mountain includes Stinson Lake and Mounts Kineo and Moosilauke.

more than the first few hikers who arrive. Wildflowers and grasses include rough-stemmed goldenrod and poverty grass, fescues, and sedges in a damp area.

On your descent, the sign indicating "Turn Right" when you reach this upper junction is intended for snowmobilers who use the old tractor road. For a different perspective from your ascent, descend via the snowmobile road to its lower junction with the hiking trail (a few damp spots). Just be careful not to miss the right turn from the road back onto the hiking trail.

OTHER ACTIVITIES

Quincy Bog, an interesting wetland with a nature center, is nearby. Follow Quincy Road from Rumney Center for 2.1 miles east and turn left onto Quincy Bog Road. Admission to the bog is free. The easy 1-mile loop trail is partly on a boardwalk.

Rumney Rocks is a popular rock-climbing area about 1 mile west of Rumney Village off Buffalo Road (parking fee of $5). Another 1.5 miles farther down Buffalo Road, Rattlesnake Mountain Trail provides a short, steep ascent to a loop trail on a ridge. The ridge provides an extensive view south over the Baker River valley and east to Stinson Mountain and other nearby peaks. Parking is free.

MORE INFORMATION

Parking is free.

If you are hiking with your dog in summer, bring extra water because the streams along the trail are likely to be dry.

You will find an assortment of restaurants and other amenities along Route 25 in West Plymouth and Rumney.

5 MOUNT ISRAEL

Mount Israel commands great views of the Sandwich Range, other peaks south of the Kancamagus Highway, and the Lakes Region. The ascent via Wentworth Trail is a moderate but steady climb.

Features 👣 🐴 💧 🔎 ✺ ⛺ ⛱

Location Sandwich, NH

Rating Moderate

Distance 4.2 miles round trip

Elevation Gain 1,700 feet

Estimated Time 3.5 hours

Maps *AMC White Mountain National Forest Map & Guide*, 4th ed., L7; AMC *White Mountain Guide*, 31st ed. Map 3 Crawford Notch–Sandwich Range, L7; USGS Topo: Center Sandwich

GPS Coordinates 43° 49.71′ N, 71° 29.06′ W

Contact White Mountain National Forest: fs.usda.gov/whitemountain, 603-536-6100; Mead Base Conservation Center: meadbase.org, 603-284-6919

DIRECTIONS

From Exit 24 on I-93, follow US 3/NH 25 east for 4.0 miles through Ashland to Holderness. Turn left onto NH 113 and follow it for 11.6 miles to Center Sandwich. Along the way you will pass the Squam Lake Natural Science Center and the trailheads for Mounts Morgan and Percival (Trip 6). Make a sharp left onto Grove Street, take it for 0.4 mile, and then continue on Diamond Ledge Road for 1.9 miles. Turn left onto Sandwich Notch Road for 0.2 mile and take a side road to the right (Diamond Ledge Road again) for 0.4 mile to Mead Base Conservation Center. This is a camp that houses trail crews and is run by the Friends of Mead Base. Park in the field below the building.

TRAIL DESCRIPTION

Wentworth Trail is a well-graded path marked with yellow blazes. It starts to the left of the conservation center and enters a deciduous woodland that has the feel of a southern New Hampshire forest due to the omnipresent oak trees. Look for hop hornbeam, a tree with shaggy, vertically peeling strands of bark. This tree is noted for its very hard wood, hence its alternative name—ironwood. Hop hornbeam is more common south of the White Mountains, so its presence here reflects the southern exposure of this trail. Ferns are plentiful along the route, including long beech, Christmas, New York, and bracken ferns. Understory herbs include wild sarsaparilla and asters.

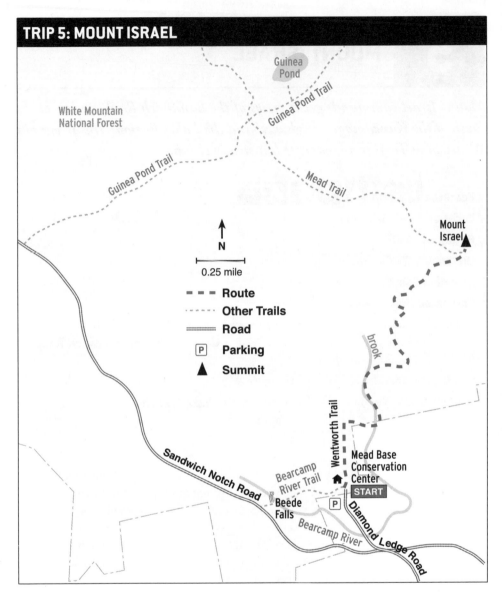

After about 0.3 mile, the trail passes through a stone wall on an old cart path, climbs up some steps above the wall, and crosses a stream at 0.5 mile. The trail then turns left to follow the stream for another 0.3 mile, making for a very pleasant walk. Note the presence of some large red pines (their long needles in bunches of two) in this area. At 0.8 mile, the trail turns right, away from the stream, and starts to climb at a slightly steeper grade. As you ascend, you will notice balsam fir trees starting to make their appearance, eventually becoming dominant.

The trail ascends on switchbacks and at 1.5 miles reaches a vista over Squam Lake and a partial view of Lake Winnipesaukee. Crinkled hairgrass, an attractive grass that grows in clumps in this ledgy area, has dark maroon flowers and seed heads in summer.

Wintry scene on the summit of Mount Israel. *Photo by Jerry Monkman.*

Shortly after the vista, the trail levels off at the top of the ridge and becomes a pleasant boreal forest walk. Cross more ledges that provide glimpses of the final view, head back into the forest for a short stint, and then reach the intersection with Mead Trail at 2.1 miles. The summit, marked with a large cairn, is about 70 yards beyond.

Sandwich Mountain, also called Sandwich Dome, is the closest large mountain to the north. Looking farther to the northeast, you can see the three summits of Mount Tripyramid with their distinct landslides on their slopes. The vegetation is a mix of red spruce and balsam fir, with a few paper birches. The pale green of reindeer lichen underlain by stones may remind you of a rock garden. Creeping snowberry, black huckleberry, lowbush blueberry, and sheep laurel make up the understory.

Head northeast from the summit cairn to find a slightly beaten trail that leads in about 100 yards to another scenic vista with views to the northeast (Mounts Tripyramid and Chocorua) and south (Squam Lake). Look for a wet area containing a lush growth of haircap moss (illustrated here). The brown capsules of this species contain a mechanism for shooting spores some distance from the parent plant, thus ensuring some measure of dispersal.

After enjoying the scenery, retrace your steps to the trailhead at Mead Base.

OTHER ACTIVITIES

A popular short extension from Mead Base Conservation Center is to walk west on Bear-camp River Trail to Beede Falls in Sandwich Town Park. This route follows the river through a dark hemlock forest and passes Cow Cave, where legend has it that a cow survived the winter. It reaches the falls 0.4 mile from Mead Base. The pool created by the falls is a popular swimming/wading area (water is thigh deep) and an ideal place to end your hike. Seeing the frozen falls in winter is a special treat. A short distance beyond the falls, Bearcamp River Trail comes out on Sandwich Notch Road.

A fine loop hike can be made by using Wentworth, Mead, and Guinea Pond trails. This requires either spotting a second car at the Guinea Pond trailhead or being willing to hike 2.2 miles along Sandwich Notch Road to Sandwich Town Park, then 0.6 mile along Bear-camp River Trail to get back to the conservation center. If you opt to spot a second car at the Guinea Pond trailhead, be aware that Sandwich Notch Road can be heavily rutted in sections, so it is best traveled by a vehicle with a high clearance (our subcompact scraped bottom numerous times).

For the loop, climb Mount Israel on Wentworth Trail as described above, but then descend via Mead Trail, a gradual descent of 1.7 miles that ends at Guinea Pond Trail. A notable feature of this route is a small ravine and stream crossing at 0.8 mile from the summit. Turn left onto Guinea Pond Trail, which is a level walk along an old forest road that leads to Sandwich Notch Road in 1.6 miles. Guinea Pond Trail passes through numerous beaver-created wetlands that are framed by nearby mountains, so the scenery is interesting and the birdlife more abundant than in other parts of the loop trail. Flooding by beavers may require relocation of some sections of the trail from time to time. Look for plentiful wildflowers, including fireweed and meadowsweet, in the right of way because it gets much more sun than the forest floor. When you reach Sandwich Notch Road, turn left for the hike back to Mead Base Conservation Center (assuming you did not spot a car at the Guinea Pond trailhead). After 2.5 miles along this road, turn left at Sandwich Town Park and follow Bearcamp River Trail for 0.6 mile past Beede Falls and back to the conservation center.

MORE INFORMATION

Parking at Mead Base Conservation Center is free, although donations are appreciated.

Three campsites are available to the public at Mead Base Conservation Center. One is a group camping site that can accommodate up to 30 people. See sites.google.com/site/friendsofmead/home for information on reserving a campsite. A picnic area and bathrooms are located there as well. The main building and many of the outbuildings are reserved for the use of the trail crew, interns, and an artist in residence.

Holderness and Ashland have restaurants, gas stations, and motels. Sandwich, a classic small New England village, has a variety of restaurants, inns, and bed-and-breakfasts.

6 PERCIVAL-MORGAN LOOP

This fine loop hike takes you over two summits with extensive views of Squam Lake. Some scrambling on rocks and by caves near the summits adds to the climbing experience.

Features 🏕️ 🎿 🥾 🐕 🔭 ❄️

Location Holderness, NH, at trailhead; Campton, NH, at summits

Rating Moderate

Distance 5.4-mile loop

Elevation Gain 1,600 feet

Estimated Time 4.5 hours

Maps *AMC White Mountain National Forest Map & Guide*, 4th ed., L6; AMC *White Mountain Guide*, 31st ed. Map 4 Moosilauke–Kinsman, L6; USGS Topo: Squam Mountains

GPS Coordinates 43° 47.53′ N, 71° 32.68′ W (Mount Percival trailhead)

Contact Squam Lakes Association: squamlakes.org, 603-968-7336; Lakes Region Conservations Trust: lrct.org, 603-253-3301

DIRECTIONS

The two small mountains reached by this loop hike have their own trailheads, separated by about 0.4 mile on NH 113 in the town of Holderness on the north side of Squam Lake. The hike up Mount Percival is somewhat steeper, with more extensive scrambling over rocks, compared with Mount Morgan, so I suggest ascending via Mount Percival. From Exit 24 on I-93, follow US 3/NH 25 through Ashland to Holderness. Turn left onto NH 113, and note your mileage. You soon pass the Squam Lake Natural Science Center and follow the northwest shoreline of Squam Lake. After about 5 miles, pass the road that goes right to the Deephaven and Rockywold camps. At 5.6 miles from the junction in Holderness, the parking areas for Mount Morgan and for West Rattlesnake will be on the left and right side of the road, respectively. Continue for another 0.4 mile to the parking area for Mount Percival on the left, which has space for about twenty cars.

TRAIL DESCRIPTION

Mount Percival Trail, marked with yellow blazes, starts on a wide carriage road through a forest dominated by white pines. From late spring through summer, two wildflowers may immediately catch your eye. Orange hawkweed, also called devil's paintbrush, resembles an orange dandelion. The bright yellow flowers of common cinquefoil may remind you of

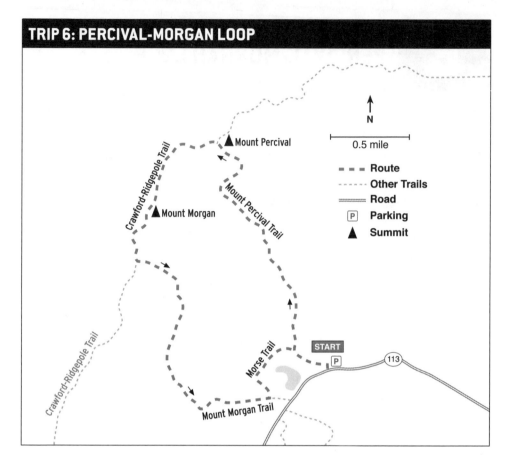

a buttercup. Note the five leaflets that give this plant its name. Other wildflowers that are notable for their leaf patterns are Solomon's plume (false Solomon's seal) and Indian cucumber-root. The former has a single arching stem with broad, lily-like leaves attached. The latter has a double whorl of leaflets.

A small patch of poison ivy grows along the side of the trail just in from the trailhead, so keep to the middle of the path here. Poison ivy's three glossy leaflets with wavy edges are the key to its identification. Another plant here that also has three leaflets is hog peanut, so this is a good spot to test your ability to discern poison ivy from similar-looking plants. Of course, it is best not to touch at all.

This lower-elevation forest is host to a symphony of bird songs from late spring through early summer. Species that are likely to serenade you include red-eyed vireo, veery, hermit thrush, black-throated green warbler, black-throated blue warbler, and American redstart. Listen for the dry, two-syllable *che-beck* of the least flycatcher, sounding more like an insect than a bird.

At 0.2 mile, Morse Trail comes in from the left. You will use that later to complete the loop but for now continue straight. As you ascend, note some very large white pines. After about 0.9 mile, the trail crosses a small brook called Smith Brook. On a hot day it is a pleasure to douse your face, neck, and arms with its cooling water. If you are hiking with your dog, give it a chance to drink. Soon after, the trail passes through an old stone wall. The pines, white birches, and stone wall suggest that this area was cleared at some point in the past 100 years.

The white pines slowly drop out as you enter a northern hardwood forest (sugar maple, American beech, yellow birch). At about 1.5 miles, the trail turns sharply right and you traverse a boulder field. After the boulder field, the trail turns left and heads steeply uphill. You'll reach a fork after about 1.9 miles. The main trail (marked "Cliff") goes right, scrambling up a steep pitch over ledges. The left fork (marked "Cave") is more strenuous, going through a boulder cave. It would be the more hazardous choice in wet weather and definitely a bad choice if you are hiking with a dog. Both lead in about 0.1 mile to the overlook, with an amazing view of Squam Lake framed by red spruces. To the west is Mount Morgan, your next destination, and to the northeast are Mounts Whiteface and Passaconaway. Some lowbush blueberries and mountain hollies grow on this ledge.

After enjoying the vista, follow the yellow blazes to the open summit of Mount Percival just beyond. Mount Percival Trail ends when it meets Crawford-Ridgepole Trail (2.0 miles). The view is similar to that from the previous ledge.

Continue on Crawford-Ridgepole Trail west (left) toward Mount Morgan. This section of the loop is a lovely boreal forest walk on the fairly level ridge between the two summits. Red spruce and balsam fir are the dominant trees. On the forest floor, look for the broad leaves of blue-bead lily (*Clintonia*) and the four or six whorls of leaflets and red berries of bunchberry dogwood. Wet swales are covered with a lush, green growth of fringed sedge.

Squam Lake from Mount Percival. The Abenaki called the lake "Keeseenunknipee," which means "goose lake in the highlands."

The birds singing here are likely to be dark-eyed juncos, several species of warblers, and golden-crowned kinglets.

At 2.8 miles (0.8 mile from Mount Percival), the trail reaches a junction with Mount Morgan Trail. Follow Mount Morgan Trail to the right to reach another excellent vista of Squam Lake about 0.1 mile ahead. Before the cliff, a spur path leads to the right to the actual summit of Mount Morgan and a view north to the Sandwich Range. A geographic marker from Boston's Museum of Science identifies the actual summit. Note the quartz and feldspar dikes embedded within the metamorphic rocks of the ledge.

If you are on these summits on a warm, sunny day without too much wind, you will likely be accompanied by butterflies and dragonflies, which seek out the warmth of sun-filled openings in a forest. Three large, common butterflies to look for are white admiral, mourning cloak, and eastern tiger swallowtail (illustrated here). Dragonflies include common baskettails early in summer and green and variable darners later on.

An alternative and more dramatic way to reach the Mount Morgan vista is to continue on Crawford-Ridgepole Trail, which at this point coincides with Mount Morgan Trail at the trail junction. The trail descends some steps and shortly reaches a junction with a spur path that ascends to the right, marked with a sign as a ladder trail. This spur path is not for anyone uncomfortable with heights. It climbs three ladders, the third of which is offset to the right, so you must be very careful where you place your feet. The trail then squeezes through a narrow cave where you may need to remove your pack to fit before coming out at the vista. Descending this way is even more challenging.

For the main descent, return to the junction with Crawford-Ridgepole Trail and turn right. Mount Morgan Trail runs together with Crawford-Ridgepole Trail for about 0.2 mile. Where they split, turn left for the 1.6-mile (one-hour) descent down Mount Morgan Trail. This is a steady downhill through northern hardwoods, becoming gradually less steep. The trail traverses a few stone walls, once again indicating the human history of the region.

Morse Trail (formerly Morgan-Percival Connector) comes in from the left near the bottom of Mount Morgan Trail. This will connect to your original trailhead at Mount Percival Trail. Turn left on Morse Trail for a pleasant 0.5-mile walk through northern hardwoods. Cross two streams, one on a wooden bridge. When you reach the junction with Mount Percival Trail, turn right and walk 0.1 mile to the parking area.

DID YOU KNOW?

On Golden Pond, the popular 1981 film starring Katharine Hepburn, Henry Fonda, and the local loons, was filmed on Squam Lake.

OTHER ACTIVITIES

The hike up West Rattlesnake Mountain on the south side of NH 113 opposite the Mount Morgan trailhead is one of the most popular family hikes in the Squam Lake region. It is a great first mountain hike for young children.

Five-Finger Point Trail is a wonderful loop hike on a promontory on the northern shore of Squam Lake. It is reached via Pinehurst Road off NH 113 about 0.75 mile west of the Mount Percival trailhead. The route provides changing vistas of the lake and several opportunities for swimming from small beaches and from one dramatic shoreline rock.

The Squam Lake Natural Science Center in Holderness has interpretive nature trails, a garden, and excellent displays on local ecology and wildlife.

MORE INFORMATION

Much of the land in this loop hike is owned by the Burleigh Land Limited Partnership. Public access comes from a conservation easement held by the Lakes Region Conservation Trust. The Squam Lakes Association provides trail maintenance. Parking is free. Holderness and Ashland, the nearest towns, have restaurants, gas stations, and motels.

7 WELCH-DICKEY LOOP

This was the most suggested family hike in the White Mountains by all the people I talked to. The summits of Welch and Dickey command excellent views for relatively modest effort. The trek is substantial enough to give hikers a feeling of accomplishment, yet is manageable for most everyone older than age 6 or so.

Features 🏃🥾🚶🐕🗺️💥💲

Location Thornton, NH

Rating Moderate to Strenuous

Distance 4.4-mile loop

Elevation Change 1,800 feet

Estimated Time 3.5–5 hours

Maps *AMC White Mountain National Forest Map & Guide*, 4th ed., J/K 5, 6; AMC *White Mountain Guide*, 31st ed. Map 4 Moosilauke–Kinsman, J/K 5, 6; USGS Topo: Waterville Valley

GPS Coordinates 43° 54.24′ N, 71° 35.31′ W

Contact White Mountain National Forest: fs.usda.gov/whitemountain, 603-536-6100

DIRECTIONS

Welch and Dickey Loop Trail is located off NH 49 at the entrance to Waterville Valley. Take I-93 to the Campton/Waterville Valley exit (Exit 28) and follow NH 49 through Campton toward Waterville Valley. Four and a half miles beyond NH 175 in Campton, turn left (northwest) on Upper Mad River Road (second intersection with this loop road) and cross the river. Follow this road for 0.7 mile and then turn right onto Orris Road. A large parking area with space for about 100 vehicles (in response to the popularity of this trail) is 0.6 mile up this road. Restrooms are at the parking area.

TRAIL DESCRIPTION

Welch and Dickey Loop Trail is a good choice early in the season, as its lower elevation and relatively southern location ensure that snow disappears sooner here than farther north. For those with less time or energy, a hike up to the first great viewpoint on Welch Mountain requires only about an hour one-way. The large areas of rocky ledges near the summits should present no problems for hikers who are comfortable with scrambling on rocks; however, they could be hazardous if the weather is wet or icy. And remember, these peaks, despite their low elevations, are still quite exposed, so bring windbreakers and rain gear and stay off the open summits if a thunderstorm threatens.

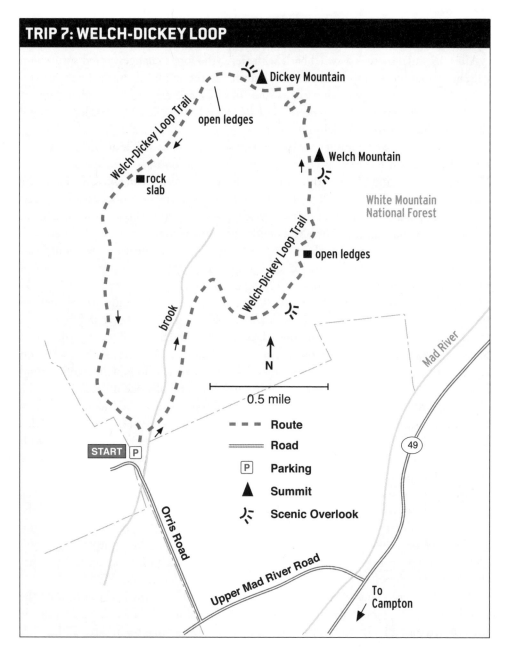

I describe going up Welch Mountain first because you'll reach a viewpoint sooner. You can turn around there if you want a shorter walk. To begin, take the right fork just beyond the display board and lost-and-found box at the trailhead. The route is marked with yellow blazes. Although its popularity has led to erosion in some places, the path is smooth for much of its length.

The trail soon crosses a stream and then follows it through a northern hardwood forest for the first 0.5 mile. Wooden boards cross several other streams. Notice the glacial erratics scattered throughout the woods. These boulders are often covered with mosses and rock tripe, the latter a type of lichen that, although edible, looks and tastes like a piece of shoe leather.

After 0.9 mile, there is a switchback with steps, the forest changes to red spruce and balsam fir, and the trail then ascends more steeply to the south ledges, the first vista (1.3 mile). Proceed upward, past other ledges, some of which are steep, and through low forests of red spruce, balsam fir, white pine, and oaks. Dogs may need help on these ledges. You'll then reach the summit of Welch (1.9 miles).

From the ledges and summit of Welch, the prominent peaks visible are Dickey Mountain, the Sandwich Range (southeast), Mount Tecumseh (north—the major ski area for Waterville Valley), and Mount Tripyramid (northeast). You also get an excellent view of the Mad River valley and a breathtaking look down into the saddle between Welch and Dickey.

Jack pine is abundant on the ledges near Welch's summit. This small tree grows in a handful of other locations in the White Mountains, including Carter Ledge and Webster Cliff. You can identify jack pine by its short, stiff needles occurring in bunches of two. It depends upon fires for regeneration because fires open up its cones for seed dispersal and perhaps inhibit other competing vegetation. According to Steven D. Smith's *The Waterville Valley Guidebook* (Town of Waterville Valley, 2020), its presence on Welch Mountain is thought to be related to a fire in 1820 that provided it with a toehold that it has never abdicated.

Recovery areas for small plants on the ledges are delineated by neat lines of small stones. Signs urge hikers to protect the plants from trampling by remaining on the trail or on exposed rocks. Two tiny alpine species preserved by this effort are mountain cranberry and mountain sandwort. The thin soil, exposure to winds, and absence of trees mimic the alpine conditions normally found above about 4,500 feet in the White Mountains, allowing these plants to thrive on Welch and Dickey, although the weather conditions at this lower elevation are not as extreme as true alpine habitat. Three-toothed cinquefoil, with small white flowers that bloom in June, is probably the most plentiful plant in the recovery areas. Each of the three leaflets of this low plant has three teeth on its outer edge.

Shrubs are a major component of the vegetation on the open ledges. Blueberries are a popular midsummer attraction, but please make sure your picking does not destroy the bushes or any other vegetation in this fragile habitat. Rhodora, a type of rhododendron, will be in glorious bloom around Memorial Day. It has large pinkish purple flowers and bluish green leaves. Labrador tea, chokeberry, shadbush, and bush honeysuckle are other shrubs on the ledges.

The trail then descends steeply to a saddle before ascending to the Dickey summit. The saddle contains a particularly attractive display of boreal forest plants. Where the shade from the red spruce is not dense, bunchberries and reindeer lichen grow in patterns that look like they were designed by a rock gardener. Mountain holly, withe-rod, the white form of pink lady's slipper, blue-bead lily, and haircap moss grow under the spruce canopy as well.

It is a 0.5-mile hike from Welch to Dickey. The view from Dickey Mountain includes much of what you see from Welch and also the Franconia Ridge. You may wonder what has caused rectangular open areas visible in the forest below. These are places where loggers have clear-cut the forest. They are in various states of revegetation, depending on how long it has been since the area was logged. A dense tangle of shrubs, such as raspberries,

Hikers arriving at the summit of Dickey Mountain. *Photo by Ryan Smith.*

blueberries, and huckleberries, will grow up within a few years, followed by early successional trees, including paper birch, aspen, and pin cherry.

The open ledges are also excellent places to look for ravens. These large, completely black members of the crow family are considered among the most intelligent of birds. They are frequently observed soaring around ledges in the mountains and sometimes cavort with one another and even fly upside down. Their voice is a hoarse call that sounds like a cross between a crow and a hog. A much smaller bird you are likely to see at higher elevations is the dark-eyed junco, a slate-gray, sparrowlike bird with a white belly and white outer tail feathers.

From Dickey, the trail, marked with cairns (piles of stones) in several places, descends through more ledges offering wonderful views, particularly of Cone Mountain. Along this stretch you can find pink corydalis, a wildflower with ferny leaves and small pink flowers that resemble the heads of birds.

About 0.8 mile below the Dickey summit, the trail crosses a particularly impressive granite slab called Dickey Cliff (3.2 miles). This is a mass of Conway granite, a type of granite formed in this region from molten magma deep within the earth during the Jurassic period 200 to 145 million years ago. Note how the granite is laced with dark gray stripes—these are sills of basalt formed from lava that penetrated cracks within the granite.

Shortly thereafter, you'll enter a forest of beech, maple, and red oak. This is a rich area for spring wildflowers and ferns. Look for Canada mayflower, wild oats, blue-bead lily, Indian cucumber-root, false Solomon's seal, King Solomon's seal, painted trillium, starflower, goldthread, and wild sarsaparilla. Partridgeberry is a small, low plant with paired dark green leaves that hug the ground and are occasionally punctuated with bright red berries. The distinctive, arrowhead-shaped leaves of rattlesnake root are present throughout the year, but its flowers wait until late summer to appear. Around Memorial Day, when the leaves of wild sarsaparilla are glossy, reddish, and in groups of three or five, you might think that you have come into contact with poison ivy. Rest assured that poison ivy does not occur at this elevation.

It's about 1 mile to the parking lot. Near the end of the hike, at 4.3 miles, make sure to stay on the trail as it passes an abandoned road and turns left onto a logging road (to the right is a mountain-bike trail).

DID YOU KNOW?

The town of Thornton, where Welch and Dickey mountains are located, is named for Matthew Thornton, one of the original settlers of the area and a signer of the Declaration of Independence.

OTHER ACTIVITIES

The resort community of Waterville Valley has restaurants, a grocery store, golf, and fishing, among other amenities. Skiing is a major activity in winter. The village of Campton has a few restaurants and a store where you can buy groceries, all near the intersection of NH 149 and NH 175.

MORE INFORMATION

A $5 user fee is required for parking.

8 MOUNT OSCEOLA

The hike up Mount Osceola from Tripoli Road may be the mellowest route up a 4,000-footer in the White Mountains. A spectacular vista greets you at the summit.

Features 🧗 🚶 🐕 💲

Location Livermore, NH

Rating Strenuous

Distance 5.8 miles round trip

Elevation Gain 2,050 feet

Estimated Time 5–6 hours

Maps *AMC White Mountain National Forest Map & Guide*, 4th ed., J6 and Waterville Valley inset; AMC *White Mountain Guide*, 31st ed. Map 4 Moosilauke–Kinsman, J6; USGS Topo: Waterville Valley at trailhead, then Mount Osceola

GPS Coordinates 43° 59.01′ N, 71° 33.52′ W

Contact White Mountain National Forest: fs.usda.gov/whitemountain, 603-536-6100

DIRECTIONS

The trailhead for Mount Osceola Trail is off Tripoli Road, 7.0 miles from its junction with I-93 (Exit 31) and 4.8 miles beyond the turnoff to Russell Pond Campground. This is close to the highest point reached by Tripoli Road in its passage through Thornton Gap. If you are coming from Waterville Valley, the trailhead is about 4.5 miles west of the junction of Tripoli Road and NH 49. Stay to the right when the road to the ski area splits off to the left.

The trailhead is on the north side of the road. Space is available for about ten vehicles in the parking area. You can also park along the side of Tripoli Road. Restrooms are available at the trailhead.

Tripoli Road is not plowed in winter, and the gates at its I-93 and Waterville Valley ends are closed in snow and mud season. Thus, a winter ascent is not feasible.

TRAIL DESCRIPTION

Mount Osceola Trail is a well-graded path for its entire length, with carefully placed switchbacks preventing anywhere from being particularly steep. However, the first section is very rocky, with some loose footing, because it passes through various boulder fields caused by landslides. Some broad, flat, slanted ledges at several places are no problem when dry but could be slippery when wet. Once you reach the ridge, the trail becomes a pleasant, gentle ascent through the boreal forest until you reach the summit ledges.

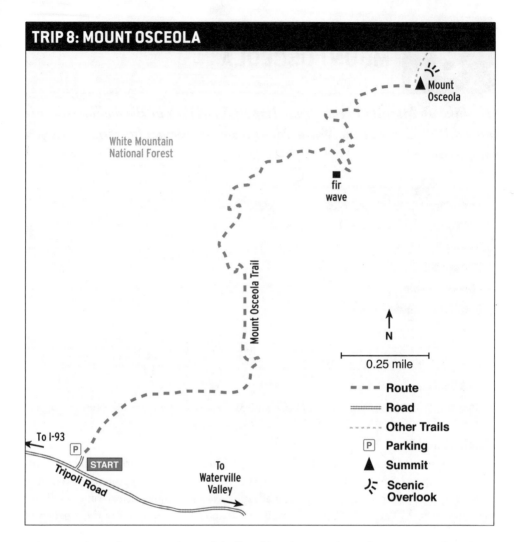

Leaving the parking area, the trail (yellow blazes) starts through a mixture of northern hardwoods and boreal forest. The forest includes American beech, hobblebush, blue-bead lily, wild sarsaparilla, and bunchberry. It quickly turns to almost complete boreal forest dominated by red spruce, balsam fir, and paper birch. Birds you are likely to hear include red-eyed vireos, hermit thrushes, black-throated green warblers, and black-throated blue warblers. In about 0.4 mile, you cross the first of several streams that tumble over and around boulders on their way down the mountain. On a hot day, pause and splash some cool water on your brow, and if you have a canine companion, allow it to have a drink.

At 1.2 miles, the trail starts a series of switchbacks and becomes less rocky. At about 2.5 miles, you attain Breadtray Ridge and the grade lessens. You can see the summit of Osceola ahead.

After passing another stream, the trail leads to a more open area on the right created by dead trees, which affords a partially occluded view across Waterville Valley to the Mount

Tecumseh ski slopes and to the broad ridge of Sandwich Dome. This opening was caused by a fir wave, a fascinating phenomenon characteristic of these high-elevation forests. For many years, fir waves were a puzzle to both forest ecologists and hikers. Scientists now have concluded that fir waves represent a common pattern of regeneration in high-elevation forests (roughly 3,000 to 4,500 feet). All the older balsam fir trees at a certain elevation die in a band parallel to the contour of the mountain. The older trees reach the end of their life span (about 80 years), die, get knocked over by winds (often bringing down their neighbors), and are replaced by regenerating saplings. Look for the many young firs growing up in the midst of the dead and dying older trees. This band of dying older trees and regenerating seedlings gradually moves up the side of the mountain, thus the term "fir wave."

At 2.9 miles, you reach the summit at a foundation of a former fire tower. Mount Osceola is the tallest mountain south of the Kancamagus Highway, so the views from its summit ledges are panoramic. A spur path to the north leads to a large rock that enables you to get above the balsam fir to enjoy superb vistas of the Franconia Range, Mount Moosilauke, South Twin, and Mount Bond.

A few yards farther along on the main trail, you'll find another open area, which was the site of a more recent fire tower. The village of Waterville Valley, the ski slopes on Mount Tecumseh, and Sandwich Dome are to the south. East Osceola and the three summits of Mount Tripyramid are to the east, with the slide on North Tripyramid particularly prominent. Farther in the distance to the east and northeast are Mounts Passaconaway, Chocorua, and Carrigain; the Moats; and the Presidential Range.

In addition to balsam fir, the vegetation at the summit ledges includes mountain cranberry, purple crowberry, and poverty grass. Birds you might encounter around the summit

The view northeast from Mount Osceola includes East Osceola and Mount Carrigain.

include white-throated sparrows, dark-eyed juncos, and yellow-rumped warblers. On a sunny day, large dragonflies (darners) are likely to be patrolling for their insect prey.

Retrace your steps to return to the parking area. Plan for about the same amount of time for the descent, due to the rockiness of the trail in its lower section.

DID YOU KNOW?

Osceola was a Seminole chief who never got within 1,000 miles of the White Mountains. The name may have been applied by a Waterville Valley summer resident in the late 1800s, but there is no obvious reason why this mountain was named for the chief.

OTHER ACTIVITIES

Mount Osceola Trail continues beyond the summit ledges to East Osceola and eventually descends to a terminus at Greeley Ponds Trail (Trip 21). This part of the route is rougher than the trip described here. In particular, the section from East Osceola to Greeley Ponds is considered one of the most difficult treks in the White Mountains.

The Waterville Valley Athletic & Improvement Association maintains a variety of pleasant trails to waterfalls and other destinations in the valley (such as Trip 1).

MORE INFORMATION

The Mount Osceola trailhead charges a $5 daily user fee for parking. The village of Waterville Valley has a grocery store, an ice cream shop and other shops, restaurants, public restrooms, and two campgrounds.

9 MOUNT MOOSILAUKE

Mount Moosilauke has a broad 4,802-foot summit that reaches up into the alpine zone on the western edge of the White Mountains and has spectacular views in all directions. This attractive loop hike follows rushing mountain streams for much of its length.

Features ❀ 🏃 🐕 💧 🍃 ✺ ↑

Location Woodstock, NH, at the trailhead, then Benton, NH

Rating Strenuous

Distance 8.3-mile loop

Elevation Gain 2,650 feet

Estimated Time 6 hours

Maps *AMC White Mountain National Forest Map & Guide*, 4th ed., I2–3; AMC *White Mountain Guide*, 31st ed. Map 4 Moosilauke–Kinsman, J/I3; USGS Topo: Mount Kineo, Mount Moosilauke

GPS Coordinates 43° 59.62′ N, 71° 48.90′ W

Contact Dartmouth Outing Club: outdoors.dartmouth.edu, 603-646-2429

⚠️ **CAUTION!** This outing takes you above treeline, where the weather can be quite harsh. It will almost always be colder and windier than at lower elevations, and the open area of alpine tundra leaves you exposed to snow (possible even in summer), rain, harsh winds, and lightning. Be prepared with extra warm clothes and rain gear, and be ready to turn back if the weather changes.

DIRECTIONS

The trailhead is at the Dartmouth Outing Club's Moosilauke Ravine Lodge. From Exit 32 off I-93 (Lincoln/North Woodstock), take NH 112 west for about 3 miles. Turn left onto NH 118 and follow it for 7.2 miles. Turn right onto Ravine Lodge Road (unpaved), and follow it to its end (1.6 miles). Use the turnaround and then find parking along the side of the road. Signs make it very clear that you should not park in the turnaround itself. Parking is shared with guests of Ravine Lodge, so you may need to park a short distance from the actual trailhead and walk back along the road. The trailhead for Gorge Brook Trail is also the trailhead for Al Merrill Loop.

During winter, the road to Ravine Lodge is not plowed. Visitors can park at the winter parking area along Ravine Lodge Road, which is about 0.85 mile from NH 118 (0.75 mile

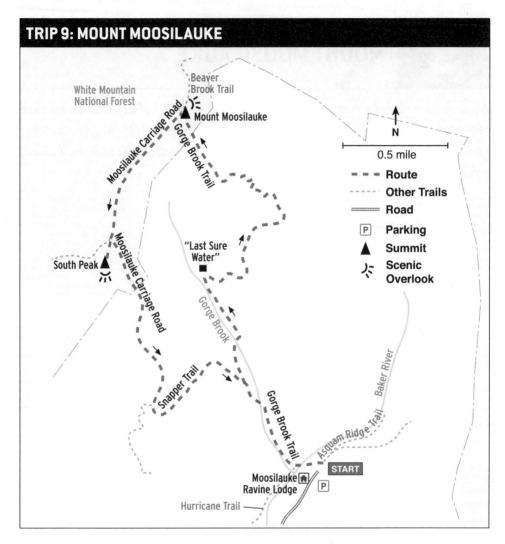

White Mountain
National Forest

Beaver
Brook Trail

Mount Moosilauke

Moosilauke Carriage Road

Gorge Brook Trail

"Last Sure
Water"

South Peak

Moosilauke Carriage Road

Gorge Brook

Snapper Trail

Gorge Brook Trail

Baker River

Asquam Ridge Trail

START

Moosilauke
Ravine Lodge

Hurricane Trail

N

0.5 mile

- - - **Route**

········· **Other Trails**

═══ **Road**

P **Parking**

▲ **Summit**

☀ **Scenic
Overlook**

from the lodge). As the sign indicates, head in, angled parking only. In winter, you must be prepared to hike or snowshoe the extra 0.75 mile each way.

TRAIL DESCRIPTION

This loop hike ascends to the summit of Mount Moosilauke on Gorge Brook Trail and then uses Moosilauke Carriage Road along with Snapper and Gorge Brook trails for the descent. The trails are well maintained and marked with signage by the Dartmouth Outing Club, so you should have no trouble following them.

From the turnaround at the terminus of Ravine Lodge Road, follow the trail beyond the barrier and descend left to a bridge across Baker River. As the big trailhead sign indicates, turn left for Gorge Brook Trail and walk a short distance across an old logging road. Turn right where Hurricane Trail continues straight ahead. This first part of Gorge Brook Trail is a gradual ascent along Gorge Brook, with many attractive small cascades and moss-covered boulders. Red spruce, balsam fir, and paper birch are the dominant trees, and hobblebush is the main understory shrub. After the first crossing of Gorge Brook on a bridge (0.8 mile), the trail continues straight ahead and coincides with Snapper Trail. An old section of Gorge Brook Trail that led to the right at this point was closed due to damage from Tropical Storm Irene in 2011. At 1 mile, this new section of Gorge Brook Trail diverges right from Snapper Trail and continues uphill high above the brook. It rejoins the original section of Gorge Brook Trail at 1.4 miles and, shortly after, crosses back over the brook on another bridge.

At 1.8 miles, at 3,300 feet altitude, the trail passes a sign reading "Last Sure Water." You will see a plaque there honoring Ross McKenny, the builder of Ravine Lodge. In winter, only experienced snowshoers should venture beyond this point. The trail turns right, away from the brook, and begins a series of switchbacks that lead up the east ridge of the mountain.

Bird songs will provide a constant symphony during your ascent through the boreal forest. Two of the most distinctive are those of the winter wren and the Swainson's thrush. The winter wren is a tiny brown bird that you almost never see, but it has a remarkable extended, sweet, twittering song of at least four subsections. You'll wonder how such a small creature does not run out of breath. Swainson's thrushes sing an ethereal, flutelike song of gradually ascending notes, appropriate for a hike to higher altitudes.

At 2.5 miles, you reach a small clearing and continue ascending at a steeper pitch. The spruce and fir trees gradually decline in stature as you climb, and the paper birches are replaced by heart-leaved birches. If you are hiking in late June or early July, you will be treated to a beautiful display of bunchberries (a tiny dogwood with four creamy white floral bracts that serve as petals). The red berries, produced in middle to late summer, are not poisonous but are at best emergency food, so leave them for the birds. Views to the south gradually open up, Mount Carr being the most prominent peak in that direction.

The next landmark (3.6 miles) is a sign that informs you that you have reached the alpine zone and therefore should stay on the trails to avoid trampling the sensitive tundra vegetation. Between here and the summit at 3.9 miles, you will find plants that thrive in alpine habitats. Two species restricted to alpine and arctic habitats that are common around the Moosilauke summit are Bigelow's sedge and highland rush. These do not have showy flowers, so they may not attract your attention, except perhaps when the rush turns a rich golden brown in late summer. Some bright flowers include three-toothed cinquefoil (white blossoms and three leaflets each tipped with three teeth) and mountain sandwort (small white blossoms and thin, opposite leaves growing in tufts). Mountain cranberry has small, glossy green leaves and red berries. Alpine (bog) bilberry is a type of blueberry with attractive, roundish blue-green leaves. (See "The Alpine Zone of the White Mountains" on page 256 for more on alpine habitats.)

Two birds that inhabit this harsh alpine environment are the white-throated sparrow (with its sweet-whistled song, *See old Sam Peabody, Peabody, Peabody*) and the dark-eyed junco (a sparrowlike gray bird that flashes white outer tail feathers when it flies).

On a clear day, Mount Moosilauke's location on the western edge of the White Mountains provides a fantastic look at several peaks. To the west, you can see the Green Mountains of Vermont and the Adirondacks of New York. The Franconia Range, Twin Range,

The grassy, alpine summit of Mount Moosilauke. *Photo by Jerry Monkman.*

and Mount Washington are visible to the northeast. If you happen to climb on a cloudy day, enjoy the plants, birds, and isolation of this alpine environment. Students from Dartmouth College serve as alpine stewards, providing trail and other information for hikers who reach the summit.

For the descent, watch for the signs for Moosilauke Carriage Road, part of the Appalachian Trail, which is blazed with white. The first 0.5 mile of this trail is on an exposed ridge, so if the weather is threatening, the best idea is to return via Gorge Brook Trail. In good weather, this section of Moosilauke Carriage Road is a pleasant, gradual descent through scrub spruce and fir vegetation with excellent vistas. At 4.8 miles (0.9 mile from the summit), you'll reach a three-way junction with Glencliff Trail (the next leg of the Appalachian Trail) and a spur path that ascends South Peak (0.2 mile each way). South Peak provides outstanding views south and back north to the summit of Moosilauke to the north, so it is well worth the detour.

After enjoying the scenery from South Peak, continue descending Moosilauke Carriage Road. The trail is relatively wide and is nowhere particularly steep. Observe how the trees gradually increase in stature as you descend.

At about 1.4 miles below the summit, note the stone barrier, which was probably erected to keep snowmobiles and ATVs from reaching the summit. Snapper Trail comes in from the left, 1.9 miles below the summit (6.2 miles total). Turn left onto Snapper Trail and continue your pleasant, gradual descent. Note the abundant hay-scented ferns along the former route of the trail. This fern favors such open, sunny locations. Stay on Snapper Trail as it crosses several bridges over a tributary of Gorge Brook.

At 7.3 miles, Snapper Trail joins the relocated section of Gorge Brook Trail that you took on your ascent. Cross the bridge over the brook (7.5 miles) and continue down Gorge Brook Trail. Turn left (upstream) when you reach a junction with a path to the Class of 1997 Swimming Hole. Cross a bridge, then follow signs to the parking area.

DID YOU KNOW?

Moosilauke is an Abenaki word thought to mean "bald place." That seems fitting given the smooth appearance of the domed summit. A minority opinion is that it means "good moose place."

OTHER ACTIVITIES

Ravine Lodge, run by students from Dartmouth College, has been open in the past to the public for overnight stays and meals. In light of the pandemic still prevalent at the time this guide was written, check outdoors.dartmouth.edu for current information.

Although the trails described in this book are not appropriate for cross-country skiing, there are a host of skiing trails around Ravine Lodge, including the unplowed access road.

MORE INFORMATION

Dartmouth College owns Mount Moosilauke; parking is free.

Find services (restaurants, motels, groceries, gas) along NH 112 or US 3 in North Woodstock or along NH 112 in Lincoln.

10 WHITEFACE–PASSACONAWAY LOOP

These two 4,000-footers within the Sandwich Range Wilderness Area both command fantastic views from ledges near their summits. From Mount Whiteface you look south over the Lakes Region. Mount Passaconaway provides a northern vista that encompasses many of the high peaks of the White Mountains. This is one of the lengthiest and most rigorous hikes in this guide, particularly the portion up Whiteface, and it should not be attempted in wet or icy conditions. If you do not have time for the complete loop, a hike to just one of the peaks is still rewarding.

Features

Location Waterville Valley, NH

Rating Strenuous

Distance 12.6-mile loop (includes spur to overlook on Mount Passaconaway)

Elevation Gain 2,950 feet

Estimated Time 7–8.5 hours

Maps *AMC White Mountain National Forest Map & Guide*, 4th ed., J8; AMC *White Mountain Guide*, 31st ed. Map 3 Crawford Notch–Sandwich Range, JK8; USGS Topo: Mount Chocorua

GPS Coordinates 43° 54.82′ N, 71° 21.47′ W

Contact White Mountain National Forest: fs.usda.gov/whitemountain, 603-536-6100; Wonalancet Out Door Club: wodc.org

DIRECTIONS

Reach the trailhead for both Blueberry Ledge (ascent) and Dicey's Mill (descent) trails off NH 113A through either North Sandwich or Tamworth.

From I-93 and points west: Take Exit 24 (Holderness/Ashland) and head east on NH 25. In Holderness, turn left on NH 113. Pass the Squam Lake Natural Science Center and follow the northwest shoreline of Squam Lake. After about 12 miles, turn left onto NH 113A. Take NH 113A for 6.6 miles. Where NH 113A makes a 90-degree turn to the east, turn left onto Ferncroft Road and follow it for 0.5 mile. The parking area for the trail is on the right.

From NH 16 and points east: At the junction of NH 113 and NH 113A in Tamworth, take NH 113A for 6.5 miles. Where the road makes a 90-degree turn to the south, go straight on Ferncroft Road. The parking for the trailhead is 0.5 mile ahead.

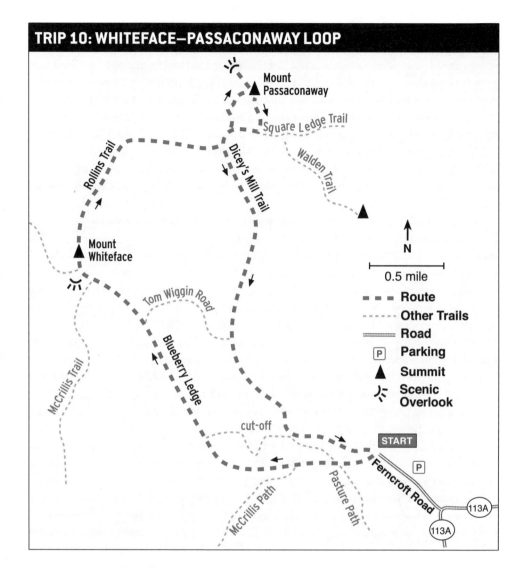

Mount Passaconaway

Square Ledge Trail

Rollins Trail

Dicey's Mill Trail

Walden Trail

N

Mount Whiteface

0.5 mile

- - - Route
- - - - Other Trails
===== Road
[P] Parking
▲ Summit
Scenic Overlook

Tom Wiggin Road

McCrillis Trail

Blueberry Ledge

cut-off

START

Ferncroft Road

[P]

113A

McCrillis Path

Pasture Path

113A

TRAIL DESCRIPTION

Trails in this hike were originally blazed in blue but are mostly faded as of this writing. The policy of the U.S. Forest Service is not to restore blazes in designated wilderness areas. Nonetheless, there is adequate signage, so following this route should not be a problem.

From the parking area, walk back to Ferncroft Road, turn right, and follow the road for about 0.3 mile. Turn left to cross Squirrel Bridge over Wonalancet River. Here, Dicey's Mill Trail, on which you will return, goes straight ahead. For Blueberry Ledge Trail, walk along a dirt road flanked by some houses, pass a sign that reads "Trail," and enter the woods. Head past Pasture Path to your left (0.5 mile) and then Blueberry Ledge Cutoff to your right (0.6 mile). A sign at this point indicates that you are now on Blueberry Ledge Trail.

The trail starts out with relatively easy grades. The forest is mixed hardwoods (American beech, sugar maple) with some scattered spruce and fir. The latter will be more prevalent as you ascend. The understory includes hobblebush and striped maple, and there are luxuriant growths of different types of ferns and wildflowers. Blue-bead lily and flowering winter-green are common. Look for Indian cucumber-root, an herbaceous plant related to lilies, with two whorls of leaves and a flower that hangs down from the upper whorl. Another interesting understory plant is princess pine (also known as ground pine). It looks like a tiny evergreen tree and is sometimes used as a Christmas decoration. Botanists classify it with club mosses, a group of ancient plants sometimes called fern allies. Another club moss on this trail is shining club moss, which has mostly unbranched stems that are covered with small, bristly leaflets.

Blueberry Ledge Trail enters the Sandwich Range Wilderness Area within the White Mountain National Forest and passes McCrillis Path (an old dirt road) to the left at 0.9 mile. About 0.3 mile later, you pass an open boulder with a restricted view of nearby mountains. The route passes a level area, reaches the bottom of the ledges at 1.6 miles, and then ascends the ledges with views of the Ossipee Mountains and various lakes and fields to the south. At 2.0 miles, you reach the upper junction with Blueberry Ledge Cutoff, where there is a large cairn. Stay on Blueberry Ledge Trail as it reenters the forest, at first at a relatively level pitch in a section dominated by hardwoods, particularly American beech. Look for white violets in the understory, especially in damp areas, and mountain wood sorrel with its cloverlike leaflets. When the trail again ascends more steeply, red spruce and balsam fir become increasingly dominant. A spur path to the right leads to a particularly scenic overlook. The route reaches the top of a ridge and then drops off a bit before ascending to the junction with Tom Wiggin Trail (3.2 miles).

As you continue on Blueberry Ledge Trail, another steep section requires some careful scrambling on rocks. In one pitch, you'll need to ascend up a crack in the rock. The reward is a pleasant view to the south. At 3.6 miles, you reach a particularly scenic overlook, although the cliff has a steep dropoff, so use caution in wet weather. Beautiful views of the lakes region to the south are here, so take a moment to enjoy them. Blueberry Ledge Trail continues up, with rough footing, until it terminates at the south summit ledges of Mount Whiteface at 3.9 miles. Here, at a junction with McCrillis and Rollins trails, pick up Rollins Trail straight ahead (north) toward the true summit of Mount Whiteface.

Rollins Trail leaves the south summit ledges in the woods and descends steeply at first, passing the junction with Kate Sleeper Trail on the left (west, 4.0 miles) and then ascending to the true but wooded summit of Mount Whiteface (4.2 miles). This is marked with a cairn.

The next section of Rollins Trail continues along the ridge that connects Mounts Whiteface and Passaconaway. It is a magical walk through a high-elevation, moss-covered forest of red spruce and balsam fir, with a gradual overall decline in elevation. Watch for a few rough short descents and ascents. To your right (east) are occasional views of the Bowl, a remote ravine scoured out by a valley glacier during the last period of glaciation, which ended some 13,000 years ago. This is the same process that formed other more famous glacial cirques in the White Mountains, such as Tuckerman and King's ravines and the Great Gulf. Through the trees you can also see Mount Passaconaway and Mount Chocorua ahead.

You need to hike down a short distance from the summit of Mount Passaconaway to reach this marvelous viewpoint north. *Photo by Alison Buchsbaum.*

Rollins Trail ends at Dicey's Mill Trail at 6.4 miles. You have descended about 600 feet from the summit of Mount Whiteface. At this point, a right turn on Dicey's Mill Trail will lead you back to the Ferncroft Road parking area in 3.7 miles. A left turn onto that trail will take you up to the summit of Mount Passaconaway.

Turn left to continue to Passaconaway. The trail starts gradually, passing a brook and the junction with East Loop coming in from the right (6.6 miles). You will use that trail later. Dicey's Mill Trail then ascends steeply with several switchbacks as it climbs 700 feet to near the summit of Mount Passaconaway, where it ends at a junction with Walden Trail (7.3 miles). Just before this junction, a short spur path leads right about 40 yards to the actual summit, which is marked with a cairn.

Like Whiteface's summit, the actual summit of Passaconaway is cloaked in forest. Follow the sign that reads "To the View," which leads you left to another spur path (rather "rooty" and sometimes muddy). The spur heads left and descends 0.25 mile (7.6 miles to this point) and about 300 feet to a small ledge. Here you have a fantastic view to the north, with Mount Carrigain, in particular, looming large. Two smaller mountains, Hedgehog (Trip 23) and Potash are in the foreground. On a clear day you can see Mount Washington and other peaks of the Presidential Range farther away.

Returning from this spur to near the actual summit (7.7 miles), take Walden Trail to make a loop around the summit. It descends somewhat steeply, but you are rewarded with views of Mount Chocorua (which you actually look down upon) and lakes to the south and east. You will also find white birches, ghost pipes, raspberry bushes, and the aptly named large-leafed goldenrod. At 8.4 miles, you reach East Loop. A sign directs you to take this to the right to return to Dicey's Mill Trail at 8.6 miles. Plan on one and a half to two hours to complete the loop over the summit from the junction of Dicey's Mill and Rollins trails, including time spent admiring the views.

Turn left on Dicey's Mill Trail to begin the 3.9-mile descent to the trailhead. The mileages below are given from this point. The descent, which mainly follows an old logging road, is gradual for most of its length, so it makes for a pleasant hike. Those interested in trail running might find this section to their liking. Pass the junction with Rollins Trail at 0.2 mile. After a little more than 1 mile, you begin to hear a river and pass a large boulder. At 1.6 miles, cross Wonalancet River on a fallen log. This is near the site of Dicey's Mill, for which the trail is named. A blue blaze on the opposite side of the river helps you know where to cross, but keep in mind that blazes are not maintained in wilderness areas, so that blaze is likely to fade into oblivion in the future.

The trail continues downhill and passes the junction with Tom Wiggin Trail at 2.0 miles. Look for ground cedar, also called fan club moss, which resembles tiny cedar trees. White violets grow in wet areas as well.

Continuing downhill, reach a junction with Blueberry Ledge Cutoff at 3.1 miles. That trail crosses Wonalancet River on a bridge to the right, but you will continue straight on Dicey's Mill Trail. This intersection is a good wading spot, so take a break, splash some water on your face, and have a snack. After that, the trail leaves the Sandwich Range Wilderness Area, and the logging road upon which you are hiking continues as Ferncroft Road past a gate and some houses and then back to the parking area (12.6 miles for the entire loop, including viewpoints).

Painted trillium is one of the showiest wildflowers in the White Mountains.

DID YOU KNOW?

Passaconaway, whose name means "son of the bear," was a legendary sachem, or chief, of the Pennacooks. His story was chronicled by C. E. Beals Jr. in his 1916 book *Passaconaway in the White Mountains* (republished in 2009 by Bibliobazaar) and was retold by Tom Eastman in a 2017 article in the *Conway Daily Sun*. Passaconaway was born sometime in the middle to late 1500s. He was the father of Wonalancet and grandfather of Kancamagus, two other chiefs for whom nearby mountains were named.

At the height of his powers in the early 1600s, Passaconaway led the Pennacooks to a decisive victory in what is now Concord, New Hampshire, over Mohawk tribes invading from New York. However, his tribe suffered during the European settlement of New England. They were decimated by diseases for which they had little resistance and from the continual appropriation of their lands by the colonists. Recognizing that his people could not defeat the colonists militarily, Passaconaway continually encouraged coexistence. "We must bend before the storm," he counseled his people shortly before he died sometime around 1669.

OTHER ACTIVITIES

The loop hike over the two summits described here can also be done as two separate day hikes.

Although Chocorua Lake, off NH 16, is not close by, a swim there is a great way to cool off after a hike if your travel plans take you in that direction.

MORE INFORMATION

Parking is free along Ferncroft Road. However, the parking area is rather small, so try to get there early to avoid having to park at a more distant trailhead.

Sandwich and Tamworth are charming New England villages located southwest and east of the trailhead, respectively. They have restaurants, inns, and bed-and-breakfasts.

The Franconia Notch region is the northwesternmost part of the White Mountains. It includes the Kinsman Range, Franconia Notch, and the Franconia Range. The latter, with its beautiful cone-shaped peaks, rises above 5,000 feet, making it the second-highest range in the White Mountains. I-93 provides easy access to the hiking opportunities described here. You'll find numerous waterfalls, rare geological formations, and gorgeous scenery. The Franconia region is a popular tourist destination and includes such well-known sites as the Flume, the Basin, Echo Lake, and Cannon Mountain.

For fishing enthusiasts with a valid New Hampshire license, Profile Lake is stocked with trout. Nonmotorized boats are permitted. The Pemigewasset River is also a popular fishing spot.

The 8.7-mile Franconia Notch Recreation Path parallels the highway through the notch and provides access to some of the hikes described in this book. The paved path, suitable for families and bicycles, can be reached from multiple parking areas in the notch.

SUPPLIES AND LOGISTICS

The village of Franconia is at the north end of Franconia Notch, off I-93; Lincoln and North Woodstock are a few miles to the south. These locations have grocery stores, pharmacies, gas stations, restaurants, motels, and inns. Visitors traveling to the notch from the north on US 3 may find it more convenient to stop for supplies in Twin Mountain, about 12 miles away.

The visitor center at Flume Gorge is open from May through the end of October. It has tourist information, snack bars, restrooms, a gift shop, and a restaurant (nhstateparks.org/visit/state-parks/flume-gorge.aspx; 603-745-8391). Profile Lake has restrooms, a small interpretive nature center, and a snack bar that serves ice cream and other treats. Echo Lake has a small snack bar, restrooms, and a swimming area. The Basin has restrooms only.

PUBLIC TRANSPORTATION

Concord Coach Lines runs from Boston's Logan Airport and South Station to Lincoln. From there, you can reserve a shuttle (the Shuttle Connection) to Franconia Notch. Check the web for details (concordcoachlines.com/stop/lincoln-nh). The AMC Hiker Shuttle

Facing page: Enjoying Stairs Falls on Falling Waters Trail.

stops at Lafayette Place (trailhead for Lonesome Lake) and the trailhead for Old Bridle Path/Falling Waters Trail; outdoors.org/shuttle; 603-466-2727.

NEARBY CAMPING

Lafayette Place Campground in Franconia Notch State Park has 97 tentsites as well as picnic tables for day use, restrooms, water, a small camp store with limited groceries, information on trails, and ranger naturalist programs. No dogs are permitted in the campground; nhstateparks.org/visit/state-parks/franconia-notch-state-park.aspx; 603-823-8800.

Several national forest campgrounds are within a 30-minute drive. Zealand and Sugarloaf campgrounds (the latter providing limited facilities for people with disabilities) are near Twin Mountain. Big Rock and Hancock campgrounds are at the western end of the Kancamagus Highway. Wildwood Campground is on NH 112, west of Lincoln. For more information, visit fs.usda.gov/activity/whitemountain/recreation/camping-cabins. Private campgrounds are available in the North Woodstock/Lincoln area.

11   FLUME GORGE

Stroll on a boardwalk along rushing water through one of the White Mountains' most renowned geological wonders: an extremely narrow gorge bounded by straight, vertical cliffs. This half-day outing also takes you past waterfalls, a giant pothole, huge boulders, and two covered bridges.

Features

Location Lincoln, NH

Rating Easy

Distance 2-mile loop

Elevation Gain 500 feet

Estimated Time 2 hours

Maps *AMC White Mountain National Forest Map & Guide*, 4th ed., H4 and Franconia Notch inset; AMC *White Mountain Guide*, 31st ed. Map 2 Franconia–Pemigewasset, H4; USGS Topo: Lincoln

GPS Coordinates 44° 05.81′ N, 71° 40.88′ W

Contact Franconia Notch State Park: nhstateparks.org/visit/state-parks/flume-gorge.aspx, 603-745-8391

DIRECTIONS

The parking area for Flume Gorge is off Exit 34A of the Franconia Notch Highway, the extension of I-93 that runs through Franconia Notch. The exit is well marked and is about 4 miles north of the exit on I-93 for North Woodstock, Lincoln, NH 112, and the Kancamagus Highway. Purchase admission tickets and pick up a trail map at the Flume Gorge Visitor Center.

TRAIL DESCRIPTION

Flume Gorge is a popular destination at the south end of Franconia Notch State Park and is a perfect half-day outing for families. You can start your hike right from the visitor center, or, if you have very young children, you can cover the first 0.7 mile on a school bus that drops you off right where the trail enters the gorge. You'll find quite a few overlooks with steep dropoffs throughout this walk, so keep an eye on younger children, especially those who like climbing on split-rail fences.

Starting from the visitor center, pass a huge glacial erratic in about 200 yards. Follow the path through the Flume Covered Bridge and the Boulder Cabin for 0.7 mile to the entrance of Flume Gorge (the school bus stop). Proceed into the Flume on boardwalks, stairs, and bridges for about 0.2 mile. The section through the gorge ends at Avalanche Falls.

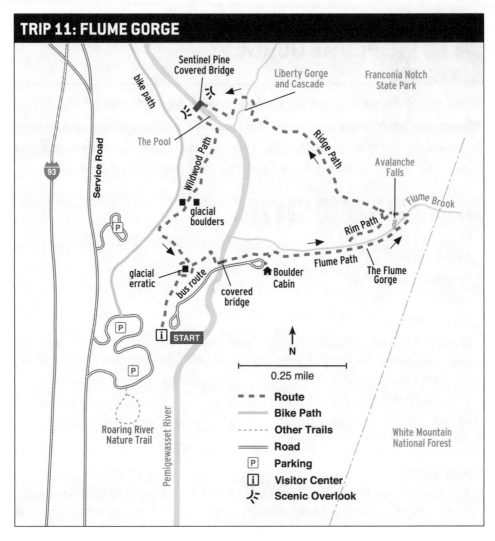

Why are the walls of the Flume so straight? The gorge was formed by erosion of a basalt dike within the granite. Two hundred million years ago, the granite, which tends to crack in straight lines, fractured vertically at the Flume. Lava from deep within the earth then flowed into the fractures, forcing the granite apart and solidifying to form a seam of basalt 12 to 20 feet wide.

Eventually, water began to flow over the granite and basalt, eroding the softer basalt and leaving the steep granite sides of the Flume. The narrowness of the gorge (at times it's only 12 feet wide) reflects the width of the original basalt dike. The straightness of the walls shows the fracture planes of the granite. In some places, you can still see remnants of the black basaltic rock.

At Avalanche Falls, you can take a shorter loop back toward the visitor center on Rim Path or continue on Ridge Path to the Pool. The Pool is as spectacular as Flume Gorge, so I highly recommend you keep going on Ridge Path.

The vertical granite walls of the Flume Gorge show where the softer basalt dike was eroded away. *Photo by Jerry Monkman.*

Follow Ridge Path for about 0.7 mile (mostly downhill) to the Pool and Sentinel Pine Covered Bridge over the Pemigewasset River. From overlooks 130 feet above the water, you can see the giant pothole 150 feet wide and 30 to 40 feet deep within the river. The Pool was created by the scouring action of sand and small stones blasted against the rock over millennia of winter snowmelts and floods.

Sentinel Pine Covered Bridge crosses the river right at the Pool. Make sure to examine the fallen 175-foot white pine that forms the base of the bridge. The best view of the tree is from a short spur path to the left after you pass through the covered bridge.

From the bridge, it is 0.6 mile back to the visitor center on Wildwood Path through a forest laced with boulders.

DID YOU KNOW?

The Conway granite that forms the walls of Flume Gorge was created from magma (molten rock) that welled up from deep within the Earth and solidified 3 to 5 miles below the surface during the middle to late Jurassic period about 180 million years ago.

OTHER ACTIVITIES

Roaring River Nature Trail, with easy access from the Flume Gorge parking area, is a quiet experience compared with the Flume. Here you can learn about the forces of destruction and renewal that shape the northern hardwood forest. Pick up a self-guided interpretive pamphlet at the visitor center. A gazebo provides a place to listen quietly to the sounds of the forest while looking out at a view of Mount Flume and Mount Liberty, two 4,000-foot peaks of the Franconia Range.

Flume Gorge is convenient to other features and activities in Franconia Notch State Park, such as the Basin, an incredible glacial pothole scoured by the Pemigewasset River; Mount Pemigewasset Trail (Trip 14), which leaves from the Flume Gorge parking area; swimming at Echo Lake Beach (admission: $4 for adults, $2 for children 6 to 12, free for children 5 and younger, free for New Hampshire residents); and the Cannon Mountain Aerial Tramway. A paved bike trail starts at the Flume Gorge parking area and runs the length of Franconia Notch.

MORE INFORMATION

The Flume Gorge Visitor Center is open from early May through late October from 9 A.M. to 5 P.M. Admission at the time of this writing was $16 for adults and $14 for children 6 to 12. Children 5 and younger with a paying adult and New Hampshire residents 65 and older may enter for free.

The visitor center has a cafeteria, gift shop, restrooms, and interpretative exhibits. Visitors can watch a short movie about Franconia Notch State Park.

In winter, the visitor center is closed, and some of the boardwalks are removed, but you can still walk in and enjoy many of the trails. The park does not charge an admission fee in winter.

Dogs are not permitted along the trails in Flume Gorge.

12 BALD MOUNTAIN AND ARTIST'S BLUFF

Bald Mountain and Artist's Bluff offer great views of Franconia Notch for relatively little effort. This ideal family outing is short, has a well-defined goal, and begins and ends near Echo Lake, a picturesque swimming beach.

Features

Location Franconia, NH

Rating Moderate

Distance 1.6-mile loop

Elevation Gain 600 feet

Estimated Time 2 hours

Maps *AMC White Mountain National Forest Map & Guide*, 4th ed., G4 and Franconia Notch inset; AMC *White Mountain Guide*, 31st ed. Map 2 Franconia–Pemigewasset, H4; USGS Topo: Franconia

GPS Coordinates 44° 10.73′ N, 71° 42.10′ W

Contact Franconia Notch State Park; nhstateparks.org/visit/state-parks/franconia-notch-state-park.aspx; 603-823-8800.

DIRECTIONS

From the south, take the Franconia Notch Highway, the extension of I-93 through Franconia Notch. As you approach the north end of the notch, the cliff of Artist's Bluff looms ahead. Take Exit 34C (NH 18/Echo Lake/Peabody Slope), drive about a half-mile west, and park in the lot (indicated by a sign) on the right (north) side of NH 18 by the Peabody Memorial Slope area of Cannon Mountain. From the Twin Mountain area, follow US 3 south toward Franconia Notch and pick up NH 18 at the entrance to the notch, where NH 3 and I-93 come together, and then follow the directions above. The trail enters the woods along the north side of the parking lot.

TRAIL DESCRIPTION

Bald Mountain, the highest elevation on this trail, is only 2,340 feet; however, it is still a good idea to throw windbreakers in your pack, particularly if you plan to have a picnic on the summit.

This loop hike has been renamed Veterans Trail in honor of New Hampshire veterans, although as of this writing, much of the signage used an old name, Loop Trail. However, Loop Trail traditionally has referred to the lower section of the loop so hikers could avoid walking back along the road. To add to the confusion, the main part of the trail is also

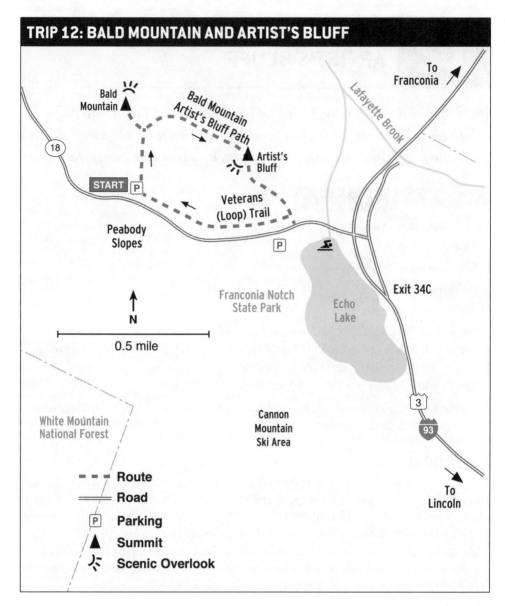

Bald Mountain

Bald Mountain Artist's Bluff Path

Artist's Bluff

18

START P

Peabody Slopes

Veterans (Loop) Trail

To Franconia

Lafayette Brook

P

Exit 34C

Franconia Notch State Park

Echo Lake

N

0.5 mile

White Mountain National Forest

Cannon Mountain Ski Area

3

93

To Lincoln

- - - Route
══ Road
P Parking
▲ Summit
Scenic Overlook

called Bald Mountain/Artist's Buff Path. Fortunately, the route, marked with red blazes, is easy to follow. It starts out fairly steeply, following an old carriage road up through northern hardwoods. After about 0.25 mile, Bald Mountain Spur, which ascends the summit of Bald Mountain, enters from the left. Follow this spur and continue ascending, now through a forest of red spruce and balsam fir. A short distance farther, the vegetation becomes scrubby, and a little bit of scrambling on rocks is required before you reach the summit of Bald Mountain, 0.4 mile from the trailhead.

From Bald Mountain, the Peabody Slopes of the Cannon Mountain Ski Area are immediately to the south. Farther to the east (your left) is the glacially carved valley that is

Franconia Notch. Try to imagine this site completely covered by ice thousands of feet thick as recently as 12,000 years ago. The glacier acted like a giant piece of sandpaper, grinding and smoothing the walls of the valley as it moved slowly through. North–south valleys in the White Mountains, such as Franconia Notch, were particularly well scoured by the north–south movements of the continental ice sheet and so have characteristically broad bottoms and steep sides.

Mount Lafayette, at 5,260 feet the highest mountain of the Franconia Range, forms the eastern wall of Franconia Notch. You will immediately be struck by how "pointy" the summits of Mount Lafayette and other peaks of the Franconia Range are, compared with the broad, smooth summits of the Presidential Range. The tops of the Presidentials were flattened out by the massive continental glacier; in contrast, the narrower Franconia Ridge was scoured from the sides by mountain glaciers. The freezing and thawing of the ice plucked out chunks of rock from both sides of Franconia Ridge, leaving behind a narrow ridge.

Another noteworthy feature of Mount Lafayette is the steep ravine carved in the side of the mountain by the rushing water of Lafayette Brook during postglacial times. Eagle Cliff is the dramatically rugged shoulder of Mount Lafayette. Legend has it that golden eagles used to nest there, and in recent years peregrine falcons have taken up residence (they're very hard to see from Bald Mountain even with binoculars).

The summit ledges on Bald Mountain are covered with stunted spruce and fir and shrubs such as mountain holly, blueberry, and meadowsweet. Three-toothed cinquefoils grow in cracks in the rocks where some soil collects. These and bunchberries form an attractive display of white flowers in mid-June. Notice the "flag trees," with branches on only one side of the trunk. The prevailing winter winds, in combination with ice, kill buds on the opposite side of the trunk, so that branches form only on the lee side (that is, the side away from the direction of the prevailing wind). On Bald Mountain, most of the "flag trees" point east, indicating that the wind is usually from the west. Exceptions do occur, perhaps where the winds whip around the side of the mountain.

If you are lucky, you may see one of the White Mountains' largest and most charismatic animals from a distance so safe that you'll need binoculars. Black bears, often mother bears with their cubs, occasionally forage for berries in the open ski trails high up on Cannon Mountain during daylight. Looking across to those ski slopes from Bald Mountain is about as good a chance as you'll have to see bears in the White Mountains, because they are usually secretive. The bears' presence along the ski trails shows that these trails are not without value to some wildlife.

After enjoying the Bald Mountain summit, retrace your steps on the spur to its junction with the main (Veterans) trail. If you have had enough for the day, take the right fork and descend to the parking area. For Artist's Bluff, 0.5 mile away, follow the left fork. The understory vegetation is particularly lush between Bald Mountain and Artist's Bluff, with abundant ferns, mosses, blue-bead lily, club mosses, false Solomon's seal, mountain wood sorrel (particularly near the junction with the Bald Mountain spur), red and painted trillium, and pink lady's slippers (both pink- and white-flowered varieties). Striped and red maples are common understory shrubs. Other plants to look for are bristly and wild sarsaparilla, goldenrod, rattlesnake root, wild oats, and Canada mayflower.

Cannon Mountain looms large from Bald Mountain. *Photo by Jerry Monkman.*

The trail passes over two wooded humps and then descends steeply for about five minutes to the junction (1.0 mile) with the short spur path that leads left to Artist's Bluff. Follow the spur to the open ledges of Artist's Bluff.

From this point, Echo Lake is immediately below, and you look directly down the notch, which is the north–south divide between two completely different drainage patterns. Echo Lake has an outlet to the northwest that flows into the Gale River, which joins the Connecticut River and flows into Long Island Sound. Profile Lake is just a little south of Echo Lake, on the other side of an almost imperceptible rise in the land. A drop of water falling in Profile Lake flows south through the Pemigewasset River to the Merrimack River and eventually reaches the Atlantic Ocean at Newburyport, Massachusetts.

From Artist's Bluff, the trail descends steeply in a gully, initially on some conveniently placed rocky stairs. At 1.3 miles it intersects with Loop Trail to the right. Going straight will lead you very shortly to NH 18, where you would need to walk back along the road to the parking area. It is much more pleasant to turn right on Loop Trail, which leads 0.3 mile back through the woods. Reward yourself with a swim in Echo Lake.

DID YOU KNOW?

Before the age of Vibram soles and Gore-Tex parkas, hikers in long, frilly dresses, starched collars, and neckties walked up Bald Mountain and Artist's Bluff from Profile House in Franconia Notch and other grand hotels. These summer guests would purchase paintings from artists who were in residence at the hotels and undoubtedly painted from Artist's Bluff.

OTHER ACTIVITIES

Bald Mountain and Artist's Bluff are very close to the scenic attractions in Franconia Notch State Park: Echo and Profile lakes, Cannon Mountain, the Old Man of the Mountain site, the Basin, and Eagle Cliff. Despite the crowds, these natural wonders are worth a stop before or after your hike.

Echo Lake has an attractive swimming beach with lifeguards and a bathhouse. The entrance fee is $4 for adults and $2 for children 6 to 11; admission is free for children 5 and younger and for New Hampshire residents. The site has a snack bar, restrooms, information service, and a picnic area.

MORE INFORMATION

This hike is within Franconia Notch State Park; parking is free.

13 COPPERMINE TRAIL TO BRIDAL VEIL FALLS

Coppermine Trail takes you on a gentle uphill grade along Coppermine Brook to Bridal Veil Falls, one of the most beautiful waterfalls in the White Mountains. It is a pleasant walk on the western side of Cannon Mountain.

Features 👥🐕))) 🏞️ ⬟

Location Franconia, NH

Rating Moderate

Distance 5.0 miles round trip

Elevation Gain 1,100 feet

Estimated Time 3–4 hours

Maps *AMC White Mountain National Forest Map & Guide*, 4th ed., G4; AMC *White Mountain Guide*, 31st ed. Map 2 Franconia–Pemigewasset, H4; USGS Topo: Sugar Hill to Franconia

GPS Coordinates 44° 10.86′ N, 71° 45.34′ W

Contact White Mountain National Forest: fs.usda.gov/whitemountain, 603-536-6100

DIRECTIONS

Coppermine Trail is off NH 116, about 3.4 miles south of the village of Franconia. If you are traveling north through Franconia Notch, take the Franconia exit on I-93 (Exit 38) and then go south on NH 116 for 3.4 miles. Alternatively, from the North Woodstock and Lincoln exit on I-93 (Exit 32), travel west on NH 112 for about 8 miles and then north on NH 116 for 7.7 miles. Look for Coppermine Road on the east side of NH 116. Park your vehicle in the ample space on Coppermine Road just after turning off NH 116.

TRAIL DESCRIPTION

The hike starts along Coppermine Road, a dirt road, so all distances are from NH 116. Be careful to avoid turning off on a road (Beechwood Lane) coming off Coppermine Road.

At 0.3 mile, Coppermine Trail, marked with yellow blazes, departs from the left side of the road (look for the hiker sign). The pleasant woodland path leads through a northern hardwood forest. Yellow birch is especially abundant, and American beech and sugar maple are also well represented. Conifers, particularly eastern hemlock but also red spruce and balsam fir, grow along the north side of the brook where the microclimate is shadier, damper, and cooler. The most prevalent understory shrub is hobblebush.

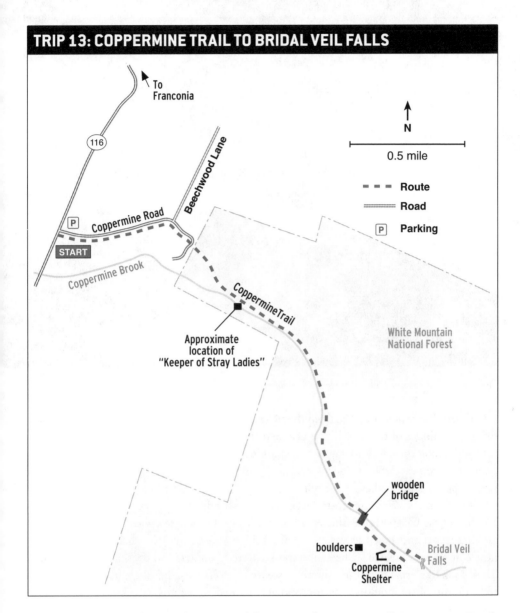

Look for circular clumps of interrupted fern soon after turning off Coppermine Road. The leafy green pinnae (leaflets) of this large fern are "interrupted" along the stalk by brownish reproductive pinnae. You may also notice the raspberries growing in disturbed areas near the road. These make a delicious treat if birds haven't gotten there first.

Most wildflowers growing along the trail bloom in May and June. These include trout lily, foamflower, lance-leaved twisted-stalk, Canada mayflower, blue-bead lily, false Solomon's seal, Indian cucumber-root, jack-in-the-pulpit, starflower, wild sarsaparilla, and American shinleaf.

The base of Coppermine Falls. *Photo by Jerry Monkman.*

Coppermine Brook comes in from the right at about 1 mile and is within sight or earshot for the remainder of the trip. If you decide to cut the walk short, several places where the trail runs along the brook make for a pleasant short (or long) stop before you turn around. Soon after, you can look for the mysterious plaque in the river (see "Coppermine Trail and the Keeper of Stray Ladies," page 68).

After 2.3 miles, the route crosses over to the south side of the brook on a wooden bridge and passes the Coppermine Shelter, a lean-to. Mountain maples, with their characteristic arching stems and lobed leaves, are at the bridge and around the shelter. You will also notice little caves created by fern- and moss-covered boulders and overhanging tree roots. These look like great dens for animals or weary elves. The small evergreen ferns that grow right on top of the boulders are appropriately named rock ferns, also known as Virginia polypody.

The trail crosses back over the stream on well-placed rocks, climbs moderately, and then ends at Bridal Veil Falls, 0.2 mile after the bridge. Bridal Veil Falls is really several connected cascades, some forming "shoots" along sloping rock faces and others tumbling over rocks into pools, such as the large one at the bottom. As with most waterfalls in the White Mountains, the best time for viewing them is when water levels are relatively high, either early in the season or just after a rainstorm. An unofficial path runs up the right side of the falls, but it is very slippery and potentially dangerous.

Retrace your steps to return to the parking area.

OTHER ACTIVITIES

The swimming area at Echo Lake in Franconia Notch State Park is about 10 miles away (admission is $4 for adults, $2 for children 6 to 11; free for children 5 and younger and for New Hampshire residents).

Lost River Reservation, 13 miles away (south on NH 116 and east on NH 112), is a gorge with lots of caves that have exotic names such as Judgment Hall of Pluto. It is run by the Society for the Protection of New Hampshire Forests and is a terrific place to take kids (admission is $18 for adults, $12 for children 4 to 12).

MORE INFORMATION

The first 0.5 mile of this hike goes through private land, so please be respectful of property owners. The remainder of the hike is in the White Mountain National Forest. Parking is free.

The village of Franconia is the closest place for food and supplies. Stores and restaurants are clustered around the junction of NH 18 and NH 116.

COPPERMINE TRAIL AND THE KEEPER OF STRAY LADIES

After hiking about 1 mile on Coppermine Trail (approximately 0.2 mile after the trail joins the brook, near where a cross-country ski trail heads left), search for a plaque on a large boulder in the streambed with an enigmatic inscription:

> In Memoriam
> to
> Arthur Farnsworth
> "The Keeper of Stray Ladies"
> Pecketts 1939
> Presented by a Grateful One

To find it, look for a steep slope that goes through an open hemlock woods down to a flat area where people might have pitched tents along the brook. You need to scramble to reach the streambed and then use caution on the slippery rocks. The boulder juts out into the water roughly halfway along the flat area. The plaque faces downstream on the same side of the brook as the trail.

For the rest of your hike, you may ponder who Arthur Farnsworth was, why the tribute was placed in this particular location, and who the "Grateful One" was who chose to eulogize Mr. Farnsworth in this manner.

The answer, according to an article by Lyn McIntosh in the autumn 1987 issue of *Magnetic North*, is that Arthur Farnsworth was a handsome young Vermonter who was employed at Pecketts, a fashionable year-round resort in the 1930s on Sugar Hill, just west of Franconia Notch. Guests of Pecketts rode on horseback to land owned by the resort on Coppermine Brook to hike, fish, snowshoe, or simply enjoy the beautiful rushing water. Farnsworth's job was to make guests feel at home at the lodge. In 1939, the actress Bette Davis came to Pecketts for a period of rest after a particularly exhausting stint of movie-making. In brief, Davis fell in love with Pecketts, the entire region, and Farnsworth. The simple life of the North Country and the strong, honest gentleman who did not find her fame particularly intimidating were just the antidotes Davis needed from her life as a movie star.

Legend has it that Davis strayed from a hiking party at Coppermine Brook, knowing that Farnsworth would be sent to find her. They were married in 1940 and lived happily in California, occasionally escaping to the White Mountains. Unfortunately, in 1943, tragedy struck. Farnsworth died after he fell down some stairs at their home on Sugar Hill. Davis continued to come back to the White Mountains for a while but eventually sold her home on Sugar Hill in 1961. The plaque mysteriously appeared at Coppermine Brook sometime around then.

14 MOUNT PEMIGEWASSET TRAIL

Mount Pemigewasset Trail ascends the 2,500-foot peak that bears the famed Indian Head profile at its summit. The climb, located at the southern end of Franconia Notch, is a good one for children because it's never very steep. The views from the top are excellent, and the combination of stream crossings and rocks in the forest makes for an interesting journey.

Features 🥾 🧑‍🦯 🐕 💧 🗺️ ✳️

Location Lincoln, NH

Rating Moderate

Distance 3.6 miles round trip

Elevation Gain 1,300 feet

Estimated Time 3 hours

Maps *AMC White Mountain National Forest Map & Guide*, 4th ed., H4 and Franconia Notch inset; AMC *White Mountain Guide*, 31st ed. Map 2 Franconia–Pemigewasset, H4; USGS Topo: Lincoln

GPS Coordinates 44° 05.87′ N, 71° 40.90′ W

Contact Franconia Notch State Park: nhstateparks.org/visit/state-parks/franconia -notch-state-park.aspx, 603-823-8800

DIRECTIONS

Reach the trailhead from the parking lot for Flume Gorge in Franconia Notch State Park. This is at Exit 34A of the Franconia Notch Highway, the extension of I-93 through Franconia Notch. The exit is about 4 miles north of Exit 32 on I-93, the exit for Lincoln, North Woodstock, NH 112, and the Kancamagus Highway. For this trail, it is most convenient to park at the northwest side of the parking lot, near the beginning of the bike path that heads north through the notch. The actual trailhead is off the bike path, so follow signs that direct you to the bike path.

TRAIL DESCRIPTION

Mount Pemigewasset Trail is marked with blue blazes, but it would be hard to get lost on this well-trod path even if you didn't see the markings. From the parking lot, start walking north on the paved bike path for about 150 yards and then follow the gravel trail to the left. The trail goes through a tunnel under US 3 (now a service road for the Franconia Notch Highway). Then it turns south for a short stretch through a forest of spruce, fir, and paper

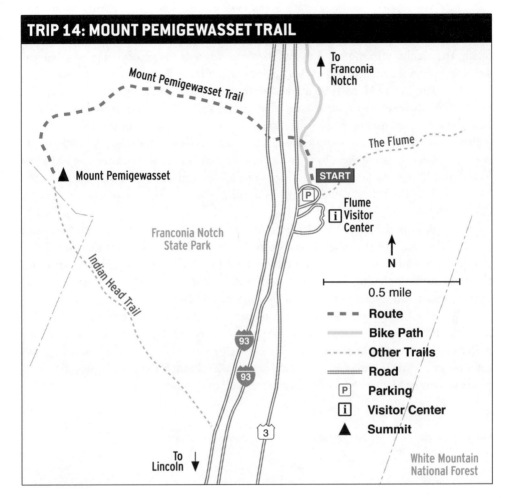

birch and crosses a small stream. You will pass through two more tunnels, which are the northbound and southbound sides of the Franconia Notch Highway.

The route then climbs on some well-placed stone slabs. After about 0.7 mile and several stream crossings, one on a log bridge, head uphill at a somewhat steeper pitch. At this point, you are walking through a northern hardwood forest, where the dominant trees are yellow birch, American beech, and sugar maple. Hobblebush, with some striped maple, forms the understory. Woodland wildflowers to look for include wild sarsaparilla, partridgeberry, mountain wood sorrel, false Solomon's seal, and white wood aster. Blue-bead lily (*Clintonia*) becomes more frequent as you ascend. Wood ferns, shining club moss, and a variety of true mosses are also quite common. Mushrooms abound from midsummer through early fall.

The birds you are likely to hear include black-throated green warblers, black-throated blue warblers, red-eyed vireos, golden-crowned kinglets, and hermit thrushes. Red squirrels and chipmunks scamper about.

Approximately 1.3 miles from the trailhead, the route passes a huge boulder, a glacial erratic, and 50 yards later veers to the left. This is a pleasant place to stop for a snack or lunch. You climb a little more steeply and then pass through an area of young trees that was a clearing when the first edition of this book came out more than twenty years ago.

At 1.7 miles, Indian Head Trail, marked with yellow blazes, comes in from the right. The northern hardwood forest is now replaced by spruce and fir. Continue straight on Mount Pemigewasset Trail for another 0.1 mile to reach the open ledges of the summit.

Panoramic views of surrounding mountains can be seen from the large, flat rocks of the summit. Mount Moosilauke is to the west, South Kinsman to the northwest, and Mounts Flume and Liberty to the east. The villages of Lincoln and North Woodstock are to the south. Some of the ledges at the summit end rather abruptly with steep dropoffs. Keep a close watch on young children.

The small, scattered trees that grow around the summit have been sculpted by the wind to form "flag trees" (that is, their branches form only on the lee side, away from the direction of the prevailing wind). Look for chimney swifts, very fast and agile birds that zoom about the summit chasing their insect prey. The left and right wings of this streamlined, dusky-colored bird sometimes look as if they move independently.

You'll find some lowbush blueberries at the summit, but you will have lots of competition from both human and nonhuman frugivores at this popular destination. The nonhuman variety include flocks of cedar waxwings—beige, crested birds with yellow bellies, red tips on some of their wing feathers, and black masks through their eyes. They also have blueberry-covered ledges, beyond human access, all to themselves.

Enjoying the view from Mount Pemigewasset. *Photo by Alison Buchsbaum.*

As you return to the start, avoid following the yellow blazes you might see at the summit ledges. These lead down the mountain on a very steep, unmaintained trail. Instead, turn right for Mount Pemigewasset Trail at its junction with Indian Head Trail. It is possible to return via Indian Head Trail, which ends up on a short gravel road just south of Indian Head Resort off US 3. But be warned that this trail is not well marked and would require a 0.75-mile walk along the highway to reach a vehicle, unless you park at its trailhead beforehand.

DID YOU KNOW?

The formation of the feature called Indian Head is the result of water seeping into cracks in the granite rock and then freezing and expanding, thereby causing pieces of the granite to break off. Although seemingly a solid, impenetrable mass, granite contains cracks (joints) along distinct planes. These cracks formed when the magma that became the granite cooled deep within the earth during the Jurassic period about 175 million years ago. Fast forward to postglacial times when water penetrated these joints. When the water froze, it expanded and broke off pieces of rock, mostly along the joints. What remained happens to resemble a human profile. The Indian Head feature is only temporary, however, and will eventually erode into something less identifiable, which happened to the Old Man of the Mountain several miles to the north.

OTHER ACTIVITIES

The Indian Head feature is not obvious from anywhere on the trail on this hike. After the hike, make sure you get a good look at it from the valley in the vicinity of Indian Head Resort.

Access to Flume Gorge (Trip 11) is available from the same parking area (admission is $16 for adults, $14 for children 6 to 12; free for children 5 and younger and for New Hampshire residents 65 and over).

MORE INFORMATION

Parking is free to use the Mount Pemigewasset Trail. The closest concentration of restaurants and other tourist facilities is off US 3 and NH 112 in Lincoln and North Woodstock.

15 LONESOME LAKE AND HUT

Lonesome Lake is a beautiful body of water reached by a short, somewhat steep climb. Swim in the lake while enjoying the spectacular view across Franconia Notch to Mount Lafayette. The shoreline abounds with interesting aquatic plants and insects. AMC's Lonesome Lake Hut provides overnight accommodations.

Features 🚶🏽‍♂️💧🐚◺🎇△🏊‍♂️🏕🔼🚌

Location Lincoln, NH

Rating Moderate

Distance 3.2 miles round trip including a short loop

Elevation Gain 1,000 feet

Estimated Time 3–4 hours loop/round trip

Maps *AMC White Mountain National Forest Map & Guide*, 4th ed., H4 and Franconia Notch inset; AMC *White Mountain Guide*, 31st ed. Map 2 Franconia–Pemigewasset, H4; USGS Topo: Franconia

GPS Coordinates 44° 08.52′ N, 71° 41.03′ W

Contact Franconia Notch State Park; nhstateparks.org/visit/state-parks/franconia -notch-state-park.aspx; 603-823-8800

DIRECTIONS

Lonesome Lake Trail starts at Lafayette Place Campground in Franconia Notch State Park. From the north, take the Franconia Notch Highway through the notch to the exit for the campground, about 1.5 miles south of the Old Man of the Mountain site. If you are coming from the south through Lincoln and North Woodstock, exit at the trailhead parking area, about 1.5 miles north of the Basin, and then cross over to the west side through a foot tunnel. The parking lots fill up early on pleasant summer and fall weekends, and parking is prohibited along the shoulder of the parkway, so you may need to park at the large lot for Bald Mountain and Artist's Bluff Trail (Trip 12). Shuttle service is available from there to the trailhead.

TRAIL DESCRIPTION

The trail begins at the picnic area at the campground's south parking lot on the west side of the highway. A large sign for the trail and yellow blazes will help you make your way past the picnic area, across the Pemigewasset River on a bridge, past Pemi Trail (paved bikeway), and through the campground without getting off track. After leaving the

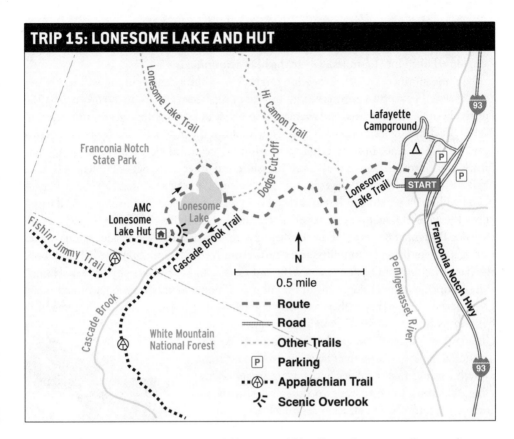

campground, Lonesome Lake Trail follows an old bridle path once used to reach a private camp on the lake.

After 0.3 mile through a dense northern hardwood forest, the trail turns left sharply and crosses a wooden plank bridge over a stream that tumbles down the mountainside. Hobblebush, violets, partridgeberry, and shining club moss are major parts of the understory. At 0.4 mile, Hi Cannon Trail departs right toward the summit of Cannon Mountain. Lonesome Lake Trail then ascends with moderate steepness via three switchbacks. While climbing, listen for the flutelike sounds of hermit thrushes and the incredible long, bubbly warble of the winter wren, two of the White Mountains' finest songsters. The trail levels off through a pretty boreal forest with red spruce and balsam fir and a lush understory of mosses, goldthread, mountain wood sorrel, and blue-bead lily. The terrain is very hummocky—it looks like the kind of place where elves might pop out from behind the trees.

Lonesome Lake Trail reaches the lake at 1.2 miles at a junction with Cascade Brook Trail. From here you loop around the water on Around Lonesome Lake Trail, a route that incorporates sections of Cascade Brook, Fishin' Jimmy, and Lonesome Lake trails. Parts of it may be soggy, particularly in spring. Because it's a loop, you can take it in either direction. I describe it going clockwise.

Turn left onto Cascade Brook Trail and follow planks along the southeast shoreline toward Lonesome Lake Hut. From vantage points along the shore you can see North and

South Kinsman mountains and the Cannonballs. At 1.4 miles, turn right onto Fishin' Jimmy Trail. In another 0.1 mile, pass the outlet of the lake and then the dock area of Lonesome Lake Hut (1.6 miles), where the best swimming is.

On a hot summer day, after sweating mightily on your ascent, nothing will feel better than a swim, but keep an eye on the kids in your group because there are no lifeguards. The lake is about 20 acres in area and averages 3 to 6 feet in depth with a maximum depth of 12 feet. Technically it's a tarn—a pond scoured out of the mountainside by a glacier. This may be the best place in New England to admire a beautiful view while practicing your backstroke. Across the notch are Mount Lafayette and other peaks of the Franconia Range. Walker Ravine in Mount Lafayette appears as a deep V in the mountainside.

You will likely see dragonflies and the closely related damselflies hovering and darting above the water. Dragonflies are strong flyers and active predators of other insects around the lake. Roughly 80 species of dragonflies were recorded in the White Mountains region during a dragonfly and damselfly survey carried out from 2007 to 2011 by NH Audubon, the New Hampshire Department of Fish and Game, and the University of New Hampshire Cooperative Extension. One of the most common you are likely to encounter is the green darner, a large dragonfly with a bright green thorax and a blue abdomen. Dragonfly behavior is fun to watch. Although you might see them chasing prey, much of their activity is related to mating. Territorial males alight on their favorite perches and chase away intruding males. Males and females mate on the wing, and you may even see two dragonflies in such a "tandem flight." The female then deposits her eggs in the water by hovering and touching it periodically with the tip of her abdomen. Some species have specialized appendages to inject their eggs into emergent vegetation.

Look for dragonfly exuviae along the shoreline. These are the discarded exoskeletons of dragonfly nymphs (larvae). The nymphs live in water as voracious predators. When it is time to molt into adulthood, a nymph crawls out onto vegetation, splits its exoskeleton ("skin"), and emerges as an adult, much like a butterfly emerging from a cocoon. The remaining exuviae, looking like pale, dried-out versions of the nymphs, are left behind on the vegetation and provide a natural record of successful breeding. The newly emerged adults, called tenerals, are soft and vulnerable for at least a few hours until their wings and new exoskeletons harden.

Shrubs growing by the dock include sheep laurel, withe-rod (northern wild raisin), sweetgale, and mountain ash. You may also observe the difference between red spruce (square needles) and balsam fir (flat needles).

After enjoying the lake, visit AMC's hut by following Fishin' Jimmy Trail to the left. Day-hikers can use the restrooms and buy trail snacks, hot and cold drinks, trail maps, T-shirts, and other supplies. Soup is sometimes available midday. Ask at the hut for information about the self-guided nature walk, which uses the next portion of Around Lonesome Lake Trail, or longer trails that take you around the lake to Cannon Mountain or other destinations.

Snowshoeing across Lonesome Lake. *Photo by Dennis Welsh.*

Very tame snowshoe hares sometimes hang out around the dock and the hut. These hares change color to match the season, turning brown in summer and white in winter. This camouflages them, although their presence around the hut suggests that they are not too worried about predators. The grassy areas provide them with forage during summer. In winter, they feed on twigs and bark.

If you visit the hut in June, you will hear a symphony of bird songs. Performers include Swainson's thrushes, winter wrens, white-throated sparrows, yellow-rumped warblers, black-capped chickadees, and dark-eyed juncos.

Leaving the hut, Around Lonesome Lake Trail continues clockwise along the western shore of the lake. Note that this is the only section of this trail that does not incorporate a part of another, longer trail. The route goes through an open boggy area on split-rail bridges and planks. The planks protect your shoes from the dampness while at the same time protecting the plants from your shoes. The most abundant shrubs are sheep laurel, sweetgale, and leatherleaf. The pink flowers of sheep laurel, produced in early July, look like smaller versions of those of mountain laurel, a close relative. The crushed leaves of sweetgale smell as delightful as those of its close relative, the bayberry.

Examine the undersides of leaves of several of the shrubs, with a hand lens if possible. Sweetgale leaves have tiny yellow resin dots. The undersides of the thick leaves of leatherleaf are covered by rusty scales. Arguably, the most interesting leaves belong to Labrador tea— they are thick and leathery with undersides covered in dense, woolly, reddish brown hairs.

Look for sundews in the wetland. These tiny bog plants capture small insects by using sticky hairs on the tips of spoon-shaped leaves. The insects are digested and provide nutrients to the plant. The low-nutrient conditions of bogs make them a haven for carnivorous plants, but it takes a sharp eye to find sundews.

Larches, also called tamaracks, grow between the plank trail and the lake. These relatives of pines, spruces, and firs are partial to bogs. Unlike pines, which have needles in bunches of two to five, larches have needles in bunches of twenty or so, which give their branches a delicate, lacy appearance.

Beavers have played a large part in creating the wetland landscape around Lonesome Lake. As of this writing they no longer inhabit the lake itself, but their legacy remains in the extensive boggy wetland created by their dams, particularly on the western and northwestern shores. You can still see the old dams too. Beavers are now active downstream from the outlet and upstream of the northwestern shore.

At about 0.3 mile from the hut, the route reaches the junction with Lonesome Lake Trail. Note the many upturned trees whose intricate root systems are exposed. It reveals graphically how shallow the root systems are due to the thinness of the soil. Here you will also find the large, cabbage-like leaves of Indian poke and an extensive cover of sphagnum moss.

Turn right onto Lonesome Lake Trail to complete the loop in another 0.2 mile. From here you can descend to the trailhead at Lafayette Place on Lonesome Lake Trail.

DID YOU KNOW?

Lonesome Lake Hut is the only one of the eight AMC huts in the White Mountains not in the White Mountain National Forest. It is in Franconia Notch State Park.

OTHER ACTIVITIES

Lonesome Lake Hut is a great place for families to have their first experience staying overnight at a backcountry hut. The hut requires a relatively short walk and is laid out so that families staying overnight often can have their own room. Hearty breakfasts and dinners are served. Throughout the full-service season, an AMC naturalist is on-site to present an evening program, lead a family-oriented nature walk, and answer your questions about the mountains. Reservations are required for an overnight stay; outdoors.org/destinations; 603-466-2727.

MORE INFORMATION

The entire hike, including the parking area, is in Franconia Notch State Park. Parking is free. Fishing is permitted at Lonesome Lake. Contact the New Hampshire Fish and Game Department (wildlife.state.nh.us) for information on obtaining a license.

AMC'S HIGH HUTS IN THE WHITE MOUNTAINS

In 1888, the Appalachian Mountain Club built a small, one-room stone hut to provide overnight accommodations at Madison Spring in the col between Mounts Madison and Adams. AMC wanted to provide a protected place that hikers could use as a base to explore the Northern Presidential Range. Numerous club members had climbed in Switzerland, and the high-mountain huts there undoubtedly inspired them. Unlike today, where visitors are greeted by an attentive crew who provide meals and manage the hut, early visitors brought their own food and were expected to take care of the premises.

Carter Notch Hut opened in 1914, using a design similar to that of Madison Spring Hut. A third hut, Lakes of the Clouds, opened in 1915, partially as a response to the tragic death of two climbers caught in a storm on Crawford Path in 1900.

The person most responsible for creating the hut system of today was Joe Dodge, who served as manager of the AMC hut system from 1928 through 1959. A legendary personality, he oversaw the creation of the four "western huts," including the acquisition of Lonesome Lake Hut and the construction of Zealand Falls, Galehead, and Greenleaf huts, expanded the existing huts, promoted the hut system throughout New England, and trained crews on managing the huts. Mizpah Spring Hut is the only addition to the system since Dodge retired. Eight backcountry huts are now available in the White Mountains.

These huts are in wonderful locations and are spaced a day's hike from each other. They provide lodging, meals, and "mountain hospitality." Guests can participate in a naturalist walk and learn about local ecology and human history from displays, books, and members of the "croo." Kids can earn a junior naturalist badge. Snacks, hot drinks, and trail information are available during the day; overnight guests are served breakfast and dinner during the full-service season (see outdoors.org/lodging/huts for information on when certain huts are closed or self-service only). Reservations are required for an overnight stay. For more information or to make a reservation, call 603-466-2727 or visit outdoors.org/destinations.

Four huts make fine destinations for day hikes as well as overnight trips. Those are Lonesome Lake (Trip 15), Zealand Falls (Trip 36), Mizpah Spring (Trip 39), and Carter Notch (Trip 47). For fans of cold-weather hiking, snowshoeing, and skiing, three of those four (Carter, Zealand, and Lonesome Lake) are open in winter on a self-service basis. All other huts close in September or October.

16 CLOUDLAND FALLS AND FRANCONIA RIDGE VIA FALLING WATERS TRAIL, GREENLEAF TRAIL, AND OLD BRIDLE PATH

The hike across Franconia Ridge from Little Haystack Mountain to Mount Lafayette is one of the White Mountains' most spectacular long day hikes, providing some of the very best scenery in the Northeast. If you want a shorter hike, the portion from Falling Waters Trail to Cloudland Falls will satisfy everyone who loves the intoxicating sound of falling water within a cool, dense forest.

Features

Location Lincoln, NH, to Franconia, NH

Rating Strenuous for the complete loop; Moderate with a few steep sections to Cloudland Falls

Distance 8.9 miles for the complete loop; 2.6 miles round trip to Cloudland Falls

Elevation Gain Mount Lafayette, 3,950 feet; Cloudland Falls, 900 feet

Estimated Time 7 hours for the complete loop; 2 hours for the round trip to Cloudland Falls only

Maps *AMC White Mountain National Forest Map & Guide*, 4th ed., H5 and Franconia Notch inset; AMC *White Mountain Guide*, 31st ed. Map 2 Franconia–Pemigewasset, H4-5; USGS Topo: Franconia

GPS Coordinates 44° 08.53' N, 71° 40.86' W

Contact White Mountain National Forest: fs.usda.gov/whitemountain, 603-536-6100; Franconia Notch State Park: nhstateparks.org/visit/state-parks/franconia-notch-state-park.aspx, 603-823-8800

⚠ **CAUTION!** The ridge has a 1.6-mile section above treeline fully exposed to the elements, so that part of this hike should be attempted only in good weather by hikers who are in good physical condition and have the proper gear.

DIRECTIONS

Falling Waters Trail departs from the Lafayette Place parking area in Franconia Notch State Park off the Franconia Notch Parkway (I-93). This is about 1.5 miles north of the Basin and 1.5 miles south of the Old Man of the Mountain site parking lot. Parking areas

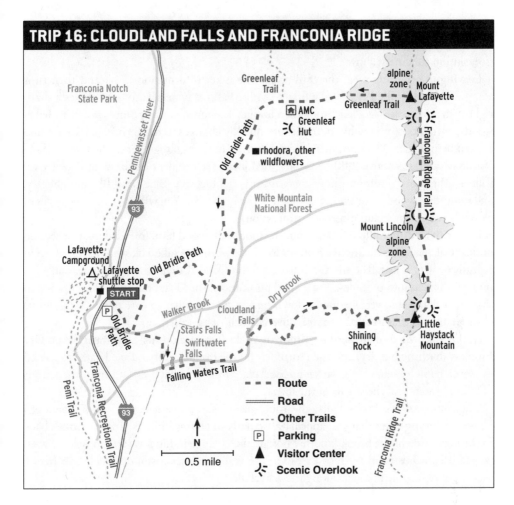

for this trail are on both sides of the highway, and which side you end up on depends on whether you are coming from the north or the south. The trail leaves from the east side of the parkway, which is where you park if you travel north through Lincoln and Woodstock. If you are traveling south on the parkway, use the same exit as for Lafayette Place Campground and park at the hiker lot on the west side of the highway. You can reach the trailhead through a tunnel underneath the highway.

Both parking areas tend to fill up early on pleasant summer and fall weekends, and parking is not permitted along the side of the highway. One alternative is to park at the large lot for Bald Mountain and Artist's Bluff Trail (Trip 12). Shuttle service is available from there to the trailhead.

TRAIL DESCRIPTION

A trip on Falling Waters Trail as far as Cloudland Falls makes an excellent family hike and should be manageable for young children. The route does have several stream crossings that could be challenging in high water, and sections can be slippery when wet. If you are considering hiking beyond the waterfalls up to and across the ridge to Greenleaf Trail, check the hiker information kiosk at the trailhead for weather conditions above treeline (see caution statement above).

Leaving the parking area, the trail passes the hiker information kiosk and then runs along with Old Bridle Path for the first 0.2 mile. Falling Waters Trail then makes a sharp right turn and crosses Walker Brook on a bridge. The forest at this point is northern hardwoods, with lots of yellow birch, but it very quickly changes to red spruce, balsam fir, and eastern hemlock as you continue to ascend. Spruce and fir go together in the forests of the White Mountains above 2,000 feet, and hemlocks are frequent denizens of cooler river valleys. The most common understory shrub is hobblebush. Blue-bead lily, bunchberry, and mountain wood sorrel compose much of the herb layer. You will also find two types of club mosses: shining club moss and princess pine.

Ferns can be difficult to tell apart, but the mountain wood fern, found along this section of this trail, has some distinctive features for those willing to take a close look. A fern frond is equivalent to a leaf. The mountain wood fern's frond is divided into pinnae, and each pinna is divided into pinnules. The second pinnules on the lowest pinna are very uneven in size, such that the lower one hangs down quite a bit. Another feature of this fern and its close relatives is that its stipe (stem) is covered with rusty scales.

At 0.7 mile, the trail crosses Dry Brook on rocks (use care during high water, when Dry Brook is anything but dry) and then turns left (to the right is an abandoned path) to ascend the south bank to Stairs Falls. This is an ideal place to sit on a flat rock and enjoy the sounds of falling waters and the smells of the forest.

Continuing above Stairs Falls, the route passes some overhanging rocks (Sawtooth Ledges), forming caves that will appeal particularly to younger hikers. Then it crosses back to the north side of the brook (another potential challenge in high water) just below Swiftwater Falls, a beautiful 60-foot cascade. The trail traverses a smooth rock slab before ascending past some boulders along the waterfall.

Beyond Swiftwater Falls, the route continues along an old, gravelly logging road, leaves the logging road, and reaches the bottom of Cloudland Falls (1.3 miles). Take a moment to enjoy the view looking up from the bottom of this 80-foot cascade and then ascend a steep and rough segment, aided by rock steps, to the top of the falls. The views here are mostly through trees across Franconia Notch in the direction of Mount Moosilauke. From this vantage point, also note the two small waterfalls at almost right angles to each other. These are brooks from two different subwatersheds. The brook to the north drains the upper sections of Mount Lincoln, whereas the other drains Little Haystack. Their flows join together to form Dry Brook, which then tumbles down Cloudland Falls and flows into the Pemigewasset River in Franconia Notch and eventually into the Merrimack River.

This is the turnaround spot for the shorter hike. For those going onward, Falling Waters Trail continues more steeply through the boreal forest. Use caution—the ledges can be slippery as the trail crosses back and forth over the brook from Mount Lincoln. After the last crossing, about 0.3 mile beyond Cloudland Falls, the route follows another old logging road, which takes it away from the stream. Leaving the logging road after about another 0.3 mile, the trail ascends a series of switchbacks. At 2.8 miles, a spur path leads to the right

Hiking through the alpine tundra along the Franconia Ridge.

to Shining Rock. This huge, steeply sloped granite slab is usually covered with a thin layer of water, so walking out on it is not recommended because it can be very slippery and dangerous. However, you can stand at the edge and look across Franconia Notch to the Kinsman Range. This provides a nice break from the enclosed forest in which you have been walking so far.

Back on Falling Waters Trail, the hike continues steeply through spruce and fir trees that are gradually becoming shorter, hinting that treeline is not far ahead. The route soon reaches treeline and shortly thereafter ends in Franconia Ridge Trail at the summit of Little Haystack Mountain (3.2 miles, 4,760 feet). This is another possible turnaround spot.

The views from Little Haystack are impressive, particularly on a clear day. Mount Lafayette, the highest point in the Franconia Range and the eventual destination for those continuing on, dominates the landscape to the north. To the east are the Twin Range, Mount Bond, and the vast Pemigewasset Wilderness. The large number of bare areas on the mountain slopes are evidence of past landslides. To the south, Franconia Ridge Trail, outlined by cairns, follows the knife-edge ridge toward the sharp peaks of Mounts Liberty and Flume. To the west, the cliffs of Cannon Mountain are particularly prominent across the glacially scoured valley that is Franconia Notch.

Note that the valleys of Walker Brook, Dry Brook, and other brooks that tumble down east to west from the Franconia Ridge are V-shaped, as opposed to the U-shaped north–south valley of Franconia Notch. The V-shaped valleys were created by erosion from the brooks after the retreat of the glaciers, so they are younger geological formations than the notch.

To continue the hike, turn left (north) on Franconia Ridge Trail, part of the Appalachian Trail. The next 1.7 miles of the hike is above treeline, with the spectacular vista as your constant backdrop. It is also completely exposed to the elements, so if the weather is deteriorating, you should return via Falling Waters Trail and not attempt the ridge. In summer, thunderstorms can be particularly dangerous and have resulted in some fatalities.

Alpine zones are one of New England's rarest communities, consisting of isolated "islands" of treeless habitat in the higher mountains of New Hampshire, Maine, and Vermont. Franconia Ridge contains about 1 square mile of alpine habitat. The broader summits of the Presidential Range support about 7 square miles and the greatest diversity of alpine species (see "The Alpine Zone of the White Mountains" on page 256 for more details). The rarity of this community makes it particularly important that visitors stay on the trail to avoid damaging the fragile vegetation.

The most distinctive alpine plant on Franconia Ridge is diapensia. Its low, rounded growth form and small, densely packed leaves resemble a pincushion and are characteristic of a variety of plant species that grow above treeline, termed "cushion plants." This growth form enables these plants to survive the strong winds and cold temperatures that characterize the alpine zone. If you are hiking in early to mid-June, you may see the small, attractive white flowers of diapensia emerge from the cushions, if the wind or a late frost haven't destroyed the petals. Another showy plant that blooms in summer is mountain sandwort. It often forms borders along both sides of the trail. Alpine avens has showy yellow flowers and large, kidney-shaped leaves. This plant is endemic to the White Mountains, meaning that it grows only here (except for a small population on an island off Nova Scotia). Knee-high balsam fir trees contorted by the strong winds on this exposed ridge are called krummholz, a German word meaning "crooked wood."

Use the cairns (piles of stones) as your guide in following the trail. In clear weather, the route is easy to follow because of the steep dropoffs on either side of the ridge, but the cairns can be lifesavers if thick clouds obscure your way. The trail takes you up and over Mount Lincoln (5,089 feet), down to a col between Mounts Lincoln and Lafayette, and finally up to the summit of Lafayette, which at 5,260 feet is the high point of this hike and 4.9 miles from the trailhead. Franconia Ridge Trail ends at the summit of Mount Lafayette, near the foundation of the old hotel that used to stand here.

The view from Mount Lafayette is one of the best in the White Mountains. Mount Garfield and its prominent cliff is the large peak to the east and slightly north of Mount Lafayette. Farther east, on a clear day, you can see Mount Washington and the other peaks of the Presidential Range. Lonesome Lake (Trip 15) is a prominent feature on a shoulder of the Kinsman Range to the west. Looking south, you see the entire length of Franconia Ridge, including the summits you just traversed.

From Mount Lafayette, follow the sign that directs you to descend to the west via Greenleaf Trail. This moderately steep grade treats you to spectacular views of the two Eagle Lakes and AMC's Greenleaf Hut immediately below and Cannon Mountain across Franconia Notch. In about 0.5 mile from the summit, you leave the alpine zone and enter an area of short spruce and fir trees. If it has been windy, this will provide a quiet break.

Just before you reach Greenleaf Hut, you pass the Eagle Lakes. These are tarns, a term used by geologists to describe glacially scoured lakes on the side of a mountain. It appears that these lakes are rapidly turning into bogs. If you look hard in the boggy areas alongside the trail, you can find cranberries. These are not the same species as commercial cranberries, but a species called small (or wren's egg) cranberries. Like their larger, lowland cousins, they grow as low, trailing vines in bogs and produce berries, but their leaves are tiny in comparison. Another interesting plant is three-leafed false Solomon's seal, similar to the false Solomon's seal (or Solomon's plume) of lowland forests except that it has three leaflets per stem.

AMC's Greenleaf Hut perches on an open ridge at 4,200 feet at 6.0 miles (roughly 1.1 miles from the summit of Mount Lafayette). This is an ideal place to take a break, enjoy the views, get some refreshments, and perhaps use the restrooms. You can also read the educational displays about the ecology of the area.

From Greenleaf Hut, continue your descent on Old Bridle Path. The first mile of this trail follows open ridges from which there are great views of Walker Ravine on the side of Mount Lafayette and across Franconia Notch. Some places are steep and require care with your footing. From late May through early June, the lovely pink flowers of rhodora, a type of rhododendron, bloom along this upper section of Old Bridle Path. Unlike the rhododendron popular in landscaping, the leaves of this shrub are not evergreen, so the flowers actually come out before the leaves do. Another spring wildflower common along this section of Old Bridle Path is trailing arbutus (mayflower). This plant grows low to the ground and has clusters of small, very fragrant white blossoms.

Shining club moss is a common inhabitant of the forest floor. It is related to an ancient group of plants that reached their zenith during the age of the dinosaurs.

The flowers along this trail can be attractive to butterflies. During one hike, we were accompanied by large numbers of eastern swallowtails feasting on nectar from blue-bead lilies.

At 7.4 miles (1.3 miles from Greenleaf Hut), the trail descends some stone steps, and you are back in the forest on a moderate grade for the remainder of the hike. At about 8.1 miles, you approach the edge of the ravine of Walker Brook. The trail continues to descend and reaches the junction with Falling Waters Trail along Walker Brook at 8.8 miles. Continue straight to the parking area 2.9 miles from Greenleaf Hut to complete your 9-mile loop.

DID YOU KNOW?

If you guessed that Mount Lafayette was named for the Marquis de Lafayette, the French general who played a key role in the American Revolution, you would be right.

OTHER ACTIVITIES

Echo Lake in Franconia Notch State Park is a wonderful place to cool off and relax after your hike. This swimming area is about 3 miles north of the trailhead. Admission for parking at Echo Lake is $4 for adults, $2 for children 6 to 11; free for children 5 and younger and for New Hampshire residents. Lafayette Place Campground (no dogs), across the highway from the trailhead, is a convenient place to camp.

Reservations are required to stay overnight at Greenleaf Hut; outdoors.org/destinations; 603-466-2727.

MORE INFORMATION

Most of the hike is within the White Mountain National Forest. The parking area for hikers (no fee) is in Franconia Notch State Park. AMC's Hiker Shuttle stops at the trailhead; outdoors.org/shuttle; 603-466-2727.

Look for information on trail conditions and the weather at the kiosk at the trailhead. A volunteer is often on duty.

The nearest stores and restaurants are on NH 112 in Lincoln and North Woodstock to the south and on NH 18 in Franconia to the north.

CLIMATE CHANGE IN THE WHITE MOUNTAINS

Earth has warmed 2.4 degrees Fahrenheit (1.3 degrees Celsius) since 1900, a more rapid rate of increase than has occurred in many millennia. Scientists agree that this rapid warming has been caused by the burning of fossil fuels by humans, something that has expanded greatly since the Industrial Revolution of the mid-1800s. Across the globe, there are many examples of species of plants and animals whose ranges and phenology (the timing of annual seasonal events in nature) have changed in response to the warming planet. The temperature is projected to increase by another 3 to 8 degrees Fahrenheit by 2100, so this global changing of species and ecosystems will likely become even more pronounced.

How has this global warming affected the White Mountains so far, and what will the future bring? That the climate is cooler as you ascend mountains is obvious to anyone who has hiked them. The vegetation zones and the fauna that are associated with particular zones occur in bands along an elevation gradient. (See "The Alpine Zone of the White Mountains" on page 256 for more details on zonation.)

Red spruce is a dominant tree in the mid-elevation boreal forest in the White Mountains. It actually expanded its range in the lowlands of New England during a time called the Little Ice Age between 1300 and 1800, when global temperatures were substantially cooler than they are now. Research on red spruce by forest ecologists Stephen Hamburg and Charles Cogbill indicates that its numbers have declined in the Northeast over the past 170 years, a decline they attribute to warming climate. It would be logical to assume that as the climate warms further, the boundaries of the elevation zones will move up the mountains, just as warmer climate zones are moving north in latitude. This could result in the "sweet spot" for red spruce moving up in elevation and ultimately the shrinkage of the alpine zone, as this arctic outpost would get squeezed between an expanding boreal forest from below and the top of the mountain.

AMC scientists and their partners have been closely monitoring the changes in vegetation, particularly the boundary between the northern hardwoods and the boreal forest (dominated by red spruce) and the boundary between the boreal forest and alpine zone, to see if this movement is in fact occurring in the White Mountains. Forestry models predict a dramatic decline in the boreal forest throughout New England over the next 100 years. Actual results so far are more complicated than one might expect. Some past studies have indicated that although lowland forests have changed in response to variations in climate since the end of the last Ice Age, high-elevation forests and the alpine zone in the White Mountains have been remarkably stable. This could be because trees growing on mountains not only have to contend with temperature changes but also with soils, moisture, wind, snow, and ice storms (see "Storms in the White Mountains," page 244). Perhaps mountains provide microclimate conditions that will allow the spruce and balsam fir to persist even as the region warms overall, at least over a time frame of decades rather than centuries. It is an open question.

While hiking in the mountains, you can contribute valuable data that could help AMC scientists evaluate the impacts of climate change in high-elevation communities. Start by downloading the iNaturalist app to your smartphone and joining the program Northeast Alpine Flower Watch. Then, during your next hike in the mountains, use iNaturalist to take photos of high-elevation plants in bloom or fruiting. iNaturalist will even help you identify a plant you have photographed if you are not sure what it is. The date and location of your observations are automatically recorded and made available to participants in the program. AMC scientists can quickly incorporate your results into the large database.

Community scientists have been recording the arrival times of birds in spring, when frogs start calling in spring, and the timing of tree leaf-out. Now, through the efforts of AMC's scientific staff and iNaturalist, you can be part of a study of blooming and fruiting times of high-elevation plants and help provide a window into the ecological future of the White Mountains.

3 // OFF THE KANCAMAGUS HIGHWAY

The Kancamagus Highway (NH 112) is a scenic road running east to west for about 35 miles between the towns of Conway and Lincoln. It provides access to many trails. The area is heavily wooded and particularly beautiful—and crowded—during fall color season. Here you can enjoy waterfalls, mountain ponds, several small peaks that have excellent views for relatively little effort, and many 4,000-footers that provide longer hikes. The eastern section of the highway follows Swift River, and the western section follows the East Branch of the Pemigewasset River, so travelers are never far from rushing water. The White Mountain National Forest maintains several picnic sites, campgrounds, and recreation areas along the road.

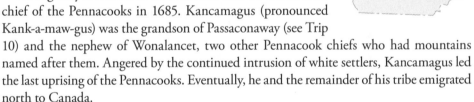

The highway is named for an American Indian who became chief of the Pennacooks in 1685. Kancamagus (pronounced Kank-a-maw-gus) was the grandson of Passaconaway (see Trip 10) and the nephew of Wonalancet, two other Pennacook chiefs who had mountains named after them. Angered by the continued intrusion of white settlers, Kancamagus led the last uprising of the Pennacooks. Eventually, he and the remainder of his tribe emigrated north to Canada.

SUPPLIES AND LOGISTICS

The Saco Ranger Station of the White Mountain National Forest is on the Kancamagus Highway at its eastern terminus near Conway off NH 16. The Lincoln Woods Ranger Station is on the highway about 4 miles east of Lincoln. Stop in for trail information and to pick up the descriptive pamphlets for the guided nature hikes along the road. The ranger stations also have water, restrooms, and displays of the local natural history. Trail information and restrooms can also be found at the Passaconaway Historical Site, about 3 miles east of Sabbaday Falls. Restrooms are located at the Rocky Gorge and Lower Falls scenic areas and at the trailheads for Sabbaday Falls, Champney Falls, Lincoln Woods, and Forest Discovery Trail.

You won't find stores or gas stations along the Kancamagus Highway, so make sure you are well supplied with lunch, snacks, and gas before heading out. If you are coming from the east, Conway and North Conway have stores, gas stations, restaurants, motels, and other amenities. Along NH 16, south of Conway, there is a small general store in Chocorua and a few others between Chocorua and the Kancamagus Highway. If you approach from the west, Lincoln has a shopping center with a supermarket on NH 112. Those coming from Crawford Notch will want to stop in Bartlett before traveling south on Bear Notch Road to the highway.

NEARBY CAMPING

The U.S. Forest Service maintains six campgrounds (more than 250 sites) and six picnic facilities spread along the Kancamagus Highway. White Ledge Campground (28 sites), also run by the Forest Service, is off NH 16 a few miles south of the highway. Campgrounds fill up on many summer weekends, so check at the information board on NH 112 just off I-93 in Lincoln (west end) or at the Saco Ranger Station (east end) for information on availability before you start your drive on the highway. You can reserve sites beforehand by calling 877-444-6777 (International 518-885-3639 or TDD 877-833-6777) or on the web at recreation.gov.

17 SABBADAY FALLS

The short hike (less than 1.0 mile) to Sabbaday Falls off the Kancamagus Highway has been a popular outing ever since tourists started to frequent the White Mountains. The wide, flat trail with minimal elevation change is an ideal walk for families with very young children.

Features 👁️🐕♿〰️🗺️🏕️💲

Location Waterville Valley, NH

Rating Easy

Distance 0.6 mile round trip

Elevation Gain 100 feet

Estimated Time 0.5–1 hour

Maps *AMC White Mountain National Forest Map & Guide*, 4th ed., J8 and Kancamagus Highway inset; AMC *White Mountain Guide*, 31st ed. Map 3 Crawford Notch–Sandwich Range, J8; USGS Topo: Mount Tripyramid

GPS Coordinates 43° 59.84′ N, 71° 23.57′ W

Contact White Mountain National Forest: fs.usda.gov/whitemountain, 603-536-6100

DIRECTIONS

The trailhead for Sabbaday Falls is on the south side of the Kancamagus Highway (NH 112), roughly 15 miles west of NH 16 near Conway and about 19 miles east of I-93 in Lincoln. For those coming through Crawford Notch or Bartlett, the trail is 3.0 miles west of the junction of Bear Notch Road with the Kancamagus Highway. The parking area, near the site of a former hotel, has space for about 30 vehicles.

TRAIL DESCRIPTION

Walk along Sabbaday Brook Trail from the parking area. The brook is bordered by hemlocks, but uphill the forest is northern hardwoods: American beech, sugar maple, and yellow birch. Hobblebush is the most abundant understory shrub.

Turn left at the sign for the falls at 0.3 mile. This is a short loop past the falls that rejoins the main trail. Very soon the loop passes a pool and an interesting small pothole. The pothole is perched above the current level of the brook, suggesting that it was created when water levels were higher than today. If it is filled with rainwater, look for mosquito larvae and other aquatic insects (see "Aquatic Insects in the White Mountains," page 7).

Ascend the stone stairs into the gorge created by the falls. It's easy to spend a long time watching the patterns of water rushing over granite ledges, through a narrow flume, and

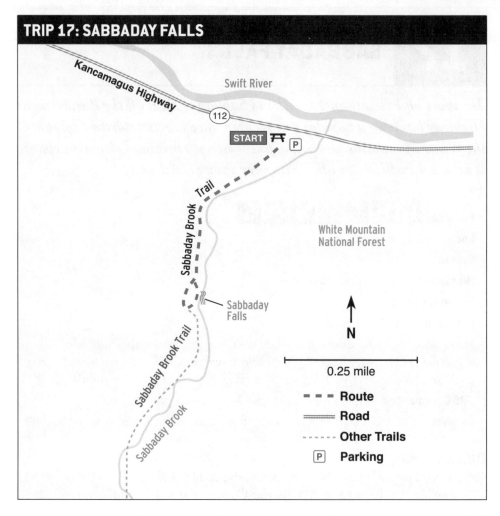

TRIP 17: SABBADAY FALLS

Kancamagus Highway

Swift River

112

START

P

Sabbaday Brook Trail

White Mountain
National Forest

Sabbaday
Falls

N

0.25 mile

- - - Route
═══ Road
----- Other Trails
P Parking

Sabbaday Brook Trail

Sabbaday Brook

into deep, clear pools. The geological features that created this environment are described on interpretive signs.

The gorge, the pools, and the small, rounded potholes in Sabbaday Brook were carved out by sand and small rocks carried by meltwater from the last continental glacier about 13,000 years ago. The floods that accompanied the melting of the glacier must have been tremendous, far surpassing anything we see today. The glacier not only unloaded vast volumes of water onto the landscape but also sand and gravel that, in combination with the fast currents, acted like sandpaper to grind down rocks, creating waterfalls, new stream channels, and pools.

The narrow and straight gorge, or flume, at Sabbaday Falls was formed by the same processes that created Flume Gorge at Franconia Notch (Trip 11). A layer of basalt that had intruded into a crack in the granite wore away during the last Ice Age, leaving steep-sided granite walls 50 feet or so above the water. You can still see remnants of the gray-black basalt within the flume where it enters the lower pool.

Sabbaday Falls, a series of lovely cascades, was formed by the erosion of a basalt dike within the granite. *Photo by Edward Quinlan.*

The loop crosses a bridge and goes past the upper pool. Both the lower and upper pools were formed by the scouring action of water melting from the glacial ice and during spring floods. Initially, the falls tumbled into the lower pool, but they eventually carved their way back through the basalt dike to form the flume. The river now makes a sharp 90-degree turn right below the upper falls, where it followed a more easily eroded geological fault in the rocks that was at a right angle to the basalt dike.

At the deep upper pool you can get a sense of the powerful erosive action of the grit-laden water by observing how the rock underwater has been carved away in a neat curve, creating an overhanging ledge. Keep in mind that the geological processes that created these marvels continue today, albeit at a slower rate than in the past because there is no glacial meltwater.

Just after the upper pool, the loop ends at the main trail. Turn right for the short walk back to the parking area.

DID YOU KNOW?

"Sabbaday" is an old New England way of referring to Sunday, or the Sabbath Day. The falls were named by settlers who were building a road through the area. It was a difficult task, and as winter approached, they left their tools near the falls on a Sunday before heading home for the winter.

OTHER ACTIVITIES

Before or after your hike, enjoy a picnic at the Sabbaday Falls Picnic Area at the trailhead. You might want to combine this walk with one of the longer treks off the Kancamagus Highway (Trips 21–24) to make a full-day outing.

Sabbaday Brook Trail continues for several miles beyond the falls, ascending Mount Tripyramid. See AMC's *White Mountain Guide* for a description of the hike beyond the falls.

MORE INFORMATION

This trail is listed by the White Mountain National Forest as being accessible, with accessible bathrooms at the trailhead. See fs.usda.gov/Internet/FSE_DOCUMENTS/stelprdb 5377702.pdf.

The trailhead and the falls are in the White Mountain National Forest. A user fee ($5 per day) is required. The parking area has picnic tables and restrooms. The nearest restaurants and other amenities are on NH 16 in Conway.

18 FOREST DISCOVERY TRAIL

Interpretive signs along Forest Discovery Trail describe different techniques employed by the White Mountain National Forest to manage the forest for multiple uses. You can walk the easy 1.4-mile loop in an hour, or linger longer if you want to sit and enjoy the view of the forest and nearby mountains from one of the many benches placed along the trail.

Features

Location Lincoln, NH

Rating Easy

Distance 1.4-mile loop

Elevation Gain 200 feet

Estimated Time 1–2 hours

Maps *AMC White Mountain National Forest Map & Guide*, 4th ed., I6; AMC *White Mountain Guide*, 31st ed. Map 2 Franconia–Pemigewasset, I6; USGS Topo: Mount Osceola

GPS Coordinates 44° 02.72′ N, 71° 33.34′ W

Contact White Mountain National Forest: fs.usda.gov/whitemountain, 603-536-6100

DIRECTIONS

Forest Discovery Trail is off the Kancamagus Highway, 7.4 miles east of Exit 32 (Lincoln, NH 112) off I-93 and 2.3 miles east of the White Mountain National Forest's visitor center at Lincoln Woods Trail. It is 0.1 mile east of Big Rock Campground on the north side of the highway.

TRAIL DESCRIPTION

Forest Discovery Trail is a wide, graded loop (wide enough for a stroller) with a spur path that is also a loop. Eleven stations with interpretive signs cover such topics as natural forest succession; selective cutting; maintaining openings for wildlife; and the values of riparian (riverside) forest, old growth, and managing for multiple-age stands. You can see examples of different management techniques along the route. As an added bonus, some of the trees are identified with labels.

The trail leaves the parking area and soon reaches the loop junction. Turn left and walk up a gradual ascent. At 0.6 mile, you reach a clearing with a view of Scar Ridge and Mount Osceola. This area was clear-cut (all trees were removed) 20 to 30 years ago. Look for pin

Forest Discovery Trail

N

500 feet

- - - **Route**
=== **Road**
P **Parking**
⅄ **Scenic Overlook**

START P

112

brook

Riparian Forest Loop

Hancock Branch

White Mountain
National Forest

cherries (brick-red bark speckled with linear pores called lenticels), trembling aspen (smooth grayish green bark), and young American beech (smooth pure gray bark) growing here. Pin cherries and aspens are characteristic early successional trees that colonize recently disturbed sites, such as clear-cuts or burned areas. Eventually these two species give way to later successional species, such as American beech. Beech does have the ability to reproduce vegetatively from root suckers when cut, which is likely why there are so many young beeches at this spot.

At 0.8 mile, you reach a junction with a spur path, a 0.3-mile loop. Turn left on the spur for an easy walk through a riparian forest. After crossing a bridge, take the left fork of the spur loop and follow it through small ups and downs. Eastern hemlock is the most common riparian tree in the White Mountains. The hobblebush leaves in the understory here are especially large.

Back at the spur loop junction, retrace your steps to the main trail. Turn left and follow it 0.2 mile back to the parking area.

DID YOU KNOW?

The effects of clear-cuts on wildlife depend on the species. Certain wildlife species, such as moose, deer, and bears, thrive in a mixture of different-aged forests and open land, rather than a continuous dense forest canopy. Some birds prefer shrublands or young forests that remain after an area of old forest is cut. On the other hand, other mammals and bird species of the White Mountains require uninterrupted forests.

OTHER ACTIVITIES

Forest Discovery Trail can be combined with one of the other walks off the Kancamagus Highway, such as Lincoln Woods Trail (Trip 20) or Greeley Ponds (Trip 21) for a longer outing.

MORE INFORMATION

Forest Discovery Trail is listed by the White Mountain National Forest as being accessible, with accessible bathrooms at the trailhead. See fs.usda.gov/Internet/FSE_DOCUMENTS/steprdb5377702.pdf.

Learn about the history of forest management at Forest Discovery Trail.

Parking at this trailhead is free, and restrooms are available. The visitor center at the Lincoln Woods Trail parking area, 2.3 miles west, has trail information and restrooms.

ROCKY GORGE AND LOVEQUIST LOOP AROUND FALLS POND

This short, easy hike takes you over a small gorge with swiftly moving water and then around a quiet, scenic pond surrounded by conifers.

Features 👤 🐕 ♿ 🏔 🍂 💧 ⛺ 💲

Location Albany, NH

Rating Easy

Distance 1-mile loop

Elevation Gain 150 feet

Estimated Time 0.5–1 hour

Maps AMC *White Mountain National Forest Map & Guide*, 4th ed., I9 and Kancamagus Highway inset; AMC *White Mountain Guide*, 31st ed. Map 3 Crawford Notch–Sandwich Range, I9; USGS Topo: Bartlett

GPS Coordinates 44° 00.16' N, 71° 16.67' W

Contact White Mountain National Forest: fs.usda.gov/whitemountain, 603-536-6100

DIRECTIONS

Rocky Gorge Scenic Area is off the Kancamagus Highway 9.5 miles west of its intersection with NH 16 just south of the village of Conway. The well-marked turnoff is about 2 miles west of the turnoff for Lower Falls, another scenic area. If you are coming from the Crawford Notch area, take US 302 to Bartlett, turn right onto Bear Notch Road, and then turn left (east) when you reach the Kancamagus Highway. The parking lot for Rocky Gorge Scenic Area is on the left in 3.5 miles. Space is available for about 40 vehicles.

TRAIL DESCRIPTION

From the parking lot, walk northeast on the paved path along the river. Plants growing here include meadowsweet, steeplebush, flat-topped aster, and dogbane (small white flowers, opposite leaves with milky sap).

Walk out on the rocks before the bridge for a view of the gorge in both directions. The walls of the canyon are mostly rectangular because granite fractures along definite joints. Notice too that the granite rocks are crisscrossed dikes of white pegmatite, an igneous "intrusion" that flowed into the cracks in the granite.

A few plants also grow here, despite the challenges of living where there is no obvious soil. Long beech ferns are especially impressive growing from cracks in the vertical walls of the gorge. On rocks that have depressions containing water and a little bit of soil, look for sweetgale (a shrub with sweet-smelling leaves covered by tiny yellow dots), red maple, wool grass (a sedge with drooping clusters of scaly brown flowers), and mosses. In cracks in the

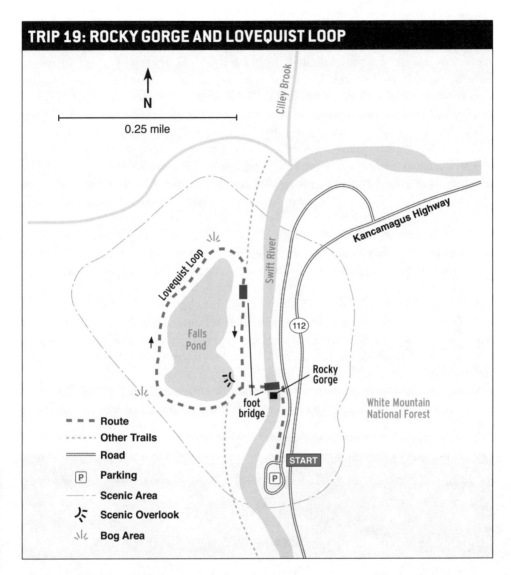

rocks, you'll find more flat-topped asters, along with goldenrods, blueberries, and small white pines. Signs warn you not to swim at Rocky Gorge, as the strong currents in the water make it dangerous.

Reach the footbridge over Rocky Gorge in 0.1 mile. Cross the river and then stroll up the graded path (with benches and interpretive signs) through hemlocks to get to the junction with Lovequist Loop Trail. Before beginning the loop, walk down to the edge of the pond. On a pleasant day, you'll likely see dragonflies patrol the shoreline, flying back and forth to hunt for insect prey, search for mates, and defend their territories. The most striking of the dragonflies are the large darners, voracious predators with very large eyes and patterns of bluish green stripes and blue speckles on their bodies. You'll also see damselflies and frogs, as well as pipeworts, aquatic plants that look like long pins.

Head clockwise around the pond on Lovequist Loop Trail, a wide yellow-blazed path that is mostly free of rocks. The ski trails that intersect this loop are marked with blue diamonds. As you go up a small hill, note the bracken ferns along the way. These are robust ferns whose main stalks divide into three equal stalks. Unlike most other ferns, bracken does not seem to mind drier habitats and thrives in sunny areas where the canopy of trees is thin. Also look for Indian cucumber-root, a lily with two tiers of whorled leaves. The top whorl supports creamy flowers in spring and black (inedible) berries later in the season.

Turn right at the next junction (straight ahead is Nanamocomuck Ski Trail) and head up a small hill onto an esker high above Falls Pond. An esker is a geological feature formed by a river flowing at the bottom of a glacier. The river here carried sand and small rocks that the walls of the glacial ice kept confined to the narrow path that the river occupied. When the glacier disappeared, it left behind the winding hill with steep sides that you now follow. As you walk along the esker, picture yourself being in a tunnel within the glacier with the river at your feet and ice walls along the banks.

The forest is dominated by tall red spruce with little understory vegetation. Red spruce is easily identified by its needles—they are individually attached on twigs and feel decidedly prickly when you grab them. White pine, another common tree along this walk, has needles in bunches of five, and the needles are flexible instead of stiff. Spruce needles are square in cross section; you can twirl them between your fingers, unlike the flat, "untwirlable" needles of hemlock and balsam fir. One way to remember all this is that to "spruce up" is to look sharp, just like spruce needles.

Red spruce is currently most abundant at middle elevations (roughly 2,000 to 3,500 feet) in the White Mountains. The elevation of Falls Pond is only 1,100 feet, so you might

Rocky Gorge, a great place to relax and be serenaded by flowing waters.

wonder why this tree is so common here. Before there was widespread logging in the White Mountains, red spruce was a dominant part of the forest, even at lower elevations. Unfortunately for the spruces, they were preferred by many loggers, and the forests that replaced them often grew up in northern hardwoods rather than spruces. Take a moment to appreciate this great stand of spruces and the fact that it is apparently sustaining itself well.

The trail goes through a small section of hardwoods roughly halfway around the loop, and then the spruces return. Woodland wildflowers include goldthread, partridgeberry, flowering wintergreen, blue-bead lily, and pink lady's slipper (blooms in mid-June).

Two short spur paths give you access to the pond shore. Take either or both for a view of the pond and for exploring its shore life. The shrubs growing in damp, boggy sections along the shore include sweetgale, Labrador tea (rusty brown fuzz on the undersides of leaves), leatherleaf (rusty scales on the undersides of leaves), sheep laurel, and huckleberry. Red maples, famous for their brilliant red fall foliage, thrive in the wet areas, and pipeworts abound in the shallow water.

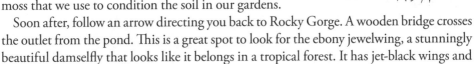

At the south end of the pond, the trail crosses a stream surrounded by a wetland with lots of sphagnum (illustrated here). Sphagnum grows well here because the topography does not allow water to drain. The moss soaks up water like a sponge and creates acidic conditions in the bog by secreting hydrogen ions. Sphagnum is the peat moss that we use to condition the soil in our gardens.

Soon after, follow an arrow directing you back to Rocky Gorge. A wooden bridge crosses the outlet from the pond. This is a great spot to look for the ebony jewelwing, a stunningly beautiful damselfly that looks like it belongs in a tropical forest. It has jet-black wings and

an iridescent blue-green abdomen, and it is common along smaller streams. It usually is very cooperative about posing for pictures (see image here). At the end of the loop, turn left to return to Rocky Gorge and the parking lot.

OTHER ACTIVITIES

Lovequist Loop Trail provides access to Lower Nanamocomuck Ski Trail. This novice-level trail runs from Covered Bridge Campground to Bear Notch Road and connects with more advanced ski trails.

You can go swimming in Swift River 2.0 miles east at the Lower Falls area. Fishing in the pond and along the river requires a New Hampshire fishing license.

MORE INFORMATION

This hike is listed by the White Mountain National Forest as being accessible up to the view of the pond. See fs.usda.gov/Internet/FSE_DOCUMENTS/stelprdb5377702.pdf.

A user fee ($5 per day) is required for parking. Restrooms are available.

20 LINCOLN WOODS TRAIL TO BLACK POND AND/OR FRANCONIA FALLS

Lincoln Woods Trail provides easy access to the Pemigewasset Wilderness, a vast protected area in the heart of the White Mountains. It follows the west bank of the East Branch of the Pemigewasset River. Explore Black Pond, a peaceful place framed by mountains, and Franconia Falls, an exciting rush of water over rocks.

Features 🚶 🐕 ♿ ♨ 💧 🔎 🎿 ✳ ⛺ 🪧 💲

Location Lincoln, NH

Rating Moderate (easy hiking but relatively long)

Distance 6.8 miles round trip to Black Pond, 6.6 miles to Franconia Falls, 8.0 miles to both

Elevation Gain Black Pond, 500 feet

Estimated Time 3–5 hours, depending on route

Maps *AMC White Mountain National Forest Map & Guide*, 4th ed., H5; AMC *White Mountain Guide*, 31st ed. Map 2 Franconia–Pemigewasset Range, I5; USGS Topo: Mount Osceola

GPS Coordinates 44° 03.84′ N, 71° 35.32′ W

Contact White Mountain National Forest: fs.usda.gov/whitemountain, 603-536-6100

DIRECTIONS

Lincoln Woods Trail is off the Kancamagus Highway (NH 112), 5.0 miles east of Exit 32 (NH 112, Lincoln) on I-93, just beyond Hancock Campground. The U.S. Forest Service operates a visitor center at the trailhead, so you can stop in to talk with the rangers about trail conditions and to pick up brochures on this and other trails.

TRAIL DESCRIPTION

Lincoln Woods Trail is great for anyone who does not like hiking uphill or on rocks but still wants to go for a long walk in the forest. It is straight and wide, and you can often see what seems like at least a half-mile ahead. The elevation gain is imperceptible. The railroad bed along which this trail was built once brought loggers and devastation to the region—sparks from a train engine ignited a disastrous forest fire (see "Logging in the Pemigewasset Wilderness," page 107). The seemingly pristine forests and mountains you now experience along this hike are a tribute to the regenerative powers of nature. The trail is heavily used, both by day-hikers and backpackers.

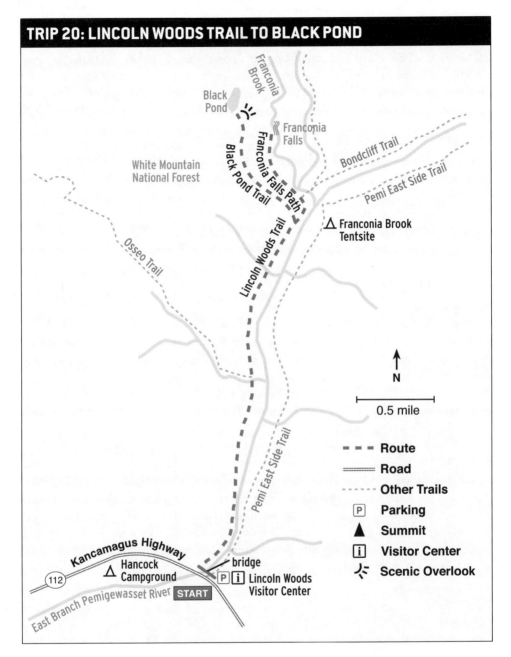

Black Pond

Franconia Brook

Franconia Falls

White Mountain National Forest

Black Pond Trail

Franconia Falls Path

Bondcliff Trail

Pemi East Side Trail

△ Franconia Brook Tentsite

Osseo Trail

Lincoln Woods Trail

↑ N

0.5 mile

- - - Route
═══ Road
- - - Other Trails
P Parking
▲ Summit
i Visitor Center
⅄ Scenic Overlook

Pemi East Side Trail

Kancamagus Highway

△ Hancock Campground

112

bridge

P i Lincoln Woods Visitor Center

East Branch Pemigewasset River START

From the visitor center at the trailhead, descend to the water, cross the East Branch of the Pemigewasset River on a suspension bridge, and then turn right. Lincoln Woods Trail never strays far from the river, which will be your constant companion on your right. For the next 2.6 miles, you'll walk on a wide, straight, flat old logging railroad bed still studded with well-preserved railroad ties made from local hemlock. Sometimes iron rails and spikes are present, and in places you can see old stone bridge abutments. (*Note*: It is illegal to disturb any artifacts.)

You'll see the influence of Tropical Storm Irene in 2011—a washout of the riverbank, uprooted trees, and a bypass—at about 0.75 mile. At 1.4 miles, Osseo Trail diverges to the left for Mount Flume and Franconia Ridge at a point where a stream also comes in from the left. Just beyond this junction, a small field on the west side of the trail provides a little diversion. This was the site of an old logging camp. It is a good place to look for butterflies fluttering around goldenrod on a sunny summer day. At 1.7 miles, Lincoln Woods Trail closely approaches the riverbank. Stop here to admire the river and the view of Bondcliff, a 4,265-foot mountain in the heart of the Pemigewasset Wilderness. Shortly after that, the trail crosses Birch Island Brook, a tributary of the East Branch. Black Pond Trail departs to the left at 2.6 miles (see below for that destination). Lincoln Woods Trail then passes through the former Franconia Brook tentsite, which has been relocated to Pemi East Side Trail on the other side of the river.

Lincoln Woods Trail officially ends at a stone wall at 2.9 miles. The spur path to Franconia Falls departs to the left. (Straight ahead, the main trail crosses Franconia Brook on a bridge and continues through the Pemigewasset Wilderness, providing access to a host of backcountry trails.)

For Black Pond

The first part of the trail to Black Pond is an old spur from the railroad that passes the ice pond used by the logging camps. This pond is rapidly becoming a marsh, and you need to be careful to follow the yellow blazes where flooding has forced the trail to be relocated. The route follows the northeast bank above Birch Island Brook for about 0.2 mile. It then crosses several small streams and passes the outlet to Black Pond, where there is a clear view of the mountain called Owl's Head. It reaches Black Pond 0.7 mile from Lincoln Woods Trail at a terrific sitting rock.

Black Pond is framed by a dense spruce-fir forest and by views of Bondcliff and West Bond. With a little bushwhacking, you can explore more of the shoreline and see other mountains, including Owl's Head. It is a wonderfully peaceful place, where dragonflies patrol over the water's surface and trout swim below. You might even see a moose. Moose tracks can be obvious in a grassy marsh northwest of the "sitting rock." Shoreline vegetation includes red and green sphagnum (a type of moss), meadowsweet, leatherleaf, and Labrador tea. These plants, along with steeplebush and sedges, also occur around the marsh at the fringes of the ice pond.

For Franconia Falls

Follow Franconia Falls Trail, which leads to the left at the stone wall marking the end of Lincoln Woods Trail. At the start of this spur path to the falls, look for a patch of helleborine orchids on the right. These 2-foot-tall plants have broad, lily-like leaves ascending their stems and a spike of small greenish orchid flowers at the top. Although native to Europe, they are established and fairly common in the United States. Just beyond the orchids, a yellow birch with a long limb over the brook provides an irresistible photo opportunity.

Continue on the short, mostly level walk to Franconia Falls (0.4 mile). You'll find plenty of flat rocks spread out over about 50 yards along the brook, so you can sit and enjoy a variety of perspectives of the falls. The smooth granite ledges and chutes of water make this a popular spot for swimming during low water and sunning in summer, so you are likely

Franconia Falls makes a fine destination from Lincoln Woods Trail.

to have lots of company. At high water, such as in spring or after a storm, it is too dangerous to venture into the water. Along the edge of the brook at the falls, look for speckled alder (rounded, toothed leaves; branchlets with speckles; cone-like fruits), withe-rod (a viburnum with opposite leaves), hobblebush, white pine, and red spruce. One of the largest trembling aspens you will ever see grows along the spur path opposite the largest cascade. Normally this tree species grows 30 to 40 feet tall and has smooth, grayish green bark. The specimen growing near Franconia Falls is more than 50 feet tall, and its bark is gray but deeply furrowed. When trees are allowed to grow old, they often take on characteristics different from those of younger ones. Hopefully, this process will be a common occurrence in the Pemigewasset Wilderness for years to come.

Retrace your steps to return to the trailhead.

OTHER ACTIVITIES

Pemi East Side Trail, also called the East Branch Truck Road, departs from the same trailhead and follows the east bank of the river. Sections of the trail were heavily undercut by Tropical Storm Irene, so use caution when near the water.

You might be tempted to make a longer loop hike starting at the Pemi East Side Trail and connecting with Lincoln Woods Trail at its terminus in the wilderness area. Keep in mind that there is no bridge for crossing back to Lincoln Woods Trail at that point. Fording the river is at best a nuisance and at worst dangerous if water levels are high.

Because it is flat and wide and has no hills, Lincoln Woods Trail is excellent for novice cross-country skiers. Intermediate skiers will prefer Pemi East Side Trail on the other side of the river because it has some hills that provide more of a challenge. Dogs are not permitted on this trail during ski season.

Fishing in the East Branch is allowed with a New Hampshire fishing license.

MORE INFORMATION

Lincoln Woods Trail is listed by the White Mountain National Forest as being accessible. There is a short nature loop near the visitor center that crosses back and forth over the East Branch. See fs.usda.gov/Internet/FSE_DOCUMENTS/stelprdb5377702.pdf.

This hike is within the White Mountain National Forest. A user fee ($5 per day) is required for parking at the trailhead. Restrooms and potable water are available at the trailhead.

LOGGING IN THE PEMIGEWASSET WILDERNESS

Logging has had a major impact on the forest around Lincoln Woods Trail and many other sections of the White Mountains. The area that is now called the Pemigewasset Wilderness was still undisturbed and known only to hunters, trappers, and a few hikers when logging baron J. E. Henry purchased the logging rights in 1892. Henry's company had been busily laying waste to the Zealand Valley since 1880 (see Trip 36), and this purchase was an expansion of his empire. He built the East Branch & Lincoln Railroad, which started in Lincoln, followed the present course of the Kancamagus Highway, and then turned north to follow the East Branch of the Pemigewasset River. One logging camp was built near the present site of the White Mountain National Forest's visitor center on the Kancamagus Highway and another near the current junction of Lincoln Woods Trail and the spur path to Black Pond.

Where Lincoln Woods Trail now ends, the railroad split into two branches, one continuing north along Franconia Brook and the other heading east along the East Branch of the Pemigewasset River. The former is now Franconia Brook Trail and the latter Bondcliff Trail. These two rail lines were further divided, like branches of a tree, as J. E. Henry's company expanded deeper into the wilderness. Along with the rail lines came more logging camps.

On weekends, the railroads carried tourists into the mountains to sightsee, visit the logging camps, and pick blueberries. Hikers, hunters, and fishers also used the railroad to gain access to the backcountry.

The logging operations laid waste to the area, and it came to be known as the "so-called Pemigewasset Wilderness." In 1917, J. E. Henry's son sold the land to Parker-Young, another logging company. Parker-Young sold the land to the U.S. government in the 1930s but retained logging rights through 1946. The railroad ceased operating in 1948. The 45,000-acre region began to recover from the logging and was officially designated a wilderness area by an act of Congress in 1984.

The large numbers of white birches, which thrive in recently logged areas, are evidence that this is second-growth forest. Along Lincoln Woods Trail, the typical vegetation is a canopy of northern hardwoods, but in many places the understory is dominated by conifers, particularly red spruces. Eventually the spruces will reclaim their dominant place here—or not, depending on the responses to global warming (see "Climate Change in the White Mountains," page 87).

21 GREELEY PONDS

In a dramatic setting near the height of Mad River Notch between Mounts Osceola and Kancamagus, the Greeley Ponds are classic mountain ponds bordered by rugged slopes that descend abruptly to the shoreline. They are reached from the Kancamagus Highway by a well-graded trail that crosses numerous split-log bridges.

Features

Location Lincoln, NH, at trailhead; Livermore, NH, at destination

Rating Moderate

Distance 3.2 miles round trip to the upper pond, or 4.6 miles to both ponds

Elevation Gain 450 feet

Estimated Time 2–4 hours

Maps *AMC White Mountain National Forest Map & Guide*, 4th ed., I6–7 and Waterville Valley inset; AMC *White Mountain Guide*, 31st ed. Map 3 Crawford Notch–Sandwich Range, I6; USGS Topo: Mount Osceola

GPS Coordinates 44° 01.89′ N, 71° 31.01′ W

Contact White Mountain National Forest: fs.usda.gov/whitemountain, 603-536-6100

DIRECTIONS

The parking area for Greeley Ponds Trail is on the south side of the Kancamagus Highway (NH 112) at a hairpin turn in the road 9.5 miles east of I-93 in Lincoln. The lot is small, and, given the popularity of this trail, it may be full when you arrive. Parking is also available about 0.25 mile to the west where the cross-country ski trail begins and at pull-offs to the east. The ski trail is marked with a sign for Greeley Ponds. If you park at the ski trail lot, walk along the road to get to the hiking trailhead. (The ski trail can be covered in knee-deep mud during hiking season.)

If you are heading west on the Kancamagus Highway, the trailhead is about 0.9 mile west of Hancock Scenic Overlook. The distance from NH 16 in Conway is about 25 miles.

TRAIL DESCRIPTION

The Greeley Ponds can easily provide a full day of swimming, picnicking, and fishing. This is a popular destination, so do not expect solitude in summer. The trail is heavily eroded due to years of tramping by hiking boots. You'll find lots of exposed tree roots, rocks, and mud, particularly in the first section. Traverse the wettest sections on split logs.

TRIP 21: GREELEY PONDS

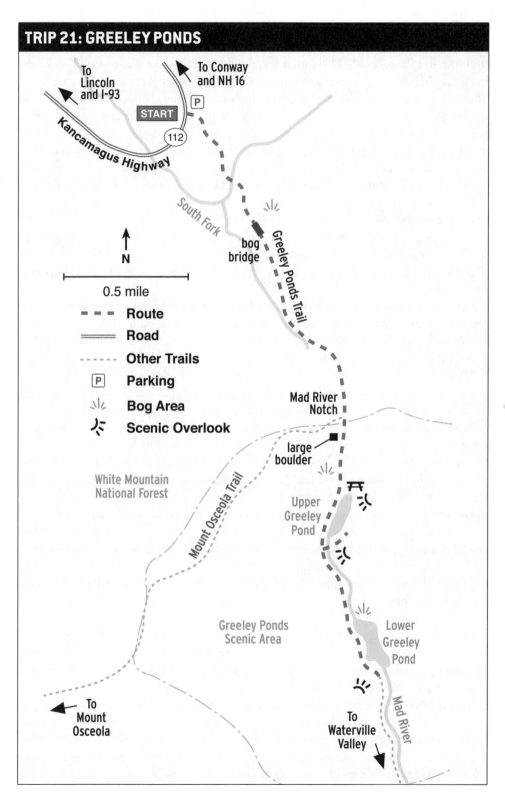

To Lincoln and I-93

To Conway and NH 16

START

Kancamagus Highway

112

P

South Fork

bog bridge

Greeley Ponds Trail

N

0.5 mile

- - - Route
═══ Road
· · · · · Other Trails
P   Parking
Bog Area
Scenic Overlook

Mad River Notch

large boulder

White Mountain National Forest

Mount Osceola Trail

Upper Greeley Pond

Greeley Ponds Scenic Area

Lower Greeley Pond

Mad River

To Mount Osceola

To Waterville Valley

Greeley Ponds Trail is marked with yellow blazes, which helps you stay on course wherever the cross-country ski trail, marked with blue diamonds, intersects it. The hiking trail starts out in a dense forest of balsam fir and soon crosses (on rocks) the South Fork of the Hancock Branch, which eventually runs into the East Branch of the Pemigewasset River. This rock crossing could be challenging in high water. After the route crosses a smaller stream, the forest changes to northern hardwoods and is carpeted with wildflowers that put on a wonderful show around Memorial Day: painted and red trillium, goldthread, blue-bead lily, hobblebush. A series of split-log bridges then traverse a damp section. On drier ground, the trail continues gradually uphill and enters the Greeley Ponds Scenic Area at the height-of-land in Mad River Notch 1.3 miles from the trailhead. Mount Osceola Trail comes in from the right and climbs very steeply to the peak of East Osceola. (This is one of the most challenging hikes in the White Mountains.)

Continuing on Greeley Ponds Trail just beyond this junction, you will pass a huge boulder. This is a glacial erratic, deposited at this site by the last glacier (see "Why Glaciers?," page 167). In late summer, look for the showy purple flowers of New England asters near the boulder.

Stay right at the next fork (with the ski trail) and cross another bog bridge. The trail then descends gently toward the ponds. At 1.6 miles, a short side path to the left descends steeply to the north end of the upper pond. A flat, sandy area here is excellent for a picnic unless the water level is too high.

After enjoying this perspective, continue south along Greeley Ponds Trail to the south side of the pond and take a short, somewhat overgrown side path leading left to open areas on the southeast shore. This provides a particularly impressive vista of craggy East Osceola looming over the western shore. Mount Kangamagus borders the eastern side. You get a sense of how the glacier that swept through this valley plucked rocks from the side of the mountain, creating the cliff you now see from what was formerly a smooth mountain slope. This also is the best place for a swim. By August, the water temperature may even be tolerable. Watch out for snags in the water. You may also discover a few leeches—or they may discover you—but they are generally small and likely won't bother you if you keep moving.

The snags that stick out of the water make terrific perches for ebony jewelwings and several different species of dragonflies. Ebony jewelwings, also called black-winged damselflies, are boldly marked with unmistakable electric green bodies and black wings, striking colors that seem more appropriate for a tropical jungle than for this relatively cold region. Damselflies hold their wings vertically when at rest, unlike dragonflies, which hold their wings horizontally.

Look for an arbor vitae, also called northern white cedar, at this side of the pond. It's a conifer tree with flat, scaly needles and is a common denizen of northern forests (as well as suburban lawns) but uncommon in the White Mountains. Other plants to look for include mountain ash, goldthread, wild sarsaparilla, and Canada mayflower.

It takes 10 to 20 minutes once you've returned to Greeley Ponds Trail to hike from the south end of the upper pond to the lower pond, depending upon how much time you spend enjoying the rich assortment of wildflowers here. You'll see lots of blue-bead lilies, goldthreads, painted trilliums, hobblebushes, lance-leaved and clasping-leaved twisted-stalks, whorled asters, and rattlesnake roots (the last having big leaves in three parts and

The East Peak of Mount Osceola dominates the view from the Greeley Ponds. *Photo by Edward Quinlan.*

drooping greenish flowers in late summer). Snowberries, with tiny rounded leaves that smell like wintergreen when crushed, are particularly abundant at the side path of the south end of the upper pond. Wet swales hold white turtleheads, sedges, sphagnum (a type of moss), and hobblebush. Look for blue-colored algae growing on damp, moldy wood, the bright blue looking more like paint than a living thing.

The lower Greeley Pond is about 100 feet lower in elevation than the upper pond. It is too shallow for swimming, but its natural features are just as interesting as those of the other pond. At its north end is a boggy area with lots of sphagnum. Leatherleaf, Labrador tea, tall meadow rue, sweetgale, and withe-rod are the most obvious shrubs, while cotton grass, white turtlehead, marsh Saint-John's-wort, bog club moss, and twig rush represent the nonwoody plants. Cotton grass (or hare's tail), actually a type of sedge, has dense balls of white, cottony hairs that surround its inconspicuous flowers.

Inspect the sphagnum mats for sundews, tiny plants whose rounded leaves are bordered with sticky hairs that trap insects. Bogs are low in nutrients, so the sundew feeds itself in a very unplantlike way: by catching and digesting insects. Be careful to avoid trampling the sphagnum when you hunt for sundews. Look for tree swallows and yellow-rumped warblers actively hunting insects over the water. Note all the standing dead trees in the water; this indicates flooding by beavers.

If you have some extra time, a small cove near a stand of paper birch at the lower pond's southwest corner offers an interesting vista.

Retrace your steps for the return trip, but be careful at the various intersections with the ski trail. Just beyond the big glacial erratic make sure you stay right at a fork and follow the yellow blazes, or you might end up on Mount Osceola Trail.

DID YOU KNOW?

The Greeley Ponds were named for Nathaniel Greeley, who ran an inn in Waterville Valley in the nineteenth century, when the valley was still a quiet, secluded place. He was one of the pioneer trail builders in this part of the White Mountains.

OTHER ACTIVITIES

A moderately difficult cross-country ski trail parallels the hiking trail and crosses it in several places. Dogs are not permitted on the ski trail.

Greeley Ponds Trail can also be approached from Waterville Valley. Sections of the trail between the ponds and Waterville Valley had to be relocated due to damage from Tropical Storm Irene, but that work has been completed. With two vehicles, you could walk or ski the entire trail from the Kancamagus Highway to Waterville Valley (or vice versa). It is 5.3 miles to hike one way. The driving distance between the two trailheads is about 36 miles.

Swimming and fishing (New Hampshire fishing license required) are possible at Greeley Ponds.

MORE INFORMATION

There is no fee for parking at the trailhead. Dogs are permitted on the hiking trail but not on the ski trail.

The nearest restaurants and other services are on NH 112 in Lincoln, about 8 miles west of the trailhead.

22 BOULDER LOOP TRAIL

Boulder Loop Trail passes jumbles of boulders during its 1,000-foot ascent to rocky ledges on a shoulder of the Moat Range. Visitors will enjoy fine views across the Swift River valley to numerous 4,000-foot peaks south of the Kancamagus Highway. An added bonus is fifteen numbered stations along the route highlighting the geology, ecology, and forest management history that can be observed in the area.

Features 👤 🐕 🔍 ✳ 💲

Location Albany, NH

Rating Moderate

Distance 3.1-mile loop

Elevation Gain 950 feet

Estimated Time 2–4 hours

Maps *AMC White Mountain National Forest Map & Guide*, 4th ed., I10 and Kancamagus Highway inset; AMC *White Mountain Guide*, 31st ed. Map 3 Crawford Notch–Sandwich Range, I10; USGS Topo: North Conway West

GPS Coordinates 44° 00.30′ N, 71° 14.35′ W

Contact White Mountain National Forest: fs.usda.gov/whitemountain, 603-536-6100

DIRECTIONS

Boulder Loop Trail is off the Kancamagus Highway (NH 112) 6.0 miles west of its intersection with NH 16, just south of Conway. Turn right at the sign to Covered Bridge Campground on Passaconaway (formerly Dugway) Road and drive through the Albany Covered Bridge (constructed in 1858, renovated in 1970). Park in the first parking lot beyond the bridge and find the trailhead at the north side of the road. In winter, the bridge is closed to vehicles, so you'll need to park before the bridge and walk a little farther on Passaconaway Road to get to the trailhead.

If you are coming from the Crawford Notch area, take US 302 to Bartlett. Turn right onto Bear Notch Road and then turn left (east) when you reach the Kancamagus Highway. Passaconaway Road is about 6 miles east.

Space is available for about twenty vehicles in the parking lot.

TRAIL DESCRIPTION

This loop is appropriate for younger hikers who have some experience on trails. Boulder Loop Trail is marked by yellow blazes. If you are interested in following the fifteen

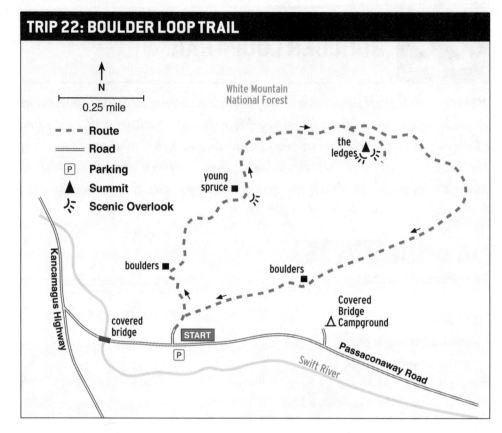

numbered interpretive signs along the route, stop at the kiosk at the trailhead to pick up a brochure or to take a picture of the posted guide on your mobile phone. The loop, which is described in the clockwise direction, begins 0.2 mile from the parking lot.

Turn left at the loop junction, and you soon pass the first large group of boulders. These and the others you see along this trail were formed by landslides. Two are especially huge: one to the left with a crack in it that forms a cave and another covered with rock-tripe (lichens), which resemble flakes of shoe leather.

The trail starts to ascend through a forest of northern hardwoods (sugar maples, American beech, and yellow birch) with an understory dominated by hobblebush and striped maple. The area was hit with a brushfire in 2016, so look for evidence of that. Common woodland wildflowers abound: Canada mayflower, blue-bead lily, painted trillium, pink lady's slipper, false Solomon's seal, spikenard, wild sarsaparilla, silverrod, various goldenrods, American shinleaf, starflower, and whorled aster. See if you can find white ash, a broad-leafed tree whose leaves are composed of many leaflets and arranged in pairs along the twigs. Its wood is used for baseball bats.

As you continue to ascend, you will notice increasing numbers of red spruce, indicating a transition to the boreal forest. After about 0.7 mile, the trail passes an opening that provides the first vista over Swift River and across to ledges that you will eventually traverse. At this and other clearings, the spruce are largely replaced by red oak and white pine, two species that survive better than spruce in drier, sunnier, warmer areas, such as these low-elevation open ledges. Some of the oaks are riddled with softball-sized holes made by pileated woodpeckers, the largest woodpeckers in the United States. Look for a distinct dark fungus called the horn of plenty, also referred to as black trumpet because it resembles that instrument. At 1.3 miles, you reach a sign reading "To the View, 0.2 mile." Follow that sign to the short spur path up the stones that take you to the ledges. The spur extends in the open for about 0.3 mile. The views are all superb, but don't get too close to the edge, particularly if it's rainy, because the dropoff is steep.

At 1,965 feet, these ledges are the highest elevation on the trail. On a clear day you can see Mounts Chocorua and Passaconaway, Middle Sister, and the three summits of Mount Tripyramid. Immediately below is the valley of Swift River. This river is a tributary of the Saco River, which flows into the Atlantic Ocean in southern Maine. The ecology at the ledges differs from the lower forest, partly because the thin soil supports only a few trees. Like the clearings described earlier, this area receives more sunlight and is drier, so red oaks and white pines are mixed in with some red spruces. Note that the white pines have relatively short needles, possibly an adaptation to reduce water loss in this wind-exposed location. Mountain ash, a small tree of the boreal forest with distinctive compound leaves, is common on the ledges. This plant is really not an ash at all, but a relative of apples and pears. In June, it displays showy white flowers; in late summer, its red berries, borne in flat-topped clusters, are relished by birds. Its twigs are a favorite food of moose. Low shrubs at the ledges include lowbush blueberry, shadbush, and dwarf juniper. Wildflowers include goldenrod and cow-wheat. Bushy, pale green reindeer lichen forms an ornate border around trees and shrubs, giving the feel of a rock garden.

A rockslide along the Boulder Loop. *Photo by Nancy Schalch.*

A large yellow spot (faded the last time we were there) marks the point where you turn around. Look for bristly sarsaparilla, a thorny relative of the more common wild sarsaparilla, near this site. After backtracking to the main trail, turn right for the 1.5-mile descent, which takes about an hour. Soon after starting down, the trail passes below the ledges you were just on, which from this perspective look as large as ten blue whales. The descent is particularly rich in hobblebush (colorful berries in late summer) and spinulose wood fern. The trail continues downhill, crosses a small stream, and enters another area of huge boulders strewn by a landslide 2.3 miles from the trailhead. An overhanging rock with a flat rock below is a good place to get out of any rain and to sit down for a bit. Beyond this, the trail flattens out and traverses a few small streams. At the loop junction, go straight to return to the parking lot.

DID YOU KNOW?
Hobblebush gets its name from the tangle of branches that would hobble a hiker or horse trying to pass through a dense stand of this shrub.

OTHER ACTIVITIES
Check out the historical interpretive signs by Albany Covered Bridge after your hike. A wheelchair-accessible fishing pier is located on the banks of the Saco River near the covered bridge.

This location is a popular place for wading in the river, enjoying a picnic on a flat rock, or relaxing with a good book while dangling your feet in the water. Access to swimming, picnic tables, and restrooms is available about 1 mile to the west along the Kancamagus Highway at the Lower Falls Recreation Area.

MORE INFORMATION
A user fee ($5 per day) is required for parking and for the day-use area around the covered bridge.

The White Mountain National Forest's Covered Bridge Campground is very close to the trailhead. Blackberry Crossing Campground is nearby as well.

23 UNH TRAIL TO HEDGEHOG MOUNTAIN

This loop hike takes you to the summit of 2,532-foot Hedgehog Mountain. Three outlooks provide impressive vistas of 4,000-foot peaks and also have some interesting wildflowers.

Features 🏃 🥾 🐕 🦌 ❀ $

Location Albany, NH

Rating Moderate, with some steep sections

Distance 4.7-mile loop

Elevation Gain 1,400 feet

Estimated Time 3.5–5 hours

Maps *AMC White Mountain National Forest Map & Guide*, 4th ed., J8 and Kancamagus Highway inset; AMC *White Mountain Guide*, 31st ed. Map 3 Crawford Notch–Sandwich Range, J8; USGS Topo: Mount Chocorua

GPS Coordinates 43° 59.66′ N, 71° 22.17′ W

Contact White Mountain National Forest: fs.usda.gov/whitemountain, 603-536-6100

DIRECTIONS

The trailhead for UNH Trail is on the south side of the Kancamagus Highway, about 15 miles west of its intersection with NH 16, just south of Conway. It is also the trailhead for Downes Brook and Mount Potash trails. Turn left (south) on a gravel road opposite Passaconaway Campground to find the trailhead. For those coming from Crawford Notch or Lincoln, the trailhead is about 1 mile west of the intersection of the Kancamagus Highway and Bear Notch Road.

TRAIL DESCRIPTION

UNH Trail should be hiked only when the weather is good, for two reasons: first, the ledges around the summit can be hazardous in wet or icy weather; second, you don't want to miss the views, which on a clear day extend as far as the Presidential Range. The elevation gain is mostly gradual, with a few short, steep sections. Some sections of the trail have been rerouted due to extensive damage caused by Tropical Storm Irene in 2011.

Leaving the parking area, the trail passes a small pond, runs with Downes Brook and Mount Potash trails for about 60 yards, and then turns left and enters the forest. Look for a dense growth of attractive dark green common haircap moss near some rocks at this point. Named for the hairs that cover the cap on its spore case, this widespread species is one of the most distinctive mosses in New England, looking like a tiny spruce tree.

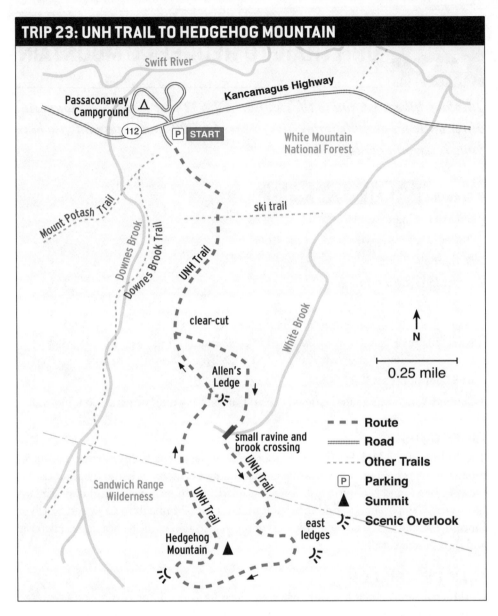

The route is well marked with yellow blazes and signs. After 0.2 mile on an old railroad bed, UNH Trail turns right (a ski trail continues straight). Continuing along an old logging road in a spruce forest, UNH Trail crosses another ski trail at 0.3 mile, heads moderately uphill, and reaches the loop junction at 0.8 mile. A large (approximately 7 acres) clear-cut to the east offers inviting views of mountains to the north and some good blackberry picking in season. The rationale for the clear-cut was to remove timber heavily damaged by Tropical Storm Irene and to attract birds and mammals that thrive in early successional habitats, such as shrublands. Blackberries, raspberries, and pin cherries are characteristic of clear-cut areas.

The East Ledges of Hedgehog Mountain afford a fine view of Mount Passaconaway and other nearby peaks.

I recommend hiking the loop clockwise by taking the left fork. This is a more gradual ascent to the East Ledges, which have the most extensive views. However, if you are short on time and still want to get to an outlook, take the right fork of the loop and go as far as Allen's Ledge, 0.3 mile from the junction. You can then backtrack to the trailhead.

For the complete loop, turn left and follow this new section of the trail. After about 0.3 mile of almost-level hiking through northern hardwoods (mostly yellow birch and American beech), the trail turns right onto the original section of the trail and starts ascending. Look for understory plants such as hobblebush, heart-leafed aster, Indian cucumber-root, King Solomon's seal, ghost pipe, and shiny club moss.

At 1.6 miles, the trail descends into a small ravine, crosses a brook (could be dry in late summer), and then begins to ascend more steeply. Note the rather abrupt change from the northern hardwood forest to a red spruce forest. The trail comes out on the East Ledges (2.1 miles). The East Ledges look down over a secluded valley bounded by Mounts Passaconaway and Paugus. Mount Chocorua is in the background, and the Moat Range is prominent to the northeast. Former clear-cuts, now covered with new growth, testify to logging in years past.

Signs at the East Ledges indicate that you are in a habitat for a rare plant and should be extra careful not to trample on the vegetation. The plant is White Mountain whitlow-wort, also called silverling, a relative of chickweed. Whitlowwort occurs in mountains from Georgia through West Virginia; however, a distinct variety is found only on rocky ledges in the mountains of New Hampshire and western Maine and, oddly, on one small island in the Merrimack River at Newburyport, Massachusetts. The low, compact plant grows where small bits of soil and moisture accumulate in cracks in the rocks. Its inconspicuous flowers are mostly hidden within silvery scales. In fact, the scientific name for this plant, *Paronychia argyrocoma*, refers to the resemblance of these silvery scales to hangnails. Other plants on the East Ledges include red spruce, black huckleberry, heartleaved birch, and goldenrod (the latter also finding a roothold in cracks in the rocks). Large dragonflies (several species of darners) patrol the open ledges for their insect prey on sunny days.

The trail follows open ledges for about 0.2 mile, providing great vistas. (Some of the ledges are narrow and could be slick in wet or icy weather.) It reenters the spruce-fir forest, descends for a short distance, and then ascends steeply to reach the summit of Hedgehog Mountain, about 0.9 mile from the East Ledges and 2.9 miles from the trailhead. Red spruce, sheep laurel, mountain holly, shadbush, withe-rod, and bracken fern grow here.

The best scenery is not at the summit itself, which is partly wooded, but at a ledge a little beyond. Turn left at an unmarked path just after reaching the high point to gain access to this ledge. To the north is a partial view of the glacially carved, U-shaped valley of Carrigain Notch, bordered by Mounts Carrigain, Anderson, and Nancy. The long ridge of Mount Hancock lies to the west of Mount Carrigain. Mount Passaconaway is particularly massive to the south. Potash Mountain, with several clear-cuts, is nearby to the west and roughly the same height as Hedgehog. Behind Potash are the three summits of Mount Tripyramid. The Swift River valley separates this assemblage of peaks from Mounts Carrigain and Hancock.

Two mountains south of the Kancamagus Highway are named after hedgehogs, presumably because the spires of spruce and fir that cover their rounded summits reminded people of that animal's quills. (Hedgehogs occur naturally in Eurasia and Africa, but bear a superficial resemblance to the North American porcupine.) While resting up before your descent, you can make a game of this by looking at the map and finding other mountains that share the same name. Owl's Head, Sugarloaf, Black Mountain, and Blueberry Mountain come immediately to mind.

UNH Trail descends steeply from the summit of Hedgehog Mountain. At 0.9 mile from the summit, watch for the turnoff to Allen's Ledge on the right, marked by a sign. Take this spur back uphill and follow the base of a massive rock to the left and up to the vista. From here Mount Washington is visible on a clear day, and Green's Cliff is prominent in front of Mount Carrigain. You also can see Bear Mountain, Mount Chocorua, and Mount Paugus.

Returning to UNH Trail, hike 1.1 miles to the parking area. The trail descends steeply, crosses a ravine, and continues to descend along a hogback ridge covered with hemlocks. It levels out on an old railroad grade, and the cross-country ski trail enters from the left. At the T junction, turn left for the short walk back to the trailhead.

DID YOU KNOW?

UNH Trail is named for a camp that was used by the University of New Hampshire's Forestry Program from the 1940s through the 1960s. The buildings, which were near the beginning of the loop, are no longer there.

OTHER ACTIVITIES

You can combine this hike with a visit to the Russell-Colbath House, a restored 1830s house that is now a museum highlighting how some of the first settlers in the area lived. It is about 1 mile east of the trailhead along the Kancamagus Highway. Swimming is allowed at the Lower Falls Recreation Area, about 9 miles east of the trailhead on the Kancamagus Highway.

MORE INFORMATION

Parking at the trailhead is free.

BIRD GUILDS IN THE WHITE MOUNTAINS

You may notice on your hikes through the White Mountains that you often go a long time without seeing or hearing any birds, and then all of a sudden you are surrounded by trees full of chickadees, nuthatches, golden-crowned kinglets, warblers, woodpeckers, and other species. They busily make their way across your trail and eventually move on. Then the quiet returns. These associations of birds of different species are called guilds, a term that comes from the old Dutch craftsmen's associations. Guilds are multispecies "teams" of birds that forage together, moving from tree to tree in the forest.

With binoculars you can observe that the different species have different ways of feeding. Chickadees and kinglets are acrobats, often hanging upside down as they inspect small twigs for insects or other edible morsels. Nuthatches probe the bark of the main trunk and large branches, while woodpeckers poke holes in branches and trunks to catch the insects deeper within the tree. Warblers and flycatchers sally for flying insects; juncos and thrushes forage among the leaf litter on the ground. By using different feeding methods, these birds reduce competition, although there is undoubtedly some overlap in their menus. The advantage to feeding in guilds is that large numbers of birds are more efficient at finding and then flushing insects than separate individuals would be. Also, there are more eyes to watch out for predators, like Cooper's hawks, and more voices to sound a warning or to drive away a predator.

If a bird guild should appear while you are walking through the boreal (spruce and fir) forest, keep your eyes open for boreal chickadees. These birds resemble black-capped chickadees, those familiar epicures of sunflower seeds at backyard bird feeders. Boreal chickadees are slightly smaller, have a brown rather than black bib, and are more at home in high-elevation forests such as those of the White Mountains. At the elevation of Hedgehog Mountain, 2,500 feet, you might very well see both species of chickadees, perhaps even together. You might also see red-breasted nuthatches along with the more familiar white-breasted nuthatches. The red-breasted nuthatch is more partial to coniferous forests, whereas its white-breasted cousin prefers broad-leafed trees. If you hear a nasal toot that sounds like a toy trumpet, that is a red-breasted nuthatch.

Boreal chickadees are similar to the familiar black-capped chickadees but you need to hike up to the spruce fir forests to see them.

24 CHAMPNEY FALLS AND MOUNT CHOCORUA

This hike takes you past waterfalls that are particularly impressive after a rainstorm and then leads to one of the White Mountains' most iconic peaks. Mount Chocorua's sharply pointed summit stands alone in the southeastern section of the White Mountains and is visible for many miles and from many other summits. For hikers with young children or limited time, the falls are a fine destination in themselves. Other hikers will want to climb the well-graded Champney Falls Trail to Mount Chocorua. A little scrambling is required near the top.

Features 🏃🚴🚶🐕 〰 🔍 ❋ $

Location Albany, NH

Rating Moderate to Champney Falls; Strenuous to Mount Chocorua summit

Distance 3.5 miles round trip to Champney Falls; 7.6 miles round trip to Mount Chocorua summit

Elevation Gain 600 feet to Champney Falls; 2,250 feet to Mount Chocorua summit

Estimated Time 2.5 hours round trip to Champney Falls; 6 hours round trip to Mount Chocorua summit

Maps *AMC White Mountain National Forest Map & Guide*, 4th ed., J9; AMC *White Mountain Guide*, 31st ed. Map 3 Crawford Notch–Sandwich Range, J9; USGS Topo: Mount Chocorua

GPS Coordinates 43° 59.40′ N, 71° 17.97′ W

Contact White Mountain National Forest: fs.usda.gov/whitemountain, 603-536-6100

DIRECTIONS

The parking area for Champney Falls Trail is on the south side of the Kancamagus Highway (NH 112), about 11 miles west of its junction with NH 16, south of Conway, and about 1.5 miles east of Bear Notch Road. Space is available for about 30 vehicles. This is a very popular trail, so vehicles may spill over onto the side of the road on summer weekends.

TRAIL DESCRIPTION

Mount Chocorua is "only" 3,500 feet in elevation, so you might be lulled into thinking that this is a relatively short and easy hike, at least compared with a 4,000-footer. Don't be fooled. The mountain is a long way from any roads, so it will take some time before you

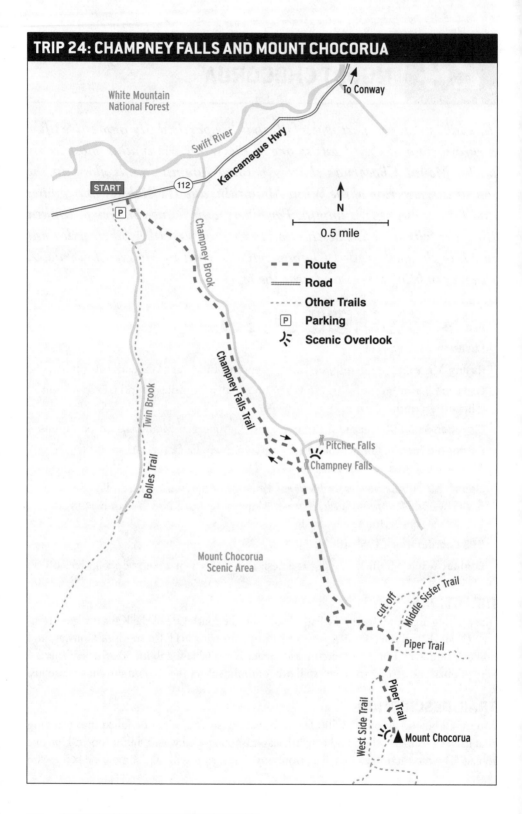

TRIP 24: CHAMPNEY FALLS AND MOUNT CHOCORUA

To Conway

White Mountain
National Forest

Swift River

Kancamagus Hwy

START

112

P

N

0.5 mile

- - - Route
——— Road
- - - - Other Trails
P Parking
Scenic Overlook

Champney Brook

Champney Falls Trail

Twin Brook

Bolles Trail

Pitcher Falls

Champney Falls

Mount Chocorua
Scenic Area

cut off

Middle Sister Trail

Piper Trail

Piper Trail

West Side Trail

Mount Chocorua

even start gaining serious elevation. Also, the bare summit cone is steep and may be uncomfortable for people who do not do well with heights or scrambling on rocks.

Snowshoeing is fine to Champney Falls. Beyond that it should be left to the experts.

Champney Falls Trail is marked with yellow blazes. It is heavily used and has a large number of exposed tree roots. It begins by crossing Twin Brook on a series of flat stones. Shortly after the crossing, Bolles Trail goes off to the right.

The forest at this point is composed of northern hardwoods with lots of hemlock, particularly along water. Hobblebush and striped maple form the understory, and Indian cucumber-root, partridgeberry, flowering wintergreen, and shining club moss are common on the forest floor. Also look for painted trillium, American shinleaf, lance-leaved twisted-stalk, jack-in-the-pulpit, wild sarsaparilla, and pink lady's slipper.

After 0.5 mile, the trail reaches Champney Brook. A newly relocated section of the trail crosses to the east bank and then back to the west bank (0.7 mile), where it remains for the rest of the hike to the falls.

At 1.4 miles, turn left at the junction with the loop trail to Champney and Pitcher falls. The loop is 0.4 mile long. Descend to cross a small brook and then pass a small waterfall—more like a shoot—that empties into a pool surrounded by moss-covered rocks. The pool is deep enough for wading, but the shade here keeps the temperature of the water at a penguin-friendly level for most of the year. Look for water striders in the pool.

Continuing on the loop, you reach Champney Falls, where water plunges (or, in dry weather, trickles) over a series of stair-like ledges. Lots of sturdy boulders provide an opportunity to sit and enjoy the scenery.

After admiring Champney Falls, walk about 100 yards east between two narrow ledges to the base of Pitcher Falls. This thin but beautiful cascade of water looks like it somehow got lost and changed its course. It is in a narrow gorge bounded by two almost-vertical side walls. Instead of being at the far end of the gorge as you might expect, Pitcher Falls plunges over one of the sides. The stream above Pitcher Falls likely did change course at some point, as erosion by water created the gorge initially.

Return to the loop trail and ascend steeply up the west side of Champney Falls to the top of the falls. You will likely find other people there, perched on rocks and gazing at the brook and the nearby mountains. Even though the view is somewhat obstructed, it is nonetheless refreshing after the long walk through a dense forest. Bunchberry, wintergreen, and hobblebush border the brook right at the ledge above the falls. Be cautious when scrambling around the rocks, because the shade tends to keep them damp and slippery. Many serious accidents have occurred here.

Follow the loop trail away from the falls to its upper junction with Champney Falls Trail (1.8 miles). If the falls is your final destination, here is where you turn right and begin the gradual 1.7-mile descent back to the parking area.

If you are heading to Mount Chocorua, turn left.* The trail continues at a moderate grade until 2.4 miles, where it turns right, passes a somewhat overgrown viewpoint, and

---

* I gratefully acknowledge input from Steven D. Smith (co-editor of AMC's *White Mountain Guide* and author of *Mount Chocorua: A Guide and History* (Bondcliff Books, 2006) and from Alison Buchsbaum and Sam Van Etten for the description of the trail and natural history from here to the summit.

Pitcher Falls tumbles over the side of a ravine along Champney Falls Trail. *Photo by Brandon O'Brien.*

starts ascending more steeply on a series of switchbacks. The forest becomes increasingly boreal (dominated by red spruce and balsam fir). You will also pass through stands of white (paper) birch, which provide evidence of past forest fires on the mountain slopes. Blueberries carpet sunny openings. At 3.0 miles, at an elevation of about 3,000 feet, Champney Falls Cutoff (also called Middle Sister Cutoff) heads left at a vista. Shortly after, Champney Falls Trail passes a junction with Middle Sister Trail and ends 80 yards beyond that at Piper Trail (3.2 miles).

Turn right to take Piper Trail the remaining 0.6 mile to the summit, following yellow blazes. The vegetation becomes scrubbier, with more vistas. At 3.4 miles, West Side Trail departs to the right. Shortly after, Piper Trail breaks out into the open and is exposed for the remainder of the hike. It ascends over ledges, sometimes steeply, and requires occasional scrambling and care to locate the next cairn or yellow blaze. The trail traverses a rocky crag with a view of the summit just ahead, descends slightly through some scrub vegetation, swings to the west side of the summit cone, and then joins Liberty Trail just below the summit. The final ascent to the summit is through a small gully.

Because it stands apart from other mountains, Mount Chocorua provides expansive and spectacular views of much of the White Mountains from its treeless summit. To the north on a clear day, you can see Mount Washington and the Presidential Range. To the northwest, Mount Carrigain is prominent. Immediately to the west, Mount Passaconaway looms large, and Mount Whiteface is nearby. The sharp, craggy eastern face of the summit of Mount Chocorua, which gives the mountain its distinctive appearance, is thought to have resulted from erosion by a mountain glacier during the Ice Age.

It is interesting to contemplate why the summit of Mount Chocorua is devoid of trees. At 3,500 feet, Chocorua's summit is not bare from a true treeline related to temperature and wind, which would generally need to be about 1,000 feet higher or more in the White Mountains, but as a result of fires that burned off both trees and the underlying soil. According to Steven D. Smith's *Mount Chocorua: A Guide and History* (Bondcliff Books, 2006), major fires occurred on the mountain in the nineteenth century and early parts of the twentieth century. The absence of tree cover has allowed some plants to flourish on the summit cone that are normally associated with the alpine zone of the White Mountains. These include highland rush, alpine (bog) bilberry, mountain cranberry, and three-toothed cinquefoil. Small shrubs in this barren area are Labrador tea (fuzzy white flower clusters and leathery leaves with rolled edges and rust-colored hairs underneath), sheep laurel (pink flowers that resemble those of mountain laurel), purple crowberry (needlelike leaves), and rhodora (a type of rhododendron).

Return to the trailhead via the same trails.

DID YOU KNOW?

According to John T. B. Mudge (*The White Mountains: Names, Places, and Legends*, The Durand Press, 1995), Chocorua was a Pequawket chief who was either killed or leaped from a cliff to his death in the early 1700s while being pursued by white settlers on the mountain that bears his name. Before dying, Chocorua cursed the settlers, and they blamed the curse for their various tribulations in subsequent years.

Champney Falls was named for Benjamin Champney, a leading artist in the White Mountains during the nineteenth century. He is considered by many art historians to be the founder of the White Mountain school of artists. They painted in the North Conway area in the second half of that century.

OTHER ACTIVITIES

Visit the Russell-Colbath Historic Site about 2 miles west of the Champney Falls trailhead along the Kancamagus Highway. The Russell-Colbath House was built in 1832 and is the only structure still standing in the town of Passaconaway from that period. It is now a museum highlighting life in the mountains at that time.

MORE INFORMATION

Restrooms are available at the trailhead. A user fee ($5 per day) is required for parking.

The Conway–North Conway region is in the southeastern part of the White Mountains and includes 3,000-foot mountains, bold cliffs popular with rock climbers, the Saco River, and a large number of ponds and streams. The distinctive summit cone of Mount Chocorua is visible for many miles in all directions. One of our suggested hikes (Trip 29) takes you to ledges with wonderful views of this peak, and another (Trip 24 in the previous section) takes you to the summit itself. The Green Hills, east of North Conway, provide superb views of the Presidential and Carter ranges for relatively little effort. You'll also find secluded areas that offer excellent wildlife observation opportunities.

SUPPLIES AND LOGISTICS

NH 16 is the main road through this region. The village of Chocorua and other nearby villages, such as Tamworth, are small and picturesque New England communities. They are wonderful places to stay, but do not expect to find a wide variety of supplies for your hike. In contrast, Conway and North Conway are among the busiest communities in the White Mountains, with extensive facilities for tourists and lots of traffic. Many outdoor opportunities and amenities for visitors are available, particularly along NH 16.

The Saco Ranger Station is on NH 112 (Kancamagus Highway) just off NH 16 south of Conway. Stop in to get the latest information on trail conditions, buy trail and field guides, and peruse displays on White Mountain ecology and geology.

NEARBY CAMPING

White Ledge Campground, a national forest campground with 28 sites, is off NH 16 about 4 miles south of the village of Conway. White Ledge Loop Trail (Trip 28) leaves from this campground. National forest campgrounds along the eastern part of the Kancamagus Highway (NH 112), such as Blackberry Crossing and Covered Bridge, are convenient to the region. Campsites can be reserved beforehand on the web at recreation.gov or by calling 877-444-6777 (International 518-885-3639 or TDD 877-833-6777).

Facing page: You can spend hours mesmerized by the flowing waters of Lucy Brook at Diana's Baths.

25 DIANA'S BATHS

Diana's Baths is a popular family destination suitable for the youngest hikers. A short, level, accessible walk along Moat Mountain Trail brings you to a former mill site where you can wade in one of the many pools among numerous cascades or explore the ruins of the old mill.

Features

Location Conway, NH

Rating Easy

Distance 1.2 mile round trip

Elevation Gain Minimal

Estimated Time 0.5–1 hour

Maps *AMC White Mountain National Forest Map & Guide*, 4th ed., I10; AMC *White Mountain Guide*, 31st ed. Map 3 Crawford Notch–Sandwich Range, I10; USGS Topo: North Conway West

GPS coordinates 44° 4.47′ N, 71° 9.84′ W

Contact White Mountain National Forest: fs.usda.gov/whitemountain, 603-536-6100

DIRECTIONS

From North Conway, turn west onto River Road, which leaves NH 16/US 302 at the traffic light just north of Eastern Slope Inn Resort. Cross the Saco River and bear right at the next two intersections. You are now headed north on West Side Road. A large, well-marked parking area is on the left about 0.9 mile past the road to Cathedral Ledge (2.4 miles from NH 16 in North Conway).

If you are traveling from the south, pick up West Side Road in the village of Conway by turning left from NH 16 onto Passaconaway Road at the intersection where NH 153 goes off to the right. Continue north (straight) as the road becomes West Side Road. About 5 miles past Conway, bear left where River Road comes in from the right. Look for the parking area 0.9 mile past the road to Cathedral Ledge.

From Crawford Notch, travel east on US 302 and turn right onto West Side Road about 4 miles east of the turnoff to Bear Notch Road in Bartlett. The large parking area is about 0.3 mile south of the Conway–Bartlett town line.

TRAIL DESCRIPTION

Diana's Baths is a pleasant spot to relax and hang out on a summer afternoon. You won't be alone, but the shady forest and the cool water make this an ideal family outing. The baths are reached by the first section of Moat Mountain Trail.

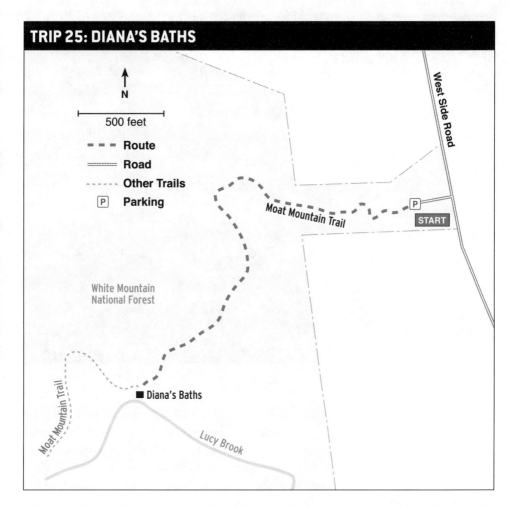

Leaving the parking area, the well-graded, crushed-stone path meanders through the forest, crossing bridges over several rivulets. Benches along the way invite you to stop and admire the impressively tall white and red pines, white ashes, and hemlocks, which make you feel like you are walking in a cathedral. You will also find big-toothed aspens and yellow birches. On the forest floor, look for flowering wintergreen (its crushed leaves smell like minty chewing gum) and partridgeberry at any season because they keep their leaves all year. You will see asters and silverrods in middle to late summer. Silverrod is actually a type of goldenrod but with silvery rather than yellow flowers.

In ten to fifteen minutes, you reach Lucy Brook. The mill site is immediately to the left, and Diana's Baths is just a little ahead, also to the left. Moat Mountain Trail continues beyond the baths, but it becomes very steep and is not recommended for families with young children, nor is it accessible.

Numerous cascades will immediately catch your attention when you arrive at Diana's Baths. Even with the crowds, you will be able to find a flat rock and an interesting stretch of water that you can claim for several hours. Kids will enjoy meandering up the granite terraces to see the wonderful assortment of waterfalls, pools, and rocks upstream. Many

The shallow pools of Diana's Baths make it a popular family destination.

small, round potholes have been carved into the flat granite. These were formed by the scouring action of small stones and sand carried by spring floodwaters. Potholes that are perched high above the current level of the water were likely formed during the melting of the last glacier, when water levels were much higher than they are now.

Some gears, pipes, and stone walls from the old mill are still present. This was a gristmill that used the waterpower of Lucy Brook to grind flour.

Diana's Baths is shaded by hemlocks, which keeps it pleasantly cool. Three interesting shrubs that grow around the water's edge are rhodora, speckled alder, and mountain holly. If you get here around Memorial Day weekend, rhodoras will be in bloom, with showy pinkish flowers that are pretty enough to make you forget the blackflies, at least for a moment. Speckled alders have distinctly spotted twigs and branches, as if they have chicken pox. Mountain hollies are particularly abundant. The leaves of these shrubs have smooth edges (that is, no serrations) and are tipped with a tiny spine (look carefully, using a hand lens if you have one). They look pale green and delicate in contrast to the dark gray branches. Look for small red berries on these shrubs in midsummer. Long beech ferns, with their lower pinnae pointing backward, grow in cracks in the rocky streambed.

Retrace your steps to return to the parking lot.

DID YOU KNOW?

Diana's Baths is named for the Roman goddess of the hunt, who was often pictured in woodland settings, surrounded by animals. Enjoy your swim and watch out for the water sprites that (according to legend) inhabit the area.

OTHER ACTIVITIES

Echo Lake State Park (not to be confused with Echo Lake in Franconia Notch), just south of the trailhead, has a swimming beach (day-use fee of $4 for adults, $2 for children 6 to 11; free for children younger than 6 and for New Hampshire residents older than 65). Cathedral Ledge and White Horse Ledge, two popular rock-climbing cliffs, are also in this state park. You need rock-climbing equipment to ascend the cliffs, but there are paths through the forest to the same fine overlooks. You can also drive to the top of Cathedral Ledge.

The North Conway/Intervale/Jackson area has a host of tourist activities, including theme parks popular with children, a scenic railroad, golf, and fishing.

MORE INFORMATION

The first section of Moat Mountain Trail as far as Diana's Baths is listed by the White Mountain National Forest as being accessible. See fs.usda.gov/Internet/FSE_DOCUMENTS/stelprdb5377702.pdf.

A user fee ($5 per day) is required for parking at the trailhead. Toilets are available at the parking area, and there are picnic benches at the baths.

26 BLACK CAP

Black Cap, a popular family hike in the Green Hills, east of North Conway, has one of the finest vistas in the White Mountains for relatively little effort. On a clear day, you can see Mounts Washington, Kearsarge North, Chocorua, and other peaks of the White Mountains from Black Cap's 2,370-foot summit.

Features

Location Conway, NH

Rating Moderate

Distance 2.2 miles round trip

Elevation Gain 650 feet

Estimated Time 1–2 hours

Maps *AMC White Mountain National Forest Map & Guide*, 4th ed., I12; AMC *White Mountain Guide*, 31st ed. Map 5, Carter Range–Evans Notch I12; USGS Topo: North Conway East

GPS Coordinates 44° 4.10′ N, 71° 4.31′ W

Contact The Nature Conservancy: nature.org/en-us/get-involved/how-to-help/places-we-protect/green-hills-preserve

DIRECTIONS

The trailhead for Black Cap Trail is on Hurricane Mountain Road, an experience in itself. This mountain road runs between Intervale and South Chatham. From the junction of NH 16/US 302 and River Road in North Conway, head north on NH 16/US 302 for 1.75 miles. Turn right onto Hurricane Mountain Road just after passing a large visitor information center and scenic overlook. From Crawford Notch or Jackson, head south through Glen on NH 16/US 302 and turn left onto Hurricane Mountain Road just south of Intervale. Wind your way up Hurricane Mountain Road for 3.8 miles (paved, but very steep in spots) to the height-of-land. The parking area has space for about fifteen vehicles.

You can also reach the trailhead from the Evans Notch area by turning right (west) off ME 113 at North Fryeburg onto South Chatham Road. After about 1.5 miles, the road turns sharply left and heads south as Robbins Ridge Road. Take this road for 2.0 miles and then follow the right fork onto Green Hill Road toward Fryeburg. Continue for 2.0 more miles and then turn right onto Hurricane Mountain Road. After 2.5 steep and winding miles on Hurricane Mountain Road, the parking area for the trail will be on your left at the height-of-land.

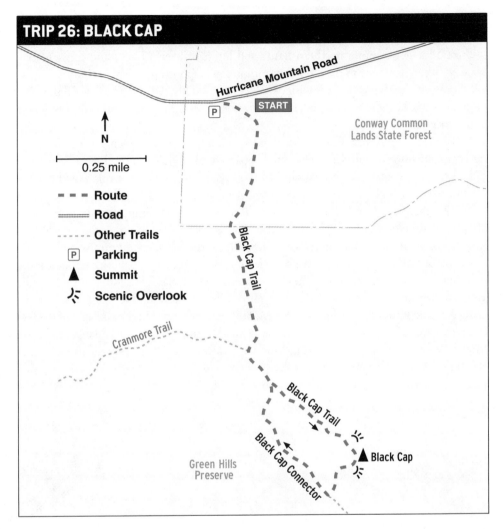

Hurricane Mountain Road is not maintained for winter travel and is closed from November through mid-May, when snowmobilers use the road.

TRAIL DESCRIPTION

Black Cap Trail, marked with red blazes and trail signs, is easy to follow and well maintained. Stone barriers channel water off during wet weather. Nonetheless, this popular trail is heavily eroded in places. Please keep to the trail itself to preserve the woodland vegetation. At a reasonable hiking pace, it should take 30 to 45 minutes to get to the summit. Bring along at least a windbreaker for this exposed summit.

Black Cap Trail begins in a spruce forest. Note the absence of any understory vegetation. This is often the case under pure stands of conifer trees, such as spruce, balsam fir, and hemlock. The dense canopy limits light to the forest floor much more completely than in a forest of broad-leafed trees. Even when the broad-leafed trees form a thick canopy, understory herbs and shrubs still get some sunlight in early spring before the trees leaf out. Not so beneath evergreens. Also, the needles that do fall off the evergreens decompose to make an acidic soil rich in tannins, which is not conducive to understory plant growth.

The trail ascends into a northern hardwood forest of beech, birch, and sugar maple. Here, light can penetrate to the ground in spring, thus supporting a lush understory. Spring wildflowers include lance-leaved twisted-stalk, blue-bead lily, painted and red trillium, and bunchberry. In late summer and fall, look for whorled aster. Striped maple is the dominant understory shrub.

At 0.5 mile, The Nature Conservancy has set up a kiosk from which you can obtain a trail map and information. Cranmore Trail departs to the right from Black Cap Trail at 0.7 mile. Look for numerous white birches blown over by the wind near this junction. The shallow roots make these trees particularly vulnerable to such mishaps.

At 0.8 mile, Black Cap Connector angles off to the right, heading around the west side of Black Cap. Continue straight, following the red blazes. Soon after, you reach open ledges with scenic vistas. The trail ends at 1.1 miles at the Black Cap summit.

Walk around the summit to get the best views in each direction. Looking north, the most prominent nearby peak is Mount Kearsarge North, which has a fire tower at its summit. You can also see the Carter and Baldface ranges. To the west are the steep rock faces of Cathedral and Humphrey ledges and the Moat Range, the latter containing one of the few large remnants of truly volcanic rock in the White Mountains. On a clear day, you can see Mount Washington to the northwest, Mounts Chocorua and Passaconaway to the southwest, and Mount Carrigain and Carrigain Notch to the west. Conway Lake is due south.

The view north from Black Cap includes Mount Kearsarge North nearby and the Presidential Range in the distance.

If you are interested in photographing the mountainous scenery to the west and northwest, plan to hike Black Cap in the morning, because the mountain views are most striking in the northwest-to-southwest direction. That way you will not be aiming your camera into the sun. A side benefit of an early morning ascent is that you are more likely to have the scenery to yourself.

At the summit, look for heart-leaved birch, balsam fir, mountain ash, white pine, red pine, red spruce, currant (a small shrub with maplelike leaves), and some blueberries and huckleberries. In spring, the white flowers of shadbush are in bloom.

A short spur path, beginning where the word *Maine* is blazed onto a rock, leads to an east outlook over the lakes and hills of western Maine. Unfortunately this outlook is now fairly overgrown. On the way to the outlook, you pass a wet swale with mosses and a distinct sedge called wool grass. It has clusters of scaly brown flowers drooping from the apex of its 3-foot-high stems.

For the descent, you can make a loop off the summit by hiking Black Cap Spur Trail to the right, which descends on granite and wooden steps about 0.2 mile to meet Black Cap Connector. Turn right on the Connector (yellow blazes, watch out for mountain bikes) and follow it for 0.4 mile back to its junction with Black Cap Trail. Turn left for the 0.8-mile descent.

MORE INFORMATION

Black Cap (2,370 feet) is part of The Nature Conservancy's Green Hills Preserve near North Conway. The preserve protects some rare plants, including the White Mountain whitlowwort, or silverling (see Trip 23). The first part of the trail is in Conway State Forest. Parking is free.

WEATHER IN THE WHITE MOUNTAINS

The summits of Black Cap and other peaks are great places to contemplate White Mountain weather—assuming, of course, that the weather is decent enough to allow you to contemplate anything. The White Mountains are famous or notorious for their weather, depending on your point of view. Often the mountains are shrouded in clouds even when it is sunny in the rest of the region.

Three of the biggest weather-related factors in the mountains are wind, temperature, and clouds. Wind is evident in the number of uprooted trees you encounter, especially near the summits. Wind speeds increase with elevation and topple trees near mountain summits because their roots have difficulty penetrating far into the ground in the thin soil. Evidence of the wind's effect is also apparent in the low, scrubby vegetation that grows on mountain summits, even those that are not technically above treeline. "Flag trees," also called "banner trees," have living branches only on one side—the lee side, which faces away from the prevailing wind direction. Winter ice that coats the windward side of the trees combines with wind to kill buds on that side.

Temperatures get cooler as elevation increases. This is caused by the decline in the density of air with increasing altitude. Air that is less dense cannot hold heat as well as air closer to sea level. A typical decline is about 3 degrees Fahrenheit for every 1,000 feet of elevation gain (or 0.5 degrees Celsius for every 100 meters, if you like to think metrically). That sounds great for hikers on a hot summer day, but plants and animals that live at higher elevations must adapt to cooler temperatures and shorter growing seasons.

The cloudiness so prevalent in the White Mountains is related to the cooler temperatures at higher elevations. It is not unusual to see clouds hovering over some of the taller peaks, even when the rest of the region is sunny. On Mount Washington, cloud cover is present an average of 75 percent of the year. As air from the west (where most of our weather systems originate) flows up and over these mountains, it cools and forms clouds. This is because cooler air holds less moisture than warm air, just as the warm, moist air inside your lungs condenses on a cold morning when you breathe out. The Presidential Range has particularly severe weather because it is the highest and therefore coolest range in the region and is positioned at the convergence of several storm tracks. Mount Washington still holds the record for the strongest wind ever recorded by humans, 231 MPH in April 1934.

Cloud shapes, wind speed and direction, and changes in temperature can help people predict the weather. As an example, big, puffy cumulus clouds generally indicate fair weather, but wispy cirrus clouds at very high altitudes indicate that although the current weather is fair, precipitation may be on its way. A change in wind direction from west to east is often associated with precipitation moving in.

27 MOUNTAIN POND LOOP TRAIL

A clear, quiet body of water surrounded by a spruce forest, Mountain Pond features beaver lodges, loons, views of mountains, and piles of boulders along the shore. A shelter makes a fine spot for a picnic or even a swim.

Features 🏊 🚶 🐕 💧 ⛺ 🦎

Location Chatham, NH

Rating Moderate

Distance 2.7-mile loop

Elevation Gain Minimal

Estimated Time 1.5–3 hours

Maps *AMC White Mountain National Forest Map & Guide*, 4th ed., G12; AMC *White Mountain Guide*, 31st ed. Map 5 Carter Range–Evans Notch, G11–12; USGS Topo: Chatham

GPS Coordinates 44° 10.21′ N, 71° 5.28′ W

Contact White Mountain National Forest: fs.usda.gov/whitemountain, 603-536-6100

DIRECTIONS

From North Conway, head north on NH 16/US 302 and turn right onto Town Hall Road in Intervale (left if you are coming south from Jackson or Glen). After 0.1 mile, the road crosses NH 16A. At 2.4 miles, the pavement ends and the road forks. Take the left fork (Slippery Brook Road) and follow it for 4.0 miles. The road passes the trailhead for East Branch Trail and then passes Forest Road 38, which goes off to the left. The parking lot and trailhead for Mountain Pond Loop Trail are on the right, about 0.6 mile past the junction with Forest Road 38. Only about the first mile of the unpaved part of the road is plowed in winter, so access to the trailhead is impossible then.

TRAIL DESCRIPTION

Mountain Pond is in a beautiful, secluded part of the White Mountain National Forest. The pond is south of the Baldface Range in the valley of Slippery Brook, east of Jackson and Wildcat mountains. Families with young children (2 to 5) can take a very pleasant short walk even if they decide not to hike the entire loop around the pond. However, this is not a great trip in damp weather. The numerous rocks on the trail become slippery, and much of the ground gets muddy. Even in dry weather, expect tired feet at the end.

From the parking lot, follow the short, wide path marked with yellow blazes to Mountain Pond Loop Trail. This first section of the trail before you reach the loop is a good place

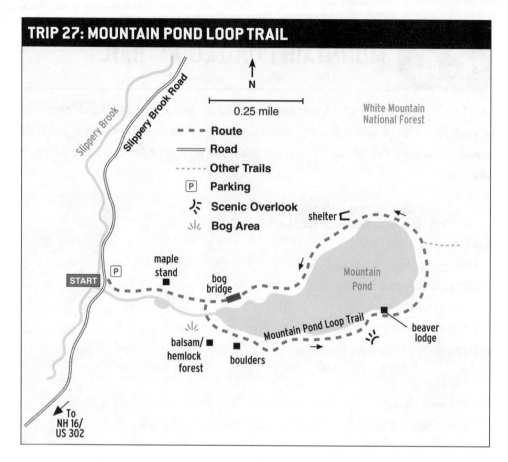

Slippery Brook

Slippery Brook Road

N

0.25 mile

- - - Route
=== Road
----- Other Trails
P Parking
Scenic Overlook
Bog Area

White Mountain
National Forest

shelter

Mountain
Pond

maple
stand

START P

bog
bridge

Mountain Pond Loop Trail

beaver
lodge

balsam/
hemlock
forest

boulders

To
NH 16/
US 302

to distinguish four species of maples. Three of them—striped, red, and mountain—grow around a small, wet area; the fourth—sugar—is a little farther down the path.

The path leads to the loop junction at 0.3 mile. Although you can walk in either direction around the pond, I suggest turning right at the fork. You will come quickly to the outlet of the pond, which could be muddy during spring thaw or after heavy rains. If passage over this damp area looks doubtful, turn around and take the shorter walk described below. Otherwise, if you start out clockwise, walk almost the entire loop, and then get to the outlet, you may discover that it is too muddy to cross comfortably.

Wetland plants occur around the pond outlet: white turtlehead, meadowsweet (a spirea with fuzzy white flower clusters), sweetgale (a shrub with leaves that smell like bayberry), alder, northern arrowwood, and bur-reed (strap-like leaves right in the stream and pond, with seed heads that resemble burrs).

Beyond the outlet, the trail is easy to follow and never far from the shore. The forest is dominated by balsam fir and hemlock, with large boulders strewn about. Trees grow directly on top of the boulders, their roots snaking down to reach the soil below. Dense growth of mosses, mountain wood sorrel, and other plants of the forest floor add to the magical atmosphere.

Autumn at Mountain Pond.

Two small, common plants—flowering wintergreen and creeping snowberry—are distinctive for their sweet, minty odors. Both have thick, glossy leaves that remain on the plant throughout winter. Wintergreen (also called teaberry or checkerberry) is the larger of the two, growing as high as 2 inches off the ground. You can crush a leaf to evoke its aroma, reminiscent of mint chewing gum. (As a conservation lesson, pick a leaf only where the plant is abundant.) The trailing vines of creeping snowberry really hug the ground. The tiny, rounded leaves are stalkless and seem to come off the stems in pairs. The "wintergreen" smell produced by creeping snowberry is not as strong as that produced by wintergreen itself.

Mountain Pond is one of the best spots in the White Mountains to find waterbirds. Look for loons, ducks, and other waterbirds whenever you pass an opening along the pond shore. If you see loons, take the time to watch these large, handsome birds as they swim silently across the pond, dive for fish, or sound their eerie cries. In summer, the loon is unmistakable with its dark head, checkered necklace, speckled back, and daggerlike bill.

On one visit, twelve common mergansers were fishing along the shores of the pond. These diving birds are ducks, but instead of having flat bills they have thin ones with serrated edges, which enables them to more easily grasp their slippery prey. Mergansers use teamwork to capture fish. They swim in a line to drive the fish toward shore and then dive in tandem to prevent fish from escaping.

Other nesters include black ducks, hooded mergansers, ruffed grouse, hairy woodpeckers, rusty blackbirds, purple finches, and numerous warblers. Beavers are still altering the local hydrology. They have dammed a tributary stream entering the pond, creating tiers of small ponds at different elevations.

When you reach the far end of the pond, stop to appreciate the great view of South Baldface to the north. The bald summit of this 3,500-foot mountain is the result of past wildfires. Back across the pond to the west are the twin peaks of the Doubleheads. A beaver lodge is near the shore here.

You'll reach the shelter at 1.7 miles. This is the best place in the pond for a swim, but you'll need water shoes to protect your feet from the rocky bottom. Another potential picnic spot is just before the loop junction (2.3 miles). Look for a short spur path heading to the left that takes you to the shore not far from the outlet. The view across the water is particularly pretty here, and it is a good place to see dragonflies, frogs, and some of the same wetland plants described earlier.

The end of the loop is at 2.4 miles. Turn right for the 0.3 mile walk back to the parking area.

For a shorter walk suitable for all ages, go left at the loop junction, walk to the shelter (maybe for a picnic), and then retrace your steps to the parking lot (a total distance of about 2 miles). Several short spurs lead down to the shore of the pond along this section of the trail.

OTHER ACTIVITIES

Fishing is permitted at Mountain Pond with the proper New Hampshire license. You can swim in Mountain Pond, but water shoes are recommended.

MORE INFORMATION

Parking is free. A latrine is located at the pond shelter.

28 WHITE LEDGE LOOP

White Ledge is an extensive open ledge with views of Moat Mountain to the north and Mount Chocorua to the south. White Ledge Loop Trail, an excellent family outing, winds through a hemlock forest, past stone walls, and then up to viewpoints.

Features 🏊 🚶 🐕 💧 🍄 🔬 ⛷ ⛺ ⛩ 💲

Location Albany, NH

Rating Moderate

Distance 4.4 miles round trip

Elevation Gain 1,450 feet

Estimated Time 3–5 hours

Maps *AMC White Mountain National Forest Map & Guide*, 4th ed., J10; AMC *White Mountain Guide*, 31st ed. Map 3 Crawford Notch–Sandwich Range, J10; USGS Topo: Silver Lake

GPS Coordinates 43° 57.26' N, 71° 12.85' W

Contact White Mountain National Forest: fs.usda.gov/whitemountain, 603-536-6100

DIRECTIONS

The trailhead is at White Mountain National Forest's White Ledge Campground off the west side of NH 16, about 6 miles north of the village of Chocorua and 5 miles south of Conway. Park in the day-use picnic area and follow the campground road straight ahead to the trailhead. Space is available for about five vehicles. If the campground is closed, park outside the gate beside NH 16, being careful not to block the gate.

TRAIL DESCRIPTION

White Ledge Loop Trail, marked with yellow blazes, departs right from the campground road between sites 6 and 7 and starts out through a dense hemlock forest with some red oaks and American beeches. Common understory herbs to look for include Canada mayflower, flowering wintergreen, ghost pipe, partridgeberry, and wild sarsaparilla. Striped maple and hobblebush form the shrub layer for the lower parts of this hike.

At 0.3 mile, the trail reaches the loop junction. At this point, it is 2.4 miles to the summit going counterclockwise and 1.4 going clockwise. I describe the loop in the counterclockwise direction.

Shortly after the loop junction, White Ledge Loop Trail crosses a stream, which can be difficult when water levels are high. At 0.6 mile, the trail passes a junction with a spur that is an alternative path from NH 16. The loop trail continues uphill and passes old stone

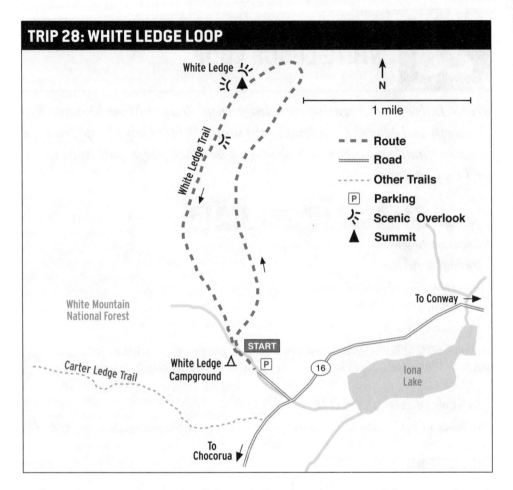

White Ledge

N

1 mile

- - - Route
═══ Road
····· Other Trails
P Parking
Scenic Overlook
▲ Summit

White Ledge Trail

White Mountain
National Forest

Carter Ledge Trail

START

White Ledge △
Campground

P

16

To Conway →

Iona
Lake

To
Chocorua ▶

walls. At about 1.2 miles it levels off, descends for a short distance, and then passes through an area of young trees, characterized by their thin trunks. The stone walls and the spindly trees give a hint that this land was formerly used for grazing cattle or sheep. New England's landscape is peppered with old stone walls—remnants of its more agrarian past—but there are not many such walls in the White Mountains. The countryside was too rugged to support more than marginal farms.

This forest is a living laboratory of ecological succession, the process by which cleared land eventually turns back in to forest. In earlier editions of this book, the area was an overgrown pasture. It is now returning to forest. Young American beech and striped maple, which were just starting to grow about twenty years ago, now form the bulk of the vegetation here. In another 20 to 30 years, the area will likely be indistinguishable from the rest of the forest.

After leaving the young forest at about 1.9 miles, the trail turns left and elevates with moderate steepness. Throughout this hike you will undoubtedly be accompanied by the staccato chips of chipmunks alerting their compatriots to your presence, but listen also for the beautiful, flutelike songs of wood thrushes (lower part of trail) or hermit thrushes (higher up).

You reach the first set of ledges at about 2.3 miles. The best view of Moat Mountain and other peaks to the north is from the ledges below the actual summit, so take time to enjoy the vistas on your way up. Moat Mountain is the only peak in the White Mountains that contains volcanic rock extruded from the earth in the Jurassic period about 175 million years ago, during the time of the dinosaurs. Other mountains you can see are Mount Kearsarge North, Bear Mountain, and Mount Cranmore (on the other side of North Conway). On a clear day the summit of Mount Washington is visible just to the east of Moat Mountain.

Follow the blazes and cairns carefully as you continue your ascent up the ledges. The ledges have interesting seeps that support the growth of sphagnum and other mosses. Common shrubs around the ledges include black huckleberry, lowbush blueberry, and sheep laurel. Three-toothed cinquefoil grows wherever its roots can find enough soil among the rocks. Anywhere along these ledges you may encounter the large dragonfly known as the variable darner.

At 2.7 miles, you reach the summit (2,010 feet). Trees to note include red and white pine, red spruce, and red oak. Follow an arrow to the best view of lakes and hills to the east. As Steven D. Smith points out in *Mount Chocorua: A Guide and History* (Bondcliff Books, 2006), White Ledge is an example of a "sheepback mountain"—gradual on its northwest side and steep on its southeast side. This shows the direction of the advance of the last glacier from northwest to southeast. Its grinding action smoothed the northwest-facing section while plucking rocks from the southeast face as it continued its advance, causing the steep dropoff there.

The trail then begins to descend and at 2.9 miles passes an excellent vista of Mount Chocorua to the south. Continuing your descent, you pass huge rocks covered with rock tripe, a lichen that looks like a piece of shoe leather. At 3.2 miles an unmarked side path leads left to a gorgeous view of lakes and hills to the southeast. As you descend, look for

The author looking northwest from the summit of White Ledge. *Photo by Alison Buchsbaum.*

some enormous white pines just after the trail makes a sharp left turn (about 3.3 miles). White pines such as these were characteristic of New England forests at the time European settlers first arrived. These huge, straight trees were sought after for use in the masts of ships, so most were cut. A double-trunked white birch in the middle of the trail has large holes and chips made by pileated woodpeckers, the largest woodpeckers in the United States. You will also pass through a boulder field that resulted from a landslide.

At about 3.6 miles, the trail bottoms out and crosses a stream, which it follows to the loop junction (4.1 miles). In our midsummer hike, we noted bunches of coral and trumpet (chanterelle) fungi in this section of the trail. Turn right at the junction to return to the trailhead (4.4 miles).

White Ledge Loop Trail provides an example of the ecological differences between north- and south-facing slopes. On your ascent, the boreal (spruce-fir) forest becomes dominant right after you pass the old pasture, at an elevation of about 1,400 feet. This part of the loop faces north, so it is often in shadow and therefore relatively cool. On the southern side of the mountain, the boreal forest gives way to northern hardwoods, the more "southern forest," almost as soon as you begin your descent, at about 1,900 feet. The southern side of the mountain is bathed in direct sunlight for a much longer part of the day, so the southern forest type occurs higher up on south-facing slopes.

DID YOU KNOW?

The French term for a sheepback mountain, such as White Ledge, is *roche moutonnée*, which means "fleecy rock." The explorer who coined that term in 1786 was struck by these mountains' resemblance to wigs worn by French aristocrats, which were smoothed with mutton fat.

OTHER ACTIVITIES

Camping at the national forest's White Ledge Campground is very convenient for hiking this trail and for other hikes around North Conway and the eastern part of the Kancamagus Highway.

Carter Ledge Trail also departs from White Ledge Campground. This trail takes you to another ledge with a vista of Mount Chocorua. At Carter Ledge you will find abundant blueberries and jack pines, a relatively rare tree in the White Mountains. Carter Ledge Trail is rougher than White Ledge Loop Trail.

A few miles east of the trailhead, off NH 113 near Madison, New Hampshire, you can see Madison Boulder, the largest glacial erratic in New England. It is the centerpiece of a small state natural area.

Swimming at Chocorua Lake, just north of the village of Chocorua, is an excellent way to cool off after your hike.

MORE INFORMATION

A user fee ($5 per day) is required for parking in the day-use area at White Ledge Campground. Conway to the north and Chocorua to the south are the nearest villages for supplies and restaurants. These can be found along NH 16.

The Crawford Notch/Zealand Notch region lies in the heart of the White Mountains. The region includes two stunning U-shaped valleys and several mountains that rise above 4,000 feet. Just getting here is a real treat because the drive up US 302 through Crawford Notch and to the Zealand Notch area is one of the most spectacular in the eastern United States. An early explorer, quoted by the Reverend Benjamin G. Willey in his 1856 book *Incidents in White Mountain History*, described it eloquently: "The sublime and awful grandeur of the Notch baffles all description. Geometry may settle the heights of the mountains, and numerical figures may record the measure; but no words can tell the emotions of the soul as it looks upward and views the almost perpendicular precipices which line the narrow space between them. . . ." The view of the narrow gap at the very height of Crawford Notch and surrounding moun-

tains has been immortalized in a 1839 painting by Thomas Cole entitled, *A View of the Mountain Pass Called the Notch of the White Mountains*. It hangs in the National Gallery of Art in Washington, D.C.

The hiking trails selected here take you to hidden ponds, breathtaking overlooks, good wildlife viewing, and some of the highest waterfalls in the White Mountains. In the secluded Zealand Valley, many trails follow old logging railroads with gentle grades perfect for young hikers.

SUPPLIES AND LOGISTICS

A variety of places provide information for hikers as well as an introduction to the rich history of the "Great Notch of the White Mountains." The Macomber Family Information Center is in Crawford Depot, a historical train station built in 1891, where guests disembarked for the Crawford House, a hotel. The depot is just north of the point where US 302 passes through the Gateway of the Notch, the highest and narrowest part of Crawford Notch. The information center is run by AMC and offers restrooms, water, and displays on the natural and human history of Crawford Notch; a store here sells some hiking supplies and souvenirs. The depot also serves as a stop on the Conway Scenic Railroad and is a short walk from AMC's Highland Center, which provides meals and overnight accommodations (see below).

Crawford Notch State Park's visitor center is at the Willey House Historic Site off US 302 and has a snack bar, restrooms, and information.

The original hotel at the Gateway of the Notch was built by Abel and Ethan Allen Crawford (father and son) in 1828 and run by Thomas Crawford, brother of Ethan Allen. It evolved into the Crawford House, which hosted presidents and other dignitaries until it closed in 1975. The building burned down a few years later.

This is an area of small communities and small stores. For picnic and other supplies, stop at one of the stores you pass on US 302 in Glen, Bartlett, Notchland (in the heart of Crawford Notch), Bretton Woods, or Twin Mountain. The communities of Twin Mountain, Bretton Woods, and Bartlett have restaurants, gas stations, motels, hotels, and tourist cabins.

THE HIGHLAND CENTER AT CRAWFORD NOTCH

This AMC destination is centrally located for day hikes around Crawford Notch and Zealand Notch. It is a few hundred yards from Crawford Depot and is near the site of the former Crawford House, a hotel. The facility, a "green building," provides lodging, meals, daily programs on the White Mountains, guided hikes, and a wealth of information for hikers. A store within the center sells hiking supplies, guidebooks, field guides, and souvenirs. The Highland Center has private rooms with baths for families as well as bunk rooms with shared baths. Breakfast and dinner are included with room packages; trail lunches are available for purchase. Shapleigh Bunkhouse, a historical building that was once the home of the artist Frank H. Shapleigh, has two bunk rooms and offers breakfast, showers, and limited facilities for heating your own food. Reservations are needed for both facilities; outdoors.org/destinations/massachusetts-and-new-hampshire/highland-center; 603-466-2727.

PUBLIC TRANSPORTATION

Concord Coach Lines runs from Boston's Logan Airport and South Station to Lincoln. From there you can reserve a shuttle (the Shuttle Connection) to Crawford Notch. Check the web for details (concordcoachlines.com/stop/lincoln-nh). The AMC Hiker Shuttle (outdoors.org/shuttle) stops at the trailhead for Zealand Trail (Trip 36), the Highland Center (Trips 29, 30, 32, 35, and 39) and the trailhead for Ethan Pond Trail (Trip 37).

NEARBY CAMPING

Dry River Campground (36 sites) on US 302 is part of Crawford Notch State Park. It is about 1.5 miles south of the turnoff to Ripley Falls and 5.5 miles south of Crawford Depot. The White Mountain National Forest's Zealand and Sugarloaf campgrounds are in the Zealand area. Zealand Campground (11 sites) is right at the junction of US 302 and Zealand Road. The two Sugarloaf campgrounds (total of 62 sites) are 0.5 mile south on Zealand Road and are accessible to people with disabilities. Private campgrounds are located near the communities of Bartlett and Twin Mountain.

29 SACO LAKE AND ELEPHANT HEAD

Wooden bridges, the chance to toss stones into the water, huge boulders, and views of the Willey Range make the walk around Saco Lake an interesting one for small children. Continue up a short climb to Elephant Head for impressive views of the famed Gateway of Crawford Notch.

Features 🚶 🐕 💧 🔍 ❄ ⛺ 🚌

Location Carroll, NH

Rating Easy

Distance 1.2 miles round trip

Elevation Gain 150 feet

Estimated Time 1 hour

Maps *AMC White Mountain National Forest Map & Guide*, 4th ed., G8 and Crawford Notch inset; AMC *White Mountain Guide*, 31st ed. Map 3 Crawford Notch–Sandwich Range, G8; USGS Topo: Crawford Notch

GPS Coordinates 44° 13.11′ N, 71° 24.63′ W

Contact Saco Lake: White Mountain National Forest, fs.usda.gov/whitemountain, 603-536-6100; Elephant Head: Crawford Notch State Park, nhstateparks.org/visit/state-parks/crawford-notch-state-park.aspx, 603-374-2272

DIRECTIONS

From the Jackson–North Conway area, follow US 302 west at Glen where it splits from NH 16. US 302 passes through Bartlett and then heads north through Crawford Notch. At the top of the notch, roughly 20 miles from the junction of NH 16 and US 302, the road goes through the narrow pass between two cliffs. If you are not staying at the Highland Center at Crawford Notch (parking for registered guests only), you can park along US 302 near the north end of Saco Lake and near the entranceway to the Highland Center. Walk about 100 yards north on the east side of US 302 until you see the sign at the trailhead: "Saco Lake, Idlewild."

From Franconia Notch and the community of Twin Mountain, the trailhead is about 8 miles south of the junction of US 3 and US 302 in Twin Mountain. Park near the north end of the lake as described above.

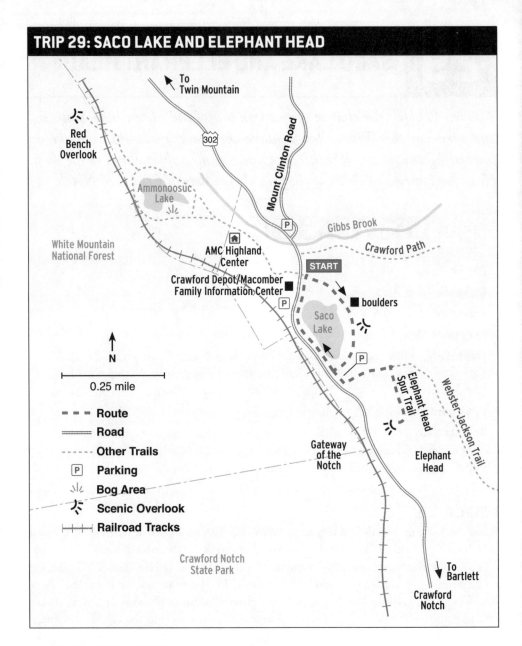

To
Twin Mountain

Red
Bench
Overlook

302

Mount Clinton Road

Ammonoosuc
Lake

Gibbs Brook

White Mountain
National Forest

Crawford Path

AMC Highland
Center

START

Crawford Depot/Macomber
Family Information Center

boulders

Saco
Lake

N

0.25 mile

- - - Route
=== Road
----- Other Trails
P Parking
Bog Area
Scenic Overlook
+++ Railroad Tracks

Elephant Head
Spur Trail

Webster-Jackson Trail

Gateway
of the
Notch

Elephant
Head

Crawford Notch
State Park

To
Bartlett

Crawford
Notch

TRAIL DESCRIPTION

This brief hike combines two short walks at the fabled Gateway of the Notch. First you walk along Saco Lake and then you walk up to Elephant Head. If you don't have much time, you can just hike around Saco Lake, but the view from Elephant Head is worth seeing.

From the trailhead, Saco Lake Trail enters the woods and soon crosses a small stream on rocks. In about 0.1 mile you reach the shoreline of Saco Lake, which is technically a pond (see "Did You Know?" on page 152 for the difference between a pond and a lake). This

Saco Lake and Mount Webster after a storm.

small, unassuming pond off US 302 is the headwater for the Saco River, which flows through Crawford Notch on the start of its more than 100-mile journey to the Atlantic Ocean. You are rarely out of sight of the road for the remainder of your walk around the pond, but you also have constant views of the Willey Range.

A plank bridge aids in traversing a rocky area with 20-foot boulders. This is a good place to study granite. Inspect its coarse texture for crystals of translucent quartz (grayish) mixed in with feldspar (white) and some biotite mica flakes (black or brownish). Also note that the vertical side of one of the huge boulders you pass is very flat, indicating that it broke off from an even huger boulder along a flat joint. Another rock overhangs the trail. The gigantic stone formations are covered with rock tripe, a lichen that looks like a piece of shoe leather. Trees somehow manage to cling precariously to life on and around the boulders with very little soil. Look for a beaver lodge tucked in among the rocks, as if designed by a landscape architect.

In summer, you are likely to see tree swallows and barn swallows soaring over the pond. These small birds are very fast and adept flyers, making aerial pirouettes as they catch insects that fly above or emerge from the water. (See Trip 41 for more on these swallows.) Dragonflies also patrol the water for unwary prey. Note the dead trees riddled with woodpecker holes that provide homes for many birds and mammals.

You'll find a variety of wetland plants along the pond shore: speckled alders, meadowsweet, water lobelia, pipeworts, flat-topped asters, goldenrods, and white turtleheads. On the upland side of the trail, look for Canada mayflowers, mountain wood sorrel, bunchberries, and occasional pink lady's slippers. Trees include yellow and white birches and balsam firs. Across the pond, there is a clear view of Mount Tom (4,051 feet), named for Thomas Crawford, who owned the Crawford House, a hotel across the road from this location.

The Idlewild Overlook is reached by a short, steep spur path. The view there has become partly obscured by plant growth. After the overlook, the trail continues along the shore, eventually crossing the inlet to the pond on another plank bridge. This is a good place to search for brook trout. Saco Lake Trail ends at the road near the Webster-Jackson Trail parking area.

To walk to Elephant Head, a round trip of 0.6 mile, continue toward the notch (south) along the highway to the trailhead for Webster-Jackson Trail. Elephant Head is a large, rocky outcropping that overlooks Crawford Notch at the east side of a narrow gap called the Gateway to the Notch. It actually resembles the head of an elephant when viewed from the highway near Crawford Depot. White lines and spots of white quartz within the gray-ish granite give the ledge its distinctive appearance. You will get a close-up view of the quartz and granite when you reach Elephant Head.

Just past a small field, note the black-eyed Susans, oxeye daisies, and goldenrods. These sun-loving plants would be completely out of place in the forest.

Take Webster-Jackson Trail for less than 0.1 mile to where Elephant Head Spur diverges right, marked with a sign that reads "Great View of the Notch." Follow the spur, pass through a damp area on wooden planks (look for northern white violets and sedges), and then ascend to an attractive knoll of spruce and fir. In the shade of the forest you will find mountain wood sorrel, spinulose wood fern, goldthread, blue-bead lily (*Clintonia*), painted trillium, shiny club moss, and dutchman's breeches.

The trail descends slightly to the open ledge at the top of Elephant Head, 0.2 mile from Webster-Jackson Trail. Views of mountains, water, and possibly some wildlife can be seen both up and down the notch. Beavers, ducks, and other animals reside in the wetland across US 302.

This is a good place to observe the drainage patterns of the land. Water in Saco Lake flows south through Crawford Notch and forms the Saco River, ultimately reaching the coast of Maine. Just north of the pond at the Highland Center, water flows north to the Ammonoosuc River and eventually to Long Island Sound via the Connecticut River. After admiring the view and the rocky ledge, retrace your steps down to the Webster-Jackson trailhead. Complete the loop and return to the trailhead by walking north along US 302.

DID YOU KNOW?

Saco Lake is called a lake, but it is really a pond. A lake is deeper than a pond and has distinctive layers of water that differ in temperature. In summer, the surface water of a lake is warm, but the deeper water remains cold, something you can experience yourself by diving deep into a lake. The two layers often have a very narrow transition between them. Ponds are shallower than lakes, and their water temperature varies little with depth.

OTHER ACTIVITIES

Saco Lake is stocked with trout. You may fish with the proper New Hampshire license. The Conway Scenic Railway drops off passengers at Crawford Depot right near the trailhead, allowing people to arrive in the style of travelers from 100 years ago.

You can combine this short hike with other hikes in Crawford Notch State Park for a longer outing. The trailheads for the Mount Willard (Trip 32) and Mount Avalon (Trip 35) trails are near the Macomber Family Information Center. For a more challenging experience, Webster-Jackson Trail in combination with Webster Cliff Trail provides access to a loop hike over Mounts Jackson and Webster. Consult AMC's *White Mountain Guide* for details.

MORE INFORMATION

Parking near Crawford Depot is free. If you park at the nearby national forest lot on Mount Clinton Road, a user fee ($5 per day) applies. The Highland Center at Crawford Notch is a stop on the AMC Hiker Shuttle; outdoors.org/shuttle. Restrooms and trail information are available at the Macomber Family Information Center at Crawford Depot; outdoors.org/destinations/massachusetts-and-new-hampshire/highland-center. This is also the place to fill up water bottles and to purchase last-minute snacks.

30 AMMONOOSUC LAKE VIA AROUND THE LAKE TRAIL

Ammonoosuc Lake feels remote from civilization, yet it is only a 15-minute walk from the Highland Center and US 302. It is a great place to look for moose, beavers, and wood ducks or to take a quick dip in the cool water. A side path leads to the Red Bench and a view of Mount Washington.

Features 🚶 🐕 💧 🔍 🎇 🏊 ⛺ 🚌

Location Carroll, NH

Rating Easy

Distance 1.2-mile or 1.8-mile loop

Elevation Gain 250 feet

Estimated Time 1–2 hours

Maps *AMC White Mountain National Forest Map & Guide*, 4th ed., G7 and Crawford Notch inset; AMC *White Mountain Guide*, 31st ed. Map 3 Crawford Notch–Sandwich Range, G7; USGS Topo: Crawford Notch

GPS Coordinates 44° 13.08′ N, 71° 24.66′ W

Contact White Mountain National Forest; fs.usda.gov/whitemountain; 603-536-6100

DIRECTIONS

Park at the Macomber Family Information Center at Crawford Depot off US 302. This is on the opposite side of US 302 from where you park for Saco Lake Trail. (See Trip 29 for directions.) An alternative is to park at the trailhead for Saco Lake Trail. Walk north behind the Highland Center and follow signs for Around the Lake Trail to your left. Another way to gain access to the trail is via AMC's Stewardship Trail. This is to the right behind the Highland Center and runs for 0.2 mile with twelve numbered stations before intersecting Around the Lake Trail. You can pick up an audio guide for Stewardship Trail at the Highland Center.

TRAIL DESCRIPTION

Around the Lake Trail travels around the shore of Ammonoosuc Lake through a shady forest of evergreens. It should take you no longer than an hour to hike the 1.2-mile loop, but allow extra time for the Red Bench overlook. Make sure you have insect repellent handy, particularly at dawn or dusk. In damp weather or early spring, expect muddy spots.

Around the Lake Trail, marked with yellow blazes, heads down toward the lake on an old road. It passes a spring (Merrill Spring) and at 0.3 mile reaches the start of the loop.

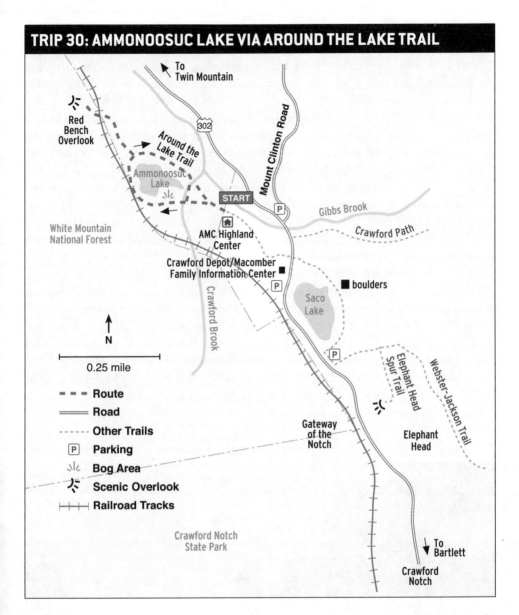

Follow the trail to the left in a clockwise direction. Cross a bridge over Crawford Brook, pass a spring, and you will then reach the west shore of the lake.

The forest near the lake is mostly red spruce, balsam fir, and paper birch. In wet areas and at the pond's edge, the understory has red-berried elder, sheep laurel, withe-rod, leatherleaf, and Labrador tea. Much of the path around the lake is lined with creeping snowberry, a small plant with tiny, rounded leaves attached to wiry stems that hug the ground. The leaves have a pleasant wintergreen scent when crushed. It is usually hard to find any of the snow-white berries that give this plant its name, but try your luck. Mountain wood sorrel, Canada mayflower, and blue-bead lily grow profusely around the lake, and you may find painted trillium and trailing arbutus there too. While admiring the flowers, you will likely be serenaded by the banjo-like plunking of green frogs.

After a few minutes you pass through a large rockslide, and at 0.6 mile, the turnoff to the Red Bench overlook heads left. This side path is 0.3 mile in each direction. Sizable patches of goldthread and hobblebush are found at this trail junction. Follow Red Bench Trail through the woods away from the lake. It jogs to the right at the railroad tracks (use caution—the tracks are still active) and crosses a wooden bridge by a small gorge. The rocky walls of this gorge are covered with ferns. Note that the spruce and fir that lined the lake have given way to deciduous trees—beech, sugar maple, and yellow birch—probably because the soil is drier. Red Bench Trail ends at a clearing in the forest. The clearing is filling in somewhat but still provides pleasing views of Mount Washington (including the cog railway that ascends that mountain). Early in the season, any breeze in this more open area will provide some relief from the blackflies and mosquitoes, which can be ubiquitous.

Retrace your steps, return to Around the Lake Trail, and turn left. Take the side path where a sign indicates "Down to the Lake" and walk to the shoreline for a view of Mounts Webster and Willard. Here is where the boat dock for the old Crawford House was. Interesting shrubs along the shore include Labrador tea, sheep laurel, leatherleaf, and northern wild raisin. Returning to Around the Lake Trail, you cross the outlet of the lake at 1.4 miles. The concrete dam with a culvert has been "improved" by beavers, which probably don't trust their human counterparts to make a structure that will last. Hotel guests would swim at this spot. They were apparently not dissuaded by occasional leeches.

Winter is a great time to explore Ammonoosuc Lake. *Photo by Dennis Welsh.*

If you look carefully at the water flowing out of the lake on the downstream side of the dam, you might notice green fuzz covering some of the rocks. This looks like algae but is actually a freshwater sponge that has green algae within its body. Most sponges are marine animals, but many species live in fresh water. The green color is from symbiotic green algae that live on the surface of the sponge. By turning sunlight into food, the algae provide the sponge with nutrition. Sponges also ingest food particles that are passively filtered out of the flowing water. Freshwater sponges thrive only in unpolluted waters, so the presence of a sponge here is a reflection of the cleanness of Ammonoosuc Lake.

Beyond the dam there was once a small clearing on your right, the location of a bath-house that was used by the hotel guests. Now it is slowly being taken over by shrubs. The wetter part of what remains of the clearing harbors yellow loosestrife plants, also known as swamp candles due to their bright yellow flowers that grow in spires 1 to 3 feet off the ground in middle to late summer. If you explore the wet meadow, be careful where you step because it's easy to trample the vegetation.

Around the Lake Trail turns away from the lake on an overgrown dirt road and then turns right off this road, crosses Crawford Brook again, and reaches the end of the loop at 1.5 miles. Turn left to get back to the trailhead.

DID YOU KNOW?

The water from Ammonoosuc Lake eventually flows southwest as the Ammonoosuc River joins the Connecticut River in the town of Woodsville, New Hampshire.

OTHER ACTIVITIES

Fishing is permitted in Ammonoosuc Lake with a New Hampshire fishing license. Like the guests from the old Crawford House, you can swim in the lake. The best swimming is by the dam. Swimmers still need to watch out for leeches, however.

After you complete this hike, stop in at the Highland Center to grab a snack, to use the library to look up any critters or unusual plants, or to plan your next hike. In the field around the Highland Center, take a moment to admire the view of Mount Tom (4,051 feet) and to enjoy the wildflowers. Mount Tom, in the Willey Range, was named for Thomas Crawford, who managed the original Crawford House. The field provides a sunny contrast to the shaded forest surrounding the lake. In midsummer, small deep crimson flowers with five petals and a black ring at the center are bound to catch your eye. These are maiden pinks, a non-native inhabitant of roadsides and fields. Other non-native eye-catchers are garden lupines, whose multicolored spikes of showy flowers put on a gorgeous display along the left side of the dirt road that takes you into the forest. Garden lupines, whose flowers resemble those of pea plants, have "escaped" from gardens and now grow along roadsides. Chipping sparrows and field sparrows flitter across the field.

MORE INFORMATION

Parking along US 302 at Crawford Depot or near Saco Lake is free. The AMC Hiker Shuttle stops at the Highland Center; outdoors.org/shuttle.

31 SAWYER POND

Sawyer Pond is a beautiful mountain pond that provides opportunities for swimming, picnicking, camping, fishing, and bird-watching.

Features 🚶🐕💧📍⛷🛶🌟⛺🏊

Location Livermore, NH

Rating Moderate

Distance 3.0 miles round trip

Elevation Gain 350 feet

Estimated Time 1.5–2 hours

Maps *AMC White Mountain National Forest Map & Guide*, 4th ed., I8; AMC *White Mountain Guide*, 31st ed. Map 3 Crawford Notch–Sandwich Range, I8; USGS Topo: Crawford Notch; Mount Carrigain

GPS Coordinates 44° 03.20′ N, 71° 24.26′ W

Contact White Mountain National Forest; fs.usda.gov/whitemountain; 603-536-6100

DIRECTIONS

The trailhead is off Sawyer River Road, a well-packed dirt road that heads southwest from US 302 about 4 miles west of the intersection of US 302 and Bear Notch Road in Bartlett. The parking area is 3.8 miles from US 302, before a gate marking the end of vehicular access. Walk around the gate and look for the trail signs. The road is not plowed in winter but is used by snowmobilers and skiers.

TRAIL DESCRIPTION

About 100 yards from the gate, Sawyer Pond Trail heads left across a narrow footbridge over Sawyer River, climbs uphill, and then turns left again. The route continues over a second bridge (0.3 mile) and turns onto an old logging road, which it follows the rest of the way to the pond.

The forest is a transition between northern hardwoods and spruce-fir, so sugar maple, American beech, yellow birch, eastern hemlock, red spruce, and balsam fir are all to be found. It is a rich forest, which C. Francis Belcher in *Logging Railroads of the White Mountains* (AMC Books, 1980) attributes to the enlightened lumbering practices of the Saunders family, who owned this region before it became part of the national forest. Unlike most loggers around the turn of the century, the Saunders family did not practice clear-cutting; instead, they engaged in selective logging. They left as their legacy the beautiful, dense forest; the painted trillium, Indian cucumber-root, and other wildflowers; and the verdant patches of shining club moss.

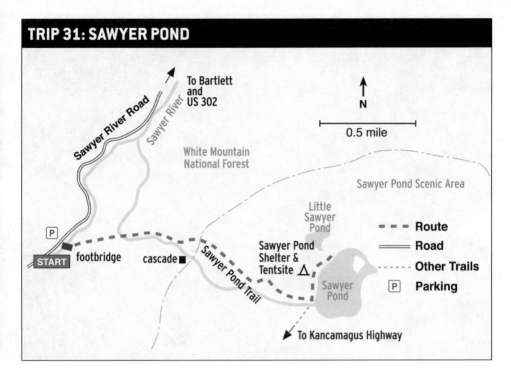

The trail approaches the outlet brook to Sawyer Pond at about 0.5 mile, where there is an attractive cascade. Look for one large glacial erratic, entwined by old roots of trees that used to grow on top but have since fallen. Nearby, some yellow birch trees appear to be on stilts, much like mangroves in the tropics. The trees probably sprouted on top of fallen "nurse" logs. As the saplings matured, their roots grew around the logs and down into the ground. Eventually the nurse logs completely decomposed, leaving the bottom of the saplings that had formerly rested on the dead logs hanging in the air and connected to the ground by roots. It is an excellent illustration of death and regeneration of the forest.

A sign states that you have entered the Sawyer Pond Scenic Area at 0.8 mile. When you pass a sign indicating the direction to one of the toilets at the campsite, you are almost at the pond. Continue to the pond's outlet and then turn left, leaving Sawyer Pond Trail. Follow the path that hugs the pond shore, enjoying the scenery and wildlife. You pass tent platforms and a shelter, the latter a particularly good place to enjoy a picnic, a snack, or a swim.

The pond is 47 acres in area, with a maximum depth of 100 feet. This is an impressive depth for a White Mountain pond (technically it's a lake—see Trip 29 for the difference), the result of glacial scouring. Owl's Cliff and the ledges of Mount Tremont form a striking backdrop at the east side of the pond.

Loons may be nesting on an island in the pond, so admire them from a suitable distance. After the breeding season they may be very friendly and swim right near you if you are quiet. You may hear the rattling calls of belted kingfishers from their perches along the shoreline as they search for fish. Lake darners (large dragonflies) patrol the pond's shore. Yellow-rumped warblers, black-capped chickadees, and golden-crowned kinglets inhabit the dense canopy of red spruce and balsam fir surrounding the water. Make sure the rather

Enjoy Sawyer Pond with your family by hiking in and staying overnight at the shelter.

tame and saucy red squirrels do not make off with your snack. As permanent inhabitants of the place, they clearly believe they are entitled to a share of whatever food visitors are toting.

Angling for brook trout is a popular activity, and the hiking distance is sufficiently short that it is possible to carry in an inflatable raft. This is a good swimming spot too, with a sandy, gravelly shoreline around a few access points, such as by the shelter.

Much of the shore is bordered with shrubs, including meadowsweet, sweetgale, witherod, leatherleaf, and mountain holly. Large floating logs from fallen trees are strewn near the shoreline and may have been there long enough to be covered with sphagnum moss and even sundews. Yellow waterlilies and pipeworts grow in the water.

A rough path continues for a short distance beyond the shelter, providing more perspectives on the pond and its surrounding mountains. This trail crosses the outlet brook from Little Sawyer Pond. Eventually, Green's Cliff will appear to the southwest. The same vantage point allows you to see a special feature of Sawyer Pond: the aforementioned island off its northeast shore. Steep-sided mountain ponds in the White Mountains rarely have islands.

Little Sawyer Pond is 11 acres in area and is more secluded than Sawyer Pond. A dense layer of shrubs limits the view of the pond except at one or two locations, but it is definitely worth seeing. To visit Little Sawyer Pond, head uphill at the Sawyer Pond shelter, pass the toilets, and then head right along an unmarked path. The pond will soon be visible through the trees on your left. Keep going until you reach a cleared space.

After enjoying the peek at Little Sawyer Pond, retrace your steps to return to the parking area.

DID YOU KNOW?

Sawyer Pond is named for Benjamin Sawyer, one of the early colonial settlers of Crawford Notch. He and a companion, Timothy Nash, brought a horse through Crawford Notch in 1772, thereby establishing a route south to north through the mountains.

OTHER ACTIVITIES

If you are interested in a longer hike, Sawyer Pond Trail continues beyond the pond and terminates at the Kancamagus Highway, a distance of 6.0 miles. This requires spotting a vehicle at each trailhead.

Sawyer Pond makes a good first overnight backpack destination for beginning hikers. The tent platforms and shelter are first come, first served, so you may want to go midweek to avoid crowds and ensure a more mellow experience.

Sawyer Pond Trail is moderately difficult for cross-country skiing. Sawyer River Road is not plowed in winter, so you need to ski in from its junction with US 302, an additional 3.8 miles.

You may fish at Sawyer Pond and Little Sawyer Pond with a New Hampshire fishing license.

MORE INFORMATION

Parking at the trailhead is free. Two outhouses are located at the campsite, but you need to supply your own toilet paper.

32 MOUNT WILLARD

AMC's White Mountain Guide *reflects: "Probably no other spot in the White Mountains affords so grand a view as Mount Willard for so little effort." The hike up this 2,865-foot spur of the Willey Range is well graded but perhaps too steep for younger children. When you reach the incredible panorama of Crawford Notch, you may declare, as my young nephew did after grumbling the whole way up, "Oh, this was really worth it!"*

Features 🚶 🐕 🔍 💧 🗺️ ❄️ ⛺ 🚌

Location Carroll, NH, to Hart's Location, NH

Rating Moderate

Distance 3.2 miles round trip

Elevation Gain 900 feet

Estimated Time 3–4 hours

Maps *AMC White Mountain National Forest Map & Guide,* 4th ed., G7 and Crawford Notch inset; AMC *White Mountain Guide,* 31st ed. Map 3 Crawford Notch–Sandwich Range, G8; USGS Topo: Crawford Notch

GPS Coordinates 44° 13.08′ N, 71° 24.66′ W

Contact Trailhead: White Mountain National Forest, fs.usda.gov/whitemountain, 603-536-6100; Summit: Crawford Notch State Park, nhstateparks.org/visit/state -parks/crawford-notch-state-park.aspx, 603-374-2272

DIRECTIONS

The trailhead for Mount Willard Trail is at the Gateway of the Notch behind Crawford Depot and the Macomber Family Information Center off US 302. From the Jackson–North Conway area, follow US 302 west at Glen where it splits from NH 16. US 302 passes through Bartlett and then heads north through Crawford Notch. At the top of the notch, roughly 20 miles from the junction of NH 16 and US 302, the road goes through the narrow pass between two cliffs. The parking area for Crawford Depot is a few hundred yards up the road on the left. The Highland Center at Crawford Notch is about 100 yards north of the trailhead.

From the community of Twin Mountain, take US 302 east. Crawford Depot is on the right just beyond the turnoff for the Highland Center, about 8 miles south of the junction of US 3 and US 302.

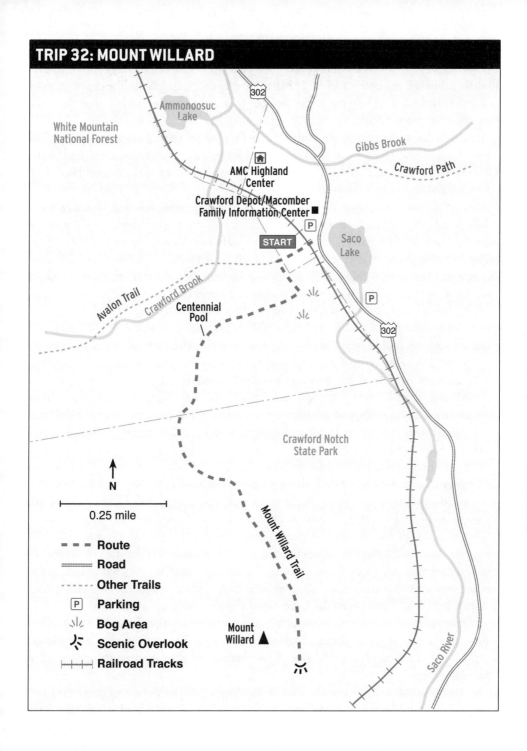

TRIP 32: MOUNT WILLARD

302

Ammonoosuc Lake

White Mountain National Forest

Gibbs Brook

Crawford Path

🏠 AMC Highland Center

Crawford Depot/Macomber Family Information Center ◼

P

START

Saco Lake

Avalon Trail

Crawford Brook

Centennial Pool

P

302

Crawford Notch State Park

N

0.25 mile

- - - Route
═══ Road
······ Other Trails
P Parking
🥀 Bog Area
🥾 Scenic Overlook
├┼┼┤ Railroad Tracks

Mount Willard Trail

Mount Willard ▲

Saco River

TRAIL DESCRIPTION

Before setting out, throw a windbreaker into your pack. On certain days the wind gets funneled through the notch and really blasts away at the open ledges. The dense cover of conifers provides some shelter near the top, but proper attire will enable you to enjoy the view in more comfort.

Mount Willard Trail starts out with Avalon Trail across the railroad tracks of the old Maine Central line. (It is unsafe and illegal to walk along the track because it is used by the Conway Scenic Railroad.) In 0.1 mile at a display board, Mount Willard Trail heads left, while Avalon Trail continues straight ahead.

Mount Willard Trail is marked with yellow blazes. It goes uphill at a steady pace, nowhere very steep or rocky but nonetheless relentless. It starts out using an old carriage path, wide enough for parents and children to walk two abreast. Mount Willard Trail crosses two streams soon after leaving Avalon Trail. At 0.5 mile, Centennial Pool will be to the right. This is a small flume with a pretty "mini waterfall" 10 to 15 feet high. Enjoy a tasty lunch or snack on the rocks here if you want a breather.

This lower part of the trail is a forest of northern hardwoods (sugar maple, American beech, and yellow birch) and paper birch, with an understory of wood fern, shining club moss, ground pine, goldthread, hobblebush, American shinleaf, and mountain wood sorrel.

At 0.7 mile, Mount Willard Trail turns right and leaves the old carriage path temporarily. At this point you will notice more and more spruce and fir. The understory now includes whorled aster, large-leaved goldenrod, and Canada mayflower. The trail makes a hairpin turn to the left at 1.2 miles, and you are completely in a boreal forest dominated by balsam fir. The understory is composed largely of sphagnum, haircap, and juniper mosses. The trail reaches the summit at 1.6 miles.

The vista from the ledges of Mount Willard is one of the most famous in the White Mountains. Before you is a breathtaking panorama of a deep, broad notch bounded by steep-sided mountains. Crawford Notch is one of the best examples of a glacially carved, U-shaped valley anywhere in the world. Because the notch runs north and south, it was a perfect channel for the continental ice sheet that covered this area as recently as 12,000 years ago. The glacier advanced along the course of a river, scouring the sides of the mountains and gouging out rocks. What had formerly been a V-shaped valley with a river at the bottom was transformed into a U. In preglacial times, Silver and Flume cascades, which you pass on US 302 just below the Gateway of the Notch, flowed gently into the river at the bottom of the notch. By steepening the sides of the notch, the glacier left the original valleys of the two streams hanging high above the floor. The two cascades now plunge steeply down the glacially scoured side of the notch, and their courses are aptly termed "hanging valleys."

Another prominent feature of the view from Mount Willard is the impressive evidence of rockslides on Mounts Webster and Willey. Many landslides and avalanches have occurred in Crawford Notch. The most famous happened in August 1826, when several days of heavy rains caused a huge slide onto the homestead of the Willey family. The entire family was killed. Moving accounts of the tragedy are in Lucy Crawford's *History of the White Mountains* (The Durand Press, 1999) and in the Reverend Benjamin G.

Willey's *Incidents in White Mountain History* (available in some libraries). The Willey House Historic Site is visible in the valley below you from Mount Willard; you can visit it after your hike.

The rocky ledges at Mount Willard support an interesting array of plants that can tolerate the exposure and thin soil. Three-toothed cinquefoil and mosses grow very neatly where small amounts of soil accumulate in cracks in the rocks. Whitlowwort, a rare plant in this region, also grows in these cracks (see Trip 23). You will find patches of meadowsweet, raspberries, poverty grass, highland rush, sedges, and hay-scented fern scattered throughout the ledges. Woody plants include heart-leaved birch and mountain ash, along with the ubiquitous balsam fir and red spruce.

Retrace your steps to return to the trailhead.

DID YOU KNOW?

The cliff below the summit of Mount Willard is a site where peregrine falcons have nested in the recent past. These spectacular birds prey on other birds by flying high up in the sky above their target and then diving down through the sky at speeds as fast as 180 to 200 mph, knocking their unfortunate victim to the ground. Of course, their actual speed during one of these "stoops" is almost impossible to measure. When peregrines were nesting on the cliff, Mount Willard Trail would be closed to protect the falcons and their young. Although the birds are not currently nesting on Mount Willard, they do nest nearby on Frankenstein Cliff (Trip 34) and hopefully will take up residence on Mount Willard again in the future.

Mount Willard provides a spectacular view of Crawford Notch. *Photo by Dennis Welsh.*

OTHER ACTIVITIES

Mount Willard Trail is an advanced cross-country ski trail, but so many winter hikers go up on snowshoes that the trail gets pretty well packed. It is best skied right after a fresh snow. Plenty of other great trails are in the area if Mount Willard Trail is closed for some reason. The Avalon Trail (Trip 35) is a longer, less-traveled alternative with a similar view of Crawford Notch.

MORE INFORMATION

Parking is free here along US 302.

The Macomber Family Information Center near the trailhead, operated by AMC, has restrooms, water, snacks, and trail information; outdoors.org/destinations/massachusetts -and-new-hampshire/highland-center. The AMC Hiker Shuttle stops at the Highland Center near the trailhead; outdoors.org/shuttle.

WHY GLACIERS?

Many of the trail descriptions in this book mention U-shaped valleys, glacial erratics, hanging valleys, cirques, tarns, kettle ponds, and eskers. These are all relatively recent features of the landscape created by the vast continental and mountain glaciers that covered much of the Northern Hemisphere as far south as Long Island, New York, peaking about 20,000 years ago.

That last Ice Age is but one of many that have occurred in Earth's long history. In fact, the first Ice Age for which there is scientific evidence occurred between 2.4 and 2.1 billion years ago. Since then, there have been times when ice reached almost to the equator and other periods when tropical plants and animals thrived even at the poles. The most recent period of glaciations consisted of several major glacial advances followed by warmer interglacial intervals.

The causes of these intermittent periods of glaciation and warming are complex, and they do interact with one another to either enhance or dampen the impacts. One major factor is the shifting of continents (see the Geology section in Appendix B, page 315). This affects ocean currents, wind patterns, and how much of a landmass there is in the Northern Hemisphere for snow accumulation and glacial formation. A second factor is the amount of greenhouse gases, such as carbon dioxide, in the atmosphere, something that naturally varies due to volcanic activity and biological activity but is now being profoundly altered by humans (see "Climate Change in the White Mountains" on page 87 and outdoors.org/conservation/approaches). A third factor is Milankovitch cycles, named for the Serbian scientist who discovered them. These are periodic differences in the shape of Earth's orbit around the sun, in the tilt of Earth's axis, and in the wobble of Earth around its axis. The cycles vary in a regular pattern and affect the strength of the sun's energy reaching Earth, thereby affecting temperatures.

During an ice age, glacial activity seems to peak approximately every 100,000 years. This corresponds with the Milankovitch cycle that describes the shape of Earth's orbit around the sun, which can vary from more elliptical to more circular. When the shape is more elliptical, Earth is in closer proximity to the sun during the northern summer, which leads to melting of glaciers and a warmer climate. The reverse happens when the shape is more circular. The causes of ice ages are still a subject of lively scientific debate.

33 SUGARLOAF TRAIL

You get impressive views from two Sugarloaf summits for relatively modest effort, but that's not all this trail has to offer. Huge boulders—glacial erratics—are scattered here, and North Sugarloaf has an abandoned quarry where you can find smoky quartz.

Features

Location Bethlehem, NH

Rating Moderate

Distance 3.4 miles round trip to both peaks

Elevation Gain North Sugarloaf, 700 feet; Middle Sugarloaf, 900 feet; both summits, 1,100 feet

Estimated Time 3–4 hours

Maps *AMC White Mountain National Forest Map & Guide*, 4th ed., F/G6; AMC *White Mountain Guide*, 31st ed. Map 2 Franconia–Pemigewasset, F6; USGS Topo: Bethlehem

GPS Coordinates 44° 15.29′ N, 71° 30.24′ W.

Contact White Mountain National Forest: fs.usda.gov/whitemountain, 603-536-6100

DIRECTIONS

The trailhead is on Zealand Road, which branches off south from US 302 at Zealand Campground, about 2 miles east of the community of Twin Mountain and about 6 miles northwest of the Highland Center at Crawford Notch. Follow Zealand Road for 1.0 mile from US 302. Park just before the bridge over Zealand River and look for the trailhead just past the bridge on the right.

Zealand Road is not plowed in winter; hikers and skiers must use the parking area across US 302, 0.2 mile from Zealand Road. That adds an extra 1.2 miles of hiking or snowshoeing to get to the trailhead.

TRAIL DESCRIPTION

Sugarloaf Trail ascends both North and Middle Sugarloaf (2,310 and 2,539 feet, respectively), and your hike could include one or both of these small mountains. If you have time for only one, the hike to North Sugarloaf takes one to one and a half hours, and the hike to Middle Sugarloaf is slightly longer.

Sugarloaf Trail coincides with Trestle Trail for its first 0.2 mile, following the west shore of Zealand River. It then branches uphill to the left, while Trestle Trail continues straight

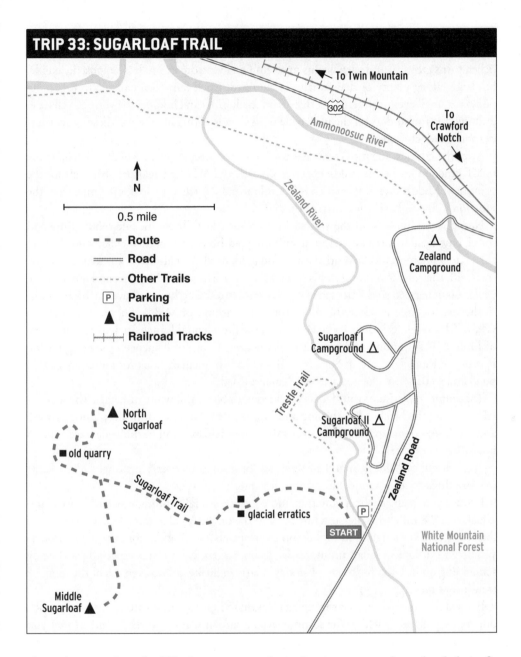

To Twin Mountain

302

Ammonoosuc River

To Crawford Notch

Zealand River

N

0.5 mile

- - - Route
Road
Other Trails
P   Parking
▲   Summit
+++ Railroad Tracks

Zealand Campground

Sugarloaf I Campground ▲

Trestle Trail

▲ North Sugarloaf

Sugarloaf II Campground ▲

■ old quarry

Zealand Road

Sugarloaf Trail

■
■ glacial erratics

P

START

White Mountain National Forest

Middle Sugarloaf ▲

along the river. Sugarloaf Trail continues with moderate steepness through a balsam fir forest and then through an area dominated by yellow and white birch.

At about 0.5 mile, the trail passes some huge boulders. These are called glacial erratics because they were picked up and carried southward for miles by an advancing glacier then deposited "erratically" on the landscape. As you wind your way around these immense boulders, you can't help but feel like a tiny ant.

Note the lush covering of mosses, rock ferns, and lichens on the boulders. One of the common lichens, rock tripe, forms flat, leathery lobes with dimples. When damp, this lichen turns greenish and even begins to resemble a living organism. It is supposedly edible, but bring along plenty of mayonnaise or mustard. Rock fern (also called Virginia polypody) is a small evergreen fern that thrives on shady cliffs and boulders. If you get a chance, examine the round dots on the underside of its fronds with a hand lens. These are clusters of spore-producing structures.

After the erratics, the trail continues to ascend at a steeper pitch. At 0.9 mile you come to a T junction in the col (saddle) between North and Middle Sugarloaf. Turn left for the summit of Middle Sugarloaf, which is 0.5 mile ahead. North Sugarloaf is 0.3 mile from the junction to the right. I will return to that later.

Note the wildflowers on the way to Middle Sugarloaf. These include mountain wood sorrel, blue-bead lily, red and painted trillium, goldthread, red-berried elder, wild sarsaparilla, King Solomon's seal, whorled aster, and goldenrod. You also pass numerous downed trees with their shallow root systems exposed to view. The soil is thin here, and much of the trail is on bare rock, so the trees are very susceptible to being knocked over by high winds.

The last 0.2 mile is relatively steep. The open summit of Middle Sugarloaf provides a vista of Mount Hale, North Twin Mountain, the Presidential Range (including a fine view of Mount Washington), and smaller peaks nearby. Look for evidence of logging on the Rosebrook Range and South Sugarloaf. If you have binoculars, look for moose in a small pond and wetland in a logged area off Zealand Road.

The granite rock under your feet is speckled with black and white minerals. The white is feldspar, and the black is hornblende and biotite mica. Granite forms deep underground and solidifies slowly, so individual minerals such as feldspar and hornblende have time to form distinct crystals.

The summit of Middle Sugarloaf provides some good blueberry picking. Other plants here are three-toothed cinquefoil, balsam fir, and sheep laurel.

Retrace your steps to the T junction and continue straight through toward North Sugarloaf. It is 0.8 mile to walk from one peak to the other. An abandoned quarry on North Sugarloaf is to your right and slightly up the slope about 0.2 mile from the T junction as you ascend. It looks like an unimpressive jumble of rocks, but kids especially will enjoy scrambling on it. Look for pieces of smoky quartz, a dusky-colored version of the familiar translucent rock.

Beyond the quarry, you pass through a pleasant red spruce forest with an interesting rock outcropping before reaching the summit. Make sure in scaling North Sugarloaf that you follow the trail to the very end—there is an open area with a vista that you could mistake for the summit just before the actual summit.

The summit of North Sugarloaf is about 200 feet lower than Middle Sugarloaf's. The views are attractive, particularly those of the Zealand Valley, the Presidential Range, and Middle Sugarloaf. Reindeer lichen abounds on this summit. This is a pale green lichen with a delicate branching structure. Lichens thrive on rocky summits with little or no soil because they have the amazing ability to revive even after being almost completely dried out. Birds you might see around both Sugarloaf summits are ravens, dark-eyed juncos, and turkey vultures.

Hunting for smoky quartz on North Sugarloaf Mountain.

Retrace your steps back to the T junction and turn left there for the walk downhill to the trailhead.

DID YOU KNOW?
Quartz is the most abundant mineral on Earth, making up about 12 percent of the planet's crust. Smoky quartz is a variety that is brown or black. It forms as a result of the natural irradiation of quartz over a long time period.

OTHER ACTIVITIES
You can use easy and level Trestle Trail along Zealand River as an extension to this hike. The route formerly crossed Zealand River on a trestle that dated to the logging railroad days (it was rebuilt a few times). Unfortunately, the trestle got washed out in 2005 and has not been replaced, so the crossing is challenging, particularly during high water.

Another short walk takes you to Wildlife Pond, 0.2 mile each way on a path heading southeast from the north side of the bridge and across the road from the Sugarloaf trailhead. This provides views of Middle Sugarloaf and its cliffs.

Wading opportunities are available in Zealand River near the trailhead.

MORE INFORMATION
A day-use fee of $5 is required for parking. Two Sugarloaf campgrounds are off Zealand Road very near the trailhead.

34 ARETHUSA FALLS AND FRANKENSTEIN CLIFF

Arethusa Falls is the tallest waterfall in New Hampshire, more than 200 feet high. The falls are an especially stunning sight early in the season. Visitors can enjoy excellent views of Crawford Notch from Frankenstein Cliff.

Features

Location Hart's Location, NH

ARETHUSA FALLS ONLY

Rating Moderate

Distance 3.0 miles round trip

Elevation Gain 950 feet

Estimated Time 2 hours

ARETHUSA FALLS TO FRANKENSTEIN CLIFF

Rating Moderate, with some steep sections

Distance 4.9 miles round trip

Elevation Gain 1,650 feet

Estimated Time 4–5 hours

Maps *AMC White Mountain National Forest Map & Guide*, 4th ed., H8 and Crawford Notch inset; AMC *White Mountain Guide*, 31st ed. Map 3 Crawford Notch–Sandwich Range, H8; USGS Topo: Stairs Mountain to Crawford Notch

GPS Coordinates 44° 08.88′ N, 71° 22.20′ W

Contact Trailhead and Frankenstein Cliff: Crawford Notch State Park, nhstateparks .org/visit/state-parks/crawford-notch-state-park.aspx, 603-374-2272; Arethusa Falls: White Mountain National Forest; fs.usda.gov/whitemountain, 603-536-6100

DIRECTIONS

From the south, take US 302 north about 8.5 miles from its intersection with Bear Notch Road in Bartlett. The turnoff on a short road to the left is well marked with a sign. From the north, the turnoff for Arethusa Falls is a right turn 6.0 miles south of Crawford Depot at the head of Crawford Notch off US 302. Park in the upper parking lot, which is closer to the trailhead. If that is full, there is ample space at the lower lot just off US 302.

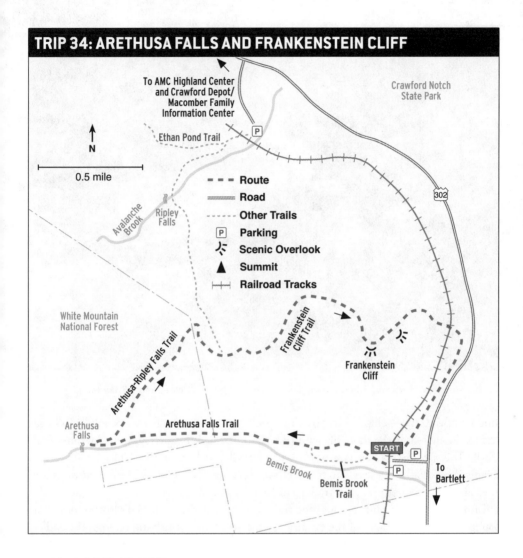

To AMC Highland Center
and Crawford Depot/
Macomber Family
Information Center

Crawford Notch
State Park

Ethan Pond Trail

N

0.5 mile

Route

Road

Other Trails

P **Parking**

Scenic Overlook

▲ **Summit**

Railroad Tracks

302

Avalanche Brook

Ripley Falls

White Mountain
National Forest

Frankenstein Cliff Trail

Frankenstein Cliff

Arethusa-Ripley Falls Trail

Arethusa Falls

Arethusa Falls Trail

START

P

P

To Bartlett

Bemis Brook

Bemis Brook Trail

TRAIL DESCRIPTION

Arethusa Falls Trail is a pleasant walk along Bemis Brook, and with additional effort, you can also visit several smaller waterfalls. Given its stature as the tallest waterfall in New Hampshire, Arethusa Falls is a popular destination, so expect lots of company, but the impressive falls and the natural history of the surroundings make it more than worth the effort.

You can hike a very scenic loop by taking Arethusa-Ripley Falls Trail from the falls to Frankenstein Cliff Trail. You will find some steep ups and downs around Frankenstein Cliff. In spring and early summer, the trail around the cliff may be closed because of nesting peregrine falcons.

Arethusa Falls Trail is marked with blue blazes and is easy to follow throughout its length. Cross the tracks of the scenic railroad and head into the forest. The route initially follows an old logging road and almost immediately passes a tree—standing right in the

At the base of Arethusa Falls, the tallest waterfall in New Hampshire. *Photo by Jerry Monkman.*

middle of the trail—chiseled out by woodpeckers. In 0.1 mile, Bemis Brook Trail heads left to closely follow the shore of Bemis Brook for 0.4 mile before rejoining Arethusa Falls Trail. This side path takes you past two beautiful small waterfalls, Coliseum Falls and Bemis Brook Falls, but it is rough and climbs very steeply with lots of exposed roots and rocks before it rejoins the main trail. Explore it if you can.

Families with young hikers could end their trip at one of these waterfalls, spend some time lounging on the flat rocks of the streambed, and still have a satisfying outing. The endless patterns that cascading water makes are fascinating no matter the height of the waterfall.

Most of the trees in the first section of the trail are northern hardwoods (sugar maple, yellow birch, and American beech). Wildflowers and shrubs include pink lady's slipper, painted trillium, blue-bead lily, creeping snowberry, hobblebush, and lowbush blueberry.

Arethusa Falls Trail continues on the side of the valley high above Bemis Brook. This section of the trail was relocated—with the help of AmeriCorps volunteers—because of concern about erosion and trampling of vegetation as well as the safety of hikers on the slippery rocks near the falls. You will pass several fairly recent landslides where paper birch fell over as the slope slipped downward due to erosion. Other birches were toppled by an ice storm in January 1998.

At 1.3 miles, the trail intersects Arethusa-Ripley Falls Trail, which comes in from the right. For Arethusa Falls, continue to the left for another 0.2 mile until it ends at the viewpoint near the falls.

Arethusa Falls, like nearby Ripley Falls and the waterfalls visible from the roadside in Crawford Notch, is the result of the last continental glacier that covered New England. By flowing in a generally southern direction, the glaciers deepened the large north–south valleys, such as Crawford Notch. Water that once flowed gently into the Saco River now plunges steeply to reach the river in the notch. Valleys of tributary streams that ran east or west, such as Bemis Brook, were not similarly gouged and so were left high above the original valley floor. Thus, geologists call them "hanging valleys." The picturesque waterfalls that flow into Crawford Notch from both sides are all hanging valleys.

At Arethusa Falls, 750 feet higher in elevation than the trailhead, the forest is a relatively even distribution of trees typically found at both higher elevations (the boreal forest: balsam fir and red spruce) and lower elevations (the northern hardwoods). The misty atmosphere around the falls supports many plants: long beech and oak fern, northern bush honeysuckle, mountain ash, whorled aster and rough aster, clasping-leaved twisted-stalk, round-leaved sundew, and mountain aven. The last has broad, kidney-shaped leaves with toothed edges and yellow flowers. It is normally an alpine species but occasionally inhabits lower elevations in the cooler atmosphere along streams. Mountain avens can also be found earlier on this hike on the wet rocks alongside Bemis Brook Falls.

Depending on the time of day and your energy level, you could retrace your steps to the parking area (1.5 miles) or hike the loop past Frankenstein Cliff (an additional 3.4 miles). A sign at the falls indicates that it is one hour or less back to the parking lot by Arethusa Falls Trail and two to four-plus hours via Frankenstein Cliff. Due to the elevation changes and switchbacks on the Frankenstein loop, it takes substantially longer than a casual glance at a map might indicate. Use extra care during winter and spring, when ice melting off the cliffs can make parts of this hike dangerous.

If you opt for the loop, return to the junction of Arethusa Falls Trail and Arethusa-Ripley Falls Trail and follow the latter to the left. Arethusa-Ripley Falls Trail, marked with blue blazes, heads gradually up the side of the valley. If you are hiking in middle to late June, this is an ideal spot to spy pink lady's slippers. Other common inhabitants of the forest floor along this trail include wild sarsaparilla, partridgeberry, mountain wood sorrel, sharp-leafed aster, shiny club moss, and hay-scented fern.

After a stream crossing, the trail climbs steeply for a short period and then levels off along the side of a slope. The trees become shorter, and you get good views over Crawford Notch through a thinning canopy. This part of Arethusa-Ripley Falls Trail is especially enjoyable—you're not in a tunnel of trees so typical at this elevation, but instead are visually connected to the surrounding landscape, even within a forest. The large number of blowdowns reveals how shallow the root systems of the trees are. Beech and yellow birch saplings are filling the voids.

Reach the junction with Frankenstein Cliff Trail 1.3 miles from Arethusa Falls. Look for red spruce, balsam fir, paper birch, yellow birch, blackberry, hobblebush, hay-scented fern, New York fern, and long beech fern at this junction.

Turn right on Frankenstein Cliff Trail. It is marked with yellow blazes and ascends slightly to the height-of-land. The trail then descends through a spruce forest and reaches the outlook ledge on top of the cliff, 2.1 miles from Arethusa Falls. The dropoff is dramatic, so keep away from the edge, particularly if you are uncomfortable with heights.

The ledge provides an expansive view of the southern part of Crawford Notch. The U-shaped valley was carved out as the last continental glacier moved south through the notch about 20,000 years ago. This is a great spot to get out a compass and a map of the region so you can identify the different peaks. From left to right are Stairs Mountain; Mount Crawford (with a distinct ledge at its summit); Mounts Hope and Chocorua (in the distance); Bear Mountain; and Mounts Bartlett, Haystack, Tremont, and Bemis. Arethusa Falls is visible below the long ridge of Mount Bemis. The Saco River threads its way south in the notch, paralleling NH 302 and the railroad. On the ledge where you sit, there are some red pines twisted by the wind and barely hanging on.

Take advantage of the wide vista to look for birds of prey and other wildlife. The cliff has been home to nesting peregrine falcons in recent years. Peregrines were wiped out in the eastern United States in the 1960s, largely because of DDT. This pesticide was picked up by the falcons in their food and caused the birds to lay eggs with thin, easily broken shells. Since DDT was banned, biologists have successfully reintroduced peregrine falcons into many of their former eastern haunts. Peregrines nest on cliffs with little or no human access, such as Frankenstein Cliff. Some rock-climbing routes up the cliff may be closed to protect nesting sites, but the hiking trail has remained open. These rare, spectacular birds may linger for a time in the area after they nest, so always keep your eyes open for them.

Red-tailed hawks are another possibility. Once I saw a family of red-tailed hawks soaring far below in the valley, their screams reaching all the way up to the cliff. Listen for the varied croaking and hoarse cawing of ravens. Sometimes these largest members of the crow family make such humanlike noises that you think you are going to run into a group of hikers on the trail. You might also see chimney swifts. On the ground, friendly chipmunks will probably greet you and expect a handout in return.

From the ledge, it is a steep descent, with steps built into the path in places. Be especially careful on the slippery, gravelly terrain.

Near the bottom, the trail passes some piles of boulders and then an exposed cliff. The cliff harbors a variety of interesting plants, including joe-pye weed, several species of aster, harebell, spreading dogbane, white snakeroot, flowering raspberry (lovely to look at, but the fruit is not edible), and northern bush honeysuckle. But the extra-special botanical treats here are round-leafed sundews, growing right in the water dripping down the cliff face. These small carnivorous plants are more typically found in bogs or wet, sandy areas.

The trail levels out, passes under the Frankenstein Trestle of the scenic railroad (the highest railroad trestle in the White Mountains and 2.8 miles from Arethusa Falls), and then heads south through a stand of northern hardwoods. Logs on the forest floor are covered with one of the more picturesque shelf fungi: turkey tail, named for its mottled pattern of brown and tan concentric layers. Just before you reach the upper parking lot, a short spur heads off left to the lower lot.

DID YOU KNOW?

In Greek mythology, Arethusa was a water nymph (nereid) who transformed herself into a fountain to escape the attentions of a river god. Arethusa is also the name of a very rare

New England orchid found in bogs and cedar swamps, but its presence in the White Mountains has never been confirmed. Godfrey Frankenstein was an artist who painted in Crawford Notch.

OTHER ACTIVITIES

Another option is to take Arethusa-Ripley Falls Trail from Arethusa Falls to Ripley Falls and then continue out to US 302 on Ethan Pond Trail. However, this would require spotting a second vehicle at the Ethan Pond trailhead on US 302. Hiking from the Ethan Pond trailhead to Ripley Falls is described in Trip 37.

Stop at Crawford Notch State Park's visitor center at the Willey House Historic Site before or after your hike for information on the history of Crawford Notch. The site, about 2.5 miles north of the trailhead on US 302, also has restrooms and a snack bar. It is open from late spring through midfall.

MORE INFORMATION

The parking area and trails are in Crawford Notch State Park, where parking is free.

Dry River Campground, part of Crawford Notch State Park, is about 0.5 mile north of the turnoff to Arethusa Falls on US 302.

35 MOUNT AVALON

The narrow summit of Mount Avalon provides excellent views of Crawford Notch, the Willey Range, and the southern Presidential Range, including Mount Washington. Avalon Trail is a longer but more interesting alternative to the very popular trail to the summit of Mount Willard. For much of its length, Avalon Trail follows Crawford Brook, which has some particularly attractive cascades.

Features 🏂 🤸 🐕)))))) 🗺 🎆 ⛺ 🚌

Location Carroll, NH, at trailhead; Bethlehem, NH, on Mount Avalon summit

Rating Moderate, with one steep section

Distance 3.7 miles round trip

Elevation Gain 1,550 feet

Estimated Time 3–4 hours

Maps *AMC White Mountain National Forest Map & Guide*, 4th ed., G7 and Crawford Notch inset; AMC *White Mountain Guide*, 31st ed. Map 3 Crawford Notch–Sandwich Range, G7; USGS Topo: Crawford Notch

GPS Coordinates 44° 13.08′ N, 71° 24.66′ W

Contact White Mountain National Forest: fs.usda.gov/whitemountain, 603-536-6100

DIRECTIONS

The trailhead for Avalon Trail is across the railroad tracks from Crawford Depot (Macomber Family Information Center) on US 302 at the head of Crawford Notch. It is the same trailhead as for Mount Willard Trail (see Trip 32 for driving directions). The Highland Center at Crawford Notch is about 100 yards north of the trailhead.

TRAIL DESCRIPTION

Two trails lead from Crawford Depot up the Willey Range to a breathtaking panorama featuring the glacially carved valley of Crawford Notch. Mount Willard Trail is the more traveled route and reaches its summit in about an hour and a half; however, there is little to see along the way. Avalon Trail is longer (three to four hours) and has a greater elevation gain, but it offers more interesting sights.

Avalon Trail runs together with Mount Willard Trail for the first 0.1 mile. Continue straight where Mount Willard Trail leaves to the left. At about 0.3 mile, Avalon Trail crosses Crawford Brook (an easy crossing unless water levels are very high). Beyond the

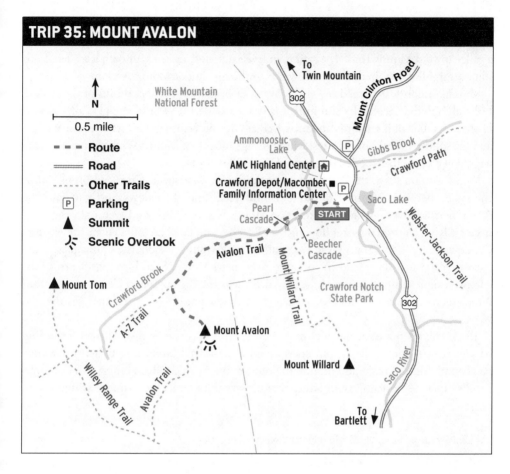

brook crossing, a side path leads left along the water and takes you past Beecher and Pearl cascades.

Beecher Cascade is named for the famous abolitionist Henry Ward Beecher, who spent many summers in the White Mountains in the latter part of the nineteenth century, along with his sister, Harriet Beecher Stowe, author of *Uncle Tom's Cabin*. Pearl Cascade is undoubtedly named for its frothy whitewater. In summer, both falls are particularly attractive after a rainstorm. At the base of Pearl Cascade, note the small tributary that flows through a mossy gorge with abundant sphagnum moss, Indian cucumber-root, and hobblebush just before it joins Crawford Brook. Sugar maple, American beech, and yellow birch dominate the canopy.

At the point where the side path rejoins Avalon Trail, you will find some handy rocks to sit on if you want to stop for lunch or a snack. Avalon Trail continues at an easy grade, always within earshot of flowing water. The large number of paper birches suggests that the area was disturbed, perhaps by fire or logging, in the early part of the twentieth century. The trail recrosses Crawford Brook at 0.8 mile. At 1.3 miles, A-Z Trail—named after its route, from Avalon to Zealand Trail—comes in from the west. The forest at this point has almost completely transitioned to spruce-fir. Continue on Avalon Trail to the left at this junction. It ascends steeply over rocks for the next 0.5 mile, with views through trees over a valley toward Mount Tom. The trail then levels out, and a steep spur path leads left, with some scrambling required, about 100 yards to the summit of Mount Avalon.

Mount Avalon was named by Moses Sweetser because it reminded him of the Avalon Hills of Newfoundland. Its summit provides a wonderful vista of the glacially carved, U-shaped valley of Crawford Notch, as well as Mount Webster, with its impressive cliffs, and the southern peaks of the Presidential Range including Mount Washington. Looking west, you can see the wooded summits of the Willey Range.

Mount Avalon sits at the boundary of two different watersheds. Crawford Brook drains the valley between Mount Tom and Mount Field and then flows north to join the Ammonoosuc River—which originates on Mount Washington—and eventually the Connecticut River. A drop of water flowing over Beecher and Pearl cascades enters the Atlantic Ocean at Long Island Sound. On the south side of Mount Avalon, the drainage is to the Saco River, which flows into the ocean off southern Maine. Saco Lake, visible from the Mount Avalon summit, is part of the Saco drainage, and the Highland Center at Crawford Notch, across the road from that lake, sits on the height-of-land that separates the two watersheds.

The small, open area at the Mount Avalon summit has scattered short trees, including balsam fir, red spruce, larch, pin cherry, and heart-leaved birch. Bog bilberry, lowbush blueberry, mountain ash, and mountain holly are the main shrubs. Flowers and low "sub-shrubs" include bunchberry, mountain cranberry, blue-bead lily, painted trillium, and

The glacially carved valley of Crawford Notch from Mount Avalon.

creeping snowberry. While searching for these plants, you could be accompanied by golden-crowned kinglets and yellow-rumped warblers.

Retrace your steps to return to Avalon Trail. Turn right for the trailhead, or, if you have time, turn left and continue west along Avalon Trail for several hundred yards beyond the spur path to an interesting flat ledge with views of Mount Avalon in one direction and the summits of Mounts Tom and Field in the other. Look here for reindeer lichen, a bushy light green lichen that thrives in sunny, dry locations with little soil. Mountain cranberry, with small, glossy, smooth-edged dark green leaves, is interspersed with the lichen. Mountain holly, a shrub noted for its red berries and leaves with a small point on the tip, is also common. Note a narrow band of quartz, which is a dike within the granite along the trail here.

When you have finished exploring, turn around and follow Avalon Trail back to the trailhead.

DID YOU KNOW?

The Avalon Hills of Newfoundland, for which Mount Avalon was named, were in Paleozoic times part of Avalonia, a small island continent between the predecessors of North America and Europe. Avalonia's rocks are now found in both North America and Great Britain, providing strong evidence for plate tectonics and continental drift, which means that Earth's continents are on plates that have floated on top of Earth's mantle since the beginning of time, constantly changing the arrangement of landmasses.

OTHER ACTIVITIES

For a longer hike, make a loop by continuing on Avalon Trail for another mile to Willey Range Trail just below the summit of 4,340-foot Mount Field. Turn right (northwest) on Willey Range Trail. After 0.9 mile, descend via A-Z Trail and Avalon Trail. The loop, which is substantially longer than just retracing your steps from Mount Avalon, is a popular snowshoe route.

MORE INFORMATION

Parking is free here along US 302. The Macomber Family Information Center at Crawford Depot, near the trailhead, operated by AMC, has restrooms, water, snacks, and trail information; outdoors.org/destinations/massachusetts-and-new-hampshire/highland-center. The AMC Hiker Shuttle stops at the Highland Center near the trailhead; outdoors.org/shuttle.

36 ZEALAND TRAIL TO ZEALAND FALLS HUT AND ZEALAND POND

This hike takes you along a former logging railroad past beaver wetlands to one of the premier locations in the White Mountains for seeing birds and other wildlife, including moose and beavers. You get a clear view of Zealand Notch from AMC's Zealand Falls Hut, and you can easily spend hours at the falls and river nearby.

Features 👫 🐕 〰️ 💧 📍 ⛷️ 📐 ✳️ 🚌 💲

Location Bethlehem, NH

Rating Moderate

Distance 5.4 miles round trip

Elevation Gain 650 feet

Estimated Time 3–4 hours

Maps *AMC White Mountain National Forest Map & Guide*, 4th ed., G7; AMC *White Mountain Guide*, 31st ed. Map 2 Franconia–Pemigewasset, G7; USGS Topo: Crawford Notch

GPS Coordinates 44° 13.49′ N, 71° 28.70′ W

Contact White Mountain National Forest: fs.usda.gov/whitemountain, 603-536-6100

DIRECTIONS

The trailhead for Zealand Trail is near the communities of Twin Mountain and Bretton Woods. From the Conway–Jackson area, take US 302 west through Crawford Notch. Turn left onto Zealand Road at Zealand Campground, about 6 miles northwest of AMC's Highland Center. Follow Zealand Road for about 3.5 miles until its end, and park in the lot. The trail is straight ahead, beyond a gate. This is also a stop for the AMC Hiker Shuttle. Zealand Road is closed to vehicles from mid-November to mid-May, and hikers and skiers must use the parking area across US 302, 0.2 mile from Zealand Road.

From Franconia Notch: Take US 3 north to Twin Mountain. Turn right (east) on US 302 and follow it for 2.0 miles. Turn right at Zealand Campground and follow Zealand Road as directed above.

From points north: Take either US 3 or NH 115 south to Twin Mountain. Turn left (east) onto US 302 and follow the directions given above.

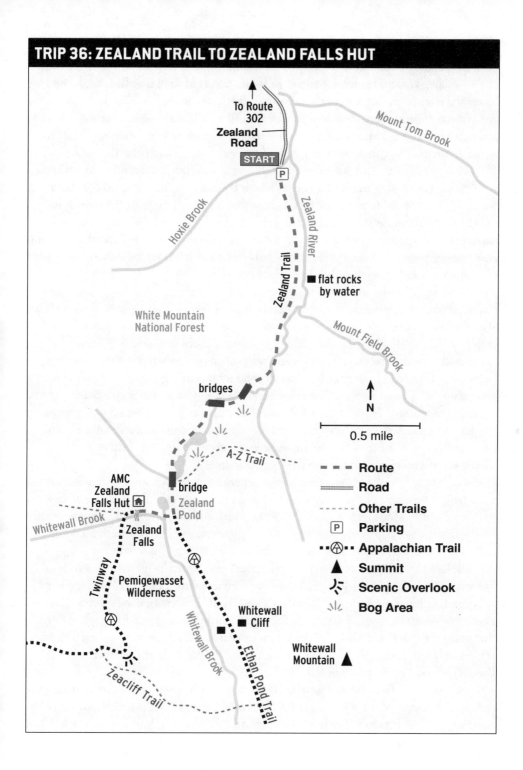

To Route
302
Zealand
Road

Mount Tom Brook

START

P

Hoxie Brook

Zealand River

flat rocks
by water

Zealand Trail

Mount Field Brook

White Mountain
National Forest

bridges

N

0.5 mile

A-Z Trail

AMC
Zealand
Falls Hut

bridge

Zealand
Pond

Whitewall Brook

Route

Zealand
Falls

Road

Other Trails

P   Parking

Appalachian Trail

Twinway

Summit

Pemigewasset
Wilderness

Scenic Overlook

Bog Area

Whitewall
Cliff

Whitewall Brook

Whitewall
Mountain

Ethan Pond Trail

Zeacliff Trail

TRAIL DESCRIPTION

Plan on spending a full day here because there is much for the entire family to see and do along Zealand Trail and around Zealand Falls Hut. Zealand Trail is well marked with blue blazes and is relatively easy, except for a steep pitch to the hut in the last 0.1 mile. It follows the bed of an old logging railroad for most of its length. The trail does traverse some soggy terrain, and despite wooden bridges and planks, it can still be a bit wet in spring or during rainy weather. Also be aware that the winter ski trail crosses back and forth over the hiking trail.

Leaving the parking area, ascend on a slight uphill through a dense forest of red spruce with young trees lining the route. You will soon enter northern hardwoods. At 0.2 mile, the trail leaves the old railroad bed on a bypass that is a little rough. At 0.6 mile, it rejoins the railroad bed, and at 0.8 mile, it approaches Zealand River, where several flat rocks are perfect for having a snack or lunch. At 1.5 miles, the trail crosses a bridge over the river. You pass through a very attractive woodland of balsam fir and white birch, with an understory of mountain wood sorrel, blue-bead lily, and hobblebush.

After about 1.8 miles, the trail crosses an open beaver swamp. The U.S. Forest Service has to constantly respond to the latest beaver engineering projects to keep Zealand Trail above water, and the elevated wooden walkway here is its most recent move. Look for stumps of beaver-chiseled trees, as well as the animals' dams and lodges.

Zealand Trail then reenters the forest and skirts open wetlands and wet meadows. At 2.3 miles, A-Z Trail enters from the left, just beyond a beautiful, grassy, wet meadow with a view across to Mount Tom. A few years back, the meadow was a beaver pond, but the beavers disappeared. As their dam fell into disrepair, the pond drained and eventually turned into a meadow. New beavers moved in, restored the dam, and reflooded the area to create the new wet meadow. In the late nineteenth century, this was neither a pond nor a meadow, but a railroad yard serving the logging industry.

Moose like to feed on tender water plants, so beaver ponds are good places to look for these largest members of the deer family. Moose tracks, resembling large deer tracks, are likely to be in muddy areas around any of the wetlands; rounded moose droppings may also be there. The sharpest-eyed member of your group may find moose teeth marks on tree bark, where it looks like someone stripped off the bark with a giant comb.

While looking for birds and moose around beaver ponds, listen for green frogs, which sound like someone plucking the strings of a banjo. Dragonflies patrol for insects over the water.

Beyond its junction with A-Z Trail, Zealand Trail then crosses the inlet to Zealand Pond, following the shore of the pond. Tall meadow rue, a plant with fuzzy white flowers, thrives on the shoreline. AMC trail crews make neat stacks of logs in this area. The wood is used to heat Zealand Falls Hut in winter. Zealand Trail ends at the junction of Ethan Pond Trail and Twinway (2.5 miles).

Turn right onto Twinway to reach Zealand Falls Hut in another 0.2 mile. The last 0.1 mile, which is part of the Appalachian Trail and blazed in white, is rough and steep, but stone steps aid your ascent. The bottom of Zealand Falls is off a short spur to the left, just below the hut. Stop to admire this waterfall either now or on the way back.

Zealand Falls is just one of the many attractive water features along Zealand Falls Trail.

Situated at 2,640 feet at the head of Zealand Notch, Zealand Falls Hut is one of AMC's eight backcountry huts, which can be reached only by hiking. Day-hikers are welcome to stop in, use the restrooms, fill their water bottles, buy snacks, peruse educational displays, and chat with the "croo" (the friendly staff).

Zealand Falls Hut provides a spectacular vista of Zealand and Carrigain notches right from the porch, although the view is gradually filling in with vegetation as of this writing. Zealand Notch, the closer of the two, is a classic glacially carved U-shaped valley. It is bounded on the left (east) by the impressive cliffs of Whitewall Mountain. Rockslides, logging, and fires have left much of Whitewall Mountain barren. The straight horizontal line on the mountainside is a former logging railroad that is now a section of Ethan Pond Trail. Places where logs were dragged down the mountain to the railroad left skid marks, some of which are still visible. The west side of Zealand Notch is bounded by Zealand Ridge, which can be reached by following Twinway on a very steep ascent beyond the hut. Carrigain Notch, in the distance, is an impressive sight.

It is hard to imagine when looking out over this verdant scenery that the Zealand Valley was completely ravaged by logging from about 1880 to 1903. During this brief period, there was a town with a sawmill, school, post office, and railroad yard just west of present-day Zealand Campground. Loggers stayed at logging camps near the falls and used the railroad to send logs to the sawmill. Zealand Falls Hut has an interesting display of old photographs from this time. Sloppy logging activity spawned numerous devastating forest fires, as sparks from the railroad ignited brush left over from the logging operations. The loggers left Zealand Valley looking like a moonscape. (See "Logging in the Pemigewasset Wilderness" on page 107 for more on logging in the White Mountains.)

Although the forest has come back, the impact of logging is still evident. The area probably once had much more spruce than it currently does, because that was the most sought-after tree. Paper birch, which is one of the first species to colonize a disturbed area, still covers large sections that had been clear-cut.

Zealand Falls Hut is popular with birders. In June and July, you can hear the songs of winter wrens, hermit thrushes, and white-throated sparrows right from the porch. These birds, along with purple finches, black-throated blue warblers, black-throated green warblers, redstarts, ovenbirds, and red-eyed vireos, can be heard singing and calling along the trail, but spotting them in the dense forest is tough. In the open areas around the beaver ponds, you'll potentially see black ducks, wood ducks, blue jays, swallows, and perhaps even a goshawk.

Just in front of the porch at the hut are a few red-berried elders. This distinctive shrub of wet areas and streamsides has compound leaves in pairs along its branches. Red-berried elders produce clusters of small white flowers that turn into small and colorful (but inedible) berries.

Explore the rocky bed of Whitewall Brook (except during extremely high water), a few yards beyond the hut. If you stand by the brook on a hot day, you will immediately feel the cool breeze streaming down from the mountain. This natural refrigerator allows alpine plants to grow at a lower elevation than usual. The showiest is the mountain avens, a wildflower with bright yellow flowers and rounded, scalloped leaves that is found virtually nowhere else in the world but the White Mountains. Mountain cranberry, a low evergreen plant with small dark green leaves, also grows here, wherever there is enough soil for it to establish roots. Other plants around the brook include three-toothed cinquefoil, meadow-sweet, mountain ash, balsam fir, and red spruce.

Many people enjoy sitting on the flat rocks in Whitewall Brook above the falls. Many pools within the brook are deep enough for swimming or wading, particularly if you walk upstream. Hearty polar-bear types will jump right in; others often join them if the weather is hot enough. The screeches you hear are decidedly human.

Retrace your steps to return to the trailhead.

DID YOU KNOW?
Rumor has it that the area was named "Zealand" after New Zealand as a testament to its remoteness.

OTHER ACTIVITIES
Zealand Falls Hut is a popular cross-country ski destination, and the hut is open on a self-serve basis in winter. Reservations are required year-round (see "More Information" below). Because the ski trail follows an old logging road, it is not difficult except for the last 0.1 mile, where you need to remove your skis. Keep in mind, however, that Zealand Road is closed from mid-November through mid-May, adding 3.5 miles to the journey.

If you have the time and energy for a longer trip (or if you are staying overnight at Zealand Falls Hut), you can combine this hike with a walk along Ethan Pond Trail from its junction with Zealand Trail to Thoreau Falls, named for the famous naturalist and philosopher (4.8-mile round trip, 300-foot elevation gain from the hut). This takes you along the side of Whitewall Mountain, a site that once was heavily logged. Another option from the hut is to hike up Twinway to Zeacliff for terrific views of the Pemigewasset Wilderness (2.4-mile round trip, 1,050-foot elevation gain from the hut).

MORE INFORMATION
Zealand Falls Hut offers overnight lodging with breakfast and dinner (reservations essential; outdoors.org/destinations; 603-466-2727). Sleeping accommodations are in two large rooms with eighteen bunks each, so the hut is not as comfortable for families with young children as Lonesome Lake Hut. But even a day trip to Zealand Falls Hut is more than worth the effort. If you do stay overnight, the hut is a base for a variety of wonderful day hikes.

A user fee ($5 per day) is required to park at the trailhead.

BEAVERS

Beavers are one of the largest members of the rodent family, which also includes mice, squirrels, and woodchucks. Their webbed feet are perfect for swimming, and their scaly, flat tails, when slapped on the water, warn other beavers of danger. Beavers use their large front teeth to feed on the nutritious inner bark of trees, favoring aspens, birches, alders, willows, and maples. Grasses and other vegetation are also part of their diet.

Beavers are one of the few animals (along with humans) that modify their entire habitat to suit their needs, building dams and conical houses of

Beavers, nature's engineers, can be found in many ponds in the mountains.

sticks and mud. As "ecosystem engineers," beavers have had a major influence on New England and the rest of the United States. Their mud-and-stick dams alter the flow of rivers, flooding forests and creating ponds and wetlands that serve not only the beavers but other wildlife as well. Their ponds trap sediments and other pollutants, playing a role in maintaining clear water downstream.

A beaver family of parents, newborns (kits), and 1-year-olds occupies a lodge. Two-year-olds are driven out of their natal lodge by their parents and may start their own colony nearby. A family will establish a new residence upstream or downstream when they have consumed many of their favorite trees. In winter, these rodents stockpile small branches underwater and then remain in their lodges most of the time, venturing out of the underwater entrance only to grab something from their food cache beneath the ice.

In the first few centuries of European settlement in this country, people trapped beavers in large numbers for their valuable fur. Beaver hats were a fashion rage in Europe, particularly through the early 1800s, so their pelts were a major source of revenue for the colonies and the young nation. Due to the intense trapping and loss of habitat, beavers had mostly disappeared from New England by the mid-1800s. Their dams fell apart, their ponds drained and the landscape became one more dominated by uninterrupted flowing streams. Beavers were reintroduced in New Hampshire around 1930 and have made a remarkable comeback in the state and throughout New England.

Although you can find ample evidence of their presence in chiseled trees, dams, and lodges, beavers are hard to spot. The best time to look is in the half-light of early dawn or dusk. Be as quiet as possible.

37 ETHAN POND AND RIPLEY FALLS

Ethan Allen Crawford described the pond that would be named for him thusly: "For beauty and grandeur it is nowhere surpassed by any spot to me known about these mountains." Ripley Falls is likewise one of the most impressive cascades in the White Mountains.

Features 🏃🏊🚶🐕〰️💧📍📐💥⛺🚌🚗

Location Hart's Location, NH, to Bethlehem, NH

Rating Moderate, with one steep section

Distance 6.0 miles round trip

Elevation Gain 1,850 feet

Estimated Time 5 hours

Maps *AMC White Mountain National Forest Map & Guide*, 4th ed., G7–8 and Crawford Notch inset; AMC *White Mountain Guide*, 31st ed. Map 3 Crawford Notch–Sandwich Range, G7–8; USGS Topo: Crawford Notch

GPS Coordinates 44° 10.05′ N, 71° 23.16′ W

Contact Trailhead and Ripley Falls: Crawford Notch State Park, nhstateparks.org /visit/state-parks/crawford-notch-state-park.aspx, 603-374-2272; Ethan Pond: White Mountain National Forest, fs.usda.gov/whitemountain, 603-536-6100

DIRECTIONS

The trailhead for Ethan Pond Trail and Ripley Falls is at the site of the old Willey House Station now along the Conway Scenic Railroad off US 302 in Crawford Notch State Park, about 1 mile south of the Willey House Historic Site. A sign for Ripley Falls and the Appalachian Trail is at the turnoff, which leads up a paved road 0.3 mile to a parking lot. If the lot is full, you can park off US 302. The turnoff is about 4 miles south of Crawford Depot and the Highland Center at Crawford Notch and 12 miles southeast of the junction of US 302 and US 3 in the community of Twin Mountain. If you are coming up through Jackson or North Conway, the turnoff is about 16 miles northwest of the intersection of US 302 and NH 16 in Glen.

TRAIL DESCRIPTION

This is a great pond-waterfall combination. Ethan Pond, a remote 4-acre pond bordered by the steep cliffs of Mount Willey and a vista across to the Twin Range, was named for Ethan Allen Crawford, who camped there during one of his hunting trips in fall 1829. After

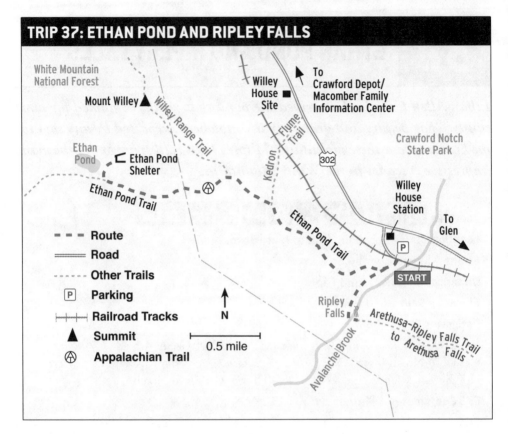

hiking to the pond, you can extend your trip by visiting Ripley Falls, only an additional 0.6 mile. Ripley Falls Trail alone is a good hike, even for younger children.

Ethan Pond Trail is part of the Appalachian Trail and is marked with white blazes. It almost immediately crosses the tracks of the Conway Scenic Railroad near a trestle. Resist the temptation to walk along the railroad tracks and on the trestle, which is dangerous and illegal. In 0.2 mile, Arethusa-Ripley Falls Trail goes left (you will return to that later), and Ethan Pond Trail continues steeply ahead. In about 0.5 mile, the trail levels off and becomes a pleasant walk, varying between a gradual ascent and level ground.

The northern hardwood forest here features yellow birches, a few larger sugar maples, many sugar maple saplings, and an understory of striped maples and hobblebushes. The shade-tolerant sugar maple saplings await the creation of a gap in the forest canopy to eventually take their place in that canopy. Gaps are created when canopy trees fall over due to wind, disease, or insects. Note a particularly distinctive uprooted paper birch along the trail about 0.5 mile from the trailhead. Its shallow root system, which led to its demise, illustrates how rocky the soil is on these slopes.

As you continue hiking, you will notice spruce and fir trees becoming increasingly dominant. Kedron Flume Trail enters from the right at 1.3 miles. (This trail leads past Kedron Flume to the Willey House Historic Site; the section between Ethan Pond Trail and this flume is steep and rough.) At 1.6 miles, Willey Range Trail intersects at a point where

Ethan Pond Trail turns left. The transition between the lower-elevation deciduous forest and the higher-elevation boreal forest is complete at this point.

Ethan Pond Trail climbs gradually for another 0.3 mile beyond the intersection and then passes through a beautiful level section of boreal forest with lots of small streams, wetlands, and bog bridges. Look for dense growth of both green and red peat mosses (sphagnum) in this damp area. These two colors actually represent separate species. Peat mosses have an amazing ability to absorb and retain water due to large vacuoles (spaces) in their cells. This is why they are so useful in gardens. Several stands of fringed sedge (long, drooping cylinders of brown flowers) are found in these wetlands too. Other plants include blue-bead lily, goldthread, bunchberry, creeping snowberry, sheep laurel, withe-rod, and whorled and purple-stemmed asters.

The trail crosses the height-of-land (about 2,900 feet) that represents the boundary between the Saco and Pemigewasset/Merrimack River watersheds. Occasional views of Mount Willey appear through the trees. At 2.6 miles, a short spur path that leads in 0.1 mile to Ethan Pond and the Ethan Pond Campsite comes in from the right. This crosses the inlet at which you get the best view of Ethan Pond and the cliff of Mount Willey. The shelter at the campsite is a good place to eat lunch, but it does not have a view of the pond.

Take some time to sit on one of the rocks by the inlet and contemplate the surroundings. You can see why this pond was so favored by Ethan Allen Crawford, who was a woodsman, guide, and innkeeper. He appreciated its beauty and its abundant fish and wildlife. Lucy Crawford's *History of the White Mountains* (The Durand Press, 1999) describes one fishing trip in which the party he guided caught about 70 "salmon trout" (native brook trout) in a very short time and broiled them over a fire on the banks of the pond. He saw ample signs of moose that fed on the waterlilies. Another story, cited in John T. B. Mudge's *The White Mountains: Names, Places, and Legends*, describes a hunting trip in which Ethan Allen Crawford's group shot two moose at the pond and then feasted on moose and trout. They eventually went to sleep within the skins of the moose, paying no attention to the howling of wolves nearby.

Wolves are long gone from Ethan Pond and the rest of the White Mountains, but visitors at the campsite must be careful to stow their food properly because of bears. A moose in this shallow pond (the greatest depth is 4 feet) is always a possibility as well.

On the opposite shore of the pond, the outlet drains into the East Branch of the Pemigewasset River. This flows through one of the largest wilderness areas in the White Mountains. In the same direction, on a clear day, you can see North Twin Mountain and South Twin Mountain. Behind you, the cliffs of Mount Willey loom above the campsite, and you may hear the hoarse cawing and croaking of ravens, which roost and possibly nest on the cliff. Peregrines periodically take up residence on the cliff as well.

The area is covered with vegetation typical of the boreal forest. Immediately along the shoreline, look for larch, Labrador tea, mountain holly, shadbush, alder, and sweetgale. Sweetgale leaves give off the pleasant aroma of bayberry when crushed. Black spruce grows along the spur path leading to the pond. This small tree has short bluish green needles and is often found in northern bogs. The upland forest surrounding the pond is characterized by red spruce and balsam fir. Birds of this forest include boreal chickadees, red-breasted nuthatches, brown creepers, and several species of warblers.

The rocks at the outlet to Ethan Pond provide a view of cliffs on Mount Willey and lead you to the shelter. *Photo by Jerry Monkman.*

Retrace your steps to start back to the trailhead. When you reach the junction with Arethusa-Ripley Falls Trail (0.2 mile from the trailhead), turn right for Ripley Falls. Arethusa-Ripley Falls Trail was marked with both yellow and blue blazes at the time of this writing. The trail proceeds high above Avalanche Brook, perched on the side of a steep slope for much of the 0.3 mile between Ethan Pond Trail and the falls.

When you approach Ripley Falls, the cool water and shady gorge may make you feel like you just walked into a refrigerator. This feeling is particularly pronounced (and welcome) on a hot day. Be careful of the slippery rocks just below the waterfall. Ripley Falls is 100 feet high and flows gracefully down a slab of granite. It is named after Henry Wheelock Ripley, who reported its existence in the 1850s. Like many other cascades in the area, Ripley Falls is a product of the last glaciations. It is called a hanging valley (see Trip 34 for an explanation).

If you have time, climb the left side of the waterfall and explore above the falls but not too close to the brink. This requires you to cross the stream, which could be difficult in high water. The hike to the top is steep, but you'll get away from the crowds and also find a few pretty pools in which you can swim. The ledges here can be slippery, so be extra careful if you explore them.

Retrace your steps to return to Ethan Pond Trail and then to the trailhead at the Willey House Station.

OTHER ACTIVITIES

Thoreau Falls can be reached by hiking an additional 2.5 miles along Ethan Pond Trail and then descending 0.1 mile along Thoreau Falls Trail.

Stop at Crawford Notch State Park's visitor center at the Willey House Historic Site before or after your hike for information on the history of Crawford Notch. The site, about 5 miles north of the trailhead on US 302, also has restrooms and a snack bar. It is open from late spring through midfall.

MORE INFORMATION

This hike begins in Crawford Notch State Park and ends in White Mountain National Forest. Parking is free. The AMC Hiker Shuttle stops at the trailhead; outdoors.org/shuttle.

The Ethan Pond Campsite has a shelter (sleeps eight) and five tent platforms.

38 MOUNT CRAWFORD

The 3,119-foot summit of Mount Crawford, surrounded by the Presidential Range and innumerable other peaks in all directions, offers one of the most stunning panoramas in the White Mountains. The hike also provides an opportunity to see birds and plants of the boreal forest.

Features

Location Hart's Location, NH, to Hadley's Purchase, NH

Rating Strenuous

Distance 5.0 miles round trip

Elevation Gain 2,100 feet

Estimated Time 5 hours

Maps *AMC White Mountain National Forest Map & Guide*, 4th ed., H8; AMC *White Mountain Guide*, 31st ed. Map 3 Crawford Notch–Sandwich Range, H8; USGS Topo: Bartlett to Stairs Mountain

GPS Coordinates 44° 07.12′ N, 71° 21.21′ W

Contact White Mountain National Forest: fs.usda.gov/whitemountain, 603-536-6100

> **⚠ CAUTION!** The trail is slippery when wet and has steep dropoffs. Do not attempt this hike in bad weather.

DIRECTIONS

The trailhead for Davis Path is off US 302, 6.3 miles north of where US 302 crosses Bear Notch Road in Bartlett and 5.6 miles south of the Willey House Historic Site in Crawford Notch. Ample parking is available at a lot on the east side of US 302.

TRAIL DESCRIPTION

Mount Crawford is reached by Davis Path, one of the oldest hiking trails in the White Mountains. The trail was completed by Nathaniel Davis in 1845 as a bridle path to the summit of Mount Washington. (It fell into disuse in the 1850s, and AMC brought it back as a footpath in 1910.) Davis was a son-in-law of Abel Crawford, the "Old Patriarch," who brought the Crawford family to the area in the 1790s. Abel built the Mount Crawford House near the current trailhead. Davis, who managed the Mount Crawford House, was married to Hannah, the sister of Ethan Allen Crawford.

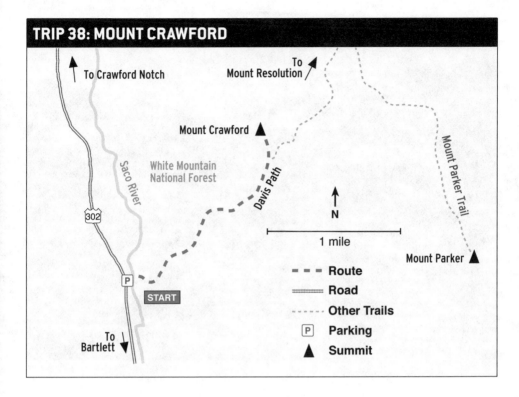

To Crawford Notch

To Mount Resolution

Mount Crawford ▲

Saco River

White Mountain National Forest

Davis Path

302

Mount Parker Trail

N

1 mile

Mount Parker ▲

START

P

To Bartlett

- - - Route
=== Road
····· Other Trails
P Parking
▲ Summit

This is a hike to save for a clear day. For much of the distance, it is a relentless ascent within a tunnel of trees, so you want to be sure that you will see something at the top. Also, the ledges near the summit can be slippery in wet weather.

Leaving the parking lot, the trail follows a dirt road along the west bank of the Saco River for a few hundred yards. It turns right to cross the river on an interesting footbridge, the Bemis Bridge. Samuel Bemis was a dentist from Boston who summered in the White Mountains from 1827 through 1840, eventually retiring here. The home he built, Notchland, is now an inn.

Beyond the bridge, the trail passes through an overgrown field (private property), turns left to follow a power-line right of way for a short distance, and then crosses a streambed that is likely to be dry by late summer. It enters the White Mountain National Forest and follows a small brook, which could also be dry. At about 0.5 mile, you pass a sign indicating that you are entering the Presidential Dry River Wilderness (groups limited to ten or fewer; no bikes, no motorized vehicles).

One special wildflower to look for in this lower section of the trail is twinflower (illustrated here), a small plant that trails along the ground. Pairs of rounded leaves with slightly scalloped edges come off the wiry stem at regular intervals. In July, you can find its two tiny, tubular pink flowers produced on a single upright stalk, hence its name. Twinflower was a favorite flower of Carolus Linnaeus, the Swedish scientist responsible for developing the

The aptly named Giant Stairs on Stairs Mountain can be seen from the summit of Mount Crawford on a clear day.

system of naming all organisms with a genus and species name in Latin. Linnaeus is often pictured holding a twinflower, or *Linnaea borealis.*

Continuing on, you pass a side path that leads to the right through red pines to a backcountry tentsite. The grade becomes moderately steep as you hike along Davis's original route. While you are chugging up the mountain, take a moment to marvel at how Davis used a series of well-placed switchbacks to traverse this steep slope so that guests from his inn could be brought up on horseback. On numerous occasions, you think you see the top of the ridge through the trees and that your climb must soon be over, but the trail then makes another sharp turn and somehow finds more mountain to ascend.

Witch hazel grows profusely along this part of the trail. This shrub has rounded, bluntly toothed leaves that are irregular at the base. Its flowers bloom later in the season than those of any other plant in the White Mountains, so look for its small, greenish yellow flowers through October and even into November.

At 1.9 miles, the trail levels off, passes through a forest of moderately sized spruce and fir, and reaches the first vista at a ledge. This is a good location to spot birds of the boreal forest. You will likely first hear their calls, and with a little patience you might see golden-crowned kinglets, red-breasted nuthatches, and boreal chickadees. If you are truly lucky, a spruce grouse could surprise you. This bird resembles a chicken and has dark bluish gray coloring with some brown and white speckling. It can seem unusually tame and unafraid of people (or lacking in intelligence, depending on your perspective).

At 2.2 miles, the spur path to the summit of Mount Crawford departs to the left at the base of an open ledge. Take care to follow the spur blazes up the ledge, and go an additional 0.3 mile to the summit. Use caution in wet weather.

The summit of Mount Crawford provides a spectacular panoramic view. Mount Hope is immediately to the south, and you can see the route of your ascent between this peak and Mount Crawford. Beyond Mount Hope in the same direction are Bear Mountain, Attitash Mountain, Mount Tremont, and the Sawyer River valley. The small clear-cuts you see near Bear Mountain are in the Bartlett Experimental Forest and are being studied by the University of New Hampshire. Farther in the distance to the south is Mount Tripyramid. To the east, the most prominent features are Mount Resolution and the steps of Stairs Mountain. To the north, the southern Presidential Range and Mount Washington frame the horizon. Crawford Notch and the Willey Range are to the northwest. Frankenstein Cliff is a prominent feature in that direction. Finally, Mount Carrigain looms large to the west.

The handiwork of the last glacier to pass through here is evident in this magnificent scenery. It smoothed out the tops of all these peaks, leaving many of them rounded, most notably Mount Eisenhower. It scooped out deep valleys, such as Crawford Notch below. The ledges around the summit of Mount Crawford bear parallel scratches etched by small stones squeezed between the moving glacier and the bedrock.

"Flag trees," or "banner trees," provide evidence of the wind's power on this exposed summit. Many of the spruce and fir here have branches on only one side, the side away from the prevailing wind. Other plants adapted to growing in these conditions include a large number of heaths: Labrador tea, bog bilberry, black huckleberry, lowbush blueberry, mountain cranberry, black crowberry, leatherleaf, sheep laurel, and rhodora. Three-toothed cinquefoil, reindeer lichen, and poverty grass also live here.

On your descent from the summit on the spur, be careful to follow the blazes back to Davis Path. Retrace your steps to the parking area.

OTHER ACTIVITIES

Stop at Crawford Notch State Park's visitor center at the Willey House Historic Site before or after your hike for information on the history of Crawford Notch. The site, about 5 miles north of the trailhead on US 302, also has restrooms and a snack bar. It is open from late spring through midfall.

MORE INFORMATION

Parking is free. The first third of a mile of Davis Path is on private land, so please respect the rights of the landowners. The remainder of the hike is in the White Mountain National Forest.

Dry River Campground, part of Crawford Notch State Park, is about 2.5 miles north of the Davis Path trailhead on US 302; nhstateparks.org/visit/state-parks/crawford-notch -state-park.aspx; 603-374-2272.

THE CRAWFORD FAMILY

Many individuals and organizations have contributed to trail-building and maintenance in the White Mountains, and it is impossible to give them all credit in a single short essay. Nonetheless, one name that has achieved legendary status is Crawford. As described in the Mizpah Spring trip (Trip 39), Crawford Path is considered the oldest continually maintained hiking trail in the Northeast. It was built by Abel and Ethan Allen Crawford in 1819. Abel, the "Old Patriarch" of the Crawford family, came to the Crawford Notch area in 1791 soon after the first road through the notch opened. Originally deeded land at what is now Fabyan's Station restaurant (site of the base station of the cog railway), Abel eventually settled in the area now known as Notchland, near the current trailhead for Davis Path off US 302. Realizing that farming was difficult in this valley, he set up an inn eventually called the Mount Crawford House, to serve the commercial traffic that used the road to travel between Portland, Maine, and points west. Eventually, enough tourists were staying at the inn that Abel and his son Ethan Allen (at 6 feet, 3 inches, called "the Mountain Giant") were motivated to build a path up the mountains. They completed the 8.25-mile path from the Gateway of the Notch to Mount Washington in 1819 and used it to guide their guests up the mountain.

Crawford Path was rough and sometimes hard to follow. No doubt the clouds and mist above treeline were similar to what hikers find today, so even the Crawfords occasionally had to stop to figure out the right direction. Two years after the completion of the original Crawford Path, Ethan Allen Crawford built a path from his inn at Fabyan's up Mount Washington. This second route, eventually taken over by the cog railway, became the more popular ascent up Mount Washington through the mid-1800s.

Abel and Ethan Allen built a hotel that would become the Crawford House at the Gateway to the Notch in 1828. It was managed by Ethan's brother Thomas, who, in 1840, smoothed and expanded the original Crawford Path into a bridle path. According to Laura and Guy Waterman's *Forest and Crag: A History of Hiking, Trail Blazing, and Adventure in the Northeast Mountains* (SUNY Press, 2019), Abel, at 74, was the first person to ride up Mount Washington on horseback.

Guests guided up the tallest mountains in New England by the Crawfords included some of the most prominent citizens of New England: Daniel Webster, Ralph Waldo Emerson, and Nathaniel Hawthorne, to name a few. The botanist William Oakes, who wrote one of the first descriptions of the flora of the White Mountains, was a frequent visitor. Many guests wrote about their experiences, enticing people to visit the White Mountains and solidifying the legendary status of the Crawfords.

39 MIZPAH SPRING HUT AND MOUNT PIERCE

Mizpah Spring Hut, located in a boreal forest clearing at an elevation of 3,800 feet, is an excellent place to see mountain birds. Continue on to 4,312-foot Mount Pierce for splendid views and a taste of alpine habitat.

Features ✿ 🏃 🚴 🎿 🐕 〰 🔍 ⚓ 🎋 △ 🌲 🚹 $

Location Carroll, NH, to Hart's Location, NH

Rating Strenuous

Distance 6.6 miles round trip

Elevation Gain 2,450 feet

Estimated Time 5–6 hours

Maps *AMC White Mountain National Forest Map & Guide*, 4th ed., G8 and Crawford Notch inset; AMC *White Mountain Guide*, 31st ed. Map 1 Presidential Range, G8; USGS Topo: Crawford Notch to Stairs Mountain

GPS Coordinates 44° 13.41′ N, 71° 24.69′ W

Contact White Mountain National Forest: fs.usda.gov/whitemountain, 603-536-6100

Lodging Mizpah Spring Hut or Highland Center: Appalachian Mountain Club, outdoors.org/destinations, 603-466-2727

⚠ **CAUTION! The summit of Mount Pierce is above treeline and therefore exposed to the rigors of alpine weather. It should not be attempted in stormy, icy, or very windy conditions.**

DIRECTIONS

The trailhead for Crawford Path is near AMC's Highland Center at the head of Crawford Notch. From the Jackson–North Conway area, follow US 302 west at Glen where it splits from NH 16. US 302 passes through Bartlett and then heads north through Crawford Notch. At the top of the notch, roughly 20 miles from the junction of NH 16 and US 302, the road goes through the narrow pass between two cliffs. If you are not staying at the Highland Center (parking for registered guests only), park in the hiker lot on Mount Clinton Road. This is a short (about 0.2 mile) distance off US 302, just beyond the Highland Center.

From Franconia Notch and the community of Twin Mountain, the hiker parking lot on Mount Clinton Road is about 8 miles south of the junction of US 3 and US 302 in Twin Mountain.

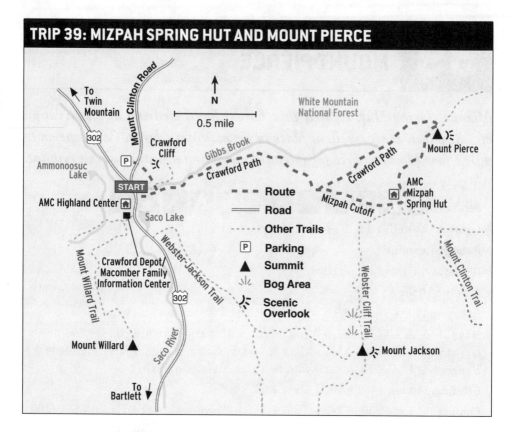

TRAIL DESCRIPTION

Much of this hike is on historical Crawford Path (see "The Crawford Family," page 198). You begin on Crawford Connector, which crosses Mount Clinton Road and links the parking area to Crawford Path. Just before the connector crosses Gibbs Brook, a spur path for Crawford Cliff diverges to the left. This follows the north bank of the brook for a short distance to a pool and then ascends steeply and roughly to Crawford Cliff, which offers a fine view of the notch and the Willey Range. The distance to the overlook is 0.4 mile, and it is worth a stop if you have the time.

Crawford Connector crosses a bridge over Gibbs Brook and ends at Crawford Path (which comes up directly from US 302 opposite the Highland Center) at 0.4 mile. Turn left and start ascending Crawford Path along the south bank of Gibbs Brook. The trail is well graded, varying between slight uphills and steeper gradients. At 0.6 mile, a short spur path leads left to Gibbs Falls, once a popular destination for guests of the Crawford House, a former hotel. Men hiked in coats and ties, and women hiked in hoopskirts.

After passing the falls, you soon enter the Gibbs Brook Scenic Area. Take note of the old-growth red spruce and some very large yellow birch. Understory plants include hobblebush, blue-bead lily, mountain wood sorrel, and a variety of mosses.

The trail eventually turns away from the brook at about 1.2 miles. At 1.9 miles, Mizpah Cutoff comes in from the right. Crawford Path continues straight for the summit of Mount

Mizpah Spring Hut is located within the boreal forest zone. It is a great place for mountain birds. *Photo by Dennis Welsh.*

Pierce, but we will save that for the descent. For Mizpah Spring Hut, take Mizpah Cutoff. This steadily ascends about 300 feet, eventually leveling out and passing across boggy sections on logs. Mizpah Cutoff joins Webster Cliff Trail 0.1 mile from the hut.

Completed in 1964, Mizpah Spring Hut was the last of the backcountry AMC huts to be constructed. It made for a convenient overnight stop for people hiking between Zealand Falls Hut and Lakes of the Clouds Hut near Mount Washington. Several tent platforms are nearby. While at the hut, you can use the restrooms, get a snack or a cup of cocoa, eat your lunch, and chat with staff and volunteers. In June, the chorus of bird songs emanating from the woods around the huts is wonderful. The singers include Swainson's thrushes, winter wrens, white-throated sparrows, dark-eyed juncos, and various warblers.

For the summit of Mount Pierce, continue ascending on Webster Cliff Trail, which is part of the Appalachian Trail, so it is blazed in white. The trail ascends steeply from the hut, and hikers are assisted at several points by ladders. After passing an open ledge with excellent views south and west, descend slightly into a col. As the vegetation becomes scrubbier, listen for the song of the Bicknell's thrush, an uncommon species whose existence high up in these mountains is threatened by the warming climate. This streaked brown bird sounds a bit like a harpsichord playing a series of notes all at one pitch. A few lovely patches of painted trillium (illustrated here) grow off the trail.

Webster Cliff Trail reaches the open summit of Mount Pierce, 0.8 mile and a 500-foot elevation gain from the hut (total of 3.4 miles from the trailhead). Formerly known as Mount Clinton, after De Witt Clinton, the governor of New York who was responsible for the Erie Canal, Mount Pierce was renamed in 1913 to honor Franklin Pierce, the only president to have hailed from New Hampshire. Enjoy breathtaking views of nearly 360 degrees, including the southern Presidential Range up to Mount Washington toward the northeast and many peaks in other directions. The summit also provides a sample of the White Mountains' rare alpine (above timberline) habitat. Note the specially adapted alpine cushion plants diapensia and alpine azalea, which bloom in early June, and low shrubs such as bog bilberry, Labrador tea, and black crowberry. (See "The Alpine Zone of the White Mountains" on page 256 for more on the alpine zone.)

From the summit of Mount Pierce, continue 0.1 mile on Webster Cliff Trail to its terminus at Crawford Path. Turn left and descend on Crawford Path. This section is a bit eroded and can be wet after heavy rains, but overall the footing is good. Crawford Path reaches Mizpah Cutoff at 4.7 miles (1.2 miles from Webster Cliff Trail). Retrace your steps down Crawford Path to Crawford Cutoff (6.2 miles) and the trailhead (6.6 miles).

OTHER ACTIVITIES

If you have two cars and extra time, you could combine this hike with the Mount Eisenhower hike (Trip 40). This should only be attempted if the weather is favorable, as much of the distance between Mounts Pierce and Eisenhower is above treeline. Leave the second car at the Edmands Path trailhead, which is along Mount Clinton Road 2.0 miles east of the Crawford Path trailhead. At the summit of Mount Pierce, instead of descending on Crawford Path, continue along Crawford Path to the northeast for 1.2 miles until you reach the Mount Eisenhower loop. After reaching the summit of Mount Eisenhower (0.3 mile), continue on the loop for another 0.3 mile to Edmands Path and descend on it for 3.0 miles to Mount Clinton Road.

DID YOU KNOW?

According to John T. B. Mudge in *The White Mountains: Names, Places, and Legends*, the name Mizpah is taken from a Hebrew word meaning "watchtower." It refers to a story in Genesis in which Jacob and Laban (Jacob's father-in-law) build a tower of stones to commemorate an agreement on the terms of the separation of their households.

MORE INFORMATION

Parking in the Mount Clinton Road lot requires a user fee of $5 per day.

THE BIRDS OF MIZPAH SPRING HUT

Mizpah Spring Hut is one of the best locations in the White Mountains to hear and see birds of the boreal forest. Many migratory birds in North America breed in the boreal forest, a vast northern belt of spruce-and-fir-dominated forest across the northern latitudes of the continent. The majority of this habitat is in central Canada and Alaska, so most people see these birds only when they are migrating north from their winter homes in Central and South America. The high elevations of the Northeast (as well as the Rocky Mountains) are their southern breeding outposts. You can pick up a bird list at the hut.

If you are at Mizpah Spring Hut during June through mid-July, you will be treated to an enchanting avian chorus, particularly early in the morning or late in the afternoon. The thrushes are arguably the top musicians. The song of the Swainson's thrush is flutelike, ethereal, and ascending in pitch, very appropriate for a bird of high elevations. The Bicknell's thrush and the veery both sound like harpsichords, giving a rolling series of notes, the former singing more or less at one pitch and the latter modulating and typically ending with descending notes. Another amazing songster is the winter wren. This tiny bird is rarely seen, but it gives a loud, boisterous, extended series of musical notes that include a variety of different phrases. You'll wonder how such a small creature has so much breath.

White-throated sparrows give several clear, sweet whistles that have been described in words as *See old Sam Peabody, Peabody, Peabody.* A musical trill at one pitch, given from the top of a spruce or fir, is likely to be a dark-eyed junco. This sparrow-sized gray bird flashes white outer tail feathers when it flies. The purple finch, the state bird of New Hampshire, gives a lively warble. The red-breasted nuthatch has a blue-gray back, orange belly, and a dark line through its eyes. This prim-looking little bird walks headfirst down the trunks of trees, searching the bark for insects. Its nasal call sounds like a child's toy trumpet. Look and listen also for several species of wood warblers that breed around Mizpah Spring Hut. These include yellow-rumped, magnolia, and blackpoll warblers. Warblers are noted for their bold color patterns (often shades of yellow, with black and white streaks) and their energetic behavior as they chase their insect prey.

If you are fortunate, you could catch a glimpse of a spruce grouse, a chickenlike bird that inhabits the spruce-fir forest.

Ascend above treeline to the alpine tundra on a path created by one of the White Mountains' master trail builders. The summit of Mount Eisenhower provides spectacular views in all directions and an area of rare alpine vegetation.

Features ❄ 🏃 ◐ ❋

Location Crawford's Purchase, NH

Rating Strenuous

Distance 6.6 miles round trip

Elevation Gain 2,750 feet

Estimated Time 6 hours

Maps *AMC White Mountain National Forest Map & Guide*, 4th ed., G8 and Mount Washington inset; AMC *White Mountain Guide*, 31st ed. Map 1 Presidential Range, G8; USGS Topo: Crawford Notch at trailhead; Stairs Mountain at summit

GPS Coordinates 44° 14.94' N, 71° 23.47' W

Contact White Mountain National Forest: fs.usda.gov/whitemountain, 603-536-6100

⚠ **CAUTION!** This outing takes you above treeline, where the weather can be quite harsh. It will almost always be colder and windier than at lower elevations, and the open expanse of alpine tundra leaves you exposed to snow (possible even in summer), rain, harsh winds, and lightning. Be prepared with extra warm clothes and rain gear, and be ready to turn back if the weather changes.

DIRECTIONS

The trailhead for Edmands Path is off Mount Clinton Road, which runs from US 302 near the Highland Center at Crawford Notch to Base Station Road for the Mount Washington Cog Railway. Mount Clinton Road is closed in winter.

From the Jackson–North Conway area, follow US 302 west at Glen where it splits from NH 16. US 302 passes through Bartlett and then heads north through Crawford Notch. At the top of the notch, roughly 20 miles from the junction of NH 16 and US 302, the road goes through the narrow pass between two cliffs. Mount Clinton Road is a short (about 0.2 mile) distance off US 302 just beyond the Highland Center. Follow this road for 2.0 miles to the trailhead on the right.

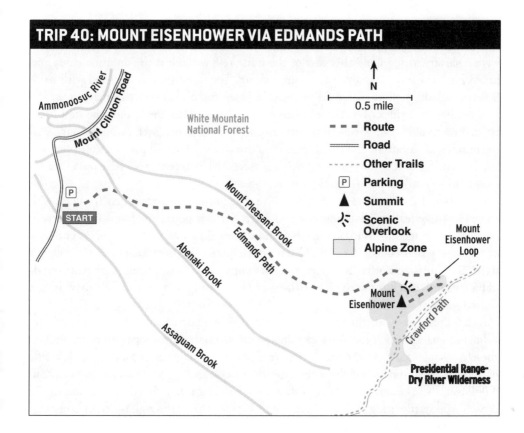

TRIP 40: MOUNT EISENHOWER VIA EDMANDS PATH

From Franconia Notch and the community of Twin Mountain, Mount Clinton Road is about 8 miles south of the junction of US 3 and US 302 in Twin Mountain. Turn left off US 302 and take Mount Clinton Road for 2.0 miles.

TRAIL DESCRIPTION

J. Rayner Edmands was one of the White Mountains' premier trail builders, active in the early part of the twentieth century. Edmands Path up Mount Eisenhower is arguably his tour de force. His style of trail-building, as outlined in Laura and Guy Waterman's *Forest and Crag: A History of Hiking, Trail Blazing, and Adventure in the Northeast Mountains* (SUNY Press, 2019), was to make the trail as easy on the hiker as possible, with well-graded pitches, carefully placed stones, and lots of switchbacks. As you might expect, constructing these types of trails is more labor-intensive than building trails that take the shortest route to a summit. As such, Edmands Path, which Edmands reconstructed from an existing route, is one of the gentlest trails to a 4,000-footer in the White Mountains. But it's no walk in the park. It ascends more than 2,700 feet, and the upper section is now rocky due to erosion. Edmands could not have anticipated how many hiking boots would eventually walk his trail. In addition, the part above treeline is exposed to the full brunt of northwest winds, so it can be uncomfortable or even dangerous if bad weather comes in from the northwest.

Edmands Path begins in a northern hardwood forest at an almost level grade and crosses bridges over two small streams. Some "sinkholes" in the forest suggest that perhaps there were once structures along this part of the trail. Yellow birch is the dominant tree and hobblebush the most abundant understory shrub. The forest floor is carpeted with wildflowers, including goldthread, wild sarsaparilla, blue-bead lily, and Canada mayflower. The trail reaches the bridge over Abenaki Brook in 0.4 mile. After the bridge, the trail turns right, onto an old logging road, and starts ascending at a steeper pitch through an increasing number of balsam fir and red spruce. (You can thank Edmands and later trail-maintenance crews for all the stone steps to help your ascent. More recent crews have put in cut-up stumps to help hikers pass through some wet areas.)

After about 1.2 miles, pass an open area with sphagnum moss and sedges. The plant with three cloverlike leaflets is mountain wood sorrel. At this point, the forest has otherwise completely changed to boreal (spruce-fir), and there is little understory vegetation because of the dense growth of conifer trees. Listen for the incredibly lively, long tune of the winter wren. Red-breasted nuthatches gives a much simpler nasal *yank, yank, yank* that sounds like a toy horn. Black-throated blue warblers and black-throated green warblers have buzzy, slurred songs.

At 2.0 miles, pass a distinctive pile of stones. This is a particularly good area to admire Edmands's handiwork. Note the rock cribbing built into the downslope part of the trail on the left to support it on either side of the stone pile. As you continue upward, the right side of the trail has abundant bunchberries, mountain wood sorrel, and snowberries. At close to 4,000 feet, these bloom much later in the season here than they do at lower elevations. To the left, you start getting glimpses of surrounding mountains through the trees, a preview of the wonderful vistas you will experience above treeline.

At 2.5 miles, reach a stream crossing lined by green alder shrubs. This crossing can be difficult if conditions are icy. Notice the large, cabbage-like leaves of false hellebore (Indian poke) here. The trail follows the streambed for a short distance and then continues its gradual ascent. The views become more and more frequent and the grade more level as you near treeline (reached at 2.8 miles as you cross a rocky talus slope). One of the first alpine plants to look for as you break out above treeline is bog bilberry, a type of blueberry with round bluish green leaves.

Edmands Path ends at Mount Eisenhower Loop at 2.9 miles at the crest of the southern Presidential Range. Turn right onto this loop trail for the final 0.4 mile (300 feet) to the summit. You immediately pass a boggy area (once known as Red Pond) full of cotton grass (actually a type of sedge), and then follow the trail, marked with cairns, to the top of the mountain.

If you are fortunate to be there on a clear day, you will have a 360-degree view and see many White Mountain peaks. The most immediate sight to the northeast is Mount Franklin; Mounts Washington and Jefferson loom large beyond it. To the south are Mounts Pierce and Jackson. The view west encompasses the Willey and Twin ranges as well as Mount Carrigain.

The broad summit is a wonderful garden of alpine wildflowers. The display changes as the season progresses. In early to mid-June, white blossoms of diapensias are abundant.

After several hours of hiking on the well-graded Edmands Path, you break out into the open with sweeping views of Mount Washington and other peaks of the Presidential Range.

This is an alpine cushion plant with small dark green leaves in a tight cluster. In midsummer, the little white blossoms of mountain sandwort line the trail in profusion, and the bright yellow flower clusters of alpine goldenrod will surely catch your eye. Another common white flower is three-toothed cinquefoil, a plant identified by its three leaflets, each with three "teeth" along their outer edges. Bearberry willow, a true willow that never grows more than a few inches above the ground, is also common here. (For more information on the alpine zone, see Trip 49 and "The Alpine Zone of the White Mountains," page 256.)

Retrace your steps to return to the trailhead. The terrain's rockiness will be more noticeable on your descent, so you should factor that in to your timing.

OTHER ACTIVITIES

For a longer trip, you could combine this hike with a descent via Mount Pierce. This is most conveniently done by having two cars, one at the Edmands Path trailhead and a second at the Crawford Path trailhead (also on Mount Clinton Road). It should be attempted only in good weather because of the extensive amount of hiking above treeline. Going over Mount Pierce adds an additional 1.5 miles to this trip. If you do not have two cars, you will need to walk 2.0 additional miles along Mount Clinton Road to get from the Crawford Path trailhead back to the Edmands Path trailhead.

For this trip, after hiking up Mount Eisenhower via Edmands Path and Mount Eisenhower Loop, continue on Mount Eisenhower Loop in a southerly direction for another 0.4 miles (350-foot descent) to Crawford Path. Head southwest on Crawford Path toward Mount Pierce for 1.2 miles. This route goes only within 0.1 mile of the summit of Mount Pierce, so you will need to take a short detour onto Webster Cliff Trail to reach the actual summit. Then retrace your steps back to Crawford Path and descend for 3.1 miles, being sure to turn right onto Crawford Connector near the bottom to get to the car at the Crawford Path trailhead. The descent of Mount Pierce via Crawford Path is described in Trip 39.

MORE INFORMATION

Parking is free in the Mount Clinton lot.

If you are coming from the Franconia Notch area, you can find hotels, restaurants, and gas stations in the communities of Bretton Woods and Twin Mountain on your way to the trailhead. If you are coming from the south, the Macomber Family Information Center at Crawford Depot has trail information, restrooms, and some basic hiking supplies. The Highland Center at Crawford Notch (outdoors.org/destinations) provides lodging and meals for registered guests, a hostel, and public programs.

The Pinkham Notch/Gorham region includes the Presidential Range, which boasts the loftiest peaks of the White Mountains. At 6,288 feet, Mount Washington is the highest mountain in the Northeast, and five other summits in the range surpass 5,000 feet. In addition to elevation, the Presidential Range is also noted for its vast bowl-shaped ravines. The Carter Range, across Pinkham Notch from the Presidential Range to the east, rises above 4,500 feet. The entire region is a magnet for day-hikers and backpackers attracted by the high elevation, rugged scenery, and broad expanse of alpine terrain with extensive vistas and rare ecological communities.

Numerous trails to ponds, waterfalls, and viewpoints are easy day hikes. These are centered on AMC's Pinkham Notch Visitor Center (PNVC) and the town of Gorham. NH 16 passes right through Pinkham Notch between Jackson and Gorham and provides access to many of the trails described here. Other trails are reached from US 2 west of Gorham.

JOE DODGE LODGE AND PINKHAM NOTCH VISITOR CENTER

PNVC is the hub of hiking activities and natural history education in the White Mountains. The Trading Post houses an information center, a store, and a dining room. Joe Dodge Lodge offers private rooms, bunkrooms, a library, and meeting rooms. Breakfast and dinner are served to overnight guests and are available to other visitors (advance notification necessary). Lunch is available for purchase. In the evenings, and sometimes during the day, there are naturalist lectures and other programs. PNVC is an excellent place to get current information on trails and the weather and to buy U.S. Forest Service parking passes, hiking guides, nature books, T-shirts, trail snacks, and other supplies. The visitor center also has restrooms and showers open to the public.

While at PNVC, do not miss the scale model of the Presidential Range, along with displays on mountain geology and ecology, to get a real perspective of the area.

PNVC is the starting point for many hikes in this book: Lost Pond (Trip 41), Square Ledge (Trip 42), Lila's Ledge (Trip 43), Low's Bald Spot (Trip 46), and Tuckerman Ravine

Trail (Trip 49). In addition to the hiking trails described in this section, PNVC is the jumping-off point for a network of cross-country ski trails for a variety of skill levels. Check at PNVC for a map. For reservations for overnight lodging at PNVC and other information, visit outdoors.org/destinations or call 603-466-2721.

SUPPLIES AND LOGISTICS

In addition to PNVC, the Wildcat Mountain Ski Area, about 1 mile north, has all the amenities you might expect in a ski resort: a restaurant, a snack bar, restrooms, coffee machines, and a gift shop. It is open all year; skiwildcat.com; 603-466-3326. If you are coming from the north on NH 16, Gorham has restaurants, inns, motels, stores, and gas stations. From the south, Jackson is the nearest town for supplies.

The Androscoggin Ranger Station of the U.S. Forest Service is on NH 16 just south of US 2 in Gorham. Stop in to ask for information, pick up trail pamphlets, or use the restrooms; fs.usda.gov/detail/whitemountain/about-forest/offices; 603-466-2713.

PUBLIC TRANSPORTATION

Concord Coach Lines operates daily bus service from Boston's Logan Airport and South Station to Pinkham Notch. Check concordcoachlines.com for schedules. Pinkham Notch Visitor Center is the terminal for the AMC Hiker Shuttle, which also stops at the Appalachia and Nineteen Mile Brook parking areas; outdoors.org/shuttle; 603-466-2727.

NEARBY CAMPING

The U.S. Forest Service's Dolly Copp Campground is at the junction of NH 16 and Pinkham B (Dolly Copp) Road between Gorham and Pinkham Notch. With 176 campsites, Dolly Copp is the largest public campground in the White Mountains; reservations can be made online at recreation.gov or by calling 877-444-6777. Large groups can camp at Barnes Field Group Area adjacent to Dolly Copp Campground.

41 LOST POND

This short hike follows Ellis River through a rich forest and ends up at Lost Pond, where you may catch a glimpse of beavers. Large rocks at the pond provide excellent perches for enjoying the view across to Huntington Ravine and Mount Washington.

Features 🚶 🐕 💧 📍 🎿 🔦 ⛺ 🚌

Location Pinkham's Grant, NH

Rating Easy

Distance 1.0 mile round trip to the pond; 1.8 miles round trip for the entire trail

Elevation Gain Minimal

Estimated Time 1–2 hours

Maps *AMC White Mountain National Forest Map & Guide*, 4th ed., F9–10 and Mount Washington inset; AMC *White Mountain Guide*, 31st ed. Map 1 Presidential Range, F10; USGS Topo: Mount Washington

GPS coordinates 44° 15.44′ N, 71° 15.17′ W (Pinkham Notch Visitor Center)

Contact White Mountain National Forest: fs.usda.gov/whitemountain, 603-536-6100; Appalachian Mountain Club PNVC: outdoors.org/destinations/massachusetts-and-new-hampshire/joe-dodge-lodge, 603-466-2721

DIRECTIONS

The trailhead for Lost Pond Trail is across NH 16 from AMC's Pinkham Notch Visitor Center (PNVC). To get to PNVC from the south, follow NH 16 north through North Conway, Glen, and Jackson. PNVC is on the left, about 10 miles north of Jackson and 0.7 mile past the turnoff to Glen Ellis Falls.

To get to PNVC from the north, pick up NH 16 in Gorham and go about 10 miles south. The visitor center is on the right, about 1 mile past the Wildcat Mountain Ski Area. Park at the large parking lot and walk across NH 16 to the trailhead.

TRAIL DESCRIPTION

Lost Pond Trail—part of the Appalachian Trail, and therefore blazed white—begins in a swampy area across from PNVC and crosses Ellis River on a wooden bridge. You may notice two "speckly" shrubs here. Speckled alder is named for its spotted bark, which makes the shrub look like it has chicken pox. The leaves of sweetgale, which grows right next to the wooden bridge, are covered with tiny yellow dots. Crush a sweetgale leaf in your

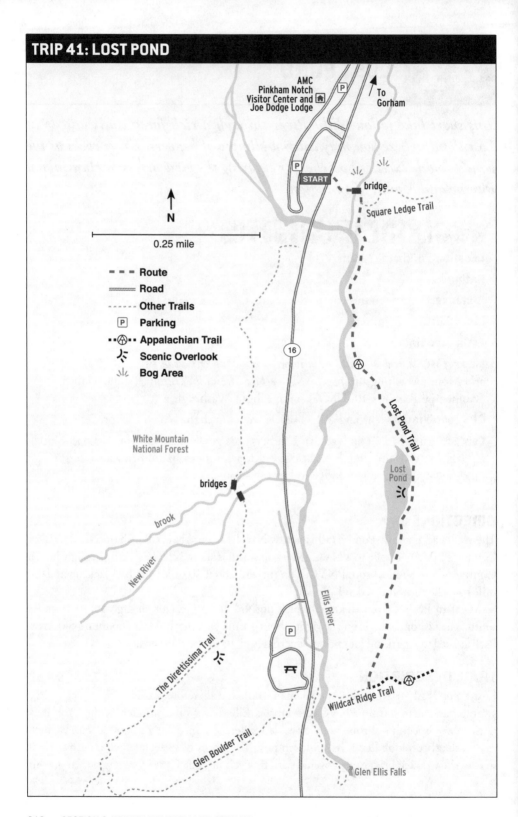

AMC
Pinkham Notch
Visitor Center and
Joe Dodge Lodge

To
Gorham

START

bridge

Square Ledge Trail

N

0.25 mile

- - - Route
——— Road
· · · · · Other Trails
P Parking
·•·Ⓐ·•· Appalachian Trail
⛸ Scenic Overlook
☀ Bog Area

16

Lost Pond Trail

White Mountain
National Forest

Lost
Pond

bridges

brook

New River

Ellis River

The Direttissima Trail

Wildcat Ridge Trail

Glen Boulder Trail

Glen Ellis Falls

fingers to get a strong, sweet scent that will remind you of bayberry. White turtlehead flowers bloom in the swamp in August.

From the wooden bridge, a beaver dam is obvious to your left. The dam is composed of mud and tree branches stripped of bark. The beavers eat the inner bark and then use the rest of the branches as lumber for the dam. They build dams to create ponds so they can swim to their supper and have a place for their lodges, safe from predators. By flooding the surrounding woodland, they can enter their lodges underwater and swim to their major foods, the nutritious inner bark of trees, grasses, and other vegetation. (See "Beavers" on page 188 for more information on these large rodents.)

Swallows are small, graceful birds you are likely to see zooming over the swamp during warm weather. Barn swallows have distinctive long, forked tails, bluish black backs, reddish throats, and buff-colored bellies. As their name implies, they sometimes nest in barns and under the eaves of buildings (such as the maintenance building at PNVC). Tree swallows also have blue-black backs but differ from barn swallows in having notched tails and being completely white underneath. They nest in tree holes and often use nest boxes. Both species of these aerial acrobats catch insects while in flight.

The trail turns right after the bridge. Square Ledge Trail (Trip 42) immediately departs left. Lost Pond Trail continues along the east side of Ellis River, initially through a forest of balsam fir and birch and eventually through northern hardwoods with a hobblebush understory. The wide trail to the pond has little ups and downs and a few rocks, but nothing major.

The flow of Ellis River is greatly increased by the addition of Cutler River flowing down from Tuckerman Ravine. Note the clarity of the water in a beautiful, deep pool in the river as you walk by. If you stand quietly by this pool for a minute or two, you may catch a glimpse of brook trout. Water striders may also be present.

In June, look for blooms of Canada mayflower, blue-bead lily, false Solomon's seal, painted trillium, and pink lady's slippers. In damp spots along the trail, smooth white violets and inflated sedges abound. Normally sedges are fairly nondescript, but inflated sedge has amusing, inflated bladders that contain its seeds.

In midsummer, mountain wood sorrel (illustrated here) blooms in profusion in this area. The three leaves of this small plant will remind you of clover, but it is not related. Other midsummer bloomers are goldenrod (several species) and tall meadow rue.

After about 0.3 mile, the trail angles away from Ellis River and crosses a wooden bridge over a tributary. You reach Lost Pond in 0.5 mile. The terrain becomes rockier as you traverse the east shore of the pond. You will pass one particularly large, flat rock that is an ideal platform for sitting quietly and enjoying the peaceful scenery, perhaps with a picnic lunch. The view of Mount Washington is impressive—Huntington Ravine stands out, and you can also see Boott Spur, the Lion Head, and the Gulf of Slides from various vantage points. Lost Pond is not far from NH 16 as the crow flies, yet it feels remote and delightfully lost.

Several more beaver lodges are at the pond. You may even see the beavers themselves cavorting about if you are there around dusk. Look for another dam at the outlet of the pond.

A peaceful winter day at Lost Pond. *Photo by Jerry Monkman.*

Two common plants in the water are waterlilies and wild celery. The leaves of waterlilies float on the surface and provide the underwater parts of the plant with air through a system of gas channels. Wild celery, with grassy, strap-like leaves, is a favorite food of ducks.

As you make your way around Lost Pond, you may observe water stains on the rocks and on tree trunks at the shore. These indicate how high the water levels rose during the past spring. Look for bunchberry (pictured here), a small relative of dogwood that produces creamy white flowers—similar to dogwood blossoms—in the latter part of June and clusters of red berries during summer. Watch for a tree that seemingly grows right out of a rock, its trunk and roots forming a little cave. Note also a dead tree laced with woodpecker holes. Holes that woodpeckers excavate in trees serve as homes not only for woodpeckers but for many other birds and small mammals, hence they are known as "wildlife trees."

Bunchberries carpet the forest floor of many White Mountain trails. Bunchberry is actually a type of dogwood.

The section of Lost Pond Trail between the south end of the pond and Wildcat Ridge Trail passes through a riot of boulders. These rocks were deposited by an avalanche off Wildcat Mountain many years ago. Skiers in winter need a fair accumulation of snow to complete this section.

Lost Pond Trail ends at Wildcat Ridge Trail (0.9 mile). From here you can retrace your steps or, if you are feeling adventurous, turn right onto Wildcat Ridge Trail and cross Ellis River to reach NH 16. The river has no bridge, so you must step carefully from rock to rock, a potentially precarious undertaking at high water. If the river is passable, you can then walk back to the trailhead along NH 16 or walk to Glen Ellis Falls, a beautiful cascade only 0.3-mile from NH 16.

DID YOU KNOW?
The swamp you cross at the beginning of this trail is at the height-of-land of Pinkham Notch. Water drains from this swamp north to Peabody River and south to Ellis River.

OTHER ACTIVITIES
Combine the hike with a visit to PNVC or extend the hike to Glen Ellis Falls and then return via Glen Boulder and Direttissima trails. Lost Pond Trail can also be combined with Square Ledge Trail (Trip 42), which takes you steeply (400 feet over 0.6 mile) to a great vista of PNVC and Mount Washington. Lost Pond Trail is suitable for skiing with sufficient snow, and there are several other ski trails in the Pinkham Notch area. Check the information desk at PNVC for more ideas for skiing and hiking opportunities.

MORE INFORMATION
Parking is free at the large lot at PNVC. However, the lot can become filled on popular weekends. The hike is within the White Mountain National Forest. PNVC has snacks, trail information, hiking supplies, and restrooms.

42 SQUARE LEDGE

This short trail to an overlook has a fantastic view of Pinkham Notch and Mount Washington. It could be an exciting first experience for young children on a steep trail.

Features

Location Pinkham's Grant, NH

Rating Moderate

Distance 1.2 miles round trip

Elevation Gain 400 feet

Estimated Time 1–2 hours

Maps *AMC White Mountain National Forest Map & Guide*, 4th ed., F10 and Mount Washington inset; AMC *White Mountain Guide*, 31st ed. Map 1 Presidential Range, F9; USGS Topo: Mount Washington

GPS coordinates 44° 15.44′ N, 71° 15.17′ W (Pinkham Notch Visitor Center)

Contact White Mountain National Forest: fs.usda.gov/whitemountain, 603-536-6100; Appalachian Mountain Club PNVC: outdoors.org/destinations/massachusetts -and-new-hampshire/joe-dodge-lodge, 603-466-2721

 CAUTION! Square Ledge has a steep dropoff; be careful when on the ledge itself. This trail is not recommended in icy or wet conditions.

DIRECTIONS

Square Ledge Trail begins directly across the road from Pinkham Notch Visitor Center (PNVC), at the same trailhead as Lost Pond Trail. (See Trip 41 for directions and parking information.)

TRAIL DESCRIPTION

Square Ledge Trail runs together with Lost Pond Trail for a short distance from NH 16 and crosses a wooden bridge over Ellis River, where there is an interesting beaver wetland (see Trip 41). The two trails make a sharp right turn, after which Square Ledge Trail makes an immediate left uphill, and Lost Pond Trail continues along the river.

The trail is initially wide, with a gradual uphill. Stop at Ladies Lookout (a short spur path to the left) at 0.1 mile for a view of Pinkham Notch. At the turnoff to Ladies Lookout, there is a particularly lush growth of striped maples. In the White Mountains, these small trees

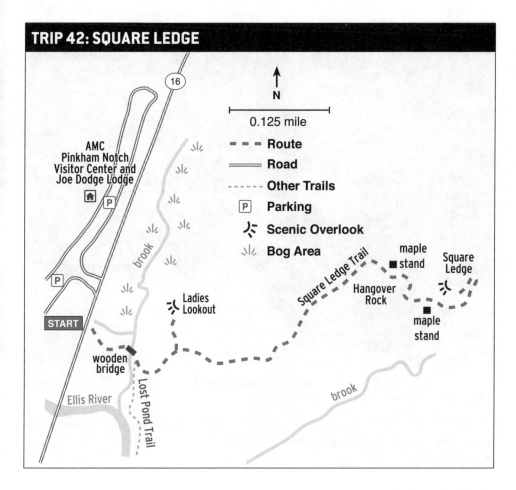

generally remain in the understory. Notice the bright green-and-white-striped bark on the branches and young trunks and the extremely large three-lobed leaves (the latter giving rise to the nickname "goosefoot maple"). Trees and shrubs growing in the shade of the understory often have very large leaves to catch the small amount of light that filters down through the canopy. Striped maple is also called moosewood because it is a favorite food of moose.

The next landmark is Hangover Rock. This large boulder projects over the trail, making a cozy shelter when it rains. If you are looking for an excuse to take a breather, slow down to enjoy the grove of paper birches nearby.

Shining club moss is abundant on the forest floor along Square Ledge Trail. This low-growing dark green plant's upright stems covered with small leaves resemble bottle brushes.

After Hangover Rock, the trail steepens and has a short section with loose rocks that may make some children (and even adults) a little uncomfortable. At 0.6 mile, it reaches Square Ledge. Use caution near the dropoff on Square Ledge.

The view of the steep headwall of Huntington Ravine is particularly dramatic from Square Ledge. A mountain glacier carved out the ravine during the last Ice Age. It is named for J. S. Huntington, a researcher who was one of the first people to spend a winter on the summit of Mount Washington (1870–1871).

A short, steep walk from Pinkham Notch Visitor Center leads you to the fantastic view of Mount Washington from Square Ledge. *Photo by Dennis Welsh.*

Square Ledge itself is composed of schist, the same metamorphic rock that underlies much of the Presidential Range. Look for red spruce, balsam fir, and heart-leaved birch around the ledge.

DID YOU KNOW?

The schist that forms Square Ledge dates back approximately 400 million years and was formed when muds beneath an ancient sea were squeezed together between two colliding continents. Schists appear laminated (in layers) and can sometimes be split apart.

OTHER ACTIVITIES

Square Ledge Trail can be combined with Lost Pond Trail (Trip 41) for a more extensive outing. In addition, there is a network of relatively easy day hikes around PNVC, such as Crystal Cascade and Lila's Ledge and Brad's Bluff (Trip 43). Check the information desk at PNVC or AMC's *White Mountain Guide* for more ideas.

Pinkham Notch has several ski trails, including Square Ledge Loop Ski Trail. This crosses the hiking trail near Ladies Lookout.

MORE INFORMATION

Parking is free at the large lot at PNVC. However, the lot can become filled on popular weekends. The hike is within the White Mountain National Forest. PNVC has snacks, trail information, hiking supplies, and restrooms.

43 LILA'S LEDGE AND BRAD'S BLUFF

These two scenic overlooks are a relatively short walk from AMC's Pinkham Notch Visitor Center. The hike makes use of three trails: Crew Cut, Liebeskind's Loop, and George's Gorge. In addition to the scenery, it features some huge rock outcroppings and boulders, a rich forest with wildflowers, and several stream crossings.

Features 🏕️🎿🚶🐕💧🔍🌿⛺🚌

Location Pinkham's Grant, NH

Rating Moderate

Distance 2.8 miles round trip

Elevation Gain 650 feet

Estimated Time 2–3 hours

Maps *AMC White Mountain National Forest Map & Guide*, 4th ed., F9–10 and Mount Washington inset; AMC *White Mountain Guide*, 31st ed. Map 1 Presidential Range, F9–10; USGS Topo: Mount Washington

GPS Coordinates 44° 15.44′ N, 71° 15.17′ W (Pinkham Notch Visitor Center)

Contact White Mountain National Forest: fs.usda.gov/whitemountain, 603-536-6100; Appalachian Mountain Club PNVC: outdoors.org/destinations/massachusetts -and-new-hampshire/joe-dodge-lodge, 603-466-2721

DIRECTIONS

The hike begins at AMC's Pinkham Notch Visitor Center (PNVC) off NH 16. (See Trip 41 for directions and parking information.) Walk past the outdoor water fountain and scale (for backpackers and kids to weigh their loads). The trail called Old Jackson Road branches off from Tuckerman Ravine Trail directly behind PNVC. As described in the trail description below, follow Old Jackson Road for 0.4 mile to begin the loop hike at Crew Cut Trail.

TRAIL DESCRIPTION

The first 0.4 mile of this hike follows Old Jackson Road. You will pass Blanchard Ski Trail at 0.2 mile. Just after crossing a bridge (0.4 mile), take Crew Cut Trail to the right. The distances described below are from this point. This blue-blazed trail starts out level with a good assortment of woodland plants: blue-bead lily, painted trillium, pink lady's slipper, starflower, lance-leaved twisted-stalk, and shining club moss. Eastern hemlock, sugar

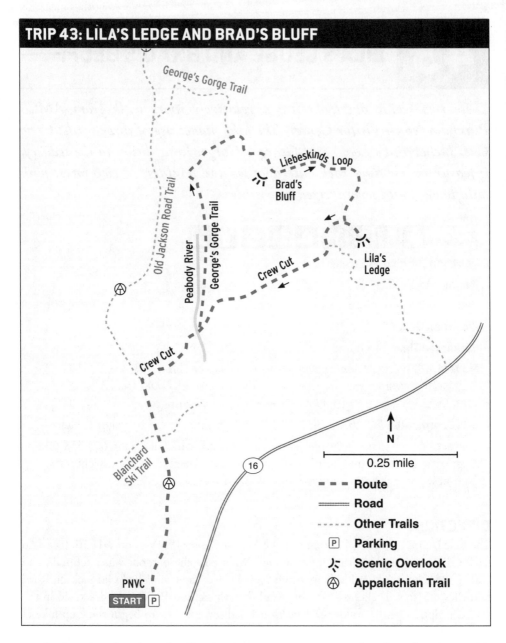

maple, American beech, and yellow birch are common trees at these low elevations, with hobblebush and striped maple forming the shrub layer.

Cross a stream—actually Peabody River—and at 0.2 mile past Old Jackson Road reach the junction with George's Gorge Trail. Turn left on George's Gorge Trail, also blazed in blue. The trail follows the river gradually uphill. It crosses the river twice and then turns away from the water and becomes rather steep. The trail reaches a junction with yellow-blazed Liebeskind's Loop at 0.7 mile from Old Jackson Road (500-foot elevation gain).

Brad's Bluff provides a great view south over Pinkham Notch.

After stopping to catch your breath from the ascent, turn right onto Liebeskind's Loop. This trail first passes through a forest of younger trees—note the thin trunks. All along the route, bold rock outcroppings studded with relatively large crystals of mica and quartz are sure to catch your eye. In several places the trail descends to boggy areas traversed by wooden planks (abundant cinnamon ferns and some creeping snowberry) and then rises up to the spruce-fir forest. Arrive at Brad's Bluff at 0.9 mile. It is a great place to have lunch. The view encompasses Wildcat Mountain and the pond across from PNVC to the east and the eastern flank of Mount Washington through the trees to the west. On a clear day, you can even see Mount Chocorua in the distance.

Liebeskind's Loop is a pleasant boreal forest walk with glimpses of the Carter Range through the trees. On one rocky cliff you can see laminated layers of rocks. These are schists that have been folded due to metamorphic processes hundreds of millions of years ago, much like rocks at Pine Mountain (see Trip 45). At 1.1 miles a spur path leading to Lila's Ledge goes off to the left. Follow that for 0.1 mile to another vista of Pinkham Notch, Wildcat Mountain, and the side of Mount Washington. A lower part of the ledge has the most open view but requires careful scrambling and should be avoided in wet or icy conditions.

After enjoying the scenery, return to Liebeskind's Loop and continue left. You will pass a very large rock outcropping that resembles the head of a tyrannosaur with its mouth open. Liebeskind Loop ends back at Crew Cut Trail at 1.3 miles.

Turn right on Crew Cut Trail to complete the loop. Follow a series of small ascents and descents, some of which are in old streambeds and aided by stone steps. After crossing multiple rivulets, pass the junction with George's Gorge Trail at 1.6 miles and then arrive back at Old Jackson Road at 1.8 mile. Turn left to return to PNVC.

DID YOU KNOW?

The names of trails and viewpoints in this hike honor AMC staff and members long associated with the Pinkham Notch area. Brad Swan was hut counselor in the early 1960s, and Lila Swan was his wife. Steve Liebeskind was an AMC member who helped build the loop that bears his name. George's Gorge was named for George Hamilton, manager of the AMC hut system in the 1960s.

OTHER ACTIVITIES

Old Jackson Road is also the start of the hike to Low's Bald Spot (Trip 46), if you are interested in a longer outing, and it is an intermediate-level ski trail as well.

MORE INFORMATION

Parking is free at PNVC although the lot can become full on popular weekends.

You can find hiking supplies, maps, snacks, restrooms, and trail information at PNVC; outdoors.org/destinations/massachusetts-and-new-hampshire/joe-dodge-lodge; 603-466-2721.

44 WATERFALL AND VISTA LOOP IN THE NORTHERN PRESIDENTIAL RANGE

The first part of this loop hike features waterfalls and many flat rocks along a brook that invite you to have a picnic, get your feet wet, and relax while listening to the sounds of rushing water. For those looking for a longer outing, the loop continues up to stunning vistas of Mounts Madison and Adams and the northern peaks.

Features

Location Randolph, NH

Rating Fallsway–Brookbank Trail, easy loop; Inlook–Kelton trails, strenuous loop

Distance 1.5 miles, easy loop; 4.0 miles, strenuous loop

Elevation Gain 400 feet, easy loop; 1,450 feet, strenuous loop

Estimated Time 1–2 hours, easy loop; 3–4 hours, strenuous loop

Maps *AMC White Mountain National Forest Map & Guide*, 4th ed., E9; AMC *White Mountain Guide*, 31st ed. Map 1 Presidential Range, E9; USGS Topo: Mount Washington

GPS Coordinates 44° 22.24′ N, 71° 17.33′ W

Contact White Mountain National Forest: fs.usda.gov/whitemountain, 603-536-6100

DIRECTIONS

Fallsway, a trail blazed in yellow, leaves from the Appalachia parking lot off US 2, about 5.4 miles west of the point where NH 16 splits off to the north from US 2 in Gorham and about 0.8 mile west of Pinkham B (Dolly Copp) Road. If you are coming from the west near the community of Twin Mountain, the trailhead is about 7 miles east of the junction of US 2 and NH 115. The parking lot is on the south side of US 2.

The large parking lot serves as the trailhead for several trails into the northern Presidential Range. Fallsway leaves from the east side of the parking lot and is well marked with yellow blazes.

TRAIL DESCRIPTION

You can make a short waterfall loop that is also suitable for children using Fallsway and Brookbank Trail, or extend it with a more rigorous hike to scenic vistas using Fallsway and sections of Inlook, Kelton, and Howker Ridge trails, then Sylvan Way and Brookbank trails. The intersections are well marked with signs, so with a little care you should have no trouble following the recommended routes.

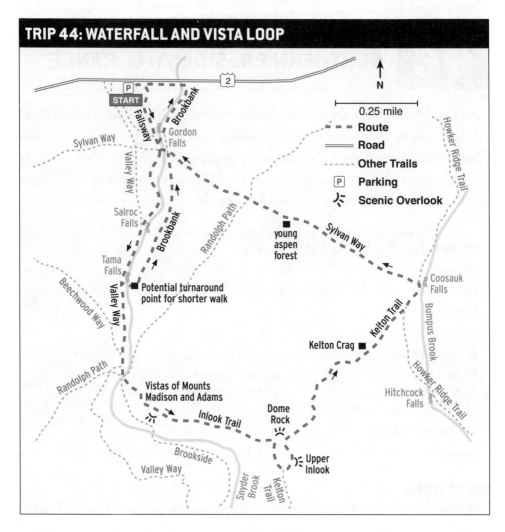

Fallsway starts through a short section of woods before turning right onto a gravel road and crossing two open areas, the first a former railroad right of way that is now the Presidential Rail Trail (a bike trail) and the second a power-line corridor. Look for birds, such as common yellowthroats and indigo buntings, and butterflies that thrive in shrubby habitats during your brief walk through these rights of way. Fallsway then enters the Snyder Brook Scenic Area of the national forest and meets up with Snyder Brook. It follows the west bank of the brook and reaches Gordon Fall, your first stop (0.2 mile). The amazing erosive power of rushing water is apparent in the channels and chutes cutting through solid rock. Mosses and ferns thrive along the sides of the waterfall.

This part of the White Mountains is laced with many short trails and trail junctions, but they are all well marked. Keep following the signs for Fallsway. The next waterfalls are Lower and Upper Salroc Falls (0.5 mile). An impressive deep plunge pool has been carved out of the streambed by Lower Salroc Falls. This pool will be over the heads of most adults, at least early in the season.

A flat rock here is ideal for a picnic if it is not underwater. Away from the water in drier, warmer habitat, northern hardwoods, particularly sugar maples and yellow birches, thrive. Hemlocks dominate along the banks of the stream because they favor the cool, shady, damp atmosphere. From just about any White Mountain outlook, dark lines of hemlock reveal the courses of streams.

Notice that the large, flat rocks below Lower Salroc Falls are crisscrossed with whitish "stripes." The stripes are dikes of pegmatite that formed when molten lava from deep within the earth flowed up into cracks in the bedrock schists and then hardened. If the lava cooled slowly, large crystals had time to form pegmatite, a combination of crystals of feldspar, quartz, and mica. A basalt dike, which appears as dark stripes, is very fine grained and occurs when lava cools rapidly near the surface of the earth.

After passing Lower and Upper Salroc Falls, Fallsway joins Valley Way for a brief stretch (for a shorter loop, you can return to the parking lot on Valley Way). At the sign for Fallsway Loop, turn left and walk 0.1 mile to Tama Fall (0.7 mile from the trailhead). Tama Fall is the tallest of the three cascades. A graceful veil of water flows down a natural granite staircase.

Here is where you need to decide how much farther you want to hike. If your group includes young children, you can make a loop by using Brookbank, which descends on the opposite side of Snyder Brook (0.7 mile back to the parking area). Cross some flat rocks in the brook (no problem except in extremely high water), turn left onto Brookbank (also marked with yellow blazes), and start your descent. Brookbank provides good access to Snyder Brook at a variety of locations and a different perspective of the same waterfalls you saw on the way up. It is an attractive, moss-laden trail with one short, rocky section that may be slick in wet weather or high water. You can also return via Valley Way, which rejoins Fallsway at Tama Fall. If Brookbank is your choice, skip the next several paragraphs and pick up the trail description two paragraphs from the end.

For those wanting a more rigorous hike, follow Fallsway past Tama Fall. It shortly ends at Valley Way, which you take uphill for another 0.2 mile. Just beyond the point where Beechwood Way comes in from the right, take the left fork onto Brookside Trail (not to be confused with Brookbank). Brookside Trail passes a huge glacial erratic in the streambed and then crosses Snyder Brook in about 0.1 mile (1.0 mile from trailhead). This crossing could be difficult in high water. The trail reaches a three-way junction with Inlook Trail in the middle and Randolph Path to your left.

Follow Inlook Trail. It starts very steeply uphill, and you will notice an increasing number of balsam fir and red spruce with the gain in elevation. At about 1.3 miles, you reach the first "inlook," an open, ledgy area providing a view across the Snyder Brook valley to the bare summits of Mounts Madison, Adams, and Quincy Adams. This is a great place to catch your breath.

Inlook Trail, marked with cairns in some places, continues uphill at a somewhat less steep pitch, alternating between boreal forest and open viewpoints. Note the Labrador tea growing along the side of the trail. This shrub has leathery leaves that are rolled along the edges. The underside of a new leaf is covered with white fuzz; in older leaves the fuzz is a rusty color.

Tama Fall, the last and highest of the waterfalls along the Fallsway. *Photo by Nancy Schalch.*

The trail reaches Dome Rock, an excellent spot for lunch, at 1.6 miles. The view to the north and east includes Pine Mountain (Trip 45), the village of Randolph, and the Crescent Range. The rock is schist, the 400-million-year-old metamorphic rock characteristic of the Presidential Range.

In another 0.1 mile, Inlook Trail ends at Kelton Trail at the Upper Inlook (1.7 miles from the trailhead). At 2,732 feet, this is the highest point of your hike. The Upper Inlook provides a fine vista west and restricted views through trees of Mounts Adams and Madison to the north.

Turn left and start your descent down Kelton Trail. It reaches the Overlook (1.9 miles), which is largely overgrown but still provides views north and east to the Crescent and Mahoosuc ranges and Pine Mountain. The trail descends more steeply now, passing a spring on your left. At 2.3 miles you reach the sign for Kelton Crag, which is just off Kelton Trail. At an elevation of just a little more than 2,000 feet, you have descended quite a bit from the Upper Inlook, and northern hardwoods are again appearing in the forest. The view from the crag is of the Androscoggin River Valley and mountains to the east. Take a moment to crush a leaf of the abundant flowering wintergreen to enjoy its pleasant minty odor. Reindeer lichen is also common on the crag.

Return to Kelton Trail, being sure not to follow a false trail on the opposite side of Kelton Crag. Kelton Trail continues at a less-steep pitch through northern hardwoods and ends at Howker Ridge Trail (2.6 miles). Turn left onto Howker Ridge Trail and follow it for 0.1 mile to the well-marked intersection with Sylvan Way coming in from the left. The sign at the intersection reads "To Gordon Fall, Coldbrook Fall, Appalachia," and you will hear the waters of Coosauk Fall through the trees. Go left onto Sylvan Way.

The next mile on Sylvan Way is a fairly level path with various wildflowers: painted trillium, false Solomon's seal, red baneberry, lance-leaved twisted-stalk, wild oats, wild sarsaparilla, and foamflower. You will see some huge white ash trees. Check out the "pimples" on the normally smooth gray bark of the American beeches. This is beech bark disease, a serious problem for these beeches that is caused by a one-two punch: a fungus infests trees that have been attacked by an insect (beech scale).

The trail passes through a logged-over area that has many young aspen saplings and then reenters the forest. Randolph Path intersects at 3.2 miles; remain on Sylvan Way. After crossing several small streams, reach Snyder Brook (3.6 miles) just above Gordon Fall, a good place to take a break. Turn right on Brookbank, which follows the east side of the brook so you do not need to cross it. You won't see a trail sign for Brookbank, but the yellow blazes are obvious. Follow Brookbank downstream.

Mosses abound in the cool woods along Brookbank and on the damp rocks around the waterfall. One of the most intriguing is named piggyback moss because new moss "plantlets" grow right out of the "backs" of older shoots. Patches of sphagnum (peat moss) also grow here.

It takes about 0.3 mile along Brookbank from Sylvan Way to reach the power-line right of way. Go through the right of way, turn left onto the Presidential Rail Trail, and cross Snyder Brook on the former railroad bridge. Turn right at Fallsway to return to the Appalachia parking area.

OTHER ACTIVITIES

You will find lots of places for wading in the cool water of Snyder Brook. The large network of trails in the northern Presidential Range provides plenty of opportunities for longer excursions to other waterfalls and beautiful scenery. Check AMC's *White Mountain Guide* for more ideas if you want to explore further.

MORE INFORMATION

The Appalachia parking area is free. After passing through a small section of private land just off the parking area, the hike enters Snyder Brook Scenic Area within White Mountain National Forest.

Gorham has restaurants, motels, and gas stations. Convenience stores are along US 2 west of the Appalachia parking area.

45

PINE MOUNTAIN FROM PINKHAM B (DOLLY COPP) ROAD

Pine Mountain is the northernmost peak of the Presidential Range. At 2,405 feet, this geological wonder is lower than its more renowned cousins, but it provides excellent views of the Presidential and Carter ranges for only moderate effort.

Features

Location Gorham, NH

Rating Moderate

Distance 3.5 miles round trip using Pine Mountain Road, Ledge Trail, and Pine Mountain Loop Trail

Elevation Gain 850 feet

Estimated Time 2–3.5 hours

Maps *AMC White Mountain National Forest Map & Guide*, 4th ed., E10; AMC *White Mountain Guide*, 31st ed. Map 1 Presidential Range, E10; USGS Topo: Carter Dome

GPS Coordinates 44° 21.23′ N, 71° 13.89′ W

Contact White Mountain National Forest: fs.usda.gov/whitemountain, 603-536-6100

DIRECTIONS

From Jackson or North Conway, head north on NH 16 past Jackson and Pinkham Notch. Turn left onto Pinkham B (Dolly Copp) Road, about 6.5 miles north of AMC's Pinkham Notch Visitor Center (PNVC). The trail to Pine Mountain is 2.4 miles from NH 16 on the right (northeast) side and opposite the trailhead for Pine Link Trail. Parking is on the left (north) side of the road. There will be signs to the Douglas Horton Center (see page 230) as well as to the trail to Pine Mountain. Pinkham B Road is not maintained for winter travel.

If you are coming from the area around the communities of Twin Mountain or Franconia, take US 3 to NH 115 in Twin Mountain and then take NH 115 about 12 miles to US 2. Turn right onto US 2 and travel about 8 miles to Pinkham B (Dolly Copp) Road, which is 0.8 mile past the Appalachia parking area. Turn right onto Pinkham B Road. The trailhead is about 3 miles on the left, opposite the trailhead for Pine Link Trail.

TRAIL DESCRIPTION

The trip described here is a loop that starts on Pine Mountain Road; it ascends to the summit of Pine Mountain via Ledge Trail and then returns via Pinkham Ledge Trail, Pine

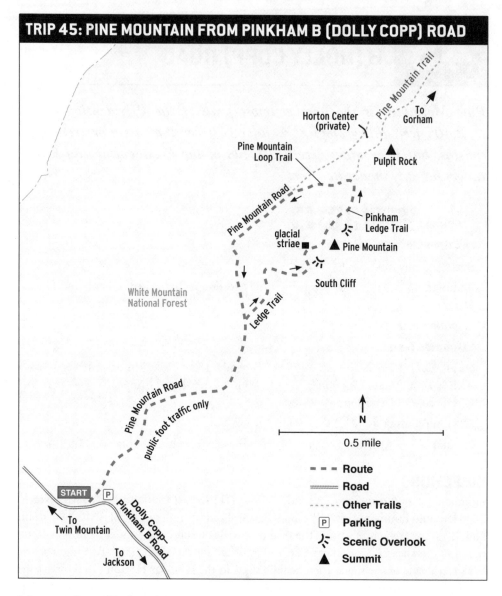

Mountain Loop Trail, and Pine Mountain Road. Pine Mountain Road is a private, un-paved road that leads to the Douglas Horton Center, a retreat run by the United Church of Christ near the summit of Pine Mountain. The center is not open to the public, and recent relocations of the trail are designed to ensure guest privacy.

This hike starts along Pine Mountain Road, which is little used, but you still need to watch out for occasional cars. The road passes through a forest formerly dominated by paper birches, but many of them were destroyed by an ice storm, so beeches and yellow birches dominate now.

Pine Mountain Road ascends gradually. A common shrub in wet swales along the road is the red-berried elder. This shrub has compound leaves that branch off in pairs along the stems. The branches themselves are covered with corky spots. Numerous white flowers, produced around early June, appear in showy pyramidal clusters. The dark red berries on the elder during summer are bitter and not fit for human consumption, unlike those of its close relative, the elderberry.

Many spring wildflowers and other small plants grow along the trail, an added feature if you are hiking in May or early June. Common ones include painted trillium, Canada mayflower, blue-bead lily, bunchberry, wild sarsaparilla, smooth white violet, and star-flower. Interrupted ferns and lady ferns (a variety with a red stem) thrive along the edge of the road, and you also should be able to find shining club moss and ground pine. Ground pine, also called princess pine, will remind you of a tiny Christmas tree. Look for pink lady's slippers in June and whorled and heart-leaved asters in late summer.

At 0.9 mile, Ledge Trail, sporadically blazed with yellow, leads off to the right. This offers a steep 0.6-mile ascent to the summit while providing excellent views from south-facing ledges along the way. It makes an interesting loop over the summit, but as its name implies, it is rocky, so it requires some scrambling and is not a good choice in wet or icy weather. Assuming the weather is cooperative, it is easiest to ascend via Ledge Trail and descend via Pine Mountain Loop Trail.

The turnoff for Ledge Trail is at a curve where Pine Mountain Road steepens a little. The forest becomes boreal (spruce-fir) almost as soon as you leave the road. When you reach the ledges (in about fifteen minutes), note the parallel stripes (called striae) embedded in the flat rocks in a northwest-southeast direction. These are scratches made by the gouging action of stones under the continental glacier as it crept along like a frozen river southwest over Pine Mountain. The rocks, stones, and other debris at the bottom of the glacier, squeezed by the tremendous weight of ice, acted like sandpaper, etching and scouring the earth below. Quartz dikes, which predate the glaciers, are also embedded in the ledges.

The best views of Mounts Washington, Adams, and Madison and of Carter Notch are from ledges off Ledge Trail just below the summit. Carter Notch shows additional clear evidence of glaciation. This beautiful U-shaped notch and the rounded summit of Wildcat Mountain on its southwest side are characteristic features of valleys and mountains smoothed by glaciers.

You reach the summit at 1.5 miles. The summit has no view, but you will find the foundation of an old fire tower.

Ravens nest on ledges on Pine Mountain, so your chance of seeing these large, black members of the crow family is good. Depending on the winds, they may effortlessly soar by any of the outlooks. They do seem to enjoy themselves.

The vegetation around the summit ledges is also interesting. Look for reindeer lichen, rhodora, blueberry, Labrador tea, heart-leaved birch, and wild currant. Reindeer lichen is a delicate lichen with thin, tangled bluish gray branches. It frequents rocky areas with thin soil in the mountains, often around and under blueberry shrubs. It usually looks so neat and prim that it is hard to believe a landscape gardener didn't deliberately place it there. Rhodora is a small, wild type of rhododendron with smooth blue-green leaves. It is common in bogs and on lower summits, such as the one on Pine Mountain. Around Memorial Day, its beautiful, large pink flowers put on a dazzling display, as befits a rhododendron.

The yellow-blazed trail, now called Pinkham Ledge Trail, continues beyond the summit. You should stop at one of several side paths that provide overlooks northeast toward the Androscoggin River valley and the Carter–Moriah Range.

Chapel Rock, which can be seen from the third of the overlooks, has a particularly fascinating geological history. Its rocks are in vertical layers, something more easily noticed through binoculars. These rocks were once horizontal beds of sandstone and mud deposited on the bottom of an ancient sea that predated the modern Atlantic. About 400 million years ago, North America and an island continent called Avalonia had a giant collision. The heat and pressure of the crash metamorphosed the deposits into schists and quartzites, folded them, and thrust them up into their present dramatic vertical position.

After the Chapel View overlook, the trail descends and reaches a four-way junction at 1.8 miles. Take Pine Mountain Loop Trail (yellow blazes) to the left. This descends to Pine Mountain Road at 2.0 miles. From here it is 1.5 miles along the road back to the trailhead.

DID YOU KNOW?

Despite its lower elevation, Pine Mountain is made up of the same types of rocks (400-million-year-old schists) as the rest of the Presidential Range.

The parallel lines on this ridge near the summit of Pine Mountain were scratched into the rock by small stones under a glacier.

OTHER ACTIVITIES

If you have extra time, take the short, steep walk along Town Line Brook Trail to Triple Falls. Its trailhead is less than a mile northwest of the Pine Mountain Road trailhead along Pinkham B (Dolly Copp) Road. Look for the sign on the left side of the road.

MORE INFORMATION

Parking is free at the trailhead.

The area around the summit of Pine Mountain and Pine Mountain Road itself are private. Please respect the privacy of guests at the Horton Center so that future hikers will continue to have access to this wonderful small mountain.

Do not confuse Pine Mountain Road with Pine Mountain Trail, which approaches Pine Mountain from the northeast. Its trailhead is in the village of Gorham.

46

LOW'S BALD SPOT VIA OLD JACKSON ROAD

Low's Bald Spot provides a terrific view of the Great Gulf and Mounts Adams and Madison. Along the way, you will cross streams and see a wide variety of mushrooms and other fungi, as well as interesting wildflowers.

Features

Location Pinkham's Grant, NH, to Sargent's Purchase, NH

Rating Moderate

Distance 4.4 miles round trip

Elevation Gain 1,050 feet

Estimated Time 3–4 hours

Maps AMC *White Mountain National Forest Map & Guide*, 4th ed., F10 and Mount Washington inset; AMC *White Mountain Guide*, 31st ed. Map 1 Presidential Range, F9; USGS Topo: Mount Washington

GPS Coordinates (Pinkham Notch Visitor Center) 44° 15.44' N, 71° 15.17' W

Contact White Mountain National Forest: fs.usda.gov/whitemountain, 603-536-6100; Appalachian Mountain Club PNVC: outdoors.org/destinations/ massachusetts-and-new-hampshire/joe-dodge-lodge, 603-466-2721

DIRECTIONS

The trail begins at AMC's Pinkham Notch Visitor Center (PNVC) off NH 16. (See Trip 41 for directions and parking information.) Walk past the outdoor water fountain and scale (for backpackers and kids to weigh their loads). The trail called Old Jackson Road branches off from Tuckerman Ravine Trail directly behind PNVC.

TRAIL DESCRIPTION

Old Jackson Road was the former carriage route from the town of Jackson to Mount Washington Auto Road. It has been incorporated into the White Mountain trail system, beginning at PNVC and meeting Mount Washington Auto Road at the latter's 2-mile marker. From there, a short section of Madison Gulf Trail leads to Low's Bald Spot. The trail ascends gradually, with a few steep sections near the end. Younger children and less-than-enthusiastic hikers might find it a bit long.

Old Jackson Road is now part of the Appalachian Trail and marked with white blazes. This hike does not begin on Old Jackson Road itself but on a link that quickly brings you to the old road. Be sure to carefully follow the signs to Old Jackson Road, which crosses a maintenance road, a ski trail (indicated by blue diamonds), and other hiking trails.

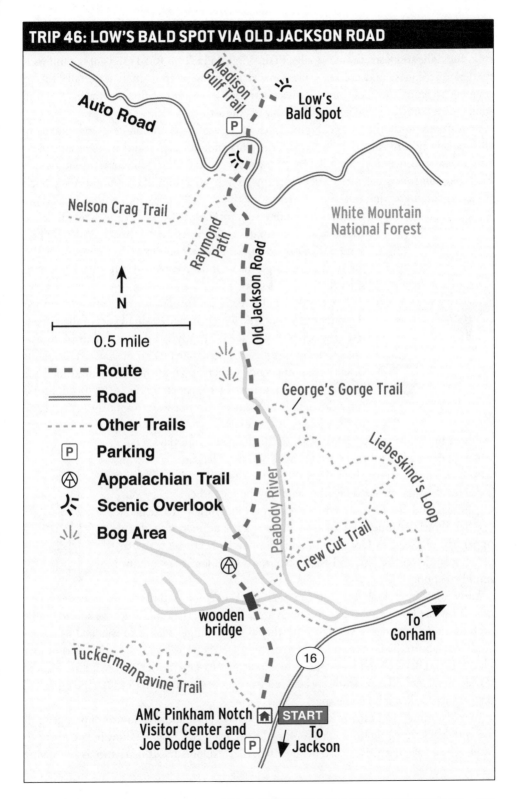

Auto Road

Madison Gulf Trail

Low's Bald Spot

P

Nelson Crag Trail

Raymond Path

Old Jackson Road

White Mountain National Forest

↑
N

0.5 mile

- - - Route

=== Road

- - - - Other Trails

P Parking

Ⓐ Appalachian Trail

⅄ Scenic Overlook

⧣ Bog Area

George's Gorge Trail

Liebeskind's Loop

Peabody River

Crew Cut Trail

Ⓐ

wooden bridge

To Gorham

Tuckerman Ravine Trail

16

AMC Pinkham Notch Visitor Center and Joe Dodge Lodge P

🏠 START

To Jackson

At 0.4 mile, Old Jackson Road widens and looks like you'd expect an old road to look. Shortly after, it crosses a solid wooden bridge at the point where Crew Cut Trail comes in from the right and leads to Lila's Ledge (Trip 43). Old Jackson Road then goes uphill with moderate steepness and crosses a pleasant, shady gorge with a small waterfall. Take a moment to enjoy the cool, mossy atmosphere and the sound of flowing water. The trail soon crosses another small gorge (likely dry in August).

Mushrooms and other fungi abound in the rich, moist soil and on decaying logs along this trail. They come in a rich assortment of colors and odd shapes and are especially plentiful in late summer and early fall. One of the most eye-catching is the coral fungus, which looks like someone stuck a piece of branching coral from a tropical ocean onto a log. Shelf (bracket) fungi growing out of dead trees sometimes reach monstrous sizes. Other types

you can find along Old Jackson Road are in the genus Russala, Mycenaea, and Amanita, the latter being almost all deadly poisonous. See Appendix C: A Primer on Flora and Fauna, page 319, for further descriptions of mushrooms. Admire them, but consider them all poisonous.

What you actually see of mushrooms or other fungi are their reproductive structures, which are only a small part of their "bodies." The soil below is laced with myriad thin filaments of numerous species of fungi. Some penetrate plant roots and aid the plants in taking up nutrients. Others, such as the coral fungus and the bracket fungus (illustrated left), penetrate into dead wood, breaking it down to basic elements. In this way, fungi play a critical role in the ecology of the forest.

Ghost pipe (illustrated right), with its distinctive white flower on a white stem, could be mistaken for a fungus because it has no green leaves. Also called Indian pipe, it is a flowering plant but gets along without leaves by "feeding" on dead organic matter in the soil rather than producing its own food. Ecologically, it functions more like a fungus than a plant.

After about 0.9 mile, Old Jackson Road reaches a junction with the upper end of George's Gorge Trail and then levels. It crosses a rivulet, passes a swale on the left, and then traverses double logs over a damp, muddy section.

Early in summer, look for white bog orchids, 1- to 3-foot-tall plants with slender spikes of small white flowers, in the damp open areas alongside the trail. Once we spotted these orchids among the dense vegetation at the edge of a large swale and watched as a tiger swallowtail butterfly flew from orchid to orchid to feed on the nectar, ignoring all the other plants. If you have a hand lens, take a close look at one of the flowers. From a distance, the flowers don't look like anything special, but close up you will see an exotic shape typical of orchids, with a lower lip and a spur.

In midsummer, you can't miss jewelweed and its delicate spurred flowers of orange spotted with black, hanging from juicy-looking leaves. Fat seed capsules follow in late summer. When these capsules are touched or squeezed, they explode, releasing the seeds and giving the squeezer a jolt like an electric shock. After trying this a few times, you can easily understand why jewelweed is also called touch-me-not.

In late summer, the white of the bog orchid is replaced by the white of the turtlehead flower (illustrated here). It may take a little imagination to see this snapdragon relative's resemblance to a turtle, but even if you decide that it looks more like a lizard's head than a turtle's, you will definitely agree that this flower has a peculiar shape. It has two lips, with the top lip overhanging the bottom.

At 1.6 miles, at a point where an old section of trail is blocked off, Old Jackson Road makes a sharp left turn and heads uphill on rock steps. You can hear vehicles from the auto road through the trees, although you still have about 0.5 mile to go before you cross it. Old Jackson Road continues straight past Raymond Path (1.7 miles), crosses logs over a few rivulets, and then passes Nelson Crag Trail. After this, the trail ascends and opens up a bit, passing through an old gravel pit with a view of Nelson Crag (a shoulder of Mount Washington).

Old Jackson Road ends at a parking area on the auto road, 1.9 miles from Pinkham Notch.

To continue on to Low's Bald Spot, walk across the auto road and follow Madison Gulf Trail (still blazed white as part of the Appalachian Trail) into the Great Gulf Wilderness. At 0.2 mile beyond the auto road, take the turnoff leading uphill to the right. You won't find a sign to indicate Low's Bald Spot, but it is easy to locate. In another few minutes you reach the viewpoint.

A vast expanse of the Great Gulf Wilderness lies before you from Low's Bald Spot. Mount Adams, the second-highest peak in the White Mountains, is particularly impressive with its symmetrical cone shape. The treeless alpine zone on the upper part of the mountain is very obvious. You can easily see the distinction between the forest dominated by broad-leaved trees at the bottom of the mountain, the boreal forest (spruce and fir) midway up, and the treeless alpine zone.

Between Mount Adams and Mount Madison is Madison Gulf, a tributary ravine of Great Gulf. Madison Gulf is a cirque—a bowl-shaped ravine carved out by a glacier on the side of a mountain. The section of Madison Gulf Trail that climbs up this ravine is one of the most difficult hikes in the White Mountains. To the southwest you'll see two shoulders of Mount Washington, Nelson Crag, and Boott Spur. Across Pinkham Notch to the east, the prominent features are Wildcat Mountain, Carter Dome, and the Imp Face. Endless peaks stretch out to the north.

The impressive vista isn't the only thing to see at Low's Bald Spot. You will probably notice a particularly gleaming white piece of quartz and several "flag trees" with their branching patterns formed by winter winds. Plants growing at Low's Bald Spot include red spruce, balsam fir, mountain holly, sheep laurel, Labrador tea, crowberry, and a few scrawny blueberries.

As for the name of this fine destination, *The Gorham Mountaineer* from September 14, 1910, provides us with the story:

Hikers arriving at Low's Bald Spot, where they can enjoy a sweeping view of the Great Gulf Wilderness and Mount Adams. *Photo by Dennis Welsh.*

"About a year ago, Mr. J. Herbert Low from Brooklyn, NY, a big man with a thousand friends, discovered the rocky knoll and was so charmed with the delightful view it affords . . . that to share his discovery he marked an easy trail to it from the carriage road. In the first party to be conducted to the outlook was Mrs. Vera Johnson of New York, who evoked peals of laughter from the party by impulsively crying out, 'Oh, Mr. Low! What a beautiful view from your Bald Spot!'"

This name was one of the unpremeditated kind that sticks, and Low's Bald Spot it has been ever since.

Return the same way you came. Within 0.4 mile of Pinkham Notch, make sure not to take the left fork where Link Ski Trail (also Connie's Way and Go Back ski trails) comes in (marked with blue diamonds). If you inadvertently end up on the ski trail, it will lead you to NH 16 about 0.3 mile north of PNVC.

DID YOU KNOW?

The destination was long called Lowe's Bald Spot. The extra 'e' likely was added because it was assumed that the name referred to the Lowe family of Randolph, New Hampshire, well-known White Mountain guides and trail builders, and not the aforementioned Herbert Low from Brooklyn, New York.

OTHER ACTIVITIES

The loop hike to Lila's Ledge and Brad's Bluff, which starts on Old Jackson Road, is described in Trip 43. Check AMC's *White Mountain Guide* or stop in at PNVC for other hiking ideas. Old Jackson Road is an intermediate-level ski trail, so you will see blue diamonds as well as the white Appalachian Trail blazes along much of the route.

MORE INFORMATION

At PNVC, you can find hiking supplies, snacks, restrooms, and trail information; outdoors.org/destinations/massachusetts-and-new-hampshire/joe-dodge-lodge; 603-466-2721. Parking is free.

47 NINETEEN MILE BROOK TRAIL TO CARTER NOTCH HUT

AMC's Carter Notch Hut is in a remote col between two 4,000-foot mountains. The notch features stunning mountain scenery, two pristine lakes, and a stark pile of boulders called the Ramparts.

Features 🐕 💧 🏞 🎿 🥾 ✴ 🚌 💲

Location Bean's Purchase, NH

Rating Moderate, with a few steep sections

Distance 7.6 miles round trip

Elevation Gain 2,000 feet

Estimated Time 7 hours

Maps AMC *White Mountain National Forest Map & Guide*, 4th ed., F10; AMC *White Mountain Guide*, 31st ed. Map 5 Carter Range–Evans Notch, F10; USGS Topo: Carter Dome

GPS Coordinates 44° 18.13′ N, 71° 13.25′ W

Contact White Mountain National Forest: fs.usda.gov/whitemountain, 603-536-6100

DIRECTIONS

The trailhead for Nineteen Mile Brook Trail is off NH 16, about 4 miles north of AMC's Pinkham Notch Visitor Center (PNVC) and 1.0 mile north of Mount Washington Auto Road. If you are coming from the north, it is about 6.5 miles south of the intersection of US 2 and NH 16 in Gorham. The large parking area (space for about twenty vehicles) is on the east side of NH 16.

TRAIL DESCRIPTION

Nineteen Mile Brook Trail is marked with blue blazes and for much of its length follows the route of an old road along the northeast bank of Nineteen Mile Brook. Sections of the trail were rebuilt after being devastated by Tropical Storm Irene in 2011. The trail ascends moderately, and the sound of flowing water is your constant companion for much of this hike. At places the trail runs very close to the brook, where ice in winter could be dangerous.

Nineteen Mile Brook Trail starts out by going up some wooden steps and on boards over a wet section before joining the old road. It crosses a bridge over a tributary at about 0.4 mile. About 0.7 mile into the hike, you pass a large rock outcropping along the side of the brook. This is schist, a metamorphic rock that underlies most of the Presidential Range (see Appendix B, page 315). Look for lines of quartz that formed in cracks within the schist.

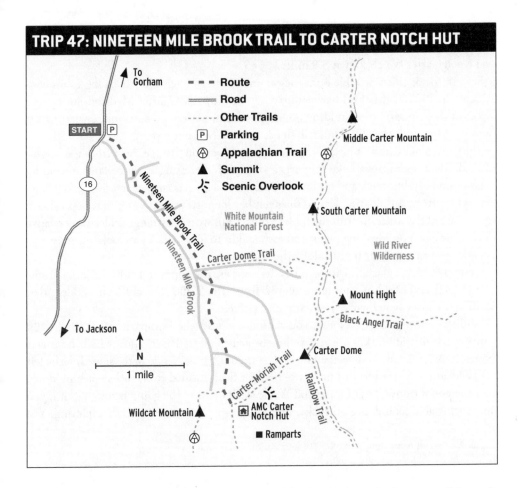

Eastern hemlocks and yellow birches dominate the forest along the first part of the trail. Hemlocks often prevail in the valleys of streams at lower elevations. Many of the yellow birches appear to be growing on stilts. These trees probably grew on top of a log that later rotted away. The roots of other yellow birches hug boulders where the trees sprouted on top of the rock.

At 1.1 miles a relocated section of the trail crosses a bridge over a tributary. (The bridge was rebuilt after Tropical Storm Irene in 2011.) After this, the trail becomes rockier, but still ascends moderately. Carter Dome Trail goes off to the left at 1.9 miles. A few steps beyond, Nineteen Mile Brook Trail crosses a wooden bridge over another tributary of the brook. A log bridge crosses a fourth tributary at 2.2 miles, and the trail then ascends away from the water. The hemlocks and yellow birches gradually give way to a spruce-fir forest with scattered paper birches, the typical forest at elevations greater than 2,500 feet.

A final stream crossing is at 3.1 miles. The trail then ascends at a steeper pitch for a short distance and then becomes a level, pleasant walk through boreal forest, where you catch glimpses through the trees of Wildcat Mountain as it dramatically slopes down to Carter Notch. A final steep section takes you to the height-of-land (elevation 3,400 feet) at the junction with Wildcat Ridge Trail (3.6 miles), where you can see the two Carter lakes below. Nineteen Mile Brook Trail then descends steeply for 100 feet to the larger of the two lakes. Carter–Moriah Trail departs to the left, and then you pass the smaller Carter Lake and reach Carter Notch Hut at 3.8 miles.

Stop in to see this venerable hut. The original Carter Notch Hut was a log cabin constructed in 1904 as the third backcountry hut built by AMC (after Madison Spring and Lakes of the Clouds). That building no longer stands, but the present stone structure was built in 1914 and is the oldest hut still in use in the AMC hut system.

The Carter lakes are an unexpected visual treat when you first see them from the height-of-land. The upper Carter Lake supports a variety of interesting aquatic plants, including yellow pond lily, bur-reed, and quillwort. Yellow pond lily has large, attractive yellow flowers and heart-shaped floating leaves. Bur-reed has long, strap-like leaves that flop over on the surface of the water. Its fruit resembles a burr. Quillwort is a strange underwater relative of club mosses (nonflowering plants somewhat akin to ferns). Its leaves look like grass and are arranged in a circular rosette along the bottom.

Carter Notch is a glacially carved valley. Its walls are the slopes and cliffs of Carter Dome (4,832 feet) and Wildcat Mountain (4,422 feet). The 1,000-foot cliffs on Wildcat that loom over Carter Notch are particularly impressive.

While you are at Carter Notch, you should not miss the Ramparts. Walk about 100 yards south of the bunkhouses on yellow-blazed Wildcat River Trail, which intersects Nineteen Mile Brook Trail at the hut. In less than 0.1 mile, a side path (signed) leads left off Wildcat River Trail to this immense boulder field, formed from rocks crashing down into the notch from Carter Dome and Wildcat Mountain. The going is rough, but if you are comfortable scrambling on rocky, uneven terrain, this place is worth exploring. You

Carter Notch Hut is surrounded by 4,000-footers in the Carter Range.

will be rewarded with a view of the hut and the two lakes and an excellent vista to the south. The two Carter lakes owe their existence to the Ramparts, which serves as a natural dam. The outlet of the lower lake flows under the boulders.

Search for caves hidden within the Ramparts, where ice can remain late into summer. Look also for large quartz crystals in the rocks. Mountain cranberry, Labrador tea, and red spruce grow around the boulders.

Another interesting side trip is to hike up Carter–Moriah Trail for 0.3 mile to an outlook near an immense boulder named Pulpit Rock. This is a very steep ascent, but the view of the notch is superb.

Listen and watch for ravens calling and soaring around the cliffs—one more element of the striking scenery of Carter Notch.

Retrace your steps on Nineteen Mile Brook Trail to return to the parking area.

DID YOU KNOW?

It is not certain who Carter was. By some accounts, he was a lonely hunter in these mountains, and by other accounts, he was a physician from Concord, New Hampshire, who used to come to the range to study plants.

OTHER ACTIVITIES

Nineteen Mile Brook Trail offers numerous swimming possibilities. The brook has many small pools deep enough for a stop on a hot day even if you do not make it all the way to the notch. The upper Carter Lake is swimmable, but has rocks and a mucky bottom. It is stocked with trout, and fishing is allowed with the proper New Hampshire license. Spring peepers (small tree frogs) also live there.

For an even longer outing, you can make a loop by taking Nineteen Mile Brook Trail to Carter Notch Hut and then hiking up Carter Dome on steep Carter–Moriah Trail. From there, Carter Dome Trail leads back down to Nineteen Mile Brook Trail at its halfway point. That adds 2.6 miles, 1,500 feet, and two and a half hours to the hike described here.

MORE INFORMATION

Parking at the trailhead has a user fee of $5 per day. The AMC Hiker Shuttle stops at the trailhead; outdoors.org/shuttle.

Carter Notch Hut is open year-round, and there are two bunkhouses along with a dining and kitchen building. During summer and fall, AMC operates it as a full-service hut, providing breakfast and dinner. For the rest of the year, it is open on a self-service basis: visitors provide their own food but have full use of kitchen facilities. Reservations are required at all times; outdoors.org/destinations; 603-466-2727.

STORMS IN THE WHITE MOUNTAINS

Storms have had a dramatic effect on the trails of the White Mountains. When Hurricane Irene came barreling through Vermont and New Hampshire from August 27 to 29, 2011, it was downgraded to a tropical storm because its winds had diminished somewhat. However, its intense rainfall, estimated as somewhere between 3 and 10 inches per hour, raised the flows in mountain rivers and creeks as much as 100 times their normal levels for that time of year. Bridges, such as those at Rocky Gorge (Trip 19), along Champney Falls Trail (Trip 24), over Nineteen Mile Brook (Trip 47), and along Tuckerman Ravine Trail (Trip 49) were carried away by the raging waters. Many trails along waterways—such Gorge Brook Trail (Trip 9), Lincoln Woods Trail (Trip 20), and Greeley Ponds Trail south of the ponds—were so badly eroded that they needed to be substantially relocated. Scouring even from relatively small streams caused a relocation of sections of UNH Trail (Trip 23). One new trail in Waterville Valley, aptly named Irene's Path, had to be cut to make up for a trail that had been completely eliminated by the widening of Flume Brook. The damage to trails took years and a tremendous effort by the Forest Service, AMC, the Student Conservation Association, and other mountain stewards, funders, and volunteers to mitigate.

How do storms like Irene affect the forest itself? The good news is that the forests of the White Mountains are remarkably resilient. According to David Publicover, AMC assistant research director, any long-lasting effects of Irene on the forest are not obvious other than

Paper birches bent by an ice storm.

along the immediate vicinity of streams that had heavy erosion and changes in location. He attributes the resilience to the ample moisture that is characteristic of the region. Fortunately for the forests, recent storms such as Irene and Sandy (2012) were more notable for their rain than wind in the White Mountains.

The storm that did have a profound impact on the forest was the hurricane of 1938. This granddaddy of all storms had winds measured as high as 186 miles per hour along the coast where it made landfall in southern New England, and it was still a Category 2 storm by the time it reached New Hampshire. According to a 2017 article by Stephen Long in *Smithsonian* magazine, the hurricane uprooted an estimated 1,000 square miles of forest. But in a strange bit of irony, this very destructive storm was responsible for rejuvenating the fall colors that we now associate with autumn in New England. It did this by flattening acres of white pines, which were the dominant trees in the forests at the time. These pines had grown up where land that had been cleared for agriculture starting in colonial times was abandoned when the Industrial Revolution hit, and much of the farming industry moved westward to richer soils. So rather than the pines dying off naturally over many years, the 1938 hurricane cleared the deck in one short burst. This allowed the maples, birches, and other northern hardwoods that form the climax forest (and beautiful fall colors) at lower elevations in New England to take over.

None of the storms since then have caused such vast destruction. Recent windstorms have had localized effects. One of these, in December 1980, caused a patchy blowdown of hemlocks in the Evans Notch region. As described in the Lord Hill hike (Trip 51), the forest varies between stands of hemlock, ash, and maple that withstood the windstorm and newer patches of aspen and birch where the blowdowns occurred.

Another storm that had regional impacts provides an important lesson for the future under climate change. An ice storm in January 1998 affected much of northern New England. The weight of ice deposited on branches snapped off crowns and branches of numerous trees. Many paper birches were bent over by the weight of the ice to the point where their crowns touched the ground. The impact of the storm on the forest was noticeable for a few years afterward, particularly in the rapid growth of the understory vegetation where the canopy had been opened up by falling trees. Yet other than the paper birches, the forest recovered from this storm. David Publicover notes that 20 years later "you would be hard-pressed to know it had even happened." A study by the U.S. Forest Service evaluating the impact 15 years after the storm concluded that the mortality of trees other than paper birches was what one would expect even in the absence of the ice storm.

Paper birches were suffering from a root rot fungus even before the ice storm and therefore suffered high mortality when the storm hit. The lesson for us as we face a future predicted to include a greater frequency of intense storms due to climate change is that a forest's resilience to these events is much stronger when trees are healthy.

48 GLEN BOULDER

Glen Boulder Trail is a steep hike to a huge glacial erratic perched on a shoulder of Mount Washington. The rock is a landmark, visible as you drive on NH 16 through Pinkham Notch. The rough climb rewards you with broad vistas and one of the shortest ascents to an alpine environment in the White Mountain National Forest.

Features ❄ 🧗 ❋ 💲

Location Pinkham's Grant, NH

Rating Strenuous

Distance 3.2 miles round trip

Elevation Gain 1,750 feet

Estimated Time 3–4 hours

Maps AMC *White Mountain National Forest Map & Guide*, 4th ed., G9 and Mount Washington inset; AMC *White Mountain Guide*, 31st ed. Map 1 Presidential Range, G9; USGS Topo: Stairs Mountain

GPS Coordinates 44° 14.75′ N, 71° 15.20′ W

Contact White Mountain National Forest: fs.usda.gov/whitemountain, 603-536-6100

DIRECTIONS

The parking area for Glen Boulder Trail is also used for Glen Ellis Falls. It is on the west side of NH 16, 0.7 mile south of AMC's Pinkham Notch Visitor Center and about 9 miles north of the village of Jackson. (See Trip 41 for directions to Pinkham Notch Visitor Center.)

TRAIL DESCRIPTION

The trail is marked with yellow blazes that have faded in places, but the route is still easy to follow. Make sure to carry sufficient water.

Glen Boulder Trail starts out with alternating level and uphill sections.* This lower part of the trail is at the transition between the lower-elevation northern hardwood forest (for example, American beech, sugar maple) and the higher-elevation boreal forest (for example, red spruce, balsam fir). The understory vegetation includes hobblebush, striped maple, painted trillium, blue-bead lily, rattlesnake root, wild sarsaparilla, Indian cucumber-root, ghost pipe, and shining club moss. Note the imposing boulders—particularly on the left

---

* I gratefully acknowledge input from Alison Buchsbaum and Gabriel Buchsbaum for the description of the trail and its natural history.

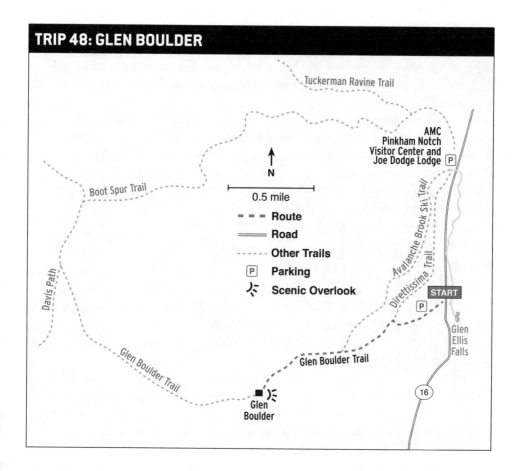

side of the trail—covered with rock tripe, a lichen that resembles a piece of shoe leather. These are the first of several such boulders you will pass on this hike.

Soon the trail begins to steepen and becomes rockier. By the time you pass the junction with Direttissima Trail (0.4 mile), which comes from Pinkham Notch Visitor Center, you have already ascended about 350 feet.

The trail turns sharply left at that junction and continues uphill. Look for a tree pock-marked with woodpecker holes along the way. Shortly thereafter, a short spur path to the left takes you to an overlook with a view of Pinkham Notch and Wildcat Mountain. The main trail becomes steeper and passes a junction with Avalanche Brook Ski Trail at 0.8 mile (600-foot elevation gain). A plant that will be your companion for this part of the hike is bunchberry, a small relative of the dogwood, with four white petals and red berries. In late summer, look also for the glossy dark blue (inedible) berries of blue-bead lily (*Clintonia*).

The route follows a stream and then turns left to cross it and a second branch of that stream (approximately 1 mile). The trail continues its steep climb, now in the spruce-fir forest. My daughter felt as if she were getting taller as she worked her way up, but she was assured that it was the trees (mostly balsam fir) getting shorter rather than any increase in her height associated with thinner air.

When you break out into the open, you are nearing your destination. Awe-inspiring views are behind you and Glen Boulder looms ahead. After some scrambling you reach the impressive boulder, which is the end of this hike (1.6 miles). Enjoy the fantastic sights of Pinkham Notch, Wildcat Mountain, and shoulders of Mount Washington; you can even see Mount Chocorua on a clear day.

The boulder was transported to this location and left behind by the last continental ice sheet approximately 13,000 years ago. (See the Geology section in Appendix B, page 315.) It is called an erratic because its final resting place is a random event, and its origin is not from the local rocks. According to J. Dykstra Eusden, a professor of earth climate and sciences at Bates College, Glen Boulder probably did not travel too far to reach its current destination because the same type of rock is exposed as bedrock within a few hundred meters.

Alpine vegetation abounds around Glen Boulder, including mountain cranberry (bright red berries and small, thick leaves), bog bilberry (a close relative of blueberry), and three-toothed cinquefoil (white flowers with five petals, leaflets edged with three teeth). An abundant grassy plant is the appropriately named highland rush. If you look carefully, you might find diapensia (clusters of small dark green leaves, white flowers early to mid-June), an alpine cushion plant that is limited to these exposed alpine environments (see "The Alpine Zone of the White Mountains" on page 256 for more information).

After soaking up the alpine atmosphere, retrace your steps to return to the parking area. Be careful of loose rocks on your descent.

Glen Boulder, an impressive glacial erratic, is perched on a shoulder of Mount Washington. *Photo by Edward Quinlan.*

OTHER ACTIVITIES

You can gain access to Glen Boulder Trail from AMC's Pinkham Notch Visitor Center (PNVC) by following Direttissima Trail for about 1 mile to its junction with Glen Boulder Trail (400-foot elevation gain). Parking at PNVC adds 0.8 mile to your overall hike, but it shaves 0.4 mile off Glen Boulder Trail. (See page 209 for more about PNVC.) Pick up Direttissima Trail by walking along NH 16 south from the PNVC parking lot for about 0.2 mile. The trailhead for Direttissima Trail is just after you cross the bridge over Cutler River.

If you park at PNVC as described above, you could make a substantially longer hike in which you ascend on Glen Boulder Trail, continue past Glen Boulder to Davis Path, mostly above treeline, and then descend to PNVC via Boott Spur and Tuckerman Ravine trails. It is a great opportunity to explore the alpine environment and to enjoy expansive views along trails that are less busy than those that lead directly to Mount Washington. However, this is a long hike (7.9 miles, 3,500-foot elevation gain, six to eight hours), with a large stretch above treeline. Only attempt it if you are in good shape, are carrying extra food and clothing, have a map of the trails, and know the weather is favorable. (See Trip 56 for precautions to take when hiking in the alpine zone.)

Glen Ellis Falls, a beautiful 64-foot waterfall on Ellis River, is reached by a gravel path that begins at the same trailhead as Glen Boulder Trail. Follow the signs through a tunnel underneath NH 16 and walk 0.3 mile.

MORE INFORMATION

The trailhead for Glen Boulder Trail has a $5 day-use parking fee. The parking area has restrooms, an information board, and a picnic site.

49 TUCKERMAN RAVINE AND MOUNT WASHINGTON

This rugged hike takes you up to Tuckerman Ravine, one of the most dramatic landscapes in New England, and then to the summit of Mount Washington, the tallest mountain in New England.

Features ❀ 🏃 🥾 🏔 〰 💧 ◣ ❋ ⬆ 🚌

Location Pinkham's Grant, NH, to Sargent's Purchase, NH

Rating Strenuous

Distance 8.4 miles round trip

Elevation Gain 4,250 feet

Estimated Time 8 hours

Maps AMC *White Mountain National Forest Map & Guide*, 4th ed., F9 and Mount Washington inset; AMC *White Mountain Guide*, 31st ed. Map 1 Presidential Range, F9; USGS Topo: Mount Washington

GPS Coordinates 44° 15.44′ N, 71° 15.17′ W

Contact White Mountain National Forest: fs.usda.gov/whitemountain, 603-536-6100; Appalachian Mountain Club PNVC: outdoors.org/destinations/massachusetts-and-new-hampshire/joe-dodge-lodge, 603-466-2721; Mount Washington State Park: nhstateparks.org/visit/state-parks/mt-washington-state-park, 603-466-3347

⚠ **CAUTION! Before beginning, check at AMC's Pinkham Notch Visitor Center (PNVC) for the weather conditions on the summit of Mount Washington, which is likely to be about 20 degrees Fahrenheit colder and much windier than at the visitor center in the valley. You can also check at the Hermit Lake Campsite at the base of Tuckerman Ravine for weather updates before ascending any farther, because the hike is well protected from the elements up to that point. The weather within Tuckerman Ravine is slightly more benign than that of the summit because it is not as affected by the westerly winds. But the weather here is notoriously fickle and can change rapidly even with a good forecast. Dense fog and slippery conditions can be hazardous on the headwall because of the steep dropoff, and thunderstorms can pop up rapidly. Don't go beyond Hermit Lake if the weather is questionable, because the route is exposed and rugged. Be prepared to turn back if the weather changes during the hike.**

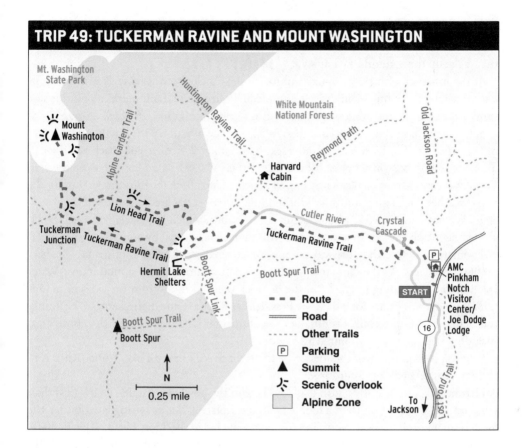

TRIP 49: TUCKERMAN RAVINE AND MOUNT WASHINGTON

Mt. Washington
State Park

White Mountain
National Forest

Huntington Ravine Trail

Old Jackson Road

Mount
Washington

Alpine Garden Trail

Raymond Path

Harvard
Cabin

Lion Head Trail

Cutler River

Crystal
Cascade

Tuckerman
Junction

Tuckerman Ravine Trail

Tuckerman Ravine Trail

P

AMC
Pinkham
Notch
Visitor
Center/
Joe Dodge
Lodge

Hermit Lake
Shelters

Boott Spur Link

Boott Spur Trail

START

16

Boott Spur Trail

Boott Spur

N

0.25 mile

Lost Pond Trail

Route

Road

Other Trails

P **Parking**

▲ **Summit**

Scenic Overlook

Alpine Zone

To
Jackson

DIRECTIONS

The trailhead for Tuckerman Ravine Trail is at AMC's Pinkham Notch Visitor Center (PNVC) on the west side of NH 16. See Trip 41 for directions and parking information. Walk past the Trading Post until you see the large sign for Tuckerman Ravine Trail.

TRAIL DESCRIPTION

This is the most popular route up New England's highest mountain and is often crowded with hikers, but it is also arguably the most "nature rich" way of ascending Mount Washington. You must have the proper gear, allow plenty of time, and be prepared for rough weather, particularly if your goal is to go beyond Hermit Lake. Make sure everyone in your group has sturdy boots and extra clothes. This trail is not appropriate for anyone who is uncomfortable hiking on rocks.

The first part of Tuckerman Ravine Trail is on an old, heavily eroded tractor road along Cutler River and is moderately steep throughout, with virtually no views. Be careful not to get sidetracked by Old Jackson Road, which goes off to the right near the trailhead, or Blanchard Ski Trail, which crosses Tuckerman Ravine Trail soon after it starts. At 0.3 mile, the trail turns sharply left and crosses a solid bridge over the river.

After a short, steep section, you reach the viewpoint for Crystal Cascade. This cascade tumbles over a black volcanic vent of basalt that formed much later in time than the schists that make up the surrounding cliffs.

At the junction with Boott Spur Trail (0.4 mile), Tuckerman Ravine Trail turns right and continues climbing relentlessly at a moderately steep rate. Landmarks along this section of the trail are the junction with Huntington Ravine Trail (1.3 mile), a bridge back over to the north side of Cutler River (1.6 mile), and the junction with Raymond Path (2.1 miles). At 2.3 miles, Lion Head Trail goes right, and at 2.4 miles you reach the floor of Tuckerman Ravine, where one of the grandest vistas in New England opens up before you. Enjoy the scenery from conveniently placed benches, and check the information hut for the latest weather. Outhouses and a well for refilling water bottles are available here.

Tuckerman Ravine is a textbook example of a cirque, which is a glacially carved, bowl-shaped ravine on the side of a mountain. This ravine was carved by a small mountain glacier sometime before the area was completely covered by the last continental ice sheet 30,000 years ago. As the climate cooled, glaciers first formed in the mountains. Water freezing and expanding in cracks in the bedrock plucked rocks from the sides of mountains, leaving the cirques for which the Presidential Range is noted: Tuckerman, Huntington, King, and Great Gulf. Eventually the continental ice sheet covered the entire area, including the summit of Mount Washington.

Follow a path past one of the shelters to the right to see Hermit Lake. Cutler River is to the left, crossed by Boott Spur Link.

Hermit Lake, technically a tarn (a glacial lake in the bowl of a cirque), is tiny (less than 0.5 acre) and shallow (less than a foot deep in most places), but its setting is exquisite. The view from Hermit Lake as you face the ravine includes the Lion Head, a particularly impressive rock face on your right that resembles its namesake when seen from NH 16 below, and the long alpine ridge of Boott Spur, with its Hanging Cliffs to the left. The headwall of the ravine is straight ahead.

Tuckerman Ravine Trail continues past the Hermit Lake area, ascending on steps over Little Headwall and then at a relatively level pitch to the base of the headwall (3.1 miles, 0.7 mile from the Hermit Lake area). A snow arch forms at the base of the headwall in winter and may still be present through early July. Although attractive to look at, it is unstable, so do not climb on it or walk under it. At least one death has resulted from falling ice.

The streamside flora is particularly interesting as you approach the headwall. Look for Indian poke (false hellebore), a large, herbaceous plant whose broad, deeply veined leaves look like those of cabbage. A plant such as this would not survive in exposed areas due to wicked winter winds, but on the floor of the ravine, the thick blanket of winter snow protects it. Green alder is a common streamside shrub. It has rounded, toothed leaves, and its cone-like fruits remain on the plant throughout summer. Meadowsweet is a type of spirea with clusters of fuzzy white flowers at the tips of its branches. This small shrub blooms in early summer at lower elevations, but at the elevation of Tuckerman Ravine, meadowsweet flowers can be found through late August. Meadowsweet is one of a variety of species in the ravine whose bloom times are late because of the heavy winter snow accumulation. In late summer, the sides of streams are lined with the purple flowers of purple-stemmed asters and clusters of the yellow flowers of large-leaved goldenrod.

Stream tumbling down the dramatic headwall of Tuckerman Ravine.

The vegetation becomes shorter in stature with an increasing number of alpine species the closer you get to the base of the headwall. The elevation at the base of the headwall is 4,500 feet, roughly treeline.

Tuckerman Ravine Trail starts ascending the headwall. Although it looks very intimidating from the base, the path is well graded and secure; however, be careful not to dislodge rocks that could potentially injure hikers below. Also, this part of the trail can be hazardous in dense fog or when wet or icy because there are steep dropoffs on either side.

The walk up the headwall, although steep and strenuous (600-foot elevation gain in 0.3 mile), is very beautiful. Wildflowers, particularly in middle to late summer, border alpine rivulets that tumble down the mountainside. Among the showiest are pale painted cup (a relative of the snapdragon) and arnica, a brilliant yellow flower that resembles a daisy. You will also see some lowland species, such as the bog orchid, that survive winter here under a protective blanket of deep snow.

At the top of the headwall, the trail levels out. On days with a westerly or northwesterly wind, you will immediately notice the wind pick up at this point. If conditions are foggy, you will need to look carefully for the cairns (rock piles) and paint blazes that mark the trail.

Tuckerman Ravine Trail passes Alpine Garden Trail at 3.4 miles (a great trail for seeing alpine wildflowers) and reaches Tuckerman Junction (3.6 mile), a major intersection for several trails heading in different directions.

Tuckerman Junction is at the edge of a broad alpine plateau called Bigelow's Lawn, which is another fine area for alpine wildflowers. Some of the botanical superstars in June are diapensia, Lapland rosebay, and mountain avens, the latter particularly partial to alpine streamsides (see "The Alpine Zone of the White Mountains," page 256). In July, mountain sandworts, delicate white flowers with five petals on small plants with thin, grassy leaves, are particularly abundant along the trail.

Continue following Tuckerman Ravine Trail as it turns sharply right and starts ascending the summit cone of Mount Washington. The trail is not well defined here but simply a way up over piles of boulders, with cairns marking the route. The boulder piles are the result of water freezing and then expanding in cracks in the bedrock, causing chunks of rock to break off.

Many of the boulders are covered by yellow-green splotches that look like paint splatters. These are map lichens, whose scientific name, *Rhizocarpon geographicum*, also notes their resemblance to a map. Lichens produce acids that break down the rocks upon which they reside, and thus perform an initial step in soil formation. Two wildflowers, mountain sandwort and three-toothed cinquefoil, also inhabit this otherwise barren area.

As you continue up the summit cone, Lion Head Trail comes in at 3.8 miles. At 4.2 miles, you cross Mount Washington Auto Road, pass a parking area, traverse the cog railway tracks, and reach the summit house. Hopefully, it will be a crystal-clear day and the view in all directions will be spectacular. You've earned it.

For your descent, start down on Tuckerman Ravine Trail but then switch to Lion Head Trail at its junction with Tuckerman Ravine Trail 0.4 mile below the summit. As you will discover on your ascent, Tuckerman Ravine Trail is narrow and particularly crowded on summer weekends, so passing a party of hikers going in the opposite direction can be troublesome. Lion Head Trail is steeper, slightly longer and rougher, and more exposed for more of its distance than Tuckerman Ravine Trail, but it is less traveled and has fantastic views of the Carter Range across Pinkham Notch. Lion Head Trail follows a ridge along the edge of the Alpine Garden, passes a knob that resembles the head of a lion when seen from below, descends steeply on well-placed steps, and enters the boreal forest. It rejoins Tuckerman Ravine Trail 0.1 mile below the shelters at Hermit Lake. From there, return the rest of the way to Pinkham Notch via Tuckerman Ravine Trail. (At less busy times, you can retrace your steps down Tuckerman Ravine Trail the entire way.)

DID YOU KNOW?

Dr. Edward Tuckerman was a professor of botany at Amherst College and a well-known lichenologist (a scientist who studies lichens). He came to the White Mountains in the 1830s to study the flora and returned many times. Tuckerman was one of the first scientists to describe the effects of elevation on plant communities of the White Mountains.

OTHER ACTIVITIES

Tuckerman Ravine makes a fine day-hike destination in its own right if you have limited time or do not want to attempt the entire hike to the Mount Washington summit.

John Sherburne Ski Trail (for advanced skiers) closely parallels Tuckerman Ravine Trail and leads downhill from Hermit Lake. The ski trail is not open to hikers, so skiers ascend via Tuckerman Ravine Trail before skiing down.

Crystal Cascade, near the beginning of Tuckerman Ravine Trail, is a popular destination for visitors of Pinkham Notch looking for a short hike.

AMC and the White Mountain National Forest run ten shelters (open on one side, they fit eight people each) and three tent platforms at Hermit Lake. If you want to spend more time exploring this fascinating area, consider camping overnight. You must purchase a ticket in person (first come, first served) at PNVC before hiking up.

MORE INFORMATION

Sections of the trail beyond Hermit Lake may be closed to hikers even in June due to heavy snow accumulation. At such times, Lion Head Trail is a logical alternative for ascending Mount Washington from Pinkham Notch. Huntington Ravine Trail is considered the most difficult hiking trail in the White Mountains and is particularly not recommended for descending.

PNVC has trail and weather information, snacks, restrooms, hiking gear, and field guides. You can also get weather information from AMC staff at the Hermit Lake Campsite; outdoors.org/destinations/massachusetts-and-new-hampshire/hermit-lake-shelters; 603-466-8116. This can provide guidance about the wisdom of hiking up to and beyond the bowl of Tuckerman Ravine.

Mount Washington State Park (New Hampshire Division of Parks and Recreation) includes about 60 acres of the summit of the mountain. The Governor Sherman Adams Summit Building at the summit has weather information, restrooms, food service, snacks, souvenirs, telephones, a post office, a museum, and lots of tourists. Nearby, the Tip Top House is a historic building that had served in various capacities in the past: hotel, bar, and printing office for *Among the Clouds*, a newspaper published on Mount Washington.

THE ALPINE ZONE OF THE WHITE MOUNTAINS

The most exciting landscape in the White Mountains (and arguably all of New England) is the land above treeline. This natural community is an arctic outpost inhabited by rare wildflowers and a few insects, birds, and mammals that are hardy enough to withstand the challenging conditions. The most extensive alpine zone in all of New England is in the Presidential Range, and you can hike to it on Edmands Path up Mount Eisenhower (Trip 40), Glen Boulder Trail (Trip 48), or Tuckerman Ravine Trail (Trip 49). Cloudland Falls/Franconia Ridge (Trip 16) takes you to the alpine zone in the Franconia Range. Mount Moosilauke (Trip 9) also hosts some alpine tundra.

When ascending to the alpine zone, you pass through three ecological zones: the broad-leafed deciduous forest (or northern hardwood forest), the boreal (montane) forest, and the alpine tundra. The boreal forest can be further subdivided into a lower montane forest dominated by red spruce and an upper montane forest dominated by balsam fir. The zonation is a response to the change in climate with elevation. On average, the temperature drops about 1 degree Fahrenheit for every 350 feet you climb, so the summit of Mount Washington is about 12 degrees cooler than a trailhead in Pinkham Notch, and a lot windier too. By hiking up 4,000 feet in elevation, you travel the equivalent of about 1,000 miles north.

The peak time to observe flowers of the alpine tundra in bloom is early to mid-June. This is early in the season for many hikers, but if you miss it, there are still many interesting plants to see all summer.

The first thing to notice about plants in the alpine zone is their small stature. Most never rise more than a few inches above the ground because of the fierce winds. Taller ones are likely to be found only where they are protected from the wind—for example, in the lees of rocks, in ravines, or where they are protected by deep snow cover. Balsam fir and black spruce grow as low, gnarled shrubs called krummholz, a German word meaning "crooked wood."

While hiking through the alpine zone in both the Presidential and Franconia ranges, you will notice cushions of dark green, tightly packed tiny leaves that hug the ground throughout the tundra. These plants, which resemble pincushions, are diapensias (illustrated here), natives of North American and Scandinavian arctic realms, as well as the high peaks of New England and the Adirondacks. If you are fortunate enough to be in the alpine zone on the Presidential or Franconia ridges in June and the wind and temperature have been cooperative, you will be treated to a profusion of small white flowers with five petals. The diapensia's dark green leaves act as passive solar collectors, absorbing solar radiation and ensuring that the plant stays warmer than the surroundings.

Alpine azalea also grows as a cushion plant. Its leaves resemble those of diapensia, but its pink flowers are tiny—no larger than the head of a matchstick. They still put on a great show when they all bloom together. Another flower that is bound to catch your eye in June because of its large magenta blossoms is the Lapland rosebay, a species of rhododendron.

In keeping with the theme that small is beautiful in the alpine garden, there are diminutive willows that never get more than 2 inches high. In June, look for pussy willow–type "buds" coming right out of the ground. These are the male and female catkins of the bearberry willow.

The big yellow flower blooming from late June throughout summer is mountain avens. This plant, with relatively large scalloped leaves, grows in only two places in the world: the White Mountains and an island off Nova Scotia. You can sometimes find mountain avens along streams at lower elevations where the microclimate is cool (see Trips 34 and 36).

In July and August, the showiest flower in the alpine zone on Mount Washington is the bluebell (harebell). This flower is common at lower elevations and may not have been native to the mountain's summit. Some people speculate that its seeds may have been carried up the mountain in the droppings of donkeys that were used as pack animals in the nineteenth century.

Donkeys are no longer part of the White Mountain landscape, and you will not see large animals in the alpine zone either. You will have to be content with the wolf spider, a large, dark arachnid that scampers over rocks; butterflies and other insects; and an occasional woodchuck or snowshoe hare. Two of the butterflies, the White Mountain butterfly and the White Mountain fritillary, are endemic to the White Mountains. The cold climate of the alpine zone is not generally friendly to amphibians; however, you can hear spring peepers, small tree frogs, into August at Lakes of the Clouds on Mount Washington and Eagle Lake on Mount Lafayette. In the lowlands, the peepers' shrill chorus of whistles from wetlands is a harbinger of spring and lasts from late March through early May. American toads occasionally wander up into the alpine zone as well.

Only two species of birds regularly build nests above treeline: dark-eyed juncos and white-throated sparrows. The junco is a small, perky gray bird with a white belly, and it flashes white outer tail feathers when it flies. The white-throated sparrow is famous for its song, a series of clear whistles. The American pipit, a sparrowlike bird with grayish or brownish streaks and white outer tail feathers, occasionally nests in the alpine area of the Presidential Range. Also watch and listen for ravens cavorting in the air, soaring over this dramatic habitat. Their characteristic throaty call sometimes sounds like the snorting of a hog.

For an in-depth look at alpine habitats in New England, see AMC's *Field Guide to the New England Alpine Summits* (AMC Books, 2014) by Nancy G. Slack and Allison W. Bell.

Evans Notch is the farthest east of the four major north–south notches that run through the White Mountains. It straddles the New Hampshire–Maine border for much of its length and provides excellent hiking and other recreational opportunities for families and hikers who prefer their mountains less crowded than those at the popular notches farther west.

The Baldface-Royce Range with peaks ranging from 2,900 to 3,600 feet in elevation is on the notch's western border. It includes North and South Baldface, Basin Rim, and East and West Royce. The mountains on the east side of Evans Notch are lower in elevation (1,000 to 2,900 feet) and include Caribou, Speckled, and Blueberry mountains and Deer Hill. Much of this area is within the Caribou–Speckled Mountain Wilderness.

The lower elevations are ideal for children. Most of the summits have excellent views, and flowing water abounds. Ample opportunities exist for picking blueberries and collecting rocks. Basin Pond is in a glacially carved bowl between West Royce Mountain and Mount Meader. The pond offers fishing (New Hampshire fishing license required), canoeing, picnicking, and chances to spot moose and other wildlife. ME 113 provides access to most of the hiking trails.

Approaching from the south, pick up ME 113 in Fryeburg, Maine. Fryeburg is approximately 8 miles east of Conway and North Conway (both in New Hampshire) along NH 113 and US 302, respectively. Keep in mind when traveling between Maine and New Hampshire that NH 113 and ME 113 are two different roads. After leaving Fryeburg, ME 113 passes through Chatham, North Chatham (both in New Hampshire), and Stow (Maine). From the north, reach ME 113 by traveling east on US 2 about 11 miles from Gorham, New Hampshire, to the former logging town of Gilead, Maine.

ME 113 is unplowed through Evans Notch and closed to vehicle traffic during winter, as are Deer Hill, Stone House, and Wild River roads. As a result, some of the trails described in this section are impassable roughly from November through early May. These include Shell Pond (Trip 50), Lord Hill (Trip 51), Basin Trail (Trip 54), Blueberry Mountain (Trip 55), and Caribou Mountain (Trip 56). Roost Trail (Trip 52) is about 1 mile south of where

Facing page: The Evans Notch region straddles the border of Maine and New Hampshire. Here, a storm has just passed by Kezar Lake in Maine.

the gate to the Roost is closed in winter. If you want to hike or snowshoe to the Roost in winter, you need to plan on walking an extra mile to reach the trailhead.

SUPPLIES AND LOGISTICS

The towns closest to Evans Notch—Chatham, North Chatham, Stow, and Gilead—are small, so you may want to pick up the supplies you need for your hike at the larger communities farther away (for example, Bethel or Fryeburg in Maine, or Gorham, New Hampshire). The Chatham Trails Association has produced a detailed trail map of Evans Notch and the Cold River valley; chathamtrails.org.

Brickett Place is a historic house in Evans Notch seasonally open to the public, just north of Basin Pond off ME 113. You can get hiking and camping information there.

Public restrooms in Evans Notch are at Basin Pond, which also has an attractive picnic area. Other public restrooms are at the campgrounds (see "Nearby Camping" below).

The Androscoggin Ranger Station on NH 16 in Gorham (fs.usda.gov/detail/white mountain/about-forest/offices; 603-466-2713) and the Evans Notch Information Center (207-824-2134) east of Bethel have pamphlets on trails in Evans Notch, as well as information on rock-collecting opportunities.

NEARBY CAMPING

Four national forest campgrounds are in and around Evans Notch: Cold River, Basin, Hastings, and Wild River campgrounds. Cold River and Basin campgrounds, with 14 and 21 sites, respectively, are both at the Basin (fs.usda.gov/activity/whitemountain/recreation/camping-cabins/?recid=74405&actid=29). Hastings Campground, with 24 sites, is located between the two ends of Roost Trail just off ME 113. Wild River Campground has 12 sites and is reached by a 5.7-mile drive down Wild River Road, an unpaved road off ME 113 (no reservations). Cold River campground, which is in the Saco District (603-447-5448) and Hastings, and Wild River campgrounds in the Androscoggin Ranger District (603-466-2713) have some accessible facilities. For campgrounds requiring reservations, visit recreation.gov or call 877-444-6777 (the National Recreation Reservation Service).

50 SHELL POND

Shell Pond is a beautiful 50-acre pond surrounded by mountains and cliffs. This trip combines two trails to make a very pleasant loop around the pond with minimal elevation gain, providing a mellow family hike. Waterbirds and beavers make their home here.

Features 👤🐕💧❋

Location Stow, ME, to Stoneham, ME

Rating Easy

Distance 3.1-mile loop

Elevation Gain 200 feet

Estimated Time 2–3 hours

Map AMC *White Mountain National Forest Map & Guide*, 4th ed., G13 and Evans Notch inset; AMC *White Mountain Guide*, 31st ed. Map 5 Carter Range–Evans Notch, G13; USGS Topo: Speckled Mountain

GPS Coordinates 44° 15.12′ N, 70° 59.46′ W

Contact White Mountain National Forest: fs.usda.gov/whitemountain, 603-536-6100

DIRECTIONS

The trailhead for this hike is at the same location as that for Blueberry Mountain (Trip 55). If you are coming from NH 16 in Conway or North Conway (both in New Hampshire), pick up ME 113 in Fryeburg, Maine, by taking either US 302 or NH 113, and head north. From Gorham, New Hampshire, or from Bethel, Maine, take ME 113 south from its junction with US 2. The trailhead for Shell Pond Trail is off Stone House Road (Forest Road 16), which heads east from ME 113, 1.3 miles north of AMC's Cold River Camp and about 0.9 mile south of the Basin Recreation Area. Stone House Road, formerly known as Shell Pond Road, crosses a small stream and then makes a sharp right and a sharp left. Park on the side of the road at a closed gate about 1.1 miles from ME 113. Walk along the continuation of Shell Pond Road for 0.5 mile until you reach the trailhead.

The trailhead and much of the trail itself are on private land. Please respect the privacy of the landowner by staying on the trail, as indicated by signs.

Stone House Road is not maintained for winter travel.

TRAIL DESCRIPTION

The mileage for this trail is described from the gate where drivers must park their vehicles. The trail is maintained by the Chatham Trails Association, and the section in the national forest is marked with yellow blazes. Be aware that ATVs are permitted on this trail.

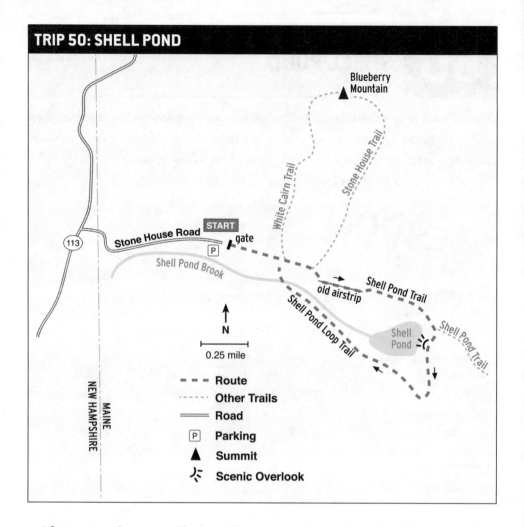

After passing the gate, walk along the road past the trailhead for White Cairn Trail (0.3 mile). Stone House Trail, which ascends Blueberry Mountain (Trip 55), goes off to the left at 0.5 mile from the gate. Follow the signs for Shell Pond Trail straight ahead, and pass the Stone House, a historical house (private) on your left. Shell Pond Trail goes straight on the path that crosses a wide field that was a former airstrip. From this open field, you can see Rattlesnake Cliff, which has been a nesting site of peregrine falcons, and Blueberry Mountain. The trail follows Rattlesnake Brook on your left and turns slightly left to pass through an old apple orchard. The landscape at this point is similar to a park, featuring older mature oak trees and a grassy understory, unlike any other trail in the White Mountains.

After leaving the old orchard, the trail crosses a bridge over the brook. This section can be a bit wet during the spring or after a rainstorm. To your right is an alder thicket. Speckled alder is named for the warty pores (lenticels) that look like white pimples on its twigs. Look also for the alder catkins that resemble small pinecones. The plant has separate male and female catkins, and the female catkins persist for a long time even after the seeds are shed. This species is very characteristic of shrubby wetlands in the lower elevations of the White Mountains. Bacteria that grow in root nodules on alder roots fix nitrogen from the air, like clover on your lawn. You might notice that other plants growing in its vicinity take advantage of this natural fertilization and are a bit greener than those farther away. Beavers favor alder wood for their dams.

The trail then enters a forest of mostly northern hardwoods with some oaks, hemlocks, and white pines. A dominant understory plant is flowering wintergreen, whose crushed leaves will release a minty scent that will remind you of chewing gum. The pond is visible through the trees, but access to it is difficult at this point. Be patient. A vista will eventually greet you.

At 0.8 mile (1.3 miles from the gate), you reach the junction with Shell Pond Loop. Turn right onto it. (Continuing straight on Shell Pond Trail would take you to Deer Hill Road.) Shell Pond Loop is an old dirt woodland road, wide, well graded, and easy to follow. It does have some ups and downs but is nowhere steep for any length of time.

At 1.5 miles, take the short spur path to the right for a grand view of the pond, which you can enjoy from a bench. This is a great place to have a snack or lunch and to enjoy the scenery of the pond and the surrounding mountains. The vista is to the west, where the peaks and ridge of Baldface–Royce Range are prominent.

The presence of beaver lodges indicates that these large rodents consider Shell Pond their home (see "Beavers," page 188). Although they are more active at dawn and dusk, you may get lucky and see them in the midafternoon, as we did one fine October day. Flocks of waterfowl, such as ring-necked ducks, hooded mergansers, and wood ducks, may visit the pond. Look for hawks soaring by and great blue herons stalking prey in the shallows, and listen for the loud drumming of pileated woodpeckers.

The pond is fringed by aquatic vegetation, particularly along its northern shoreline. One of the most numerous is bur-reed, a wetland plant whose roots are submerged in the shallow water while its strap-like leaves emerge above. Note the round, spiky seed heads that give the plant its name. Another plant that grows at the water's edge is meadowsweet, which has fuzzy white flowers in midsummer.

From the outlook, the trail swings away from the pond for a little while and at 1.9 miles makes a sharp right and crosses a bridge over a stream coming from Deer Hill Bog. The trail continues along the southwest shore of the pond but high above it.

The pond becomes narrower and eventually transitions into Shell Pond Brook, which is the outlet to the pond. This flows west and will be within earshot for much of the rest of the hike. Several unmarked intersecting trails and forest roads lie around the pond, so be careful to follow the yellow blazes. At 2.7 miles, cross a bridge over the brook, turn right, go through some openings, and reach Shell Pond Road (2.9 miles). Walk 0.2 mile west (left) to the gate where drivers must park their vehicles.

DID YOU KNOW?

The Stone House near the trailhead was built from granite carted down from the Baldface mountains by oxen about 200 years ago. Looking across to the ledges across the notch, you cannot help but be impressed by what a task that must have been.

A beautiful fall day at Shell Pond.

OTHER ACTIVITIES

For a longer outing, this trip could be combined with Stone House Trail, which takes you to the summit of Blueberry Mountain (Trip 55).

Deer Hill Bog, the outlet stream of which you cross in this trip, is a fine wildlife-viewing area off Deer Hill Road. If you have time, visit the bog after your hike.

MORE INFORMATION

As mentioned above, much of this hike is on private land, so respect the rights of the property owners by remaining on the trails. This helps ensure that the trails stay open to the public in perpetuity. Some sections, marked with signs and yellow blazes, are within White Mountain National Forest. Parking is free.

51 LORD HILL

The excursion up Lord Hill combines a relatively short uphill walk to an excellent outlook with a visit to an abandoned mine. Amateur rock hobbyists are permitted to collect samples for their personal use.

Features 🚶 🐕 ☀

Location Stoneham, ME

Rating Easy

Distance 2.8 miles round trip

Elevation Gain 750 feet

Estimated Time 2–4 hours

Maps AMC *White Mountain National Forest Map & Guide*, 4th ed., G13 and Evans Notch inset; AMC *White Mountain Guide*, 31st ed. Map 5 Carter Range–Evans Notch, G13; USGS Topo: Center Lovell

GPS Coordinates 44° 14.14′ N, 70° 56.67′ W

Contact White Mountain National Forest: fs.usda.gov/whitemountain, 603-536-6100

DIRECTIONS

From the Conway/North Conway area in New Hampshire, take US 302 to Fryeburg, Maine, and then head north on ME 113. Turn right (east) onto unpaved Deer Hill Road (Forest Road 9), approximately 4.9 miles north of the little village of Stow, Maine. (If you pass AMC's Cold River Camp, you have gone 0.8 mile too far.) Follow Deer Hill Road past the wildlife-viewing area (2.6 miles from ME 113) to the trailhead for Horseshoe Pond Trail on the right, 4.4 miles from ME 113. The trailhead is located in a bend in the road where there is room on the right for vehicles to park. After parking, look for yellow blazes heading off into the forest if a trail sign is not obvious (it seems to keep disappearing!). If you reach an unpaved road heading sharply to the right (Forest Road 50), you have gone about 0.1 mile too far.

From the north or west, take US 2 through Gorham, New Hampshire, and turn south onto ME 113, which is about 11 miles east of the junction of US 2 with NH 16. Travel 13.7 miles on ME 113 through Evans Notch. Turn left onto Deer Hill Road approximately 0.8 mile south of AMC's Cold River Camp and follow the directions above. Deer Hill Road is not plowed in winter.

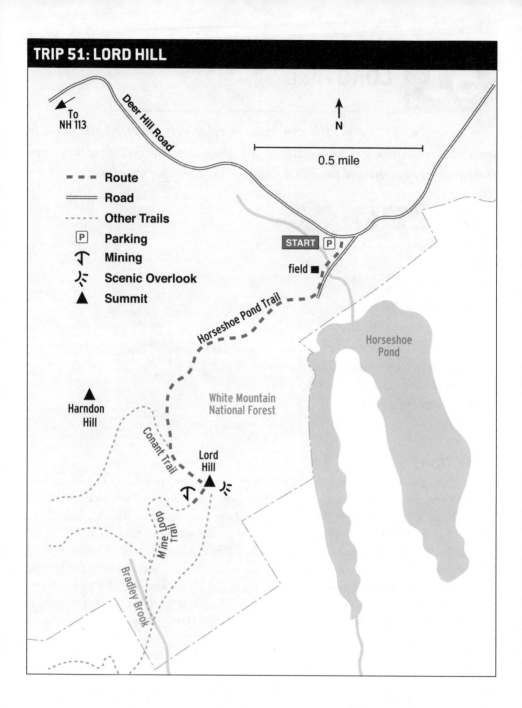

TRIP 51: LORD HILL

To NH 113

Deer Hill Road

N

0.5 mile

- - - Route
═══ Road
· · · Other Trails
P Parking
⊤ Mining
⅄ Scenic Overlook
▲ Summit

START P

field ■

Horseshoe Pond Trail

Horseshoe Pond

White Mountain National Forest

▲ Harndon Hill

Conant Trail

Lord Hill ▲

Mine Loop Trail

Bradley Brook

TRAIL DESCRIPTION

The hike to the summit of Lord Hill (1,257 feet) uses Horseshoe Pond and Conant trails. Horseshoe Pond Trail, marked with yellow blazes, starts off with a short downhill section through a beautiful forest of white pines. The trail passes the Styles gravesite, which dates to 1851. After 0.1 mile, turn right onto a forest road and then stay straight through a fork. Just before the road widens into what appears to be a parking area, turn right onto a wide, grassy path through a field. Then turn left onto the old trail and watch for the yellow blazes.

The trail ascends, first through fields and raspberry brambles, then open woodlands, and eventually an evergreen forest. Observe the interesting forest dynamics as you climb the hill. Stone walls indicate that the area was farmed at one time, and you also may notice an old house foundation in the woods. The forest returned after the farms were abandoned. In December 1980, an intense windstorm hit the area. The storm was very patchy in its impact, so the forest now alternates between older stands of white pines, hemlocks, and sugar maples that survived and newer patches of aspens and birches.

Look for piles of hemlock bark that were harvested but never made it to the tannery. Hemlocks, identified by their short, flat, single needles (not in clusters like pines), were extensively logged for tannins before the advent of synthetic substitutes. After trees were cut, the bark was stripped and placed in piles before being transported to tanneries. Tannins extracted from the bark were used to preserve leather.

Two sweet-smelling plants are common along the trail. Sweet fern, a small, sun-loving shrub with fernlike leaves, grows in the open patches in the forest. Crush a leaf for its bayberry-like scent. The crushed leaves of flowering wintergreen, a low plant with evergreen leaves that grows in shaded parts of the trail, have a pleasant, minty odor that will remind you of chewing gum. Other growing things of note in the understory are goldthread, whorled aster, and boletus mushrooms. The latter have pores instead of gills on the undersides of their caps.

This trail is a good low-elevation spot for red spruce, a tree that covered much of the lower elevations in the mountains before it was intensively logged. If you feel so inclined, you can make spruce gum out of globs of the resin sticking to the bark. This used to be a popular treat before Mr. Wrigley's creation. You'll need to work it over in your mouth, spitting out the grit. Eventually it will soften up and look like regular chewing gum. For those with less adventurous gustatory inclinations, wait for the blueberries near the summit.

Horseshoe Pond Trail ends at a T intersection with Conant Trail (also called Pine-Lord-Harndon Trail or Pine-Lord Loop). Watch for the pileated woodpeckers that live in the area. Multiple trees with softball-sized holes chiseled out and large flakes of wood piled up on the ground below are evidence of these birds' presence. If you are fortunate, you might catch a glimpse of this crow-sized woodpecker with a flaming red crest.

Turn left and follow Conant Trail (yellow blazes) for about 0.2 mile. At the summit (1,257 feet), go left to see the best scenery from open ledges. The vista includes Horseshoe Pond immediately below; long, sinuous Kezar Lake a little farther; and a ridge that includes Speckled Mountain (2,906 feet), Red Rock Cliff, and Blueberry Mountain.

Large "books" of mica are one of the treasures at the old mine on Lord Hill.

An attractive stand of red pines greets hikers at the summit of Lord Hill. This tree has distinctive reddish bark in "plates" and two long needles per bunch. It is often planted as an ornamental.

Take Mine Loop Trail to the right for a 0.1-mile walk to the abandoned mine. Visiting the old mine on Lord Hill is a dream come true for rock hunters young and old. Many early explorers of the White Mountains came seeking riches from minerals locked up in the rocks. Although there is little commercial mining in the White Mountains now, in the past, mining probably ranked second behind lumbering in local commerce. Lord Hill is one of several mines in western Maine, some of which are still in operation. The region remains a major source of amethysts and other semiprecious gems.

The White Mountain National Forest allows visitors to dig for common minerals for their own use without a permit (except for smoky quartz in the Saco Ranger District). Power tools and explosives are forbidden, and a prospecting permit is required if you plan to sell the minerals.

The Lord Hill mine is actually an open depression in the hill rather than a deep, dark shaft. On hot and sunny summer days, bring a hat and plenty of water. The floor of the mine is littered with small pieces of rock, the remnants of past blasting. Miners at Lord Hill were particularly interested in the large chunks of muscovite, silvery mica that can be divided into paper-thin, flat crystals, like the pages of a book. The crystals were used as capacitors in electronics; capacitors now are made of ceramic. Mica is a common mineral constituent of granite throughout the White Mountains; however, the "books" at Lord Hill are particularly large and impressive. The feldspar at Lord Hill is a white and opaque mineral. At one time it was mined here for use as a material similar to porcelain for sinks and bathtubs.

Two gems found at Lord Hill are beryl, a greenish quartz that is high in the element beryllium, and topaz. Beryl crystals 10 to 12 feet long have been found in this part of Maine—one is now at the American Museum of Natural History in New York City. You might initially mistake the clear topaz for quartz because it is also uncolored and translucent, but if you look closely, you can see the difference in the arrangement of the angles of the crystals. Topaz also has a smoother feel to it. Smoky quartz is common at Lord Hill, and purple amethyst can be found as well.

These beautiful crystals were formed beneath the earth within the granite that makes up much of the White Mountains. Eons ago, molten rock bubbled up through cracks in the granite, forming pegmatite dikes. Within these dikes, crystals of feldspar, quartz, mica, and other minerals formed, becoming large because they cooled very slowly. Later, erosion from water and ice and scouring by glaciers broke up the rock, revealing the minerals.

Retrace your steps down Mine Loop Trail, Conant Trail, and finally Horseshoe Pond Trail to return to the trailhead.

DID YOU KNOW?

You can find specimens of beryl and amethyst from Lord Hill and other nearby mines at the American Museum of Natural History, Harvard's Mineralogical and Geological Museum, and the Smithsonian Museum of Natural History.

OTHER ACTIVITIES

The Forest Service has set up a wildlife-viewing area on the shores of Deer Hill Bog, a wooded pond along Deer Hill Road (Forest Road 9), not far from the trailhead for Horseshoe Pond Trail. It makes an excellent stop before or after your hike. Wildlife that frequent the pond and its surrounding shoreline include moose, great blue herons, wood ducks, hooded mergansers, Canada geese, tree swallows, kingbirds, red-winged blackbirds, and warblers. Bring your binoculars.

If you really get inspired by rock collecting, be sure to visit the Maine Mineral and Gem Museum (mainemineralmuseum.org) in nearby Bethel, Maine.

MORE INFORMATION

The U.S. Forest Service has produced a guide for rockhounding in the White Mountain National Forest. Go to fs.usda.gov/activity/whitemountain/recreation/rocks-minerals for guidelines and rules for collecting rocks and minerals as well as for a list of sites, such as Lord Hill, for amateur rock hounds to visit.

Parking is free at the trailhead. This trip is in a relatively remote area, so make sure you pick up supplies in one of the towns you pass through on your way to the trailhead. The nearest restrooms are at Basin Pond, about 2.8 miles north of Deer Hill Road on ME 113.

52 THE ROOST

The Roost is a small hill (1,374 feet) north of Evans Notch that provides splendid views of the Wild River and Evans Brook valleys. It is reached by a short, steep trail off ME 113 near Hastings Campground at the abandoned village of Hastings.

Features 🏔️🏊🚶🐕🌊☀️🏕️

Location Batchelder's Grant, ME

Rating Moderate

Distance 2.1 miles round trip

Elevation Gain 700 feet

Estimated Time 1–1.5 hours

Maps AMC *White Mountain National Forest Map & Guide*, 4th ed., E13; AMC *White Mountain Guide*, 31st ed. Map 5 Carter Range–Evans Notch, E13; USGS Topo: Speckled Mountain

GPS Coordinates 44° 21.58′ N, 70° 59.45′ W

Contact White Mountain National Forest: fs.usda.gov/whitemountain, 603-536-6100

DIRECTIONS

Roost Trail forms a semicircle with two trailheads on the east side of ME 113. The north trailhead is about 2.7 miles south of US 2 and 0.1 mile north of the bridge over Evans Brook and the junction of ME 113 with Wild River Road. This is 7.0 miles north of the turnoff to Basin Pond. Parking is available for only one or two vehicles opposite the trailhead, so you may need to park at the more substantial turnoff on the south side of the bridge. The south trailhead is 0.7 mile south of the north trailhead on ME 113, about 0.1 mile north of its intersection with Little Lary Road. The road through Evans Notch is closed during winter from roughly 1 mile north of the Roost. If you want to snowshoe or hike the trail in winter, you will need to park at the gate and walk that mile along the road.

TRAIL DESCRIPTION

The distance to the summit of the Roost is 0.5 mile from the north trailhead and 0.7 mile from the south trailhead. From the north trailhead, Roost Trail immediately climbs some steps that will definitely raise your pulse rate. Pass through a diverse forest of beech, sugar maple, paper birch, white ash, hop hornbeam (note the vertically scraggly bark), and aspen.

The summit (0.5 mile) is in a red spruce forest and has only a restricted view. Follow the sign that reads "To the Scenic View" and descend 150 feet (0.1 mile) on a rather steep side path to open ledges that overlook the Wild River and Evans Brook valleys.

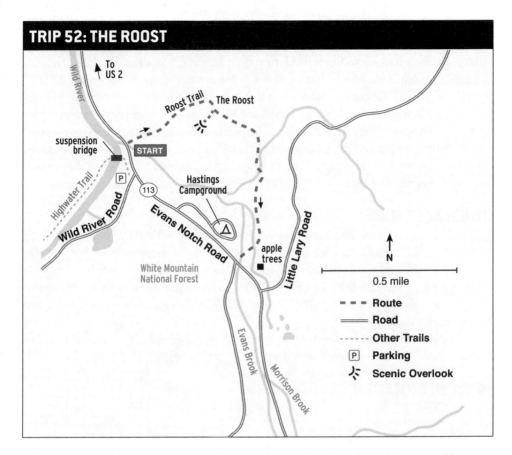

The Roost is situated above the confluence of Evans Brook and Wild River, enabling you to clearly see both valleys. The Wild River valley, angling off to the southwest, is broader, looking as if glaciers did not carve it quite as deeply as they carved the Evans Brook valley, which runs near ME 113 to the height-of-land in Evans Notch. The tall peaks on the west slope of the Wild River valley are in the Carter–Moriah Range. The land immediately below you is one of the few level areas in this mountainous region; thus the first record of human activity in this location is of farming (see "Wild River, Logging, and the Town of Hastings," page 273). Walk down the ledges as far as you safely can for the best look at the Evans Brook valley toward Evans Notch. You'll be rewarded with the sight of several small ponds and an oxbow (very sharp curve) in Evans Brook.

From the Roost, look down and see the leaves of trembling aspens shimmering in the breeze. These trees have smooth, light grayish green bark, but their most notable feature is their leaves. A very gentle breeze that hardly ruffles the leaves of other trees induces aspen leaves to shake violently and evoke the sound of the wind. This is because the leaf stalk is flattened rather than rounded as in most trees. The flattened stalks enable aspen leaves to bend more readily in the wind. What function this serves for the aspen is anybody's guess, but what it does for us is to reveal even the slightest breeze.

Aspens, like paper birches, are early colonizers of land where the trees have been cut or blown down. The aspens on the Roost probably moved in after the area was heavily logged from 1891 to 1917. Other trees of note at the ledges are mountain ash, red and white pine, and red spruce. Lowbush blueberry and reindeer lichen are also common.

After climbing back up to Roost Trail, turn right for the remainder of the loop. The trail descends through birch, beech, and sugar maple forest and then crosses a stream 0.3 mile from the summit. Like most streams in the White Mountains, this one could cause hikers trouble early in the season when water levels are high. The trail then turns right on a dirt road and passes some very tall white pine, hemlock, and red spruce. It crosses a second stream (fairly flooded the last time we were there) and passes through an area of small balsam fir. The main road is just after an old apple grove (another indication that a town once existed here). Turn right onto ME 113 for the walk back to the hike's beginning.

OTHER ACTIVITIES

Take a detour along ME 113 to walk out on the bridge over Wild River near the parking area for the north trailhead. This bridge recently replaced a suspension bridge that was destroyed by Tropical Storm Irene in August 2011, showing that Wild River is still capable of living up to its name. A large log near the water on the opposite side of the river is a great place to rest at the end of your hike. Some deeper pools in the river are good for wading and perhaps even a complete dunk.

Hastings Campground is off ME 113 between the two trailheads. Visit recreation.gov or call 877-444-6777 to make reservations.

MORE INFORMATION

Parking is free.

Wild River Valley from the Roost.

WILD RIVER, LOGGING, AND THE TOWN OF HASTINGS

The following is based on *The Wild River Wilderness* by D. B. Wight (Courier Press, 1971) and *Logging Railroads of the White Mountains* by C. F. Belcher (AMC Books, 1980).

Wild River looks quiet and peaceful now, but it once was a hub of human activity and industry in the mountains. In the mid-nineteenth century, as legend has it, the floodplain where Evans Brook joins Wild River (now Hastings Campground) was farmed by an escaped slave until he had to abandon his farm and flee the area when his former master came looking for him. Then the loggers came.

Before 1890, logging operations in the Wild River valley were small. Logs were either floated down the river or dragged by teams of horses to a mill at the village of Gilead, Maine, where currently ME 113 joins US 2. In 1891, the Wild River Railroad was built to transport wood products down the valley, and logging efforts began in earnest. Hemlock bark was taken for tanneries and red spruce for pulp. The village of Hastings, Maine, with a population of more than 300, sprang up almost overnight at the intersection of the two rivers. The village had sawmills, a school, a post office, houses for workers, and a plant that produced wood alcohol. The Wild River Railroad ran alongside Wild River about 15 miles south into the valley, following the course of present-day ME 113 south from Gilead, and then Wild River Road and Wild River Trail.

As in Zealand Valley (Trip 36), there were numerous logging camps, trestles, railroad yards, and spur lines along the railroad. Also as in Zealand Valley, the logging activity removed many acres of trees and spawned fires and erosion, causing devastation where a few years before a pristine wilderness had existed. Disaster came in 1903 when Wild River lived up to its name. A tremendous flood from March 11 to March 20 inundated Hastings and destroyed much of the Wild River Railroad. This was followed by many forest fires later in 1903 and in 1904.

When the loggers left, the wilderness returned. Today, it is hard to imagine a village existed there. The abandoned apple groves near Hastings Campground are one of the few reminders of that once thriving community. Even with the landscape returning to a more forested condition, the river continues to alter its surroundings, particularly during major storms. From the bridge over Wild River, you can see evidence of new landslides from the erosion of riverbanks. And as previously mentioned (Trip 52), in 2011, Tropical Storm Irene destroyed a bridge over Wild River where the village of Hastings once stood.

53 DEER HILL

The hike up Little Deer and Big Deer hills on Deer Hills Trail is a pleasant half-day outing through forests of maple, beech, birch, and hemlock to a summit with seasonal blueberries and excellent views of Baldface–Royce Range. You can continue on to Deer Hill Spring, a magical place, and loop back to the trailhead on Deer Hills Bypass.

Features

Location Chatham, NH, to Stow, ME

LITTLE DEER HILL AND BIG DEER HILL LOOP

Rating Moderate

Distance 4.3-mile loop

Elevation Gain 1,250 feet

Estimated Time 3–4 hours

ABOVE LOOP WITH EXTENSION TO DEER HILL SPRING

Distance from Trailhead 5.1 miles round trip

Elevation Gain 1,600 feet

Estimated Time 4–5 hours

Maps AMC *White Mountain National Forest Map & Guide*, 4th ed., G13 and Evans Notch inset; AMC *White Mountain Guide*, 31st ed. Map 5 Carter Range–Evans Notch, G13; USGS Topo: Chatham to Center Lovell

GPS Coordinates 44° 14.25′ N, 71° 00.90′ W (Deer Hills/Baldface Circle trailhead); 44° 13.26′ N, 70° 59.33′ W (Deer Hill Spring Trailhead)

Contact White Mountain National Forest: fs.usda.gov/whitemountain, 603-536-6100

DIRECTIONS

Deer Hills Trailhead

From the North Conway area in New Hampshire, take NH 113 or US 302 to Fryeburg, Maine. Take ME 113 north from Fryeburg, Maine, along the Maine–New Hampshire border. After about 11 miles you pass through the village of Stow, Maine. The parking area for Deer Hills Trail is on the right about 6 miles north of Stow and 0.2 mile north of AMC's Cold River Camp (facilities for registered guests only). Look for the sign for Baldface Circle Trail, because there is no sign for Deer Hills Trail at the parking area.

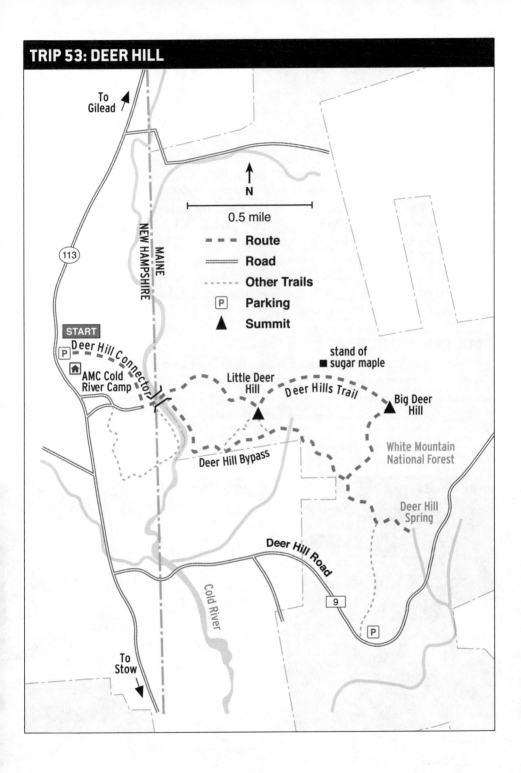

TRIP 53: DEER HILL

To Gilead

NEW HAMPSHIRE
MAINE

113

N

0.5 mile

- - - Route
═══ Road
····· Other Trails
P Parking
▲ Summit

START
P
Deer Hill Connector

AMC Cold River Camp

Little Deer Hill

stand of
■ sugar maple

Deer Hills Trail

Big Deer Hill

Deer Hill Bypass

White Mountain National Forest

Deer Hill Spring

Deer Hill Road

Cold River

9

P

To Stow

From Gorham or Bethel in Maine, take ME 113 south from US 2 in Gilead. The trail-head is about 2 miles south of the turnoff to Basin Pond. This approach from the north on ME 113 is closed in winter.

Deer Hill/Deer Hill Spring Trailhead

Deer Hill Spring is a fascinating destination and can be combined with the hike to Little Deer and Big Deer hills or visited on its own. You can walk all the way to Deer Hill Spring from the trailhead for Deer Hills Trail on ME 113 using the trail description below. To return to a parked car, you will then walk back to the trailhead using the Deer Hills, Deer Hill Bypass, and Deer Hill Connector trails. Another option is to leave a second vehicle where Deer Hills Trail comes out on Deer Hill Road and finish your hike there. To reach this Deer Hill/Deer Hill Spring trailhead, drive south on NH 113 from the Baldface Circle/Deer Hills Connector parking lot for about 1 mile, turn left onto Deer Hill Road (Forest Road 9, not maintained in winter), and continue for 1.3 miles, then park where you see the signs for Deer Hills Trail/Deer Hill Spring on the left. Of course, you can always make the short walk to Deer Hill Spring from that trailhead as a separate outing after your hike up the Deer Hills or on its own.

TRAIL DESCRIPTION

You'll see a number of interesting sights as you climb Little Deer and Big Deer hills, so this hike is worthwhile even if you decide not to complete the entire trip. The 1,000-foot rise in elevation up Big Deer Hill is manageable for most families with children but still enough to make you feel like you have gotten sufficient exercise. The trail is in relatively good

Deer Hill Spring bubbles up mysteriously from the side of Deer Hill.

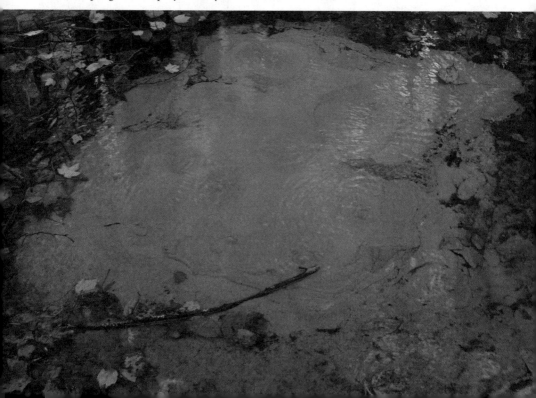

condition and is easy to follow, with some moderately steep, rocky sections and a few sections with roots. A heavy layer of leaves in some steep sections makes the trail slippery when wet.

From the parking area, look for yellow blazes heading east (on the same side of the road) because there is no sign there for Deer Hills Trail or Deer Hills Connector. A sign about 0.1 mile from the parking area leads you left down to Cold River. This section of Deer Hills Connector was seriously damaged by Tropical Storm Irene in 2011 and subsequently repaired. In 0.4 mile, the path from AMC's Cold River Camp comes in from the right (not open to the public) at a dam over the river. Here, pick up Deer Hills Trail and follow it across the dam (an excellent place for a swim).

After crossing the river, bear right at the double yellow marker and pass the stone that indicates the border of New Hampshire and Maine. Few can resist the temptation to have one foot in New Hampshire and the other in Maine. Painted trillium, blue-bead lily, and hobblebush grow abundantly here.

Notice how the river has formed flat, parallel terraces at different heights above its current banks. Each terrace was built up when the river flooded and deposited sand, silt, and mud along its shores. During the melting of the last glacier about 12,000 years ago, Cold River was much deeper and wider than it is today. The terraces it formed at that time are now stranded high above the present water level.

Look for the sign for Little Deer Hill after crossing an old logging road. Yellow blazes mark the trail as it goes uphill at a moderate grade. Several dead trees stand along the trail between Cold River and Little Deer Hill. Observe the softball-sized holes in these trees and the large wood chips at the base, both the handiwork of pileated woodpeckers. Many small mammals and birds depend on woodpecker holes like these for their own nests.

The route goes through a northern hardwood forest. Many wildflowers grow alongside the trail, but unfortunately for summer visitors, most bloom in May and June. You can see blue-bead lily, painted trillium, Canada mayflower, Indian cucumber-root, pink lady's slipper, wild anemone, dwarf ginseng, partridgeberry, and wild sarsaparilla. The dominant understory shrub is hobblebush.

About halfway up the trail to Little Deer Hill, look to the right for a hemlock with four separate trunks united at the base. More than likely, insects or wind damaged the original trunk, and none of the four branches could dominate and take over. Other trees in the area have double trunks, probably for the same reason.

Where the woods start to thin out as you continue your climb, look for trailing arbutus (mayflower) and flowering wintergreen. Deer Hills Trail then passes over several ledges with views. These ledges also sport blueberries, chokeberries, and reindeer moss. At 1.3 miles, you reach the summit of Little Deer Hill (1,090-foot elevation). The views and blueberries alike are excellent here, so it is a handy place for a picnic and a possible turnaround spot. The bare summits of North Baldface and South Baldface mountains and the impressive cliff face of the Basin are to the west.

The summit of Big Deer Hill is another 0.7 mile beyond. The trail descends about 200 feet into the col between Little Deer and Big Deer hills in a forest dominated by sugar maples, crosses a stream, and then ascends about 400 feet to the summit of Big Deer Hill (2.0 miles, 1,367-foot elevation). The best vista is about 50 yards east of the true summit.

Looking eastward, you'll see hills, lakes, and bogs in Maine. With binoculars you may be lucky enough to see a moose in one of the bogs.

Continue on Deer Hills Trail beyond the summit, and reach Deer Hills Bypass at 2.5 miles (0.5 mile from Deer Hill). Here is where you need to decide whether you want to add Deer Hill Spring to your hike (another 0.8 mile and 350 feet of elevation).

If you decide to go to Deer Hill Spring, continue for another 0.2 mile on Deer Hills Trail and reach the spur path to the spring at 2.7 miles. Turning left, descend about 150 feet and reach the spring in 0.2 mile. Deer Hill Spring, also called Bubbling Spring, is in a shady hemlock grove, where you are likely to be serenaded by the beautiful flutelike sounds of the hermit thrush or the energetic song of the winter wren. Nothing alerts you that something odd is nearby.

Then you notice a porridge of bubbling yellow sand contrasting sharply with the dark surroundings. Water percolates out of the side of the mountain with enough force to keep sand constantly in suspension. Finer particles pass out of the spring with the outflow. You might think you have been magically transported to one of those muddy hot springs at Yellowstone National Park.

Although the bubbling sand looks like it might be solid, you certainly do not want to walk on it. According to a local story, a horse was swallowed up by this "quicksand" years ago, and its remains still lie somewhere below. That would be a hard rumor to verify.

After enjoying the spring, go back to Deer Hills Trail, turn right, and return to the junction with Deer Hills Bypass. Taking Deer Hills Bypass enables you to make a complete loop while avoiding having to hike back over Little Deer and Big Deer hills. The trail starts out on easy grades, crossing over several streams and passing trail junctions for Frost Trail (0.6 mile) and Ledge Trail (0.8 mile). It descends to meet an old road along Cold River at 1.0 mile from the start of the bypass. The trail follows this road for 0.4 mile to the junction with Deer Hills Trail at the dam you used to cross over Cold River near the beginning of your hike. Return across the dam and turn right on Deer Hills Connector to get back to the trailhead.

OTHER ACTIVITIES

As an alternative to the hike over Little Deer and Big Deer hills, you can do a shorter hike to only Deer Hill Spring by parking at a trailhead on Deer Hill Road. Follow the directions above for the Deer Hill Spring trailhead. Park where you see the signs for Deer Hills Trail/ Deer Hill Spring. The route, which is part of Deer Hills Trail, follows an old logging road 0.6 mile (300-foot ascent) to the spur path to the spring. The 0.2-mile walk on the spur (150-foot descent) should take about 30 minutes.

Visit Basin Pond about 2 miles north of the Deer Hills Trail/Baldface Circle trailhead after your hike. You can go fishing (New Hampshire license required), paddle around in your canoe, and look for moose and water birds. Two campgrounds in the Basin Pond area are convenient for hiking Deer Hills Trail and other trails in the Evans Notch region.

The wildlife-viewing area on Deer Hill Road is a good stop after a visit to Deer Hill Spring. It is 1.3 miles east of the Deer Hill Spring trailhead.

MORE INFORMATION

Parking is free.

54 BASIN TRAIL TO BASIN RIM

The Basin is an impressive glacial cirque (a bowl-shaped ravine carved out by a glacier) in the Evans Notch region. The best view of it, which includes impressive cliffs and Basin Pond, is from the Basin Rim, a ridge in the Baldface–Royce Range.

Features 🏃🚴🧗🥾🐕💧❄️⛺🌲💲

Location Bean's Purchase, NH

Rating Moderate

Distance 4.6 miles round trip

Elevation Gain 800 feet

Estimated Time 3.5–5 hours

Maps AMC *White Mountain National Forest Map & Guide*, 4th ed., F12; AMC *White Mountain Guide*, 31st ed. Map 5 Carter Range–Evans Notch, F12; USGS Topo: Wild River

GPS Coordinates 44° 18.38′ N, 71° 03.85′ W

Contact White Mountain National Forest: fs.usda.gov/whitemountain, 603-536-6100

DIRECTIONS

The drive to the trailhead includes a 5.7-mile stretch on unpaved Wild River Road (Forest Road 12) that follows the route of the former Wild River Railroad. The road, marked by a sign to Wild River Campground, heads southwest off ME 113 (Evans Notch Road) 2.8 miles south of the town of Gilead, Maine (where ME 113 intersects with US 2), and about 7 miles north of Basin and Cold River campgrounds. The parking area for hikers is at the end of the road, just before you enter the campground. Wild River Road and ME 113 through Evans Notch are closed to vehicle traffic during winter, so this trail is impassable then.

TRAIL DESCRIPTION

Basin Trail runs 4.5 miles from the Wild River valley up and over the Basin Rim and then down to Evans Notch by the Basin Campground and Recreation Area, so you can ascend to the rim from either direction. The approach from the Wild River valley is more gradual and allows you to hike along Blue Brook for a good distance. That approach is featured here. With two vehicles, you could hike the entire trail.

Yellow-blazed Basin Trail is mostly within the Wild River Wilderness. It starts out as a gentle path through a rich deciduous woodland with several bog bridges. Expect some muddy spots in spring or after rain. Signs of moose are everywhere. Look for their very

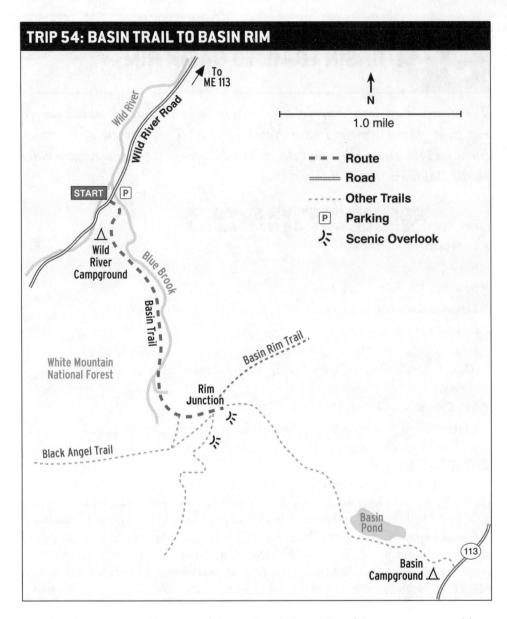

large hoofprints in muddy parts of the trail and their piles of droppings scattered here and there.

Wildflowers flourish along the trail. Look for the cloverlike three leaflets of mountain wood sorrel. It produces white flowers lined with pink from late June through early August. Bunchberry, painted and red trillium, blue-bead lily, Indian cucumber-root, and pink lady's slipper may be in bloom, depending on the time of year. Cinnamon ferns are common in damp areas. These large ferns are named for the cinnamon-colored fertile frond (the part that bears the spores) that rises straight up from a circle of green fronds. The fern's stipe (stalk) is covered with cinnamon-colored chaff.

Looking down at Basin Pond from the Basin Rim.

At 1.3 miles, the trail crosses Blue Brook (this is a good lunch or snack spot) and then begins to ascend on the east bank of the brook. This 0.3-mile part of the trail may delight you as much as the vista from the Basin Rim. The water rushes through some small canyons, forming miniature waterfalls and quieter pools. When water levels are low, there are places where you can rock-hop across the brook. Small caves and passageways between large boulders invite investigation. Bring a bathing suit if you want a chance for the brook to turn you the color of its name. One particularly good place to explore is where the brook flows near an impressive cliff face that rises up on the opposite bank. It could be a turn-around point if you need a shorter hike.

Basin Trail then turns away from the brook and ascends more steeply. At 2.0 miles, Blue Brook Connector comes in from the right. Basin Trail reaches Rim Junction at 2.2 miles, where it intersects with Basin Rim and Black Angel trails.

An excellent overlook is about 0.1 mile south of Rim Junction on Basin Rim Trail. For a second overlook, continue on Basin Trail for about another 0.1 mile east past Rim Junction to a small, open ledge facing eastward, slightly off the trail and just before it begins to descend into the Basin. The vistas include the cliffs of West Royce, Basin Pond, Blueberry Mountain, and other peaks in Maine.

These overlooks are great places to contemplate the glacial geology of the Basin below you. The Basin is the Evans Notch counterpart to Tuckerman Ravine, an east-facing bowl created by a mountain glacier during the last Ice Age (1 million to 12,000 years ago). The carving of the steep headwall occurred over a long period of time as a result of the abrasive action of small stones, pebbles, and sand within the ice. Rocks were plucked from the side of the mountain when ice at the bottom of the glacier thawed and the water flowed into cracks in the rocks and then refroze. The plucked rocks collected in a heap toward the bottom of the bowl. The flat bottoms of glacial cirques are frequently filled with ponds called tarns.

From these viewpoints, Basin Pond and its surrounding wetlands stand out like gems. On a warm, sunny day, you will probably see people down below in canoes fishing or paddling. If you have a pair of binoculars, you may even be lucky enough to spot moose in marshy areas of Basin Pond.

The Basin Rim provides a bird's-eye view of birds too. On a sunny day in June, I watched four turkey vultures soaring majestically with outstretched wings, at eye level, over the valley. These birds are master gliders, riding warm thermal air currents created as the day heats up. It enables them to save energy that would be required for flapping while they search for their lunch of dead animals. You might also see ravens, swifts, and peregrine falcons, all of which build nests on the cliffs. A variety of warblers—yellow-rumped, magnolia, black-throated green, and black-throated blue—as well as American redstarts flitter around the trees on the ridge.

This is a good location to have lunch before retracing your steps. On the way back, follow the sign for Basin Trail (not to be confused with Basin Rim Trail) and Wild River Campground at Rim Junction.

About 0.2 mile from the parking lot, be sure to follow an arrow pointing to the right at a fork with the old trail.

For those who have spotted a second vehicle at Basin Pond and are hiking the entire Basin Trail, it is a 1,300-foot, steep descent and 2.3 miles from Rim Junction to the parking area at Basin Pond. Be aware of loose footing at the upper part of this descent. You can reach Hermit Falls by a short loop trail to the right during your descent.

OTHER ACTIVITIES

Basin Pond invites exploration, either by driving there after the hike or, if you have spotted a second vehicle at the pond, by hiking down its steep headwall. It has picnic tables, restrooms, a campground, and canoe access. Walk out on the dam, stroll along the shoreline, or look over the pond for ducks, spotted sandpipers, swallows, signs of beavers, or an elusive moose. Bring your canoe if you have one. It makes a fitting end to a great day of hiking.

MORE INFORMATION

A parking fee ($5 per day) is required at the trailhead. Wild River Campground (twelve sites) is adjacent to the trailhead.

55 BLUEBERRY MOUNTAIN VIA STONE HOUSE TRAIL

Blueberry Mountain, 1,781 feet in elevation, is loaded with blueberries and commands superb views of the Baldface–Royce Range and the hills around the Cold River valley. The first part of Stone House Trail passes a gorge and a deep pool in Rattlesnake Brook.

Features 🏃 🎿 🚶 🐕 〰 ☀ 🌲

Location Stow, ME, to Stoneham, ME

Rating Moderate, with some steep sections

Distance 4.0 miles round trip

Elevation Gain 1,150 feet

Estimated Time 3–5 hours

Map AMC *White Mountain National Forest Map & Guide*, 4th ed., F13 and Evans Notch inset; AMC *White Mountain Guide*, 31st ed. Map 5 Carter Range–Evans Notch, F13; USGS Topo: Speckled Mountain

GPS Coordinates 44° 15.12′ N, 70° 59.46′ W

Contact White Mountain National Forest: fs.usda.gov/whitemountain, 603-536-6100

DIRECTIONS

If you are coming from NH 16 in Conway or North Conway (both in New Hampshire), pick up ME 113 in Fryeburg, Maine, by taking either US 302 or NH 113 and head north. From Gorham, New Hampshire, or Bethel, Maine, take ME 113 south from its junction with US 2. The trailhead for Stone House Trail is off Stone House Road (Forest Road 16), which heads east from ME 113, 1.3 miles north of AMC's Cold River Camp and about 0.9 mile south of the Basin Recreation Area. Stone House Road, formerly known as Shell Pond Road, crosses a small stream and then makes a sharp right and a sharp left. Park on the side of the road at a closed gate about 1.1 miles from ME 113. Walk on that road past the trailhead for White Cairn Trail (0.3 mile) until you reach Stone House Trail going off to the left, about 0.5 mile from the gate. The road continues as Shell Pond Trail (Trip 50) past the Stone House and a private airstrip. Stone House Road/Shell Pond Road is not maintained for winter travel.

TRAIL DESCRIPTION

Blueberry Mountain conjures up images of an August afternoon blissfully spent picking sweet blue morsels from low shrubs while gazing over a lovely valley and surrounding

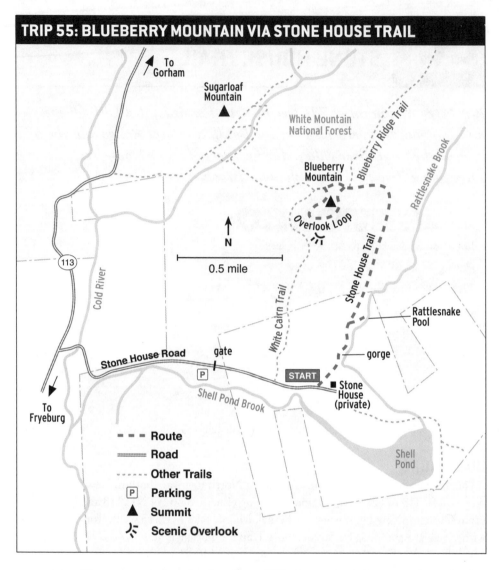

mountains. The next morning there's a feast of blueberry pancakes around a campfire. Well, that aptly describes the experience on this trail.

Stone House Trail, named for an attractive stone building (private) near the trailhead, provides the easiest ascent of Blueberry Mountain and is the most suitable for children. The ascent is gradual, but the upper part is steeper and has a few rocky sections. A 0.6-mile loop around the summit gives you access to several outlooks.

Stone House Trail is marked at its lower end with Chatham Trail Association (CTA) signs and some yellow blazes. The route passes through private land for the first mile, so stay on the main trail marked by the CTA signs and blazes, except when taking detours to Rattlesnake Flume and Pool. The trail eventually enters the Caribou–Speckled Mountain Wilderness. In keeping with U.S. Forest Service policy, trail blazes are no longer maintained in wilderness areas so be careful in following the trail through the wilderness area.

The distances provided below are from the trailhead at Stone House Road and do not include the 0.5 mile from the parking area. The first part of the trail is a very gradual uphill on an old logging road. After 0.2 mile, a private path from the Stone House enters right. A few paces beyond, a spur path to the right marked with an arrow leads you to a view of Rattlesnake Flume. It is definitely worth the 30-yard detour to a little wooden bridge over the flume. Here you can watch the waters of Rattlesnake Brook rushing through a narrow gorge with straight walls rising about 25 feet above the water. Rock ferns and rock tripe (a lichen) cover the damp walls of the flume. On the opposite side of the brook, look for the exquisite blossoms of trailing arbutus (in May) and twinflower (in July). Like the well-known flume of Franconia Notch, Rattlesnake Flume was created by the erosion of a narrow dike of softer rock that had intruded into the granite.

A whole network of trails beyond the bridge could easily lead you astray, so return to Stone House Trail the way you came and continue uphill. At 0.5 mile, the trail crosses a small wooden bridge and then passes a sign: "Stone House Trail to Blueberry Mountain." Shortly after, a spur path on the right leads you 0.1 mile to Rattlesnake Pool.

Rattlesnake Pool is actually a series of small pools connected by cascades and chutes. The setting is a shady woods of hemlock, beech, yellow birch, and striped maple. This is a good place for a snack, lunch, or, if you are truly daring, a plunge into the icy waters. The first pool is fairly deep (probably about 15 feet) and has remarkably clear water. The pools farther downstream are shallower and more suitable for young children, but be prepared for some scrambling over boulders that may be slippery.

A young hiker picks blueberries on Blueberry Mountain. While picking the fruit seems irresistible, keep in mind that wild creatures depend on these bushes for survival and we do not.

After Rattlesnake Pool, return to Stone House Trail. This is a possible turnaround point if you are hiking with children who have reached their limit. If not, continue uphill on the trail, being sure to stay left at a fork as indicated by a CTA sign.

The next section of the trail is a gradual uphill with a pleasant hemlock forest to your right and a babbling brook to your left. At 0.8 mile, the trail enters the Caribou–Speckled Mountain Wilderness and becomes steeper, passing through a thick forest of beech. Here you will find beechdrops, a unique plant that grows only under beech trees. All you ever see of this 6- to 18-inch plant are its small white flowers with reddish brown splotches scattered along a pale stalk. It has no green leaves because it gets all of its nutrition by parasitizing the roots of the beech tree. Beechdrops plants do no obvious damage to the host trees. Wherever there are beechdrops, you are bound to find beeches.

Listen for bird songs in June and July, and you may hear the flutelike sounds of hermit thrushes near the trailhead and Swainson's thrushes higher up. Also, keep your eyes open for guilds of forest birds (see "Bird Guilds in the White Mountains," page 122), including chickadees, nuthatches, downy woodpeckers, blue jays, and some finches.

At 1.2 miles, a newly relocated section of the trail swings to the right to avoid a heavily eroded section. Remember, the trail is no longer blazed at this point, so you need to follow the path carefully. Here the forest has become almost completely red spruce and balsam fir. The trail loops around to the left and steepens, with a few sections requiring a bit of scrambling on ledges. Stone House Trail ends at its junction with Blueberry Ridge Trail 1.7 miles from the start of the trip (2.2 miles from the parking area) and near the 1,781-foot summit of Blueberry Mountain. For the best vistas and blueberries, turn left (west) onto Blueberry Ridge Trail and follow it past a few small cairns for about 50 yards to its junction with Overlook Loop. Take Overlook Loop to the left.

Overlook Loop around the summit of Blueberry Mountain has awe-inspiring views from several open, rocky ledges. I first visited the summit on a magical day in fall when the scene was at first muted and dull because of fog. Then the fog began to lift, unveiling incredibly vivid fall foliage. To the southwest, the peaks of the Baldface–Royce Range slowly came into view and eventually loomed over everything. Shell Pond and Little Deer and Big Deer hills are prominent to the south. Special moments like this can make you forget all the damp days of hiking in the mist when you cannot see much past your own nose.

Lowbush blueberry shrubs are everywhere on Blueberry Mountain. Huckleberries grow here too. They are darker in color and seedier than blueberries but also quite tasty. They can be distinguished from blueberries by their leaves; the undersides of huckleberry leaves are covered by small yellow resin dots (easier to see if you have a hand lens). Other plants to note from the Overlook Loop are rhodora, which has beautiful, large pink flowers around Memorial Day weekend; three-toothed cinquefoil; sheep laurel, which looks like a miniature mountain laurel; red pine; white pine; and red spruce. Birds and mammals in this area include ravens, dark-eyed juncos, and snowshoe hares.

Overlook Loop passes a small bog that provides a good illustration of why bogs form where they do. The water that collects in this depression is stagnant, with no flow to replenish nutrients once plants use them up. The several species of sphagnum mosses that grow so profusely in the bog make life even more difficult for plants and for the fungi and bacteria that decompose dead leaves and recycle nutrients, because they increase the acidity of the water. As a result, plants that live in bogs must be able to tolerate acidity and very low levels of nutrients.

One beautiful tree that manages to grow quite well in this and other bogs is larch, also called tamarack (illustrated here). This conifer has gracefully curved branches with 10 to 30 needles per bunch. Unlike other conifers such as spruce and fir, larch needles are actually shed in winter. Look also for cotton grass, with its unmistakable cottony white balls at the top of leafless, grasslike stems. Bog bilberry and mountain holly also grow here.

Overlook Loop ends in 0.4 mile back at Blueberry Ridge Trail. Turn right for the 0.2-mile walk back to the intersection with Stone House Trail and then your descent.

DID YOU KNOW?

Not surprisingly, given how common these plants are on mountain summits, there is another Blueberry Mountain in the White Mountains. The other Blueberry Mountain is in the westernmost part of the national forest in the town of Benton, New Hampshire. Between these two peaks, which are at opposite corners of the east–west extent of the White Mountains, you are still never far from a place to pick blueberries.

OTHER ACTIVITIES

Stone House Trail can be combined with Blueberry Ridge and White Cairn trails to make a loop, but be aware that White Cairn Trail has some steep, rocky sections that could be a problem, particularly in wet weather. In addition, beaver activity may make it necessary to bushwhack around flooded sections near the bottom of the trail. If you choose this option, it is best to ascend via White Cairn Trail and descend via Stone House Trail.

You can also combine this hike with a much more level hike around Shell Pond (Trip 50).

MORE INFORMATION

The trail begins on private land and enters the White Mountain National Forest after about 0.5 mile. Parking is free.

The area around the summit of Blueberry Mountain is part of the Caribou–Speckled Mountain Wilderness. Hiking groups are limited to ten or fewer individuals and geocaching is prohibited; fs.usda.gov/detail/whitemountain/specialplaces/?cid=stelprdb5186041.

56 CARIBOU MOUNTAIN

This loop hike takes you through a wilderness area past beautiful cascades to the broad, open summit of Caribou Mountain (2,870 feet), one of the highest peaks in the Evans Notch region. The summit has breathtaking views as well as uncommon alpine plants.

Features 🏂 🏃 🏊 🚶 🐕 ♨ ☀ 🌲

Location Batchelder's Grant, ME

Rating Strenuous

Distance 6.9-mile loop

Elevation Gain 1,950 feet

Estimated Time 6 hours

Maps AMC *White Mountain National Forest Map & Guide*, 4th ed., E13; AMC *White Mountain Guide*, 31st ed. Map 5 Carter Range–Evans Notch, E13; USGS Topo: Speckled Mountain

GPS Coordinates 44° 20.16′ N, 70° 58.52′ W

Contact White Mountain National Forest: fs.usda.gov/whitemountain, 603-536-6100

DIRECTIONS

The same parking area serves both Caribou Trail and Mud Brook Trail, the two trails used for this loop. From Gorham, New Hampshire, follow US 2 east to Gilead, Maine (about 11 miles) and turn right onto NH 113. Travel about 4.7 miles south. The parking area is on the left. Space is available for about fifteen vehicles.

From the North Conway area in New Hampshire, pick up ME 113 in Fryeburg, Maine, after taking either US 302 or NH 113 to Fryeburg and head north. ME 113 follows the Maine–New Hampshire border, passing through the Maine villages of North Fryeburg and Stow. The trailhead is on the right about 5.5 miles north of the national forest's Basin Pond picnic and camping area. ME 113 is not plowed through Evans Notch in winter, so this is only a three-season hike.

TRAIL DESCRIPTION

This loop hike ascends via Caribou Trail and then uses Mud Brook Trail for the final climb to the actual summit and for the descent. Much of the route is within the Caribou–Speckled Mountain Wilderness. Caribou Trail leaves from the left (north) side of the parking area.

The trail begins by descending slightly and reaches Morrison Brook at 0.4 mile. Rock-hop to cross the brook. (The former bridge here washed out in a storm.) This is the first of at least

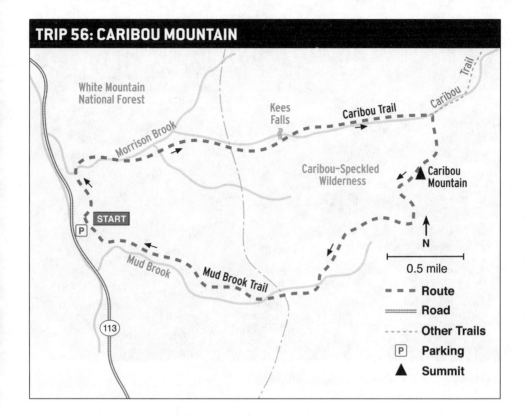

six stream crossings, none of which should present difficulties except in extreme high water. In about 0.8 mile, the trail returns to the side of the brook and begins a long ascent alongside it. It enters the Caribou–Speckled Mountain Wilderness after about 1.5 miles.

At 2.0 miles, the trail approaches Kees Falls, a beautiful 60-foot cascade. It follows the right side of the falls and then crosses the stream at the top. Get the best view of the falls by scrambling down (carefully) after crossing the stream. This is an ideal lunch spot, and a pool at the bottom of the falls is deep enough for a swim.

After you have enjoyed the falls, continue on the trail by crossing over to the right side of the brook, then back to the left, with waterfalls on all sides from two streams that join up. Large yellow birches and hemlocks dominate the forest. The trail continues ascending and finally turns away from the stream. It steepens and then levels out before reaching the junction with Mud Brook Trail at 3.0 miles. A small, wet, grassy swale at this junction may even harbor a moose.

Turn right onto Mud Brook Trail to continue your ascent. (Caribou Trail descends from this point to a second trailhead on a dirt road off US 2, a long way from the parking area, so be sure to follow Mud Brook Trail here.) As you keep ascending, the northern hardwoods give way to boreal forest (red spruce and balsam fir) characteristic of higher elevations in the White Mountains. See if you can detect the former location of a shelter in a flat area about 0.3 mile beyond the trail junction. Caribou Spring is there as well, but it is an unreliable water source during the dry days of summer.

A well-deserved rest on the way to Caribou Mountain.

Reach an open ledge providing a vista to the north shortly beyond the spring, and then arrive at the summit of Caribou Mountain at 3.6 miles. The 360-degree panorama from the summit includes many White Mountain peaks. Immediately to your south is Speckled Mountain. Looking west, you can see Evans Notch between Speckled and East Royce mountains. North Baldface and South Baldface mountains are behind them, and the Carter Range forms the long ridge farther to your west. Note the remote Wild River valley between the Carter Range and East Royce Mountain. On a clear day, Mounts Madison, Adams, and Washington are visible beyond the Carter Range. Lakes dominate to the southeast. To the north are the peaks of the Kilkenny and Crescent ridges.

After enjoying the scenery, take a moment to appreciate the plants that inhabit this open summit. Signs here explain that this is a special habitat for rare alpine plants, so please avoid trampling the plants. Several of the species on the Caribou summit are common in the higher elevations of the Presidential Range, so it is a treat to see them at this relatively low elevation. One of the most eye-catching is mountain sandwort, a short, delicate plant that forms clumps with small white flowers and fine leaves. Three low, shrubby plants that produce edible berries are lowbush blueberry, bog bilberry, and mountain cranberry. A rare species that occurs only in the White Mountains (except for one clump on an island in the Merrimack River at Newburyport, Massachusetts) is White Mountain whitlowwort (also called silvering; see Trip 23). This low, compact plant has inconspicuous flowers mostly hidden within silvery scales. Reindeer lichen, a light bluish green species that looks like a tiny bush, is interspersed with whitlowwort, making the area look like a rock garden. In late June or early July, the bright pink flowers of sheep laurel will be in bloom. They resemble a smaller version of their close relative, mountain laurel. Bird songs that might accompany you as you enjoy the summit include the flutelike sounds of Swainson's and hermit thrushes and the clear-whistled notes of the white-throated sparrow.

The trail can be a little difficult to follow from one side of the broad summit to the other. Let the occasional cairns be your guide, and watch for any remnant yellow blazes. As mentioned in Trip 55, the policy of the U.S. Forest Service is to not replace blazes in wilderness areas, so these are gradually fading. Look for a small, boggy area with cotton grass, Labrador tea, and leatherleaf near a second high point on the summit.

Continue following Mud Brook Trail when you are ready to descend. The trail passes open ledges that provide a vista east at 3.9 miles, but be careful of the dropoff. Then descend steeply through an attractive boreal forest with lots of blue-bead lily, which produces glossy but inedible blue berries in summer. The boreal forest is more extensive on the descent than on the ascent, but eventually you return to northern hardwood forest, which you will recognize by the increasing numbers of sugar and striped maples, yellow birches, and American beeches.

After about an hour of a fairly steep descent, the trail levels out somewhat and reaches the first of several crossings of Mud Brook (5.0 miles). Soon after, you pass a sign indicating that you are leaving the wilderness area. The route follows the brook for most of the remainder of the descent, often high above it. At about 6 miles, the trail widens and the grade becomes even gentler. At 6.6 miles, it swings away from the brook and shortly thereafter arrives at the trailhead (6.9 miles).

DID YOU KNOW?

Caribou do not currently inhabit the White Mountains, although they did in the immediate aftermath of the last Ice Age. According to the White Mountain National Forest website (fs.usda.gov/whitemountain), Caribou Mountain got its name after two brothers shot what was considered to be the last caribou in the White Mountains in 1854.

OTHER ACTIVITIES

Basin Pond, about 5.5 miles south of the trailhead, is a pleasant place for a picnic. You can canoe and fish (New Hampshire license needed) there or camp at the Cold River or Basin campgrounds nearby.

A variety of places along Wild River offer visitors the opportunity to hang out on flat rocks by the edge of the water. Park near Hastings Campground, about 1.5 miles north of the trailhead, and walk across the bridge to find your spot.

MORE INFORMATION

A large portion of this hike is through the Caribou–Speckled Mountain Wilderness (fs.usda.gov/detail/whitemountain/specialplaces/?cid=stelprdb5186041). Group sizes should be fewer than ten people. Signage and blazes are kept to a minimum to enhance the wilderness experience so more care is needed to follow your route.

An outhouse and a kiosk with trail information are at this trailhead. Parking is free.

8 // NORTH COUNTRY

The North Country is the northernmost section of the White Mountains, above US 2 and Gorham, New Hampshire. It tends to be less crowded than the busy regions farther south because it is a longer drive for visitors from the south, its mountains are not as tall as those of the Presidential or Franconia ranges, and it is still a center of logging operations. Much of the land is wild and not well developed for tourists. Nevertheless, the North Country has a certain mystique for backpackers and others who want to escape crowds. It is the White Mountains as they might have been 70 years ago. Several peaks in the Kilkenny Range, which forms the central "spine" of this region, are more than 4,000 feet.

SUPPLIES AND LOGISTICS
Berlin is the largest city in this part of the White Mountains. Pick up supplies there or in other towns you pass through on your way up, such as Gorham, Lancaster, or Twin Mountain. The nearest community to the South Pond Recreation Area (Trip 57) is Stark, several miles west of the access road to the recreation area. You will find a bathhouse, restrooms, and picnic tables at South Pond.

NEARBY CAMPING
No national forest campgrounds are in this region that are set up for car camping. Moose Brook State Park in Gorham has 42 tentsites. Numerous private campgrounds are available in the region, such as Nay Pond Campground in West Milan off NH 110.

Facing page: The North Country is the most remote and least traveled region of the White Mountains. *Photo by Ryan Smith.*

57 DEVIL'S HOPYARD

This hike takes you along South Pond and then into the Devil's Hopyard, a narrow, picturesque gorge where ice may linger even in summer and a flowing stream disappears beneath moss-covered boulders. The section of the trail along South Pond is universally accessible.

Features 🏕🚶🐕♿💧📍🎣🏊⛺💲

Location Stark, NH

Rating Easy

Distance 2.6 miles round trip (4.6 miles if the gate is closed)

Elevation Gain 200 feet

Estimated Time 1–2 hours, longer if the gate is closed

Maps AMC *White Mountain National Forest Map & Guide*, 4th ed., Kilkenny Region inset, B8; AMC *White Mountain Guide*, 31st ed. Map 6 North Country–Mahoosuc Range, B8; USGS Topo: West Milan

GPS Coordinates 44° 35.87′ N, 71° 22.09′ W

Contact White Mountain National Forest: fs.usda.gov/whitemountain, 603-536-6100

 CAUTION! The Devil's Hopyard is always wet and slippery; be careful on the rocks.

DIRECTIONS

Take NH 16 north from Gorham 4.5 miles to Berlin. Bear left on NH 110 heading north (to West Milan). It is a little tricky following NH 110 as it winds its way through Berlin because the directional arrows are rather tiny. Turn left onto Madigan Street and right onto Wight Street. Stay on NH 110 through West Milan. South Pond Road is on the left 14.7 miles after you turn onto NH 110 in Berlin. Several mailboxes and a hiking sign are at the intersection, but the sign for the South Pond Recreation Area may not be there in the off-season.

Bear right at a fork in 0.7 mile. During the off-season, there will be a closed gate a short distance after the fork. Park your vehicle outside the gate and walk the remainder of the distance to the pond (about 1 mile). If the gate is open, continue to the large parking area.

From Franconia Notch or the community of Twin Mountain, take US 3 north about 25 miles past Twin Mountain to its intersection with NH 110 in Groveton. This drive passes near the town of Guildhall, Vermont, notable as the ancestral home of the Crawford family before they settled in the notch that now bears their name (see "The Crawford Family," page 198). Follow NH 110 through Stark, another 8.0 miles, and turn right onto South

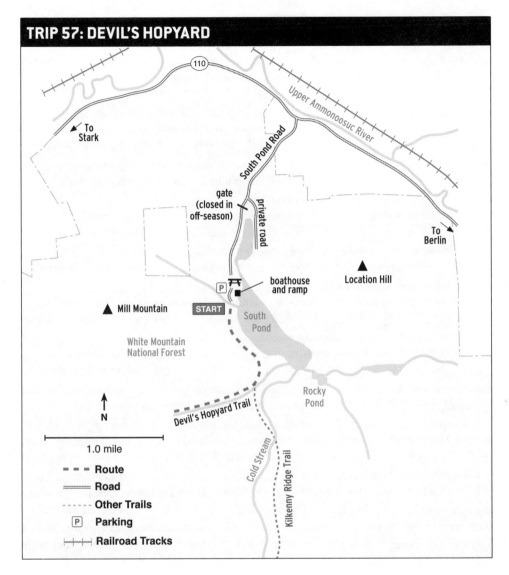

Pond Road about 1.7 miles past a historical marker along the road. Follow the directions above from there.

TRAIL DESCRIPTION

The beginning section of the trail to the Devil's Hopyard is an accessible path (880 feet), which means it is also ideal for strollers and very young walkers. Within the Devil's Hopyard itself, the trail requires some scrambling on rocks, so this section is not recommended for families with young children (2 to 5 years old). Caution is required at all times for everyone because the rocks in the shady gorge are almost always wet and slippery. The Devil's Hopyard is an exquisite spot, however, and it is certainly worth the walk, even if you don't get very far into it.

To start the hike, walk past the bathhouse at the South Pond Recreation Area, following signs to Kilkenny Ridge Trail (yellow blazes) and the quarter-mile accessible trail. These start out together along South Pond as a level gravel path. Along the way there are benches at which you can stop and admire the pond, pull out a fishing rod (New Hampshire license needed), or throw stones into the water.

The rich deciduous forest here is the type that dominates the lower elevations of the White Mountains. Trees include American beech, sugar maple, yellow birch, and eastern hemlock. Beech trees have distinctive, smooth gray bark that looks like it was meant for someone to carve their initials into (of course you won't do that!). Sugar maples have the familiar five-lobed leaves. The bark of yellow birch, which peels naturally, is yellowish brown and marked with short horizontal lines.

Two shorter woody plants along this part of the trail are striped maple and hobblebush. Striped maple is a small tree with distinctly green-and-white-striped bark and large, lobed leaves that look like a goose's foot. Hobblebush forms impenetrable thickets that will hobble anyone who dares to lumber through. It has large, rounded leaves that are arranged along its skinny branches in pairs.

The flowers of the hobblebush show a fascinating division of labor. Flat-topped white clusters bloom in May. The outer flowers are all show but no business. They serve to attract insects to the cluster but are themselves sterile. The innocuous-looking flowers in the center of the cluster lack the showy petals but have the stamens and pistils needed to produce fruits and seeds. Insects attracted to the cluster by the showy flowers brush up against the inner ones, pollinating them. Later in the season, clusters of fruits that start out red and eventually turn bluish black show that this special arrangement does work.

Kilkenny Ridge Trail extends as a path beyond the accessible trail and could be muddy in spots. You might see American shinleaf, a common woodland wildflower with roundish leaves that hug the ground and a spike of nodding flowers with five white petals in midsummer.

Kilkenny Ridge Trail crosses Devil's Hopyard Stream, and at 0.7 mile, take Devil's Hopyard Trail, which forks off to the right where Kilkenny Ridge Trail continues straight. Shining club moss is abundant on the forest floor at this junction. It resembles an upright moss with erect 6-inch stems that are covered by tightly whorled "leaves," each from ⅛- to a ¼-inch long, giving them the appearance of bottle brushes. Today the little plants are easily overlooked, but millions of years ago their distant relatives were as large as trees. Much of the coal burned for fuel comes from these mosses' fossilized ancestors.

At 0.8 mile, Devil's Hopyard Trail crosses Devil's Hopyard Stream on a bridge. Beyond the bridge the gradient steepens, and the stream alternates between fast-moving riffles and calm pools. Aquatic insects and other invertebrates show distinct preferences for either riffles or pools. Water striders, for example, will seek out the calmer pools, whereas blackfly larvae attach themselves to rocks where the current is strong.

The trail enters the gorge, and you will instantly notice that it gets cooler, as if you've just walked into a refrigerator. The drop in temperature results from the cold water of the rushing stream and the dense shade within the steep walls of the gorge. Even in midsummer, lingering ice can be found in holes between the rocks. At times you might feel as if you are

Devil's Hopyard Stream disappears under boulders in the Devil's Hopyard. Mosses and ferns abound in this damp environment.

walking on top of the stream—and indeed you are. The water is often hidden underneath a jumble of boulders that are part of the trail. Gurgling sounds from holes between the rocks reveal that the stream has gone underground.

Mosses and ferns thrive in this cool, damp habitat. One of the most abundant mosses is piggyback moss, named so because the delicate new branches ride directly on top of the old ones. This common moss is also called fern moss because of its ferny appearance. It covers many of the boulders in a lush coat of green.

Devil's Hopyard Trail becomes increasingly steep before ending at 1.3 miles, having climbed about 200 feet. The shady gorge remains damp long after rainstorms have passed. Use your judgment to determine how much farther everyone should scramble before turning around.

DID YOU KNOW?

Hops are cultivated to be used in brewing beer, so a hopyard is a field where hops are grown. What that has to do with the White Mountains, where hops are not cultivated, is a mystery. You can decide after exploring this beautiful but dark and slippery gorge if the "Devil" moniker is warranted.

OTHER ACTIVITIES

The South Pond Recreation Area is ideal for families either before or after a walk to the Devil's Hopyard. This developed Forest Service recreational area with picnic tables, a swimming beach, a bathhouse, and boater access is easy to get to. A family can plan an entire day's outing, hanging out at the recreation area for part of the time and hiking for the remainder.

Dogs are not allowed on the beach or in the bathhouse, but they are allowed on the trails. If you have your dog with you, tell the person at the gate that you are hiking the trails.

If you enjoyed exploring the Devil's Hopyard, a longer, more challenging hike into a similar gorge is Ice Gulch Path in Randolph off US 2. See AMC's *White Mountain Guide* for details.

MORE INFORMATION

The White Mountain National Forest lists South Pond and its bathhouse as an accessible swimming area with a quarter-mile gravel-packed shoreline trail along the pond. See fs.usda.gov/Internet/FSE_DOCUMENTS/stelprdb5377701.pdf.

The recreation area is open from 10 A.M. to 8 P.M. during the summer season. At the time this guide was written, the recreation area charged an entrance fee of $7 per vehicle. It is possible that a White Mountain National Forest parking pass will get you in if you tell the person at the gate that you are just hiking and do not plan to use the beach facilities. Before 10 A.M. and during the off-season, a barrier blocks the access road about a mile from the parking area. Hikers can go around the barrier but need to walk about 1.1 mile to get to South Pond and to Devil's Hopyard Trail.

58 MOUNT CRAG

Mount Crag is a small mountain that affords a superb vista of the Androscoggin Valley and surrounding peaks for very little effort. The hike described here is a pleasant, well-graded trail through hemlocks and northern hardwoods to the outlook at the summit.

Features 👣 🐕 💧 🔖 ❋

Location Shelburne, NH

Rating Moderate

Distance 2.4 miles round trip

Elevation Gain 700 feet

Estimated Time 2 hours

Maps AMC *White Mountain National Forest Map & Guide*, 4th ed., E12; AMC *White Mountain Guide*, 31st ed. Map 6 North Country–Mahoosuc, E12; USGS Topo: Shelburne

GPS Coordinates 44° 24.75′ N, 71° 04.09′ W.

Contact Shelburne Trails Club: shelburnetrails@gmail.com

DIRECTIONS

From the intersection of US 2 and NH 16 in Gorham, head east along US 2 toward Bethel, Maine. After 3.4 miles, turn left onto North Road. This crosses the Androscoggin River near a dam site. Continue for 3.2 miles along North Road. The trailhead for Austin Brook Trail is just before the road crosses Austin Brook. Several cars can park in spaces on either side of the bridge. Walk through a turnstile to start your hike.

TRAIL DESCRIPTION

Blue-blazed Austin Brook Trail is an old forest road running along the brook. Note the dam and waterfall at the beginning of the trail just after passing through the turnstile. Walk past a small pond and some lawns and then enter a forest of hemlocks.

At 0.4 mile you reach the junction with Yellow Trail, which originates at Philbrook Farm Inn. Turn left for Mount Crag. Yellow Trail, a woodland path with yellow blazes, starts out in a dark hemlock forest, but the forest changes to northern hardwoods (primarily American beech and yellow birch) as you begin your ascent. The well-graded trail is never too steep, but still enough of a climb to make you feel like you earned your lunch or snack at the top.

Beechdrops, a plant that is parasitic on the roots of beeches, is particularly abundant along the trail. The small herb, typically about 6 inches high, has a reddish brown stalk

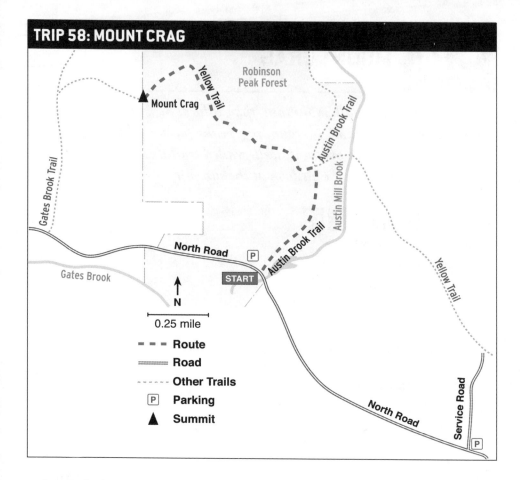

with a small white flower with brownish spots on top. Because beechdrops gets all its nutrition from the beech it parasitizes, it has no green leaves.

Yellow Trail reaches the summit ledges of Mount Crag at 1.2 miles. This is 0.8 mile from its junction with Austin Brook Trail. Enjoy the lovely view of the Androscoggin River valley. The last time we were there, someone had even provided lawn chairs to enhance the experience. The Androscoggin River has its source in Lake Umbagog, north of Mount Crag. It flows south past the New Hampshire towns of Berlin and Gorham and then east into Maine, where it turns southeast and joins the Kennebec River in Merrymeeting Bay near the town of Bath.

Mount Moriah, a 4,000-footer, is the prominent peak across the valley to the southwest. By walking out on the ledge and looking west, you can see the peaks of the Northern Presidentials.

The vegetation at and near the summit of Mount Crag differs from that on your ascent. Summit trees include red spruce, red and white pine, hemlock, and red oak. Trailing arbutus, sheep laurel, huckleberry, lowbush blueberry, Canada mayflower, flowering wintergreen, and reindeer lichen form much of the understory.

Retrace your steps to the trailhead. The 1.2-mile descent should take about 40 minutes.

OTHER ACTIVITIES

You can also pick up Yellow Trail at Philbrook Farm Inn, which is on North Road about 1 mile east of the trailhead for Austin Brook Trail. This is a somewhat longer hike (3.6 miles) and requires a crossing of Austin Brook that could be challenging during high water. It is a good idea to stop at the inn before starting your hike to check on where you should park.

The trailhead for Yellow Trail is not obvious from the inn itself. You need to walk along a service road that starts at the west side of the inn. It passes several cottages, enters the woods, and reaches the joint trailhead for Yellow, Red, and Blue trails. Follow the yellow blazes. Most of Yellow Trail in this section is along a grassy woodland road, but watch those blazes carefully to avoid turning off on unmarked paths.

Recent logging activity is evident along the route. Yellow Trail reaches Austin Brook in about 0.9 mile, where you can either ford by carefully stepping on rocks or take a slight detour and use a special hand-powered cable car to aid your crossing. (A sign indicates that you use the cable car at your own risk.) Once safely across the brook, you enter a hemlock forest and reach the junction with Austin Brook Trail, 1.0 mile from Philbrook Farm Inn. From this point, follow the original trail description above.

MORE INFORMATION

Mount Crag and the trails that lead to its summit are all on private conservation land, so please respect the privacy of residences near the trailhead and along the trail. The trails are maintained by the Shelburne Trails Club, which also constructed the aforementioned cable car at Austin Brook.

Gorham, New Hampshire, the nearest town, has motels, restaurants, gas stations, and other stores.

The Northern Presidential Range in the clouds, as viewed from Mount Crag.

59   LOOKOUT LEDGE

Lookout Ledge is a rocky outcropping on the side of Mount Randolph that affords a wonderful view of King Ravine and Mounts Adams and Madison, plus some of the peaks of the Carter Range. Ledge Trail provides a relatively direct ascent, steep in a few places but for the most part well graded.

Features 🪜 🧍 🐕 🔖 🔍 ❄️

Location Randolph, NH

Rating Moderate

Distance 2.6 miles round trip

Elevation Gain 950 feet

Estimated Time 2.5–3.5 hours

Maps AMC *White Mountain National Forest Map & Guide*, 4th ed., E9; AMC *White Mountain Guide*, 31st ed. Map 6 North Country–Mahoosuc Range, E9; USGS Topo: Mount Washington to Pliny Range

GPS Coordinates 44° 22.48′ N, 71° 17.48′ W

Contact Randolph Community Forest: info@randolphforest.org

DIRECTIONS

The trailhead for Ledge Trail is at the Ravine House site on Durand Road in Randolph. From Franconia Notch, Crawford Notch, and the community of Twin Mountain, take US 3 north at its junction with US 302 in Twin Mountain. After about 2 miles, turn right onto NH 115 and take it for about 10 miles to US 2. Turn right onto US 2, take it for about 6 miles, and then turn left onto Durand Road, which closely parallels US 2. The Ravine House site is well marked with a historical sign on the left in about 1.6 miles. The trailhead is on the west side of the Ravine House site. Parking areas are on both sides of the road. (Durand Road eventually rejoins US 2 about 1 mile east of the Ravine House.)

From North Conway and Pinkham Notch, take NH 16 into Gorham, where it meets US 2. Travel west on US 2 for about 4.5 miles past its split with NH 16. Turn right at the east intersection of Durand Road with US 2 and take it for 1.1 miles to the Ravine House site on the right.

TRAIL DESCRIPTION

Much of Ledge Trail is within the Randolph Community Forest. This 10,000-acre tract, formerly owned by a timber company, is now owned and managed by the Town of Randolph with a conservation easement held by the state of New Hampshire. More on that below.

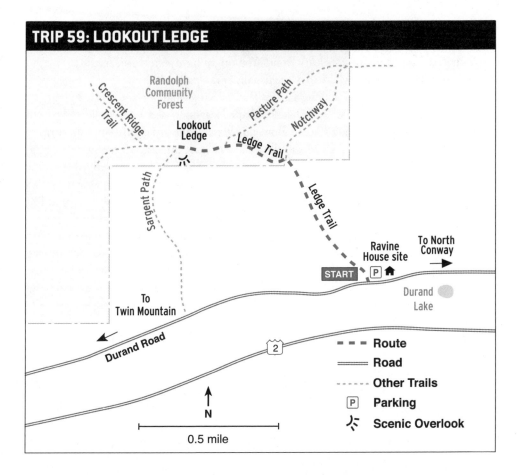

Crescent Ridge Trail

Randolph Community Forest

Pasture Path

Notchway

Lookout Ledge

Ledge Trail

Sargent Path

Ledge Trail

Ravine House site

To North Conway

START

To Twin Mountain

Durand Lake

Durand Road

2

- - - Route
—— Road
.... Other Trails
P Parking
Scenic Overlook

N

0.5 mile

Ledge Trail is well marked with orange blazes. The trail begins in the woods between two driveways and joins an old logging road. The pitch varies from moderately steep to gently uphill throughout this hike. The dominant trees along most of the route are sugar maple, American beech, and yellow and paper birch. Look also for the tall, straight trunks of white ash. The bark of this tree has distinct vertical ridges, and its compound leaves attach to its branches in pairs.

The forest was severely affected by an ice storm in January 1998 that downed many trees. The ice storm was actually part of the story of the creation of the Randolph Community Forest because it convinced the timber company that owned the land to sell it. Much of the forest is regrown now, but gaps still exist where sunlight penetrates to the forest floor, and this has stimulated the rampant growth of hay-scented ferns. These ferns are able to exploit forest gaps because once they take root they spread rapidly. All the hay-scented ferns in a forest opening may actually be connected by underground rhizomes and therefore be one individual plant. Eventually, however, saplings of sugar maple, yellow birch, and American beech, spawned from nearby trees that survived the ice storm, will fill in the open patches, perhaps preceded by paper birch. Trees in the White Mountains must be able to tolerate periodic setbacks from storms (see "Storms in the White Mountains," page 244), harsh winters, drought, flooding, disease, and insect outbreaks.

Two other types of ferns grow along the trail. Look for New York fern, with its smallish, lacy frond tapered at both ends. Sensitive fern produces clusters of small, round spore cases (sori) on a stem separate from its leafy frond. You might have seen these "fertile fronds" in dried flower arrangements, where they are usually spray-painted silver.

A wildflower that flourishes along Ledge Trail is King Solomon's seal. This plant has unbranched, arching stems with broad, lance-shaped leaves. It used to be considered part of the lily family but now is thought to be more closely related to asparagus—but don't try to eat it. In spring, pairs of small greenish yellow flowers hang underneath the stem. In summer, these turn into blue-black berries. The name King Solomon's seal is derived from the pattern of the scar left on the rootstock when the stem is broken off. It presumably resembles an official seal of the ancient king. Other wildflowers to look for include blue-bead lily, doll's-eye (white baneberry), wild sarsaparilla, white lettuce, and whorled aster.

In 0.6 mile, Notchway comes in from the right, and Ledge Trail then makes a sharp bend to the left. The trail continues climbing steeply, sometimes with minor scrambling over rocks, and then joins another old logging road for a time. Look carefully for bear claw marks on tree trunks and for bear "nests." The latter are not places where bears sleep but are clusters of broken branches that bears pull together when they are sitting at a crook in a tree while feeding on nuts, buds, and leaves.

Ledge Trail reaches a junction with Pasture Path at 1.1 miles. Very soon after, the northern hardwoods you have been walking through give way to spruce-fir forest. You may particularly enjoy looking at the caves made by rocks and tree roots.

After another steep section, Ledge Trail turns left, passes a wonderful viewpoint with a bench (the Eyrie), and reaches Lookout Ledge at 1.3 miles. This is where the trail meets

Lookout Ledge provides a dramatic view of King Ravine and Mount Adams. *Photo by Nancy Schalch.*

Crescent Ridge Trail and Sargent Path. The large, flat ledge is an inviting place to sit and enjoy both your lunch and the scenery.

The most striking sight from Lookout Ledge is the cirque of King Ravine on the upper slope of Mount Adams. It is a classic glacier-carved, bowl-shaped ravine on the side of a mountain, as if it were taken straight from the pages of a geology textbook. (See "Why Glaciers?" on page 167 for more on glaciation.) With binoculars you can easily see the boulders that fell from the sides of the ravine and now litter its floor. Although they seem small from Lookout Ledge, they present a serious challenge to hikers in King Ravine. Notice the cairns that mark the trails up the ravine. Crag Camp, a cabin operated by the Randolph Mountain Club, overlooks the ravine on its right wall.

Lookout Ledge is an ideal place to work with your compass and a map of the region to identify mountains, ridges, valleys, and streams. Mounts Adams and Madison, with their pointed, picturesque summits, loom large in the foreground. The col between the two peaks is the location of AMC's Madison Hut (not visible from Lookout Ledge). From west to east are Castellated Ridge, Nowell Ridge, Durand Ridge, Snyder Brook, Gordon Ridge, and Howker Ridge. To the southeast are Pine Mountain (Trip 45) and Imp Mountain of the Carter–Moriah Range. The Mahoosuc Range and the Androscoggin River valley are to the east. Durand Lake is right below you.

Retrace your steps to return to the parking area.

DID YOU KNOW?

John Durand, for whom the road, ridge, and lake were named, was a Londoner who received the original grant to settle in the region. The town of Randolph was originally known as Durand.

OTHER ACTIVITIES

A network of trails in this area could make for a longer hike. You could use Sargent Path for the descent, but you would need to spot a second vehicle at its trailhead or walk the 0.75 mile along Durand Road. Sargent Path is steeper than Ledge Trail.

MORE INFORMATION

The Randolph Community Forest through which much of Ledge Trail runs includes most of the northern part of the town of Randolph. This is the largest town-owned forest in New Hampshire, quite an accomplishment for a community of only 300 residents. Read about the forest's creation in 2001 by downloading a pdf at randolphforest.org/wp-content/documents/miscellaneous/Randolph_Community_Forest_Story.pdf. The lower part of the trail and Lookout Ledge itself are privately owned.

Lookout Ledge can be approached by numerous trails north of US 2 that are maintained by the Randolph Mountain Club (randolphmountainclub.org). Parking is free.

The town of Gorham seven miles east has restaurants, motels, gas stations, and other stores.

THE RAVINE HOUSE

The Ravine House site at the trailhead for Ledge Trail should be a prime destination for anyone interested in the history of trail-building in the White Mountains. First opened to guests in 1877, it became a summer hangout for people who built and hiked trails in the northern Presidential Range and the Randolph area. According to Guy and Laura Waterman's *Forest and Crag: A History of Hiking, Trail Blazing, and Adventure in the Northeast Mountains* (SUNY Press, 2019), the Ravine House was not an opulent hotel cut from the Gilded Age, such as the extant Mount Washington Hotel in Bretton Woods; rather, it was a comfortable, rambling inn, grand in its own way. Like visitors today to AMC huts, people back then must have looked forward to returning to the Ravine House each evening for dinner and discussions with other guests about the trails they had hiked and what they were planning next. When they were done with such discussions, they might get together to play music.

If the guests at the table included one of the premier trail builders, such as Laban Watson, there was undoubtedly conversation about new trails needing to be built or a report on a trail in progress. Watson's trails were legendary for being the shortest, steepest, and most direct routes to a summit.

Perhaps someone might have bantered, "You can't be serious about building such a steep trail up Mount Adams!" J. Rayner Edmands, another master trail builder, preferred smoother, more graded paths—harder to construct, but easier on weary hikers' legs.

The Ravine House closed in 1960, but the town of Randolph continues the tradition of trail work and community spirit fostered by the Ravine House and several other now-defunct hotels in the area. Many of the trails in Randolph and the northern Presidential Range across US 2 are maintained by the Randolph Mountain Club, which was formed in the early 1900s to restore and maintain trails that had been obscured by logging activity at the turn of the century.

AMC's flag flies in front of the Ravine House in this photo from the early 1900s. *Photo courtesy of AMC Archives.*

60 UNKNOWN POND FROM MILL BROOK ROAD

This pleasant hike follows a stream and then ascends through an attractive paper birch forest to a remote boreal mountain pond bordered by conifers. At the pond you have a good chance of encountering some of the rare birds and wildlife of this region in a beautiful setting.

Features 👪 🐕 💧 🗺️ 🎇 ⛺

Location Stark, NH, to Kilkenny, NH

Rating Moderate

Distance 4.4 miles round trip

Elevation Gain 1,450 feet

Estimated Time 3.5 hours

Maps AMC *White Mountain National Forest Map & Guide*, 4th ed., Kilkenny Region inset, C8; AMC *White Mountain Guide*, 31st ed. Map 6 North Country–Mahoosuc Range, C8; USGS Topo: Stark

GPS Coordinates 44° 33.23′ N, 71° 24.62′ W

Contact White Mountain National Forest: fs.usda.gov/whitemountain, 603-536-6100

DIRECTIONS

Reach the trailhead from NH 110 on Mill Brook Road. The unpaved road is in good condition but is not maintained for winter travel.

Take NH 16 north from Gorham 4.5 miles to Berlin. Bear left onto NH 110 heading north (to West Milan). It is a little tricky following NH 110 as it winds its way through Berlin because the directional arrows are rather tiny. It turns left onto Madigan Street and then right onto Wight Street. Once out of Berlin, stay on NH 110 past the road to the South Pond Recreation Area. Mill Brook Road is on the left about 3 miles past South Pond Road, about 18 miles from Berlin, and just before the village of Stark Bridge. A hiker sign is at the intersection.

Follow Mill Brook Road (unpaved) south for 4.6 miles. Park just past the second bridge (space for several vehicles) and walk back over the bridge. The trailhead is on the east side of the road (right side if you are facing north) just before the bridge. A hiker sign is a little obscured by vegetation, so you might not see it at first glance.

TRAIL DESCRIPTION

Part of the charm of Unknown Pond is that it is in a quiet part of the White Mountains. You are likely to run into few fellow hikers here. Unknown Pond Trail begins as a

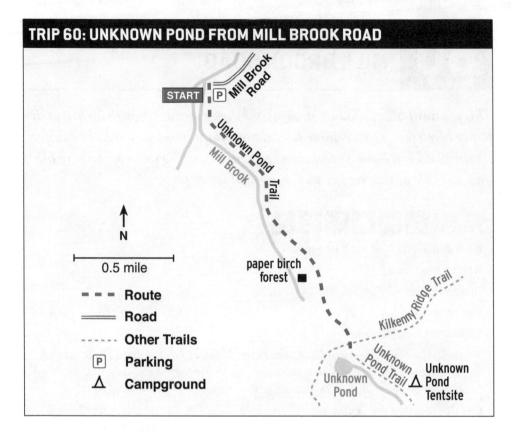

well-graded path along one of the branches of Mill Brook. The spruce-fir forest at the trail-head quickly changes to a rich northern hardwood forest with abundant wildflowers: Indian cucumber-root, painted trillium, bunchberry, and foamflower, to name a few. This first section of the trail can be muddy, particularly right after a rainstorm.

This section of the trail also had one of the greatest concentrations of moose droppings and hoofprints that I have ever seen, so keep your eyes open for moose. On the other side of the size-and-grace spectrum, watch for the white admiral butterfly, a large brown butterfly with a bold white stripe on its forewings and hind wings. Oddly, the butterflies have an affinity for the moose droppings, and it is not uncommon to see clusters of these creatures wherever there are such deposits.

In about 1 mile, Unknown Pond Trail reaches a small clearing where another branch of Mill Brook comes in, and the more serious ascent begins. This is accompanied by yellow and paper (white) birches. Eventually, the yellow birches drop out and the forest becomes almost all paper birches, a beautiful backdrop to your climb. The presence of these trees is a legacy to logging activities that formerly occurred in this region. Red spruces and balsam firs, the dominant trees above about 2,500 feet, will eventually replace the birches. Where the trees are a little thin, you get occasional views of the nearby ridge of the Pilot Range to the southwest.

Mist over Unknown Pond. At an elevation of 3,200 feet, the pond is in the heart of the boreal (spruce-fir) forest.

At about 2 miles, the trail levels out and crosses a small, rushing stream in an open area. This is a pleasant place to take a short break. The vegetation along the stream includes goldenrods and asters that provide midsummer color, tall meadow rue (fuzzy white flowers), and lady ferns. Bunchberries, whose flowers have long since bloomed near the trailhead, may still be in bloom here, a result of the delayed season at higher elevations. Shortly after the stream, you pass a sign providing information about backcountry camping opportunities at Unknown Pond, so you know you are getting close.

Unknown Pond Trail intersects Kilkenny Ridge Trail at 2.2 miles at the northeast corner of the pond. For a good view of the pond, turn right (south) on Kilkenny Ridge Trail for about 100 feet and then walk a few paces to the left to the water's edge. On a clear day, the Horn, an impressively sharp peak that is part of the Kilkenny Ridge, makes a striking backdrop to the pond.

Campers and hikers straying off trails have seriously eroded the shoreline at Unknown Pond. The Forest Service has addressed this by clearly marking camping and revegetation areas. As the signs indicate, avoid entering the revegetation areas and, for those who are camping, stay in the designated areas.

Return to the trail junction and continue to the right. At this point, Unknown Pond and Kilkenny Ridge trails run together for about 100 yards. For the second excellent outlook, follow Unknown Pond Trail past where Kilkenny Ridge Trail departs to the north. Look for an open area on the right just beyond where the spur path to the tentsites goes off to the left. This is the best lunch spot.

The shoreline is fringed with Labrador tea, a shrub with thick, leathery leaves that have rolled edges and white or rust-colored woolly hairs on their undersides. Yellow waterlilies grow in the shallows.

At an elevation of 3,170 feet, Unknown Pond is noted for its boreal birdlife. Rusty blackbirds, looking like red-winged blackbirds without the red wing markings, nest around the south side of the pond. Boreal chickadees, with their brown caps, are a high-elevation spruce-fir counterpart of the familiar black-capped chickadees. Swainson's thrushes, winter wrens, and white-throated sparrows vie for the title of the most accomplished songster at Unknown Pond. Yellow-rumped and blackpoll warblers, cedar waxwings, and dark-eyed juncos can also be found.

Retrace your steps to return to the trailhead.

DID YOU KNOW?

According to Steven D. Smith's *Ponds & Lakes of the White Mountains* (Backcountry Publications, 1998), Unknown Pond did not make it into AMC's *White Mountain Guide* until 1940—hence, the appropriateness of its name.

OTHER ACTIVITIES

Nearby South Pond Recreation Area (see Trip 57) offers swimming and boating. It has a bathhouse and restrooms (entry fee charged). The White Mountain National Forest has designated six tentsites off Unknown Pond Trail for backcountry camping at the east side of the pond. Camping is permitted only at those sites.

For a more extended hike, the Horn is about 2 miles south of Unknown Pond via Kilkenny Ridge Trail and a spur path. It provides an outstanding view of the pond and some peaks of the North Country, but you'll find some difficult scrambles to reach its summit.

Unknown Pond Trail continues past the pond for another 3.3 miles to a second trailhead on York Pond Road, 2.1 miles past the Berlin Fish Hatchery. Although you could spot a second vehicle at that trailhead, the gate at the fish hatchery is open only between 8 A.M. and 4:30 P.M., so you would need to finish your hike before closing time.

MORE INFORMATION

Parking is free at the trailhead.

Unknown Pond Trail is in a region of very small villages and limited services, so you may want to pick up supplies in Gorham or Berlin on your way up. Given the remoteness of this region, the outhouse at the camping area at the pond can come in handy.

APPENDIX A: HIKING WITH CHILDREN

Hiking with children requires flexibility, a sense of humor, and patience. You need to slow down and encourage children to explore the natural world around them—the sights, the sounds, and the smells—even if it means you might not make it to that scenic overlook or waterfall. You have a wonderful opportunity to not only expose a child to the wonders of the natural world at an early age but also to enjoy nature as a child sees it.

Our recommendations are based on our experiences and those of many AMC staff and friends, but please keep in mind that it's difficult to generalize about what a child can handle at a given age. Some precocious and energetic 5-year-olds may be ready for a 4,000-footer. Some 10-year-olds may not be willing to hike very far at all.

Don't be afraid to start your kids early. Our daughter slept through her first hike in a front carrier at 2 months of age. Hiking with a 1-year-old in a backpack is actually much easier than negotiating with a toddler. Pack diapers, baby food, and other items just as you would on any daylong outing, and be prepared with extra clothes.

WHAT KINDS OF HIKES DO KIDS LIKE?

With the right spirit, every trail can be fun for adults and children alike, but some trails will engage children more easily than others. In our hikes with children, we've noticed a few especially winning features.

Most children love to be around water. The White Mountains have an abundance of waterfalls and lakes that are popular destinations for family hikes. You can swim or wade, look for small critters, throw stones into the water, or have a picnic or a snack on big, flat boulders while dangling your feet in the water. It is also much more fun to hike along a flowing river or a bubbly stream than through unchanging woodland.

Most children love to walk on wooden plank bridges that cross streams and wetlands and on split logs that traverse muddy areas. (Covered bridges are even better, but there are only a few in the White Mountains.)

Most children like to stop and examine little things, such as an odd-looking bug on the path, a colorful leaf in autumn, or a brightly colored fungus. It is hard to predict what will strike their fancy. One friend remembered her nephew's fascination with small conifer trees that were his own height. Take the time to enjoy those things with children rather than hurrying off to the next destination.

Most children like climbing. Rocks and big boulders so common along many trails in the White Mountains are great opportunities for climbing and exploration. Especially intriguing are those that form caves or overhang the trail. Beginning hikers will proudly show you how they have "conquered" even a small rock in the middle of a trail.

Similarly, most children love scrambling around rocky ledges, particularly after they have been hiking through a dense forest. At a scenic overlook, the scenery itself is likely to play second fiddle to the scrambling. Rocky ledges are like a substitute jungle gym. (Of course, if the adults ooh and aah over the views, children may get curious and eventually start oohing and aahing too.) Remember to pay attention to children even as you admire the scenery, however, because there are no railings on most trails.

Most children love picking and eating fruit, such as blueberries. They may not persevere long enough to collect a stash for tomorrow morning's blueberry pancakes, but they will certainly enjoy this activity for a while. The summits of many of the smaller mountains listed in this book are loaded with ripe blueberries toward the end of July and throughout August. Huckleberries, blackberries, and raspberries are also available for picking.

Most children love bright colors. Some children will be attracted to wildflowers and brightly colored mushrooms, although others may not notice them. Preventing children from picking flowers may be the hardest job you'll have on the trail, but once they get into the habit of just looking, they'll keep it for life.

Most children like to see natural creatures. In the White Mountains, squirrels, chipmunks, toads, red efts (salamanders), and butterflies are usually popular in a child's bestiary. Look for tadpoles, frogs, fish, and water striders along the edges of ponds. Trees riddled with woodpecker holes, trees with bark stripped by moose, or trees scarred by bear claws are interesting sights to point out. Birds in the White Mountains are sometimes hard for

Inspecting a mushroom. This young hiker has mastered the art of "look, but don't touch," which is vital for protecting the natural environment.

children to enjoy because they are much more often heard than seen. Encourage children to listen to the beautiful bird songs in the forest, but don't push it. You'll be more successful if you can show them either the big birds of open spaces and wetlands—such as hawks, herons, and ducks—or the smaller, sassy, tame birds, such as gray jays and chickadees, which seem as curious about you as you are about them.

Many people who hike seek out quiet backcountry trails to get a refreshing break from their hectic work lives and their crowded urban or suburban surroundings. Children are less likely than adults to feel the need for such a solitary wilderness experience. In fact, they may enjoy the crowds at such places as the Flume or Sabbaday Falls.

Few people enjoy walking through an endless tunnel of trees with no scenery to admire. Adults can tolerate monotonous trails in anticipation of a reward at the end in the form of a summit, a waterfall or lake, or a breathtaking vista. When you are hiking with children, however, there is no guarantee that they will stick with the hike until that reward, so pick a trip that won't be disappointing even if you don't complete it.

Navigating can be a fun challenge. Some younger kids will be motivated by the responsibility of spotting the next blaze or trail marker. Older kids may want to learn how to read trail maps and use a compass and GPS. They may enjoy helping to plan the hike as well.

Invite one of your children's friends on the trip. Your children may enjoy the hike more if they have a friend along. They can chat, joke together, and encourage each other on the trail. Of course, you need to be sure that the friend is someone who likes hiking or this could backfire.

FAVORITE DISTRACTIONS

Inevitably, kids will hit a low point on some hikes. Here's where you need to be creative and prepared.

Some children love singing songs on the trail. Camp songs and songs they have learned in school are great when the trek seems never-ending. Let them pick out the songs, but be ready with your own.

Stories and tales of what you did when you were their age work wonders at distracting children. Ask them a nature question they can answer along the hike—look at the trip descriptions for ideas. Often there's something close at hand that can be made into a game, such as scraping resin off red spruce bark and chewing it to make spruce gum, or popping jewelweed seed pods to make them explode.

Make the hike into a scavenger hunt. Have a list of items kids can search for, and be ready to pull it out at a strategic moment. Possible items are toads, spiderwebs, ghost pipes, pinecones, princess pines, maple leaves, or whatever you can glean from reading the trip descriptions. You can also impart a valuable conservation lesson if you encourage children to leave the items in the forest or simply point them out, rather than collecting them in a bag.

ADDITIONAL THOUGHTS

Be flexible and allow plenty of extra time. Be ready to change your plans midhike, and always encourage kids to investigate the natural world. Time spent spying on a moose feeding on water plants or watching a moth caught in a spiderweb will likely be remembered much longer than seeing that third waterfall.

Be goal oriented if doing so can stimulate your children to overcome those first pangs of tiredness or a lack of motivation, but also be ready to bail out if it isn't working or if the children get engrossed in little things they see along the trail and time runs out before you reach that goal. The idea is to have fun, not to make this into a forced march. On the other hand, don't necessarily turn back at the first complaint either, particularly if there is something you're sure the children will really enjoy with just a little more effort.

Children have an amazing ability to do a complete 180-degree recovery just after they have insisted that they can't possibly move their legs another inch. We've been saved many times by something like a toad magically appearing on the trail and stimulating a mood change just when it seemed all was lost.

Sometimes picking kids up, clowning around, and carrying them for a short period will get them back on track. And be liberal with praise for how well they are doing.

Trips in this book with the "good for kids" icon have interesting things for both adults and children to see along the way so that the trip will be worthwhile even if you do not complete it. The text sometimes suggests logical places at which to turn around before reaching the end, such as at an attractive view or a pool of water in which toes can be immersed.

Remember, it is much more important for you to instill an appreciation for the natural world in your children than to impart facts about nature. Besides, sooner or later a kid will ask a question that even the most expert naturalist can't answer. Make it into a game and help them look up the answer after the hike. A pad and pencil are useful to record field notes and questions. Although it is better if everyone can get away from their cell phones during a hike, the app iNaturalist does an amazing job of identifying mysterious plants, insects, fungi, and other organisms.

Your own enthusiasm for the hike will rub off on them.

APPENDIX B: NATURAL HISTORY OF THE WHITE MOUNTAINS

The White Mountain region is a special place, not only for the scenery and outdoor recreational opportunities but also for the wonderful diversity of natural history. This brief description of the region's geology, plants, and animals hopefully will enrich your hiking experience. Look for more information in the individual trip descriptions, in the essays, and in the references. A complete guide to the natural history of the White Mountains would take up several volumes, so seek out additional books if you'd like to know more.

GEOGRAPHY

The White Mountains of north-central New Hampshire and western Maine are the largest expanse of mountains in New England. Forty-eight peaks exceed 4,000 feet in elevation and seven exceed 5,000 feet. Most of the region is included in the White Mountain National Forest and several state parks. The national forest and many volunteer organizations, such as Appalachian Mountain Club and the Randolph Mountain Club, maintain an extensive network of hiking trails.

Because of their elevation, the White Mountains have a cooler climate and a more "northern" ecology than one would expect at their latitude. Snow remains in some mountain ravines into June, and trees generally do not grow above an elevation of 4,500 feet. The higher peaks are notorious for damp, misty, and windy weather, so you should particularly cherish a beautiful summer day when there are extensive views. Mount Washington still holds the record for the strongest wind ever recorded by a human in the United States: 231 MPH on April 12, 1934.

A major geographic feature is the north-to-south-running valleys (called notches) that separate the major mountain ranges. From west to east, these are Franconia Notch, Zealand Notch, Crawford Notch, Pinkham Notch, and Evans Notch. Roads traverse all except Zealand.

GEOLOGY

Where did the White Mountains come from? The latest hypothesis is described in *The Geology of New Hampshire's White Mountains* by J. Dykstra Eusden and seven other geologists (The Durand Press, 2013). It is a fascinating story involving drifting ancient continents and oceans that formed and then disappeared. About 500 million years ago, Ganderia, a ribbonlike micro-continent, split off from Gondwana, the huge southern supercontinent located somewhere south of the equator at the time. The split formed an ocean, the Iapetus Ocean. Ganderia drifted across the earth and eventually fused with

Laurentia, which is the ancient continental mass that makes up most of today's North America. About 400 million years ago, the thick layers of sand and mud that had accumulated at the bottom of the Iapetus Ocean were squeezed between Ganderia and an ancient island continent called Avalonia that had also split off from Gondwana and was drifting in Ganderia's direction. This event is called the Acadian Orogeny. Under immense pressure, these layers hardened to form the schists, gneisses, and quartzites of today's Presidential Range and were then uplifted to the surface of the Earth. Pine Mountain and Stinson Mountain are great places to see how these layers of metamorphic rock were actually twisted by these powerful forces.

A second major geological event occurred 230 to 180 million years ago when the granite that forms the bedrock of much of the rest of the White Mountains solidified from molten rock deep within Earth as ancient continents split apart. Subsequent uplift and erosion of layers of softer, overlying rocks brought the granite to Earth's surface. Volcanic eruptions at that same time created additional rocks.

The rocks along the trails in the White Mountains are almost all granites or schists. Both have a salt-and-pepper appearance because they are composed of different-colored minerals. Granites are composed primarily of crystals of feldspar (whitish or pink) and quartz (translucent white or gray). Usually there are smaller amounts of mica flakes (biotite if brown or black; muscovite if white or silvery) and hornblende (black). The mineral crystals in schist are smaller than those in granite.

Gleaming white quartzes and glossy mica flakes are evident along just about any trail. Rock hounds will especially enjoy a visit to one of the abandoned mines, such as those on Lord Hill or North Sugarloaf. At these mines you can find large crystals of mica, feldspar, and, if you look hard enough, topaz, garnet, beryl, smoky quartz, and even amethyst.

When hiking through White Mountain forests, you will undoubtedly come upon some monstrous boulders. Jumbles of huge rocks at the base of a mountain, such as on Boulder Loop Trail or Mount Osceola Trail, probably tumbled down during landslides. Isolated boulders may be glacial erratics, carried to their destination by a glacier and left behind when ice in the glacier melted. You'll find large glacial erratics at the Flume, at "the Boulder" near Cascade Path in Waterville Valley, at Goodrich Rock, on Greeley Ponds Trail near its intersection with Osceola Trail, on Sugarloaf Trail, and at Glen Boulder.

Many of the hikes take you past huge outcroppings (visible exposures) of bedrock. Famous profiles such as the Indian Head near Franconia Notch and the Elephant Head at Crawford Notch are gigantic outcroppings of bedrock that are visible from highways. On most outcroppings of bedrock you can find narrow bands of white or black rocks, called dikes, crisscrossing the grayer granite. Dikes form when molten rock, heated by forces deep within the earth, flows into cracks in the granite and then cools. Pegmatite dikes are typically white and contain relatively large crystals of feldspar, quartz, mica, and sometimes other minerals. Basalt dikes are black and do not appear to have any crystalline structure at all, because the magma (molten rock) flowed near the surface of the earth and cooled so rapidly there was no time for crystal formation. Narrow, steep-sided gorges, called flumes, form where flowing water has eroded the softer dike and left the relatively harder granite wall. The Flume (at Franconia Notch) is the most well-known example, but there are other places where you can see a similar phenomenon (for example, Sabbaday Falls, Basin Trail).

The erosive action of glaciers had a profound effect on the White Mountain landscape. Mountain glaciers high up on the sides of peaks carved the now-famous bowl-shaped ravines called cirques in the Presidential Range. (The word cirque is derived from the same root as the word circus.) These include Tuckerman, Huntington, and King ravines and the Great Gulf. They face in the north, northeast, or east direction where snow from the broad uplands could accumulate, driven by prevailing western and southwestern winds and exposed to only limited direct solar radiation. Mountain glaciers also carved the sharp, narrow ridge of the Franconia Range, but its topography and orientation was not conducive to cirque formation.

The continental glaciers that covered much of North America during the last Ice Age had an even more widespread impact than the mountain glaciers. Four separate advances and retreats of glaciers occurred between 1 million and 13,000 years ago. The final glacier, which has been dated from 30,000 to 13,000 in the White Mountains, covered even Mount Washington under several thousand feet of ice. Its erosive action smoothed the summits of the Presidential Range and carved U-shaped north–south valleys, such as Crawford and Zealand notches. Pine Mountain is a good place to see scratches in the bedrock etched by stones dragged along by the movement of ice.

Erosion by streams in postglacial times has created V-shaped valleys, such as those evident in the Franconia Range and along the Valley Way in the northern Presidential Range. Waterfalls, such as Arethusa Falls, were created as east–west flowing streams dropped substantially over the sides of the north–south notches that had been deepened by the continental glaciers.

Recent investigations by the New Hampshire Historic Preservation Office have shown that people inhabited the area around what is now Jefferson, New Hampshire, about 11,000 years ago, indicating that the glaciers were no longer covering the White Mountains by then. Archaeological investigations since 1995 have uncovered tools, fluted spear points, and other artifacts.

FORESTS

The White Mountains are densely forested, a fact many easterners may not appreciate unless they have spent time in the Sierra Nevada or other western ranges. Many walks described in this book pass through two different types of forest: the northern hardwood at lower elevations and the boreal forest higher up.

Three broad-leaved trees dominate northern hardwood forests: sugar maple, American beech, and yellow birch. Eastern hemlock, a needle-bearing tree, is plentiful along streams in shady gorges. Hobblebush and striped maple are common shrubs in the understory. Northern hardwoods cover a wide band of the northern United States and southern Canada from Maine through Minnesota. This forest glows with beautiful colors in autumn—a great, insect-free time to hike.

Lower-elevation trails have abundant oaks and white pines mixed in with the northern hardwoods. These species are more characteristic of southern New England forests.

As you ascend above 2,000 feet, you will notice an increasing number of conifers—cone-bearing trees with needlelike leaves. The two most common species are red spruce and balsam fir. Spruce and fir, along with pines, are often called evergreens because they keep their needles year-round; however, conifer is a better term because some broad-leafed shrubs, such as rhododendrons, are also "evergreen."

Above 2,500 to 3,000 feet, a dark forest of conifers—the boreal forest—completely replaces the northern hardwoods. Boreas, the Greek god of the north wind, was portrayed in mythology as blowing a cold wind across the land, and, indeed, the boreal forest occurs in colder places, such as the middle latitudes of Canada and Russia. An ascent of several thousand feet in the White Mountains is ecologically equivalent to traveling several hundred miles north of Montreal. The summit of Mount Washington, the highest point in the White Mountains at 6,288 feet, is roughly equivalent to the environment of northern Labrador.

The boreal forest, also called the spruce-fir forest, is a fantasyland of dense "Christmas" trees with a soft, dark, mossy understory. Red spruce (illustrated at right) tends to dominate the lower part of the boreal forest (below 3,500 feet), which is also called the lower montane forest. Balsam fir (illustrated below) dominates the upper montane forest. Scattered throughout the forest, particularly in clearings, are a few broad-leafed trees and shrubs, such as paper birch and mountain ash. The upper part of the boreal forest grades into dwarf trees and scrub near treeline. The Ger-

man word krummholz, which means "crooked wood," is used to describe the low, twisted trees around treeline.

Humans have had a major impact on the character of White Mountain forests. Red spruces at lower elevations were logged heavily in the late-nineteenth and early-twentieth centuries. Since then, northern hardwood forests have grown up in many places where spruces once dominated. Fire has been the other major human impact. The most notorious fires occurred during the logging era in the Zealand and Wild River valleys, but very few areas were not touched by fires at one time or another. Many of the lower-elevation summits below 4,000 feet are now "bald" because the forest cover was burned off. (The true alpine zone, where weather conditions are too harsh to support tree growth, begins at between 4,200 and 4,800 feet in the White Mountains.)

The natural events that can affect the forests are windstorms, ice storms, and floods. These are discussed in "Storms in the White Mountains" on page 244. Although you can sometimes see patches where trees have been blown over by a windstorm or uprooted by floods, overall the forests are resilient to these events and recover within a few decades.

On summits, trees are often contorted into odd shapes because of wind exposure. "Flag trees" (also called "banner trees") have branches on one side only. This phenomenon occurs when a combination of ice and wind kills the branches that attempt to grow into the prevailing winds, which are generally from the west or northwest. The surviving branches point away from the wind, just like a flag extends in a stiff breeze.

APPENDIX C: A PRIMER ON FLORA AND FAUNA

COMMON TREES

Maples are characterized by three- or five-pointed palmately lobed leaves, brilliant fall colors, and helicopter-like winged seeds that spin as they are carried by the wind. Another distinguishing feature is that their leaves and twigs are attached to the stems in pairs, what botanists term an "opposite" pattern of branching.

Four species of maples are found in the White Mountains:

Sugar maple (illustrated at right) is a large tree of the forest canopy at lower elevations. Leaves have five pointed lobes, like the shape of a hand. The leaves turn brilliant yellow and orange in fall. And, of course, the concentrated sap of this tree is something many people adore, particularly on blueberry pancakes.

Red maple is equally at home in wetlands and on mountain slopes. Red maples can grow as fairly large, straight trees in the forest or as shrubby, multiple-trunked individuals in wetlands. Leaves are smaller than those of striped maples and are three-pointed, with sharp angles between the lobes. Red maples turn spectacular shades of red in fall. Their wine-colored flowers bloom before their leaves come out in spring and add a splash of color to wetlands early in the season.

Striped maple (illustrated at left) is particularly striking and easy to identify. This small tree, often a major component of the understory, is named for the distinctive white striping along its young bright green stems and branches. Striped maples' large leaves (up to 10 inches across), with three relatively small pointed lobes, resemble the webbed feet of geese, which is why they are also called goosefoot maples. Another name is moosewood. Drooping clusters of flowers are present in spring.

Mountain maple grows only as an understory shrub. Its leaves tend to be three-pointed and rounded, and its twigs are hairy. Mountain maples have long clusters of flowers in spring and early summer, and seeds can be seen in middle to late summer.

American beech has distinctive, smooth gray bark. The combination of smooth gray bark and long, pointed buds makes this an easy tree to identify, even in winter. The edges of its elliptical leaves are coarsely serrated (toothed). It is a major component of the low-elevation northern hardwood forest.

Paper birch has unmistakable white bark that peels into large horizontal strips. The bark is lined with distinct horizontal pores called lenticels. Young saplings and the branches of adult trees are a rich reddish brown color. Leaves of paper birch are oval or egg-shaped with serrated edges. A high-altitude form, which is now considered a separate species, has heart-shaped leaves. Paper birch is often the first tree species to colonize an area clear-cut by loggers.

Yellow birch also has lenticels like white birch but has yellowish brown or gray bark. Its bark peels in small, thin pieces. Its twigs taste like wintergreen when chewed. It is a major component of the low-elevation forest.

Eastern hemlock is a sprawling evergreen conifer of cool ravines and streamsides at lower elevations. It has 0.5-inch needles with two white lines underneath.

Balsam fir is one of the two major trees of the boreal forest. Balsam fir's flat needles are longer than hemlock needles (up to 1.5 inches) and emit a wonderful balsam fragrance when crushed. It is the only conifer with cones that sit upright on branches.

Red spruce is the other major tree of the boreal forest. Its 0.75- to 1.5-inch needles are attached singly to branches, are square in cross section, and are sharp to the touch. If you can roll a needle between your thumb and forefinger, it is a red spruce needle.

White pine has needles in bunches of five. The 3- to 5-inch needles are soft and flexible, so they won't prick you. A dominant component of New England lowland forests, white pine is often found on lower summits. In the right conditions, it can grow more than 200 feet tall.

Larch, also called tamarack, is a tree of open, boggy areas. The 1-inch needles grow in clusters of 10 to 30. The larch is unique among conifers in that it drops its needles in fall after they turn bright yellow.

COMMON SHRUBS

Blueberries of several species occur on summits and ledges, where they are often less than a foot high. Delicate white clusters of small, bell-shaped flowers in May and June precede the berries, which ripen in July through about mid-August.

Hobblebush is the one of the most abundant shrubs in the forest understory. Rounded, paired leaves with finely toothed edges and heart-shaped bases run along straggling stems. Hobblebush produces flat-topped white clusters of flowers in May and clusters of berries during summer that start out red and then ripen to dark purple.

Raspberry and **blackberry** grow as thin, arching "canes" covered with thorns and prickles. White flowers appear in June and the fruits in July and August. Raspberries and blackberries are colonizers of forest clearings, roadsides, and recently logged areas.

Labrador tea is a small (1 to 2 feet) shrub of bogs, boggy shorelines, and the alpine zone. Its leathery dark green leaves are rolled underneath at the edges and remain on the plant all year. The undersides of the leaves are covered with dense rust-colored hairs (white on new leaves).

SPRING WILDFLOWERS

Blue-bead lily, also called *Clintonia*, is a lily with large, shiny, smooth-edged leaves that hug the ground. The plant was named for DeWitt Clinton, a former governor of New York and the "father of the Erie Canal." A single flowering stalk produces several yellowish green flowers with six "petals" in late May through June. Glossy blue-black berries, which are inedible, appear in summer.

Painted trillium is one of the grandest of the White Mountain woodland wildflowers. It is unmistakable, containing a whorl of three leaves on a 1-foot stem. The stem is topped by a single three-petaled white flower with a purple center. In summer, a large red berry replaces the flower.

Pink lady's slipper is a native orchid and is one of showiest flowers at low elevations in the mountains. The hanging flower is shaped like a shoe or moccasin. A typical pink lady's slipper has a pair of large, smooth, glossy, almost round leaves that hug the ground and a single flowering stalk. The flower has a distinctive pink pouch that resembles a shoe (more like a heavy clog than a slipper). As many as one in four of the pink lady's slippers in the White Mountains is not pink but white. The pouch is lined with dark pink veins. The flower also contains three thin greenish sepals. Another name for pink lady's slipper is moccasin flower.

Canada mayflower is a small plant that flourishes in many woodlands at both low and high elevations. It has two or three smooth-edged, heart-shaped leaves. Its fuzzy white spike of small flowers develops into white-and-red-speckled berries that eventually turn all red.

Goldthread (illustrated here) is a small flower of shady, mossy woods with three small, rounded leaflets, each with scalloped edges. In spring, a single white flower with five to seven petals arises from a separate stem. Goldthread has a bright yellow underground stem that connects different individual plants.

Starflower has delicate white flowers that really do resemble stars. Typically, two white "stars" with six to eight petals each are on top of a whorl of five to seven narrow, pointed leaves on a 4- to 8-inch stem.

Alpine wildflowers have always been a key enticement for climbing to higher elevations in the White Mountains. Several showy species bloom in early to mid-June. See "The Alpine Zone of the White Mountains" on page 256 for more information.

SUMMER WILDFLOWERS

Bunchberry is a cheery white wildflower that usually occurs in large colonies on the forest floor. The plant is also called Canada dogwood because it is related to the flowering dogwood tree. Bunchberry produces a whorl of four or six smooth-edged leaves. It blooms in June at low elevations and in July at higher elevations. Look for its bright red berries in middle to late summer.

Mountain wood sorrel, another wildflower of the forest floor, will remind you of a shamrock. Its three leaflets, notched at the apex, are a common sight in cool woods. Mountain wood sorrel has attractive, delicate white flowers with five petals inscribed with thin pink lines and (usually) a pink circle surrounding the center.

Ghost pipes occur in isolated small groups in the forest. They are easily mistaken for a fungus because of their ghostly white color and lack of green leaves. Drooping white flowers are produced on top of a 6- to 8-inch stem.

Bluet flowers have four light blue petals surrounding a yellow center. They are less than 0.5 inch in diameter and 3 inches tall but grow in dense colonies that can be quite impressive. Look for bluets in sunny areas along trails, roadsides, and fields.

Jewelweed grows in wet areas and has delicate orange flowers with a spur and that hang down on long stalks from the stem. When their pods are ripe, the seeds "explode" in all directions when touched. This is why it is also called touch-me-not.

Whorled aster is the most common aster in the northern hardwood forest. Its leaves appear to be whorled (attached at or near the same point) around the stem. Its other name, sharp-toothed nodding aster, relates to its coarsely toothed leaves that are tapered at both ends. The flowers, which bloom from mid-August through September, resemble daisies.

Goldenrod is a flashy late-summer flower of fields, roadsides, and, occasionally, sunny spots in forests. Distinguishing the many species is challenging, but it is not hard to enjoy the bright yellow color they add to the landscape in August and September and the pollinating insects they attract.

Orange hawkweed (illustrated here) looks like a small orange dandelion. It is not native to North America but provides a striking splash of color along roadsides and in cultivated areas, such as along ski trails and around AMC huts.

FERNS AND LYCOPHYTES

Ferns have attractive, feathery leaves called fronds that are divided into leaflets called pinnae. The pinnae in most species are further subdivided into pinnules. Spores used for reproduction occur in clusters.

Long beech fern is very common in moist forests and on damp ledges around waterfalls. It is roughly triangular in shape, with its two lowest pinnae pointing downward.

Rock fern, also called Virginia polypody, grows on rocks wherever enough soil has accumulated. It is a small (1 foot) evergreen fern whose fronds are divided only once. Look at the underside of a frond to see the round spore clusters.

Interrupted fern is a large (3 to 4 feet) fern. It gets its name from the brown, spore-containing section of fertile fronds that occurs between the green pinnae along the stem. This fern grows in wet areas, often in clearings and along roadsides. A similar species, **cinnamon fern**, has dense tufts of rust-colored hairs where the pinnae join the stem.

Hay-scented fern is a lacy, medium-sized fern that grows in dense colonies in small clearings in the woods, such as those created by fallen trees. It gives off the sweet smell of freshly mown grass when the fronds have dried out in late September and October.

Bracken fern is a robust fern with a triangular frond divided into three parts. Unlike most ferns, it grows in sunny, weedy locales, such as along roadsides.

Wood ferns of several species are common on the forest floor. These large ferns have finely cut fronds and brown scales along the stem.

Club mosses are a group of primitive plants that are not actually mosses but are in their own group, the lycophytes. In prehistoric times they formed trees, but the current living species are never more than a few inches tall, even though they look like miniature cedars, pines, or spruces. Two of the most common are **princess pine**, which resembles a miniature spruce, and **shining club moss**, which resembles a green bottle brush.

MOSSES

Mosses are small, primitive plants that provide a beautiful cover of greenery in damp forests. In the boreal forest they cover rocks, logs, and old stumps, often being the only understory vegetation.

Haircap moss is one of the most common woodland mosses. Its upright branches are covered with small, needlelike leaves. This moss gets its name from the hairy cap that covers its spore-containing capsules. The spores are shot out of the capsule as it dries.

Fern moss, also called piggyback moss, is feathery and fernlike. Smaller "plantlets" grow by piggybacking on top of larger ones.

Sphagnum, or peat moss, is the most economically important moss. It has a tremendous capacity to hold water, which is why it is so useful to gardeners as a soil conditioner. Sphagnum covers bogs with green or red colors, depending on the particular species.

FUNGI AND LICHENS

Fungi come in an assortment of odd shapes with occasionally vivid colors. They are like icebergs—what you see above ground, their reproductive structures, is only a small part of the whole. Below the ground or within a decaying log, myriad fungal filaments break down dead plant matter, helping to create soil. Other types of fungi live symbiotically within plant roots, where they aid plants in taking up nutrients from the soil.

Mushrooms are the best-known fungi. They are eye-catching but can be a challenge to identify, often changing shape as they develop. And, of course, even some of the common ones are deadly poisonous, sporting names like death cap and destroying angel. Most of the widespread mushrooms in the mountains have umbrella-shaped caps with gills on the underside. The gills radiate around a central axis, like spokes of an umbrella. These include *Russula* (a genus of robust mushrooms with wide reddish brown or yellow caps and thick stalks), *Mycena* (a genus of delicate mushrooms with thin stalks and conical caps), and *Amanita* (a genus of mostly poisonous mushrooms that typically grow out of a fleshy cup and have a collar around their stalk). Mushrooms in the genus *Boletus* have pores rather than gills on their undersides. Two uniquely shaped mushrooms of the forest floor are black trumpets (shaped like funnels) and coral fungi (tangles of pale branchlets resembling coral).

The best time to find a variety of mushrooms in the White Mountains is in late summer through early fall, particularly after damp weather. Leave picking and eating wild mushrooms to the experts.

Lichens are fungi that have the trapped cells of algae within them. The tiny algal cells produce food for the fungus, and the fungus in turn provides the algae with some nutrients and protection from the environment. Lichens can live in harsh places, such as on bare rocks above treeline, because they provide for their own nutrition and have an amazing ability to resuscitate after being almost completely dried out. These symbiotic organisms grow so slowly and live so long that individual ones can be used to track the slow, frost-induced movement of the rocks upon which they live. Lichens are abundant on rocky ledges, on summits, and in drier forests of the White Mountains. They come in three general types: crusty, leafy, and bushy.

Map lichen creates green and yellow splashes of color with a black background on boulders on open ledges and summits. These brightly colored lichens grow as flat crusts in patches that resemble the patterns of rivers, oceans, and islands on a map.

Rock tripe is a leafy lichen that flourishes on boulders in the forest. It looks like overlapping pieces of black or dark brown shoe leather, each 1 to 2 inches across and irregular in shape. Each piece is attached to a rock by a central stalk.

Reindeer lichen is bushy, with many pale yellow-green entangled branches arising from individual stalks. It grows on open, scrubby ledges, often in large patches that look so neat and well manicured that you might think a gardener deliberately planted them there.

British soldier, a bushy lichen, consists of gray green stalks no more than 3 inches high that are topped by bright-red reproductive structures. It was first described scientifically by botanist Edward Tuckerman (for whom Tuckerman Ravine is named) in 1858.

ANIMALS

Insects, Spiders, and Other Invertebrates

More people might admire the insects in the White Mountains were it not for two notorious inhabitants: **blackflies** and **mosquitoes**. Learn more about them and other aquatic insects in "Aquatic Insects in the White Mountains" on page 7.

Butterflies are sometimes called flying flowers, a reference to their lovely colors and perhaps their affinity for feeding on the nectar from flowers. **Eastern tiger swallowtails** are yellow with black stripes and have two "tails," one projecting from each hind wing. Boldly patterned **mourning cloaks**, with brownish purple wings edged with bright yellow, dart from flower to flower. Some years, **white admirals** are abundant. These brown butterflies have bold white bands across their forewings and hind wings. The caterpillars of butterflies and moths are essential food for most birds that nest in the forests of the White Mountains.

Dragonflies and **damselflies**, members of the insect order Odonata, are common around the edges of ponds. They are striking insects, often colored with iridescent blues and greens with bold yellow stripes. Some are red or orange and black. Dragonflies are strong flyers, moving straight ahead rapidly on outspread wings like little airplanes and changing direction abruptly. They have very large eyes that for most species touch each other. Darners, which are big dragonflies with mottled blue-and-brown abdomens and green or blue stripes on their thoraxes, can often be seen hunting insects on summits and rocky ledges or along the shores of mountain ponds. Damselflies are smaller and more delicate than dragonflies, and their smaller eyes are well separated on their heads. Their flight is typically erratic, like a butterfly's. Dragonflies hold their wings horizontally when at rest, whereas damselflies bring their wings together over their bodies.

Large black **wolf spiders** are often observed scurrying across rocks on open summits and ledges. These eight-legged relatives of insects are predators of insects. Unlike most spiders, wolf spiders catch their prey without the use of a web. Of course, you can also find many spiders in the White Mountains that spin traditional webs.

Fallen trees often harbor a variety of invertebrate life that aids in decomposing the trees and recycling nutrients. **Ants** and **termites** create networks of chambers under bark and scatter wildly when you uncover them. **Centipedes, millipedes, sowbugs (pillbugs), slugs**, and **worms** of various sorts take up residence in decaying logs. (Make sure you return any logs you overturn to their original positions.)

Reptiles and Amphibians

The long, cold winters and damp summers of the White Mountains do not make an ideal climate for reptiles. These scaly vertebrates are more common and diverse in drier, warmer climates. No poisonous snakes live in the White Mountains.

If you do find a snake, it is likely to be an **eastern garter snake**, which is brownish with three yellow stripes running along the entire length of its body. Although harmless, this snake won't like being picked up and may try to bite or rub a very stinky fluid on you if you try. Garter snakes feed on insects and small vertebrates.

Painted turtles are occasionally seen basking on rocks and logs in ponds at lower elevations. Their heads are marked with short yellow stripes, and their shells are bordered with red.

Amphibians, which include frogs, toads, and salamanders, are much more tied to water than reptiles. Almost all species lay their eggs in water, and their larvae (frog larvae are called tadpoles) have gills and develop in water. Many species remain in, or close to, water as adults, even though they breathe air.

American toads are the most wide-ranging amphibians in the region. You'll often find them along trails in the forest far from water, as high up as treeline. They blend in very well with the dead leaves of the forest floor, and usually your first clue to them is a rustling sound as they move about. Their leathery, warty skin allows them to wander farther from dampness than most amphibians, although they must return to water to lay their eggs.

Frogs of various species inhabit ponds and wetlands of the White Mountains. It is much easier to identify them by sound than by sight. In early spring, the birdlike chirping of **spring peepers** is a familiar chorus. ("Early spring" is a relative term in the White Mountains, so spring peepers can be heard in April at low elevations and in July at high-elevation ponds.) **Green frogs**, which sound like someone plucking a string of a banjo, can be heard in late spring and throughout summer.

Salamanders are creatures of damp woods, mountain streams, and ponds. They generally remain hidden and are difficult to find unless you look under dead logs in the woods or flat stones by water. Despite their secretive habits, the abundance of some species, particularly the **red-backed salamander**, makes them very important to nutrient cycling in the soil and leaf litter of White Mountain forests.

The only salamander bold enough to cross a trail out in the open is the **red eft**. This bright red salamander with greenish spots can afford to be more brazen than others because it is very toxic. The red eft is actually a juvenile, the land stage of the **red-spotted newt**, an aquatic salamander common in both mountain and lowland ponds, such as East Pond (Trip 3).

Birds

Birds are more often heard than seen in the White Mountains. Their calls and songs fill the forests and summits. A few songs are particularly characteristic and easy to identify.

White-throated sparrows sing a variety of clear, sweet-whistled notes varying in pitch, followed by several wavy notes. Their song sounds like *See old Sam Peabody, Peabody, Peabody* and is very easy to imitate.

Winter wrens have an amazingly extensive, bubbly song that varies in pitch. They make a lot of noise for such small birds.

If you hear repeated nasal notes that sound like a child's toy horn, that is a **red-breasted nuthatch**.

The song of the **hermit thrush** is flutelike and ethereal. It starts with a long, high note, followed by shorter notes that modulate up and down in scale. Usually hermit thrushes sing from shrubs or the lower branches of trees in the northern hardwood forest. At higher elevations in the boreal forest, the thrush you are most likely to encounter is the **Swainson's thrush**. Its song is similar to that of the hermit thrush but ascends up the scale and lacks the characteristic long opening note.

Ovenbirds belt out a raucous two-syllable *t'cher, t'cher, t'cher* that increases gradually in volume. These warblers sing from the ground.

Black-capped chickadees are a favorite of children because they are perky, relatively tame, and are constantly saying their own name. You'll see and hear them on most hikes.

Dark-eyed juncos are sparrow-sized gray birds with white bellies and white outer tail feathers. They spend much of their time on summits and ledges. Their song is a musical trill on one note.

Ravens make a hoarse *caw caw* or a series of piglike snorts as they fly overhead. They can sometimes sound like a screaming person.

The presence of woodpeckers is evident not in song but in dead trees riddled with the holes they create. The little **downy woodpecker** is the one you are most likely to see. It is about the size of a cardinal and is speckled with black and white. These birds produce a lively descending whinny when they land.

Woodpeckers are essential to the ecology of the forest because many kinds of birds and mammals use their holes as homes. Because of this, the Forest Service has a policy of protecting these hole-ridden "wildlife trees."

Mammals

In the White Mountains it is not easy to see many types of mammals, particularly large ones. Nonetheless, they leave ample signs of their presence in tracks, holes in trees, scratch marks on bark, and dams.

Beavers are abundant but rarely in view. Many trails take you by beaver ponds where you can see their wooden lodges, dams of sticks and mud, canals, and chewed trees. The animals themselves can sometimes be seen around dusk or dawn. Zealand Pond (Trip 36), Lost Pond (Trip 41), and Shell Pond (Trip 50) have been good places for beaver sightings in recent years.

Red squirrels are the most frequently encountered mammals in the White Mountains. They scold hikers entering their territories with a rattling chatter, usually delivered from a red spruce or balsam fir.

Chipmunks are popular campground rodents. They chirp like birds, scamper on the forest floor over fallen logs, and dive into holes in the ground.

Snowshoe hares look somewhat like cottontail rabbits of lowlands but with larger ears and feet that appear a bit too big for their bodies. Those feet act as snowshoes, helping them to stay on top of deep snow in winter. Snowshoe hares are white in winter and turn brown in summer.

Watching **moose** has become a popular pastime in the White Mountains as their population has increased. These largest members of the deer family occasionally can be seen along roadsides around dusk. The wetlands along the Kancamagus Highway near the Passaconaway Historic Site are particularly good places to look for moose. In fall rutting season, males can be ill-tempered, so give them a wide berth. Moose leave characteristic stripe marks on trees with their teeth.

Hikers on the trails rarely encounter **black bears**, but you may see the claw marks they leave on trees to claim their territories or the clusters of branches they pull together when sitting in trees and eating buds, nuts, and catkins. Bears are omnivores, feeding on a variety of mammals, insects, fruits, and nuts.

APPENDIX D: SELECTED RESOURCES

NATURAL HISTORY GUIDES

DeGraaf, Richard M., and Yuriko Yamisaki, *New England Wildlife: Habitat, Natural History, and Distribution*, Lebanon, NH: University Press of New England, 2000.

Eusden, J. Dykstra, et al., *The Geology of New Hampshire's White Mountains*, Etna, NH: The Durand Press, 2013.

Haines, Arthur, *Flora Novae Angliae: A Manual for the Identification of Native and Naturalized Higher Vascular Plants of New England*, New Haven, CT: Yale University Press, 2011.

Johnson, Charles W., *Bogs of the Northeast*, Lebanon, NH: University Press of New England, 1985.

Marchand, Peter J., *Nature Guide to the Northern Forest*, Boston: Appalachian Mountain Club Books, 2010.

Murray, Tom, *Insects of New England and New York*, Boston: Kollath-Stensaas Publishing, 2012.

Native Plant Trust, "Go Botany," accessed [10/12/2021], gobotany.nativeplanttrust.org.

Newcomb, Lawrence, and Gordon Morrison, *Newcomb's Wildflower Guide*, Boston: Little, Brown & Co., 1989.

Pope, Ralph, *Lichens above Treeline: A Hiker's Guide to Alpine Zone Lichens of the Northeastern United States*, Lebanon, NH: University Press of New England, 2005.

Raymo, Chet, and Maureen Raymo, *Written in Stone: A Geological History of the Northeastern United States*, Hensonville, NY: Black Dome Press Corp., 2001.

Sibley, David, *The Sibley Field Guide to Birds of Eastern North America*, 2nd ed., New York: Alfred A. Knopf, 2014.

Slack, Nancy G., and Allison W. Bell, *Field Guide to the New England Mountain Summits*, 3rd ed., Boston: Appalachian Mountain Club Books, 2014.

Sperduto, Dan, and Ben Kimball, *The Nature of New Hampshire: Natural Communities of the Granite State*, Lebanon, NH: University Press of New England, 2011.

Various authors, *Peterson Field Guides*, Boston: Houghton Mifflin Co.

NATURE WITH CHILDREN

Cornell, Joseph, *Sharing Nature with Children*, 2nd ed., Nevada City, CA: Dawn Publishing Co., 1998.

Hipple, Ethan, and Yemaya St. Clair, *Outdoors with Kids Maine, New Hampshire, Vermont: 75 of the Best Family Hiking, Camping, and Paddling Trips*, Boston: Appalachian Mountain Club Books, 2014.

WHITE MOUNTAINS GUIDES AND HISTORIES

Bolnick, Bruce, and Doreen Bolnick, *Waterfalls of the White Mountains: 30 Trips to 100 Waterfalls*, 2nd ed., Woodstock, VT: Backcountry Publications, 1999.

Crawford, Lucy, *History of the White Mountains*, Etna, NH: The Durand Press, 1999.

Dickerman, Mike, *White Mountains Hiking History: Trailblazers of the Granite State*, Mount Pleasant, SC: The History Press, 2013.

MacGray, Ken, and Steven D. Smith, *White Mountain Guide: AMC's Comprehensive Guide to Hiking Trails in the White Mountain National Forest*, 31st ed., Boston: Appalachian Mountain Club Books, 2022.

Mudge, John T. B., *The White Mountains: Names, Places, and Legends*, 2nd ed., Etna, NH: The Durand Press, 1995.

Randall, Peter E., *Mount Washington: A Guide & Short History*, Woodstock, VT: The Countryman Press, 1992.

Smith, Steven D., *Mount Chocorua: A Guide and History*, Littleton, NH: Bondcliff Books, 2006.

Smith, Steven D., *Ponds & Lakes of the White Mountains: From Wayside to Wilderness*, 2nd ed., Woodstock, VT: Backcountry Publications, 1998.

Smith, Steven D., *The Waterville Valley Guidebook*, Town of Waterville Valley, NH, 2020.

Waterman, Laura, and Guy Waterman, *Forest and Crag: A History of Hiking, Trail Blazing, and Adventure in the Northeast Mountains*, 30th anniversary edition, Albany, NY: SUNY Press, 2019.

Wivell, Ty, *Passport to AMC's High Huts in the White Mountains*, Boston: Appalachian Mountain Club Books, 2011.

INDEX

J

jack pine, 34
jewelweed, 236–237, 322
Joe Dodge Lodge, xxvi, 209–210. *See also* Pinkham Notch Visitor Center

K

Kancamagus Highway region
  camping in, 90
  easy hikes in, 91–94, 95–97, 98–101
  moderate hikes in, 102–106, 108–112, 113–116, 117–121, 123–127
  region description, 89–90
  strenuous hikes in, 123–127
  trip planning, x–xi
Kilkenny, hikes near, xiv–xv
King Solomon's seal, 304

L

Labrador tea, 77, 320
Lafayette Place Campground, 74
Lakes of the Clouds Hut, 79
larches, 78, 287, 320
Leave No Trace principles, xxvi–xxvii
lichen, 323–324
Lila's Ledge, xii–xiii, 219–222
Lincoln, hikes near, viii–ix, x–xi, 55–58, 70–73, 74–78, 80–86, 95–97, 102–106, 108–112
Lincoln Woods Trail, x–xi, 102–106
  logging on, 100
Little East Pond, viii–ix, 14–18
Little Haystack Mountain, 83
Livermore, hikes near, viii–ix, x–xi, 14–18, 37–40, 108–112, 158–161
logging, 97, 107, 158
  in Evans Notch, 273
Lonesome Lake and Hut, viii–ix, 74–78
long beech fern, 322
Lookout Ledge, xiv–xv, 302–305
Lord Hill, xiv–xv, 265–269, 316
Lost Pond, xii–xiii, 211–215
Lost River Reservation, 67
Lovequist Loop, x–xi, 98–101
Lower Falls Recreation Area, 121
Low's Bald Spot, xii–xiii, 234–239

M

Macomber Family Information Center, 147, 153, 166, 208. *See* also Highland Center at Crawford Notch

Maine. *See* Evans Notch region
maple trees, 319
map lichen, 324
McKenny, Ross, 43
Mead Base Conservation Center, 23–26
mica, 268, 316
Mill Brook Road, xiv–xv, 307–310
Mizpah Spring Hut, xii–xiii, 79, 199–202
  birdwatching at, 203
moderate hikes
  in Conway-North Conway region, 134–137, 139–142, 143–146
  in Crawford Notch/Zealand Notch region, 158–161, 162–166, 168–171, 172–177, 178–181, 182–187
  in Evans Notch, 270–272, 274–278, 279–282, 283–287
  in Franconia Notch, 59–63, 64–67, 70–73, 74–78, 80–86
  along Kancamagus Highway, 102–106, 108–112, 113–116, 117–121, 123–127
  in North Country region, 299–301, 302–305, 307–310
  in Pinkham Notch region, 216–218, 219–222, 229–233, 234–239, 240–243
  in Southwestern White Mountains, 9–13, 14–18, 19–22, 23–26, 27–31, 32–36
moose, 184, 327
Moose Brook State park, 293
Moosilauke Ravine Lodge, trips from, 41–45
mosses, 323
mountain avens, 186, 257
mountain hollies, 132
mountain maples, 319
Mountain Pond Loop Trail, x–xi, 139–142
mountain wood fern, 82
mountain wood sorrel, 206, 213, 321
Mount Avalon, xii–xiii, 178–181
Mount Chocorua, x–xi, 123–127
Mount Crag, xiv–xv, 299–301
Mount Crawford, xii–xiii, 194–197
Mount Crawford House, 198
Mount Eisenhower, xii–xiii, 204–208
Mount Israel, viii–ix, 23–26
Mount Lafayette, 84, 86
Mount Moosilauke, viii–ix, 41–45
Mount Morgan, 27–31
Mount Osceola, viii–ix, 37–40
Mount Osceola Trail, 40
Mount Pemigewasset Trail, viii–ix, 70–73
Mount Percival, 27–31
Mount Pierce, xii–xiii, 199–202, 207–208

ABOUT THE AUTHOR

Robert N. Buchsbaum has both a professional interest in and a passion for the natural history of New England. He received a bachelor of science degree in natural resources from Cornell University and a PhD in marine ecology from the Boston University Marine Program at Woods Hole, Massachusetts. A native New Yorker, he moved to New England in 1978 and has since spent many of his free weekends and vacations exploring the White Mountains. As an AMC volunteer naturalist, Buchsbaum presented programs in huts, lodges, and other locations in the White Mountains on a wide variety of topics, including botany, alpine ecology, birds, and geology.

Buchsbaum resides in Beverly, Massachusetts, with his wife, Nancy Schalch. Their two children, Alison and Gabriel, were along for many of the hikes described in this updated guide and contributed their insights. Buchsbaum recently retired from Mass Audubon, where he worked for more than 30 years as a conservation scientist. He has written numerous magazine articles on natural history and has published extensively in technical journals and books.

AMC BOOK UPDATES

AMC Books strives to keep our guidebooks as up-to-date as possible to help you plan safe and enjoyable adventures. If we learn after publishing a book that relevant trails have been relocated or route or contact information has changed, we will post the updated information online. Before you hit the trail, visit outdoors.org/books-maps and click the "Book Updates" link.

While hiking, if you notice discrepancies with the trip descriptions or maps, or if you find any other errors in the book, please let us know by submitting them to amcbookupdates@outdoors.org or to Books Editor, c/o AMC, 10 City Square, Boston, MA 02129. We will verify all submissions and post key updates each month. AMC Books is dedicated to being a recognized leader in outdoor publishing. Thank you for your participation.

ABOUT AMC IN NEW HAMPSHIRE

The Appalachian Mountain Club's New Hampshire Chapter has more than 10,000 members and offers hundreds of trips each year. Well-trained and dedicated leaders guide hiking, paddling, skiing, and climbing excursions. The chapter is also active in trail work, conservation projects, and instructional programs. You can learn more about this chapter by visiting outdoors.org/community/chapters. To view a list of AMC activities in New Hampshire and other parts of the Northeast, visit activities.outdoors.org.

White Mountain Guide, 31st Edition

Compiled and edited by Ken MacGray and Steven D. Smith

For day-hikers and backpackers alike, AMC's *White Mountain Guide* has remained the most trusted and indispensable resource for 115 years. This 31st edition has been updated and revised with turn-by-turn descriptions of more than 500 trails, as well as trip planning advice, safety information, and a checklist of New Hampshire's 4,000-footers. Included in this boxed set are six pull-out topographic maps, updated to reflect the latest trail openings, closings, and reroutings.

$26.95 • 978-1-62842-140-8 • ebook available

Best Backcountry Skiing in the Northeast, 2nd Edition

David Goodman

Thirty years after his first guidebook became a cult classic among Eastern powder seekers, David Goodman has revised and expanded his "bible of Northeastern backcountry skiing" for the next generation of winter adventurers. From thrilling day trips in the East's highest mountains to hut-to-hut wilderness journeys, this is the only comprehensive guide to the best backcountry ski and snowboard tours in New Hampshire, Maine, Vermont, New York, and Massachusetts with description, distance, elevation, difficulty rating, and topographic map included for each tour.

$21.95 • 978-1-62842-124-8 • ebook available

This Wild Land

Andrew Vietze

Almost twenty years ago, Andrew Vietze made an unexpected career change: from punk rock magazine editor to park ranger at Baxter State Park in Maine. From midnight search-and-rescue missions to trail maintenance to cleaning toilets, Baxter rangers do it all…and over the decades Vietze has seen it all. In *This Wild Land*, Vietze tells his story with humor, action, and an eye for the compelling details of life as a park ranger, making it the perfect read for outdoor and armchair adventurers alike.

$18.95 • 978-1-62842-132-3 • ebook available

Outdoors with Kids Maine, New Hampshire, and Vermont

Ethan Hipple and Yemaya St. Clair

Written with families in mind, this guide from the Appalachian Mountain Club features 75 kid-sized adventures, both close to home and farther afield, from hiking and paddling to biking and camping. This must-have resource offers tips and tricks, safety and planning information, educational essays, and activity ideas, including the ever important "Plan B" to shorten or lengthen your day.

$18.95 • 978-1-62842-003-6 • ebook available